Culture and Subjective Well-being

Well-being and Quality of Life

During the past century, psychology has helped unlock many of the mysteries of human behavior and clarified the sources of many illnesses of the mind. But, until recently, this young science did not have much to say about what made life worth living. Happiness, hope, courage, and other positive experiences that are so important to our private existence were considered too subjective to be amenable to rigorous investigation. Only in the last decade have scholars recognized that quality of life is too important to be ignored any longer. New techniques and new conceptual frameworks have emerged for studying the large variety of human strengths and their impact on physical and mental health. Comparative studies of happiness, of the neurophysiology of optimal experiences, and of the role of altruism, forgiveness, and gratitude in improving the quality of lives, have begun to open up exciting new directions for cognitive, neuroscientific, and social research.

The MIT Press Well-being and Quality of Life series, edited by Mihaly Csikszentmihalyi, intends to take a position of leadership in charting the progress of this new domain, in order to advance our knowledge of the objective bases of subjective well-being.

Culture and Subjective Well-being
Ed Diener and Eunkook M. Suh, editors

Culture and Subjective Well-being

edited by Ed Diener and Eunkook M. Suh

17020l

A Bradford Book
The MIT Press
Cambridge, Massachusetts
London, England

This book was set in Sabon on '3B2' by Asco Typesetters, Hong Kong.
Printed and bound in the United States of America.

Library of Congress Cataloging-in-Publication Data

Culture and subjective well-being / edited by Ed Diener and Eunkook M. Suh.
    p.   cm.
  "A Bradford book."
  Includes bibliographical references and index.
  ISBN 0-262-04182-0 (hc. : alk. paper)
  1. Happiness. 2. Culture—Philosophy. 3. Anthropology—Philosophy. I. Diener, Ed.
II. Suh, Eunkook M.
  B187.H3C85   2000
  306—dc21   00-035155

Contents

Contributors

Ed Diener
University of Illinois
Psychology Department
603 E. Daniel St.
Champaign, IL 61820

Carol Gohm
University of Illinois
Psychology Department
603 E. Daniel St.
Champaign, IL 61820

Alexander Grob
University of Bonn
Institute of Psychology
Develop/Education Psychology
Roemerstrasse 164
D-53117 Bonn
Germany

Ronald Inglehart
University of Michigan
Institute for Social Research
Ann Arbor, MI 48106-1248

Shinobu Kitayama
Kyoto University
Department of Psychology
Faculty of Integrated Human Studies
Sakyo-ku, Kyoto 606-11
Japan

Hans-Dieter Klingemann
Wissenschaftszentrum Berlin
Germany

Natalia Kouznetsova
San Francisco State University
Psychology Department
1600 Holloway Ave.
San Francisco, CA 94132

Richard Lucas
University of Illinois
Psychology Department
603 E. Daniel St.
Champaign, IL 61820

Hazel Rose Markus
Stanford University
Department of Psychology
Jordan Hall, Building 420
Stanford, CA 94305

David Matsumoto
San Francisco State University
Psychology Department
1600 Holloway Ave.
San Francisco, CA 94132

Gila Melech
The Hebrew University of Jerusalem
Department of Psychology
Mount Scopus, Jerusalem
Israel 91905

Shigehiro Oishi
University of Illinois
Psychology Department
603 E. Daniel St.
Champaign, IL 61820

Jacques Raroque
San Francisco State University
Psychology Department
1600 Holloway Ave.
San Francisco, CA 94132

Charlotte Ratzlaff
University of Michigan
School of Education
1225 SEB
Ann Arbor, MI 48109

Rebecca Ray
San Francisco State University
Psychology Department
1600 Holloway Ave.
San Francisco, CA 94132

Shalom H. Schwartz
The Hebrew University
Department of Psychology
Mount Scopus, Jerusalem
Israel 91905

Eunkook M. Suh
University of California, Irvine
Department of Psychology and Social
Behavior
3357 Social Ecology II
Irvine, CA 92697-7085

Harry C. Triandis
University of Illinois
Psychology Department
603 E. Daniel St.
Champaign, IL 61820

Ruut Veenhoven
Erasmus University Rotterdam
Postbus 1738
NL 3000 DR Rotterdam
Netherlands

Acknowledgments

We wish to thank Steve Heine, Susan Nolen-Hoeksema, and Michael Robinson who provided valuable suggestions for improving some of the chapters in this book. Our sincere thanks goes to Kris Eaton who helped throughout with the compilation of this volume. Her organizational ability, along with good spirits, made editing this book a pleasure.

I

Introduction

1

Measuring Subjective Well-being to Compare the Quality of Life of Cultures

Ed Diener and Eunkook M. Suh

The question of what is the "good life" has been contemplated for millennia. The classic Greek philosophers concluded that the good life resides in virtue. Similarly the Confucian school in ancient China described the good life in terms of an orderly society in which individuals correctly performed their roles and responsibilities. The Utilitarians such as Jeremy Bentham characterized the good life as one replete with happiness and pleasure, and the desirable society as one that maximizes pleasure for all people. Although the search for the ingredients of quality of life is ancient, only in the last decades has the empirical study of well-being become a systematic scientific endeavor. The present volume is devoted to the idea that we can empirically study quality of life and make comparisons of the subjective well-being (SWB) of societies. It is unclear whether we will ever be able to conclude in a definitive way that one society is better than another in terms of overall quality of life because this judgment is so dependent on values. We can conclude, however, which societies have greater subjective well-being—people in them evaluate their lives in positive terms. Someday it may be possible to make cross-cultural comparisons of subjective well-being with a degree of certitude.

In confronting the question of the good life and the successful society, we encounter the vexatious question of cultural relativism. If societies have different sets of values, people in them are likely to consider different criteria relevant when judging the success of their society. In one community equality may be most important, for example, whereas in another location more weight may be placed on economic prosperity. In yet another culture love might be considered most important. Thus people in various nations might consider their own society to be better than the others because they use a criterion on which their nation is performing well. The concept of cultural relativism thus points to the need for internal standards when judging societies—are citizens able to accomplish their own values and goals, and therefore judge their own lives and community to be successful based on their own standards? In this approach, an unsuccessful culture is one that possesses values and goals that it fails to reach. Because people who cannot attain their values and goals are likely to be less satisfied and happy, it is likely that measures of subjective well-being to some degree represent a judgment of the culture from an internal perspective, from the viewpoint of the members of that society. Therefore, if we assess various aspects of subjective well-being such as whether people believe they are living correctly, whether they enjoy their lives, whether important others think they are living well, as well as whether they possess a sense of fulfillment, we may have one set of measures by which we can compare the success of societies. In other words, SWB can represent the degree to which people in each society are accomplishing the values they hold dear.

Some might argue that subjective well-being is just one value among many, competing with all the others in an endless cacophony of competing concerns. There are reasons to argue, however, that subjective well-being has a privileged place at the table. First, societies throughout the world are becoming increasingly democratized, and subjective well-being is a particularly democratic scalar. It is based on the idea that how each person thinks and feels about his or her life is important. It is not just the opinion of a power elite, or an intellectual class, or psychologists who are experts on "mental health" but through the standards and values chosen by the person herself that societies are evaluated. Second, SWB can take people's values into account, and give a summary of whether their lives fulfill these standards, because individuals' own views of their well-being reflect their values. Thus SWB can reflect success at achieving the numerous values that people seek. Finally, subjective well-being includes components that are dependent on pleasure and the fulfillment of basic human needs, but also includes people's ethical and evaluative judgments of their lives. Thus SWB reflects to some degree how much people are living in accord with evolutionary imperatives and human needs, but also represents judgments based on the particular norms and values of each culture.

Measures of subjective well-being that are dependent on happiness and pleasure might be necessary in fully evaluating the quality of life of societies, but they will never be sufficient (see Diener and Suh 1997; Diener, Sapyta, and Suh 1998) because all people have values in addition to hedonism and satisfaction. We hope for low infant mortality, a degree of human equality, and respect for nature, regardless of whether these things will make people happier or more satisfied. Further we want to achieve subjective well-being through our relationships and attainment of goals and values, not simply from drugs. Thus a full set of measures of SWB will include judgments of whether people are living the "good life" from the frame of reference of that society, and include evaluative judgments that go beyond hedonism.

The degree to which subjective well-being arises from meeting inherent human needs versus from acquiring cultural imperatives is an issue that is not yet resolved. In either case, subjective well-being is one outcome measure by which to judge successful living. We need criteria by which to determine whether humans are living in accord with "human nature"—what better place to start than whether people feel happy and satisfied. A problem with an unswerving cultural relativism is that every outcome is as good as every other; a Hitler is judged to be as good as Francis of Assisi. In this view, every type of life is equally desirable depending on the framework for evaluation. While respecting many differences between cultures, we reject all-out cultural relativism because it is too accepting of terrible people and sick societies. But in rejecting complete cultural relativism, we must have some criteria by which societies can be judged. We agree with Edgerton (1992) that human health and happiness are two good standards with which to start in judging a society, and we would add the long-term well-being of the planet and the happiness of people in other communities as two other standards.

We may discover that there are many types of good societies that can produce happy citizens. Just because diverse societies can be good, however, does not mean that all societies are good. There can be bad societies that produce bad outcomes on many dimensions (e.g., see Edgerton 1992). Cultural relativism points us to the idea that there are alternative paths that can accommodate human needs and desires, but we cannot take this to mean that all institutional arrangements are equally good. We may discover that some types of societies are inferior in producing health and happiness.

Methodological Issues

When examining subjective well-being, a number of thorny methodological issues arise, and these concerns are exacerbated when the researcher wants to formulate conclusions that are generalizable across cultures (for a comprehensive discussion, see Vijver and Leung 1997). First, the question of measurement: Do the subjective well-being scales yield scores that are comparable across individuals and societies? Most extant evidence on this issue is encouraging. For example, Sandvik, Diener, and Seidlitz (1993) found that self-report SWB scales correlated well with a number of non-self-report measures of well-being such as informant reports, experience sampling, smiling, memory measures, and interviews. Balatsky and Diener (1993) found that memory measures, in which people must remember good versus bad events from their lives, yielded scores that converged with self-reports of SWB collected in the former Soviet Union and in the United States. Thus there are some limited data from other measures of SWB besides global self-reports, but these alternative forms of assessment must be utilized much more frequently in cross-cultural research. We may also be nearing the time when biological measures such as hormone assays, evoked potentials, and brain imaging can also produce measures of happiness. Although subjective well-being is of course experiential, this does not mean that self-report need be the only measure of the experience. We will find ourselves standing on more firm ground if we find that our conclusions converge across measurement methods. Currently virtually all of the conclusions in this book, save several notable studies, are based solely on global self-report measures, and thus our inferences must be accepted with caution at this time.

Questions arise about measurement artifacts when conducting cross-cultural studies. A major question is whether translation into different languages might influence research results. Ouweneel and Veenhoven (1991) review evidence from countries in which more than one language are spoken, showing that the SWB scores across language groups are similar. Shao (1993) administered our life satisfaction scale to bilingual individuals in both Mandarin Chinese and English, and found much the same results regardless of language. Despite the encouraging findings, more research needs to be performed in this area. Not only is translation an issue, but the comparability of well-being concepts across cultures is an important consideration. In order to explore this issue, we will need to compare emic measures that are created in diverse communities and administer them in other cultures, explore the semantic evaluations of the measurement concepts, and so forth. This, in combination with the addition of non-self-report measures, should yield a theoretical network to help understand the meaning of the self-report measures across societies.

Other self-report artifacts have also been explored across cultures. Diener, Suh, Smith, and Shao (1995) examined whether humility produced lower subjective well-being scores in the East Asian cultures compared to the United States. They used several strategies for analyzing this question, including examining scores for domains in which the respondent was more or was less responsible. They found little evidence that humility was a significant influence on responding. Several potential artifacts were explored such as the differential use of extreme numbers, and little evidence was found that these artifacts produce the national differences in SWB.

Diener et al. (1999) did find evidence, however, that satisfaction scales might have a somewhat different meaning between cultures, related to a global positivity response tendency. Whereas individuals in western cultures were slightly more positive about concrete, narrow domains of their lives, they were much more positive about the broader domains that subsumed the narrower ones. Further this difference tended to predict the life satisfaction of nations. It suggested to the authors that two forms of SWB—one based on a bottom-up consideration of one's objective life circumstances, and another following a top-down evaluation of one's overall life—are differentially influenced by a positivity disposition that varies across individuals and across cultures. Disposition toward positivity does not have as large an influence on a person's satisfaction with narrow life domains, which might be more grounded in concrete reality, as on global ratings in which there is more latitude of judgment. This set of findings obviously requires replication and future research, but represents a provocative possible interpretation of some of the differences in SWB reports across cultures.

Diener and Oishi (chapter 8 this volume) report one methodological finding that is troubling. They found that various self-report items produce somewhat different scaling of the SWB of nations. This finding is troubling in part because we have virtually no understanding of how various questions or response options might produce different scores for various nations. Item response theory applied to scales across cultures may help address this question, as will focus groups and interviews combined with the existing scales. Statistics such as latent class analysis (Eid and Diener 1999) might also help in comparing responses across cultures.

Besides issues of measurement, there are additional methodological questions that must be addressed. One is the issue of causality. In most of the cross-sectional research reviewed in this book, one-time cross-sectional research is used, and thus it is impossible to draw conclusions about causal direction. In rare circumstances actual experiments have been conducted, and a few longitudinal or panel studies also exist that give us some hints about causal direction. Much more work, however, needs to be accomplished in this area, and most statements in this book must be qualified by the fact that they are both correlational and cross-sectional.

A further methodological and conceptual complication is defining and measuring the cultural and societal variables that predict well-being. In some cases we have relatively objective indicators for nations such as GNP per capita and infant mortality rates, although these measures do differ in quality and subjectivity. For example, measures of GNP include some products and services of a society and purposefully exclude others (e.g., housework). Further, when we examine predictor variables such as freedom, it is not always clear exactly which variables should be measured, and often no single variable is a completely valid index of an underlying construct. For example, what measures are best in terms of indicating equality between the sexes in nations?

Sampling is another topic that invariably arises in discussions of methodology. Although some of the studies of SWB reviewed in this publication relied on samples of college students that are typical in psychological research, the area of SWB is fortunate to have its roots in survey research. Thus many of the surveys in the field are based on large probability samples of nations. Originally, the sample of nations for which SWB data were available was small, and most studies came from highly industrialized western countries. In recent years, however, larger samples of nations are available (and the diversity of countries employed in these modern studies can be seen in chapter 7 by Inglehart and Klingemann). Nevertheless, very poor countries such as those in Africa are still underrepresented. In addition preliterate societies are virtually absent from this area of study, and this is especially unfortunate for a volume on cross-cultural differences.

A final methodological topic is the use of process measures to understand how reports of SWB are generated. For example, What information is used when respondents formulate their responses to life satisfaction scales (e.g., Suh and Diener 1999)? Related to this issue, we need procedures by which we can assess the influence of memory biases in mood reports, determine the influence of impression management in responding, and assess the impact of current events and mood on the responses given. For example, Schwarz and Strack (1999), show that situational factors can have an influence on SWB responses. An important task is to understand how such transient, situational factors interplay with more chronic cultural influences in affecting SWB responses. Another topic that begs for systematic research is the influence of the social settings on SWB reports across cultures. East Asian cultural members who are highly sensitive to self-presentational concerns (Suh 1999), for instance, may report their SWB differently depending on the nature of the interpersonal survey setting. An example of a method to assess the influence of impression management is to vary the degree of anonymity in responding and determine how it influences the reports (Park, Upshaw, and Koh 1988). Research paradigms used in social cognition, such as reaction time measures, delayed memory paradigms, and priming methods (e.g., see Oishi, Wyer, and Colcombe 1999; Robinson 1999) can also be used to assess the cognitive processes leading to satisfaction responses. If we understand the processes by which SWB judgments are made, we will be in a much stronger position to understand the differences in the responses between individuals and between cultures.

Although many of the methodological problems have been barely addressed in empirical research, we feel that the chapters in this book indicate that interesting findings have nevertheless emerged. The measures and methods seem sufficient to have produced some meaningful and fascinating results. We believe, however, that it is time for more rigorous methodology in this area, and we suggest that definitive conclusions will be possible only after this occurs. In-depth ethnographic work can help craft measures that are appropriate to various cultures, but we also need to develop these measures into batteries for assessing subjective well-being that can be used across cultures. We believe that some of the greatest progress on subjective well-being in the decades to come will be based on sophisticated measurement work across societies in which the scales derive from sophisticated theories.

Overview of the Book

We begin the book with a chapter by Harry Triandis (chapter 2) because this work presents an extensive overview of many of the factors that might influence subjective well-being across cultures. There are data to support some of Triandis's conjectures; other variables represent promising avenues for future research. As always, Triandis, one of the leading figures in cross-cultural psychology, brings creativity to his broad model of SWB. Chapter 3 by Charlotte Ratzlaff, David Matsumoto, and colleagues provides a definition of culture and SWB, and highlights the importance of considering the significant individual variation that exists within all cultures.

The second section of the book is focused on differences in how SWB is experienced across cultures. Eunkook Suh (chapter 4) addresses one important variable, the self. He finds that factors such as self-esteem and self-consistency, which are both believed to be central to optimal functioning in the western nations of Europe and North America, are not such strong correlates of life satisfaction in East Asian cultures. Suh also shows how the relation of affective happiness and life satisfaction varies across societies. In brief, individualists use their emotions more to judge their life satisfaction, whereas collectivists tend to rely more heavily on social appraisals. Following this lead, Shigehiro Oishi (chapter 5) demonstrates that feelings of autonomy are correlated with well-being in individualistic cultures, but not in collectivistic cultures. Oishi finds that positive social relationships, however, are equally important in both collectivistic and individualistic cultures, suggesting the idea that some variables may be universally related to the experience of well-being. Shinobu Kitayama and Hazel Markus (chapter 6) take the most radical cultural position in advancing the notion that both "well" and "being" must be defined in cultural terms, and therefore that the very texture of subjective well-being varies across cultures. These authors suggest that well-being is necessarily defined in social terms in all societies, and that a person's quality of life is defined collaboratively with others, not simply from an internal frame of reference. This argument meshes nicely with Suh's finding that respondents in collectivistic cultures are more likely to use norms and the social appraisals of others in evaluating their SWB, whereas those in individualistic societies are more likely to heavily weight the internal frame of reference arising from one's own happiness.

The next section of the book contains four chapters that ask whether specific societal conditions generally lead to SWB in the nations of the world. Ronald Inglehart and Hans-Dieter Klingemann (chapter 7) propose several provocative hypotheses, and marshal evidence for them. First, they suggest that SWB is necessary for stable democracy, and that political systems are likely to collapse if many people within a nation are dissatisfied over a period of time. Their second finding complements the first: stable democracies are likely to experience higher levels of SWB, and unstable political circumstances lead to very low average levels of SWB. Thus SWB may be both a cause and consequence of stable democratic governance. Because the conditions of nations so clearly influence average levels of well-being, Inglehart and Klingemann deduce that genetic influences are not the sole contributors to long-term subjective well-being.

In chapter 8 Ed Diener and Shigehiro Oishi review evidence on the relation of income to SWB: between nations, within countries, and over time. Two findings are noteworthy: wealthy nations are happier on average than poor ones, and yet SWB increased very little in the richer nations over the last several decades, even though wealth expanded spectacularly. Shalom Schwartz and Gila Melech (chapter 9) introduce worry as one aspect of subjective ill-being. They demonstrate that micro worry—concerning threats to self and close others—and macro worry—concerning threats to society or the world—are distinguished in fourteen nations. They discuss how violations of human rights, income inequality, and inflation lead to high levels of micro worry but have little effect on macro worry. Strikingly, cultural values affect worry levels more powerfully than objective life conditions do. Cultural egalitarianism and harmony lead to low micro worry and to high macro worry. In chapter 10 Ruut Veenhoven provides an examination of how freedom may influence feelings of well-being. Although Veenhoven finds that the economic freedom of nations is related to the average levels of well-being in them, he finds that broader notions of freedom, including political and personal freedoms, are related to higher SWB in wealthier nations but not in poorer ones.

In the final section of the volume, several individual difference variables are discussed in terms of their relation to subjective well-being across nations. Richard Lucas and Carol Gohm (chapter 11) use a meta-analytic strategy in which nations are treated as separate studies in order to analyze differences in subjective well-being due to sex and age across countries. In two data sets several general trends appear to occur across most nations. Alexander Grob (chapter 12) explores the relation of feelings of control to happiness in European adolescents, and hypothesizes that feelings of control are increasingly important as societies become more individualistic. Thus the chapters of the book examine broad factors that influence the general well-being of most nations, as well as variables that have a differential influence across cultures.

We hope that readers from all societies will gain a degree of subjective well-being from reading the chapters of this volume.

The Authors

It is fitting that a book on culture and well-being be authored by scholars from diverse nations. Ed Diener is from the United States. Although Eunkook Suh recently joined the faculty at the University of California, Irvine, in the United States, he was born and grew up in South Korea, and also lived for a time in Indonesia. Although several of the authors hail from North America (Gohm, Inglehart, Lucas, Ratzlaff, and Markus), two of the Americans have their roots in other nations: Triandis is originally from Greece, and David Matsumoto is of Japanese ancestry and has lived in that nation. The other authors, and the nations of which they are citizens, are Alexander Grob (Switzerland), Shinobu Kitayama and Shigehiro Oishi (Japan), Shalom Schwartz and Gila Melech (Israel), Hans-Dieter Klingemann (Germany), and Ruut Veenhoven (the Netherlands).

References

Balatsky, G., and Diener, E. 1993. Subjective well-being among Russian students. *Social Indicators Research* 28: 225–43.

Diener, E., Napa-Scollon, C. K., Oishi, S., Suh, E. M., and Dzokoto, V. (in press). Positivity and the construction of life satisfaction judgments: Global happiness is not the sum of its parts. *Journal of Happiness Studies.*

Diener, E., Sapyta, J., and Suh, E. 1998. Subjective well-being is essential to well-being. *Psychological Inquiry* 9: 33–37.

Diener, E., and Suh, E. 1997. Measuring quality of life: Economic, social, and subjective indicators. *Social Indicators Research* 40: 189–216.

Diener, E., Suh, E. M., Smith, H., and Shao. L. 1995. National differences in reported subjective well-being: Why do they occur? *Social Indicators Research* 34: 7–32.

Edgerton, R. B. 1992. *Sick Societies: Challenging the Myth of Primitive Harmony.* New York: Free Press.

Eid, M., and Diener, E. 1999. The derivation of latent class analysis for comparisons across cultures: The case of subjective well-being. Manuscript, University of Trier, Germany.

Oishi, S., Wyer, R. S., and Colcombe, S. 1999. Cultural variation in the use of current life satisfaction to predict the future. Manuscript, University of Illinois at Urbana-Champaign.

Ouweenel, P., and Veenhoven, R. 1991. Cross-national differences in happiness: Cultural bias or societal quality? In N. Bleichrodt and P. J. D. Drenth, eds., *Contemporary Issues in Cross-cultural Psychology,* Amsterdam: Swets and Zeitlinger, pp. 168–84.

Park, K. B., Upshaw, H. S., and Koh, S. D. 1988. East Asian's responses to western health items. *Journal of Cross-Cultural Psychology* 19: 51–64.

Robinson, M. D. 1999. Short-duration valenced primes can influence life satisfaction: Normative and personality influences on judgment. Manuscript, University of Illinois at Urbana-Champaign.

Sandvik. E., Diener, E., and Seidlitz, L. 1993. Subjective well-being: The convergence and stability of self-report and non-self-report measures. *Journal of Personality* 61: 317–42.

Schwarz, N., and Strack, F. 1999. Reports of subjective well-being: Judgmental processes and their methodological implications. In D. Kahneman, E. Diener, and N. Schwarz, eds., *Well-Being: The Foundations of Hedonic Psychology.* New York: Russell Sage Foundation, pp. 61–84.

Shao, L. Multilanguage comparability of life satisfaction and happiness measures in mainland Chinese and American students. Unpublished master's thesis, University of Illinois at Urbana-Champaign.

Suh, E. M. 1999. Culture, identity consistency, and subjective well-being. Manuscript. University of California at Irvine.

Suh, E. M., and Diener, E. 1999. The use of emotion and social appraisal information in life satisfaction judgments: Joining culture, personality, and situational influences. Manuscript. University of Illinois at Urbana-Champaign.

Vijver, F. V. D., and Leung, K. 1997. *Methods and Data Analyses for Cross-cultural Research.* Thousand Oaks, CA: Sage.

2

Cultural Syndromes and Subjective Well-being

Harry C. Triandis

This chapter attempts to construct a useful theory on the relationship between culture and subjective well-being. It will consider many factors, but the picture is more complex. The chapter's purpose therefore is to initiate further research in the theoretical aspects of SWB.

Culture is to society what memory is to individuals. It refers to tools and ideas that are shared and transmitted to succeeding generations because they were once practical at some point in time. The construct is always fuzzy, and one way to focus it is to examine cultural syndromes.

Meaning of Cultural Syndromes

A cultural syndrome is a *shared* pattern of attitudes, beliefs, categorizations, self-definitions, norms, role definitions, values, and other subjective elements of culture that is organized around some theme; it can be found among those who speak a language dialect, in a certain historic period, and in a definable geographic region.

We will consider three such syndromes:

1. *Complexity–simplicity.* The roles and choices in information societies are very large, but among hunters and gatherers they are relatively small. The theme is the complexity in the culture.

2. *Tightness–looseness.* Tightness is associated with dependable sanctions if people do not follow the norms of a society; looseness is associated with tolerance for deviations from the norms of a culture. The theme is the culture's tolerance (looseness) or nontolerance (tightness) for deviations from norms. Additionally tight cultures have many rules and norms about social behavior; loose cultures have fewer rules and norms.

3. *Individualism–collectivism.* Individualism is found in societies in which the self is regarded as autonomous, personal goals have priority over in-group goals,

attitudes are the most important determinants of behavior, and social exchanges characterize interpersonal relationships. The theme is the centrality of the individual in the culture. Collectivism is found in societies where the self is regarded as an aspect of groups, interdependent with members of those groups, in-group norms have priority over personal needs, norms are as important as attitudes in determining behavior, and relationships are communal, including a lot of sharing, and little concern for the costs of the relationship to individuals. The theme is the centrality of the group.

Triandis (1994, 1995) hypothecized that individualism is maximal in complex, loose societies (e.g., among Hollywood stars), and collectivism is maximal in simple, tight societies (e.g., in theocracies). As data become available on Michele Gelfand's project that measures tightness in several cultures, it will become possible to correlate gross national product per capita (GNP is a proxy for complexity) and tightness with measures of individualism–collectivism and to test this hypothesis.

In the meantime let us look at some relationships between existing measures of individualism and SWB. We will remain open to the possibility that tightness and complexity might turn out to be even better predictors of SWB.

In reviewing the literature we will keep in mind that "culture" is often indexed by "nation." This we admit is not ideal, but it is the only way to do this kind of research with limited funds. Statistics about nations have been compiled by the United Nations and other agencies. There is relatively little work on measuring cultural attributes, since there are at least 650 known cultures (Triandis 1995) and innumerable subcultures (e.g., physicians have a different culture than lawyers). Each nation includes many cultures, so it is only in future work that we will be able to obtain relatively "pure" measures of cultural attributes. There are a few studies where this has already been done, so we will review these studies in some detail. In any case, when we refer to the literature, most of the time we will be dealing with national cultures, even though they are theoretically unsatisfactory entities. Before we consider the literature, we need to have a better idea about the meaning of SWB.

Meaning of Subjective Well-being (SWB)

Subjective well-being comprises people's evaluations, both affective and cognitive, of their lives (Diener and Fujita 1994). Diener (1984) presented a discussion of the major theoretical perspectives and methodological issues in the study of SWB.

Ryff and Keyes (1995) proposed that well-being has six aspects: self-acceptance, positive relations with others, autonomy, environmental mastery, purpose in life, and personal growth. It would be interesting to examine if these components are found in all cultures, and whether additional components might be found in certain other cultures. Also the relative weight of these components is likely to vary with culture.

One good way to understand the meaning of a construct is to look at the factors associated with it. The factors that predict SWB may be different across cultures. This was clearly evidenced in a study by Suh and Diener (1997) who found that emotions predicted the SWB of people in individualist cultures, while both emotions and behaving according to the norms of the society predicted the SWB of individuals in collectivist cultures (61 nations, $N = 62,446$). A similar point was made by Suh, Diener, Oishi, and Triandis (1998).

SWB is related to the common term "happiness," and it can range from depression to elation. It can have both "affective" aspects (I feel good about my life) and cognitive aspects (I think that the various aspects of my life, i.e., family, job, education, etc., are satisfactory). A distinction between the two is desirable, since sometimes they are not the same. For example, Campbell, Converse, and Rodgers (1976) found that Americans younger than 35-years-old were the happiest age group, while those over 75-years-old were the least happy group. Yet the satisfactions expressed by the older group were higher than the satisfactions expressed by the younger group. They interpreted these findings by noting that the young may be happy, but they have not yet achieved their aspirations. Therefore they may feel less satisfied than the older group who may find in their later years that they are better off than they had anticipated and thus feel satisfied with their lives.

Diener, Diener and Diener (1995) investigated the factors that lead to SWB. They found that high income, individualism, human rights, and social equality are connected with SWB. Individualism is an important component of SWB even after income is controlled statistically. However, rapid increases in income seem to lower SWB, suggesting that expectations can rise too fast and not be realized. In general, developed countries enjoy high incomes, value human rights and social equality, so they have high levels of SWB. Underdeveloped and developing countries of the third world which do not emphasize these factors show lower levels of SWB.

Distinction between the Ecological and Individual Levels of Analysis   It is important to distinguish analyses at the cultural (ecological) level from analyses at the individual level. At the cultural level, we deal with attributes that refer to entities such as gross national income per capita, average longevity, and expenditures on the environment as a percentage of national income. At the individual level, we refer, for example, to the attitudes, beliefs, perceptions, and values of individuals.

Hofstede (1980) identified individualism and collectivism at the level of culture by summing the responses of the individuals in each country to the attitude and value items that were used in a survey. In such a study responses to n items over the N people who responded to each of the n items in a culture are summed and divided by N. Thus one has n means per culture. If there are k cultures, one can compute the n by n matrix of correlations based on k observations per variable. Hofstede subjected this matrix to a factor analysis, from which he extracted the individualism–collectivism factor.

The results obtained at the cultural level can vary greatly from the results obtained at the individual level of analysis. To deal with this problem, Triandis, Leung, Villareal, and Clack (1985) introduced the terms *idiocentrism* and *allocentrism*. These terms refer to the personality attributes that correspond to individualism and collectivism. There are many studies showing that individualism is related in one way to some other variable and that idiocentrism is related in a different way to the same variable. For example, Hui, Yee, and Eastman (1995) found that individualism is positively related to job satisfaction at the cultural level, but in Hong Kong idiocentrism is negatively related to job satisfaction. One interpretation is that people in individualist cultures are more socially mobile and have more choices, so they settle on jobs that are more satisfying. Hence there is a positive correlation between individualism and job satisfaction at the cultural level. But in Hong Kong, which is generally a collectivist culture, people are expected to be allocentric (Triandis, Chen, and Chan 1998) and to pay much attention to interpersonal relationships. Thus in Hong Kong the idiocentrics are countercultural. Idiocentrics are people who are too concerned with getting the job done and not sufficiently concerned with interpersonal relationships. So they do not receive social support and may even be disliked by their coworkers. As a result they often become dissatisfied with their jobs.

Diener, Diener, and Diener (1995) did not find social comparison theory useful in providing explanations for the differences in the levels of SWB across countries (ecological analyses). On the other hand, Diener and Fujita (1997) argue that at the individual level, social comparisons predict SWB.

SWB and Other Variables at the Ecological and Individual Levels   There is research that attempts to determine which theories are best in predicting SWB at the cultural level of analysis. Veenhoven (1995) tested social comparison, folklore, and livability theories at the ecological level. He did not find support for the first two as explanations for differences in SWB but did find support for the last theory. Livability can be indexed by real income per capita, social security, gender equality, freedom of the press, political democracy, high levels of education, media attendance, and the like. These attributes are more common in developed countries than in the developing and third world countries.

Diener (1995) developed a quality of life index, reflecting social statistics that correspond to Shalom Schwartz's (1992) values. Statistics such as number of physicians per capita, college attendance rates, income equality, number of environmental treaties, monetary saving rate, and purchasing power parity were used to construct a quality of life index. This index was related to income levels. The countries that had incomes of about 40 percent or less than the U.S. standard had lower quality of life index scores than the countries with more than 40 percent of the U.S. standard. However, purchasing parity power income was linearly related to the quality of life index, showing no asymptote at high levels of income. Wealth, of course, was correlated with the quality of life index (Diener and Diener 1995a). Staudinger, Fleeson, and Baltes (1997) also found that well-being was predicted from socioeconomic level, both in Germany and the USA.

At the individual level of analysis Diener and Diener (1995b) found that self-esteem and SWB were correlated, and that the correlation between satisfaction with different aspects of life, such as self, family, and friends, and SWB, was higher in individualist than in collectivist countries. Oishi, Diener, Lucas, and Suh (1999) found that values mediate SWB. In poor countries satisfaction with finances is a better predictor of SWB than in rich countries. In rich countries, which of course are individualistic, there is emphasis on the self, freedom, and recreation. In individualistic countries, those who are satisfied with self, freedom, and recreation have high SWB.

Diener (2000) reports that in the developed countries the correlation between self-esteem and SWB is around 0.65, whereas in the less developed countries it is around 0.15. It may be that when basic needs are satisfied, self-esteem is salient, but when basic needs are not satisfied, self-esteem is not salient, so it does not correlate with SWB. This Maslowian view of the relationship between self-esteem and SWB is testable.

Diener, Diener, and Diener (1995) showed that at the cultural level there is a positive connection between individualism and SWB but that at the individual level, it may be negative. An explanation for this may be that the more allocentric the person is, the more social support that person is likely to receive (Triandis, Bontempo, Asai, and Lucca 1988), and the more satisfaction that person will derive from close social relationships. This is a factor that should increase SWB. The Diener, Diener, and Diener argument is in agreement with the findings of Verkuyten and Lay (1997). They found that allocentrism is related to SWB, and they also showed that relationships at the cultural level are not always consistent with relationships at the individual level.

Verkuyten (1995) found that in collectivist cultures idiocentrism and allocentrism are unrelated; in individualist cultures they are negatively related. This difference may be related to the fact that people in collectivist cultures tolerate inconsistencies more than people in individualist cultures (Fiske, Kitayama, Markus, and Nisbett 1997). Allocentrism is related to sensitivity to friends, having fewer friends but feeling closer to them, perceiving less intimacy with all who are not "best friends," and endorsing rules about relationships with others more than idiocentrism. Idiocentrism is related to less sensitivity to the needs of friends, the use of more personal attributes to describe friends (idiocentrics in general use more internal factors to explain behavior), the use of less intimacy in general, and less intimacy with friends in particular than is found among allocentrics. Thus allocentrics probably derive more pleasure from interpersonal relationships, which increases their SWB.

Diener, Suh, Smith, and Shao (1995) examined the possibility that some artifact might explain the cultural differences in SWB. For example, is it more desirable to say "I am happy" in some countries than in other countries? Is there a fear that if one says "I am happy" such certainty will bring on unfortunate life events, which Lyubomirsky (1997) has reported is a typical Russian superstition? Is there a norm that requires people, in some cultures, to deny that they are happy? Are there norms for the expression of happiness that are reflected in lower scores? Are cultural differences likely to explain differences in SWB across nations? And is SWB of equal importance in every culture? Are there differences in the social desirability of saying "I am happy?"

After an analysis of Michalos's data from several countries, and their own data from China, Korea, and the United States, these authors discount most of these explanations, with few exceptions. The exceptions were that they found that there are cultural differences in the importance of SWB (the Chinese do not consider it so important), and that people in Asian cultures have such high aspirations and expectations that they frequently do not realize their hopes. For this reason they often have lower SWB.

Even when objective living conditions (having opportunities for education, health services, good housing, good transportation, and good recreation) are relatively good, people in East Asian countries react to these conditions as if they are inadequate. For example, the objective evidence shows that many people in East Asia have excellent educational systems, and yet they rate their educational systems as unsatisfactory (Stevenson, Chen, and Lee 1993). Here again a distinction is needed between the cultural and the individual levels of analysis. It may be, and this needs to be checked in future research, that China or Japan have as excellent educational systems as other countries. But in circumstances where too many Chinese and Japanese are unable to enter the existing highly competitive universities, they judge their own educational systems as inadequate. Expectations are important determinants of SWB. Expectations may not be realized because of difficulties encountered in everyday life, perhaps because of the high population density that makes the specific sources of satisfaction less available to individuals.

SWB is high in all countries (Diener 2000). The high levels of satisfaction in countries with limited resources suggest that when expectations are low and/or when people have relatively low levels of desires for things that require resources, they will have high SWB. This supports the Buddhist emphasis on limited desires that can lead to nirvana. (Actually this is the opposite of what advertising does, so it would be interesting to do a study of expenditures on advertising in relation to SWB.)

Future research should investigate if there is a "halo effect" that makes people with a high SWB likely to see most of the elements of their life as more satisfactory than they are objectively. This effect may be especially strong for elements that are closest to the individual, such as my school or my congressional representative. These data may explain why Americans are satisfied with their schools even when their children score at the bottom in international comparisons on mathematics and science (Stevenson, Chen, and Lee 1993). This discrepancy may in part reflect ignorance of such comparisons, but a gradient of a halo effect may operate and account for the fact that parents think that their own school (or member of Congress) is fine, while other schools (or members of Congress) are not.

Relatively low SWB may result in a negative halo effect. East Asians may be dissatisfied with their educational systems, health services, housing, transportation systems, and so on, because of negative halo effects. In this case "my school" may seem less good than other Chinese or Japanese schools, while schools that are far away may look exceptionally good.

Some researchers have investigated SWB in relation to "objective" indexes. For example, Sagan (1987) provided an analysis of well-being that depends entirely on life expectancies. He reports that with the decline of infectious diseases during the twentieth century, life expectancies have increased dramatically in many parts of the world. The high levels of SWB in most countries may reflect comparisons with the life expectancies of previous generations, which of course were quite low. Sagan (1987) further argues that shifts toward individualism, with the related decreases of family cohesion and increased frequencies of divorce, attenuate the positive effects of affluence on SWB. After 1900 the upper classes in most countries improved their life expectancy much more than the lower classes. A good research project would examine if the correlation between individualism and SWB might be related, in part, to longevity. Since individualism and affluence are related, high levels of SWB may be correlated with individualism because people in the individualist cultures live longer than people in most collectivist cultures.

Affluence also increases well-being because it protects people from some natural disasters (better controls of floods, earthquakes, and warnings about bad weather). Veenhoven (1994) found that the greater the number of vulnerabilities (floods, hurricanes, and tornadoes) in a particular place, the lower is the SWB ($r = -0.71$, $N = 27$).

Slottje, Scully, Hirschberg, and Hayes (1991) considered several dimensions that determine SWB: physical well-being, political rights, male life expectancy, infant mortality, calorie consumption, female literacy, and gross domestic product. They developed models for combining these and for ranking countries. Their general conclusions, however, are not different from the conclusions of other researchers: the economically developed countries have high SWB and the less developed countries low SWB.

One may wonder if the indexes of SWB with which psychologists work are reliable and valid measuring tools. Apparently they are, since they correlate with a number of variables in ways that make sense. For example, across many studies (Veenhoven 1994), SWB has positive correlations with amount of education, income, employment, and health status, and it has negative correlations with unemployment, suicide (Moum 1996), war conditions, violations of civil rights, riots, income inequality, oppression of the political opposition, undemocratic governments, and the like. The more "vulnerabilities (floods, hurricanes, tornadoes, etc.) in a particular country, the lower is the SWB of the country.

In sum, it appears that economic and social conditions are major factors in SWB. But even when economic factors are controlled statistically, individualism is still positively related to SWB. Personality factors such as self-esteem, optimism, and extroversion have been found, in some cases, to predict SWB. In addition, relationships found at the ecological level of analysis are not necessarily found at the individual level of analysis. Thus it is important to keep the levels of analysis separate. In short, we need to analyze the factors that increase and decrease SWB at both the cultural and the individual levels of analysis.

Subjective Well-being as a Quasi-stationary Equilibrium

Kurt Lewin's (1952) concept of a quasi-stationary equilibrium is especially appropriate in examining complex social phenomena. The idea is that there are forces that push SWB toward higher levels, and other forces that push it toward lower levels. At some point the two sets of forces are in balance. When that happens, SWB is at a temporary equilibrium. But the equilibrium is only quasi-stationary because sooner or later one of the forces will change and that will change the level of the equilibrium. Changes can occur when forces become stronger or weaker, and affect equilibrium. Thus we can conceive of SWB as a dynamic state that depends on the temporary balance among different sets of forces.

For example, at the cultural level, a force that increases SWB is income, and a force that decreases it is war. At the individual level, a force that increases SWB is openness to new experiences, and a force that decreases it is stress. We will review many forces that work in both directions at each of the above levels of analysis.

Cultural Factors That May Influence Subjective Well-being

In the previous sections the focus was on research that provided a background for understanding SWB. Here the focus will be on cultural and personal factors that may be associated with SWB. The effect size of some of these forces may be small, but their theoretical significance is often large.

Tightness   The literature indicates that at the cultural level individualism is correlated with SWB, even when the economic level is controlled statistically. According to Triandis (1994, 1995) collectivism is correlated with tightness. Thus we can expect tightness to be related to lower levels of SWB. This prediction is consistent with the findings of Arrindell, Hatzichristou, Wensink, and Rosenberg (1997). These researchers checked the correlations of Hofstede's (1980) four dimensions of national culture and cultural level SWB. They found that uncertainty avoidance, a dimension that Hofstede equated with tightness, was related to low SWB.

In tight societies people experience high levels of anxiety. They fear that they may not be "correct" and "proper" in their behavior, that they may be criticized, rejected, or even ostracized as a result. Iwao (1993) discusses the extent to which people in Japan, a very tight culture, live in terror that they will commit a social error and be criticized. Fear of criticism occurs especially when there is a difference in social status. If the other person is higher in social standing, one may risk not expressing sufficient deference; if the other person is lower socially, one may not be a sufficiently good model of correct behavior. Similarly Kitayama, Markus, and Kurokawa (in press) report that the second most frequent emotion for both men and women in Japan is an anxiety about the consequences of one's own actions on others.

Thus it is only with peers, for example, in pubs with one's friends or in high school reunions, that the Japanese are relaxed and can escape the fear of inappropriate action. When alcohol is involved, one is forgiven for acting inappropriately. Furthermore, in Japan one has many obligations to others (*giri*), and one may well worry about not being able to meet all of these obligations.

Since tightness results in people fearing that their behavior is going to be inappropriate, there is the supposition that they may escape from this actuality by engaging in fantasies. So far, however, there is very little research on fantasies, though fantasies are an important aspect of subjective experience. It would be interesting to study fantasies in relation to SWB, since then one can be totally free. There are no unpleasant consequences in fantasies. Thus it seems reasonable to hypothesize that the frequency of fantasies will be higher in tight than in loose societies.

However, a high frequency of fantasies has consequences. Fantasies are generally pleasant, so the framework for evaluating events becomes quite positive. When a new event is perceived that is relatively lower in affect than the mean of the framework, the event is perceived as undesirable (Parducci 1995). Thus too many pleasant fantasies can lead to low SWB.

Parducci (1995) has shown that people have a tendency to choose alternatives that are immediately pleasing, but establish contexts against which their future outcomes compare unfavorably. His contextual theory of happiness suggests that people will be happier if they have many moderately positive experiences rather than many positive experiences as well as one *very* positive experience. This result is counter-intuitive. Yet his data are very clear.

To use some numbers to make the point: Suppose that people in a country earn $5, 90 percent of the time, and $0, 10 percent of the time. They will be happier than people who earn $10, 90 percent of the time, and $15, 10 percent of the time. That is counterintuitive because the people in the second country earn more. But the average pleasantness rating on a 9 point scale is 3.6 for the latter and 6.4 for the former (Parducci 1995, p. 89).

In short, if one has many pleasant fantasies, reality is likely to appear rather unpleasant. If it is true that people in tight cultures have more fantasies, then their SWB will be lower than the SWB of people in loose cultures. This is a testable hypothesis. Tightness can be studied in a number of ways as Michele Gelfand has done. For example, one could ask what deviations from norms are punishable? One could present several examples of deviations from norms and ask if one unit of punishment is appropriate for the least offensive deviation, how many units of punishment might be appropriate for each of the offenses. In tight cultures there should be a sharp increase in the number of units of punishment that are assigned to relatively minor offenses, whereas in loose cultures the sharp increase will occur only for the relatively serious offenses. The distance between the place in the rank-order of offenses where the curves shift from few to many units of punishment in any two cultures is a measure of the difference in the tightness of the two cultures.

Fantasies may have also a reciprocal causal relationship with SWB. Having fantasies decreases SWB, but also low SWB may lead to more fantasies. This kind of reciprocal causation may result in lower SWB.

Another hypothesis is that tight cultures have rules not only about most social behavior but also about who the "appropriate" comparison others ought to be. This restriction in the ability of individuals to chose comparison others who will make them feel good about themselves is likely to result in a low SWB.

While social comparison theory has not received support in the literature when cultural level studies were carried out, there is the argument of Diener and Fujita (1994) that at the individual level this theory predicts SWB. In short, if we compare ourselves to others who are less fortunate, we increase our SWB, at the individual level but this does not carry all the way to the cultural level of analysis.

In summary, a number of hypotheses suggest that cultural tightness is related to low SWB.

Cultural Complexity SWB is high when one's children "turn out" the way we want them to turn out. Ryff (1995) found that about a quarter of the variance in SWB is due to this factor. My hypothesis is that the simpler the culture, the fewer the desirable ways for the children to turn out. In short, in simple cultures the definition of what it is to "turn out well" is more limited, and thus there is likely to be more dissatisfaction with the way children turn out. For example, if the parent hoped that the child will become a physician and instead the child became a famous actor, the parent may well be dissatisfied. In a complex culture there are fewer clear expectations of how the child will "turn out." On the other hand, it may be the case that in simpler cultures children do turn out frequently the way parents expect them to turn out. In that case simplicity should increase SWB. Future studies should examine the "how children turn out" factor in relation to both cultural complexity and tightness.

Cultural complexity may lead to anxiety. Also, if cultural complexity is related to individualism, which is often related to competitiveness, there may be pressures to achieve that at times reduce SWB. Anxiety and stress will of course result in low SWB. Furthermore individualism is related to a fast pace of life (Levine and Norenzayan 1999) and that may also increase stress. On the other hand, in complex societies one has more comparison others to chose from. One can chose comparison targets that will increase one's self-esteem and result in higher SWB. In short, there are some very interesting ways of linking cultural complexity to SWB.

Also further research should investigate situations where people have few choices as opposed to many choices and simultaneously situations where people have many comparison others as opposed to few comparison others. It is likely that in the high-high cell SWB will be average. However, there will be many choices for the few comparison others cell that show very low SWB, and in the low-low cell, low SWB. In the few choices associated with many comparison others cell, there will be high SWB.

Individualism Individualism is closely linked with affluence. In this regard Hofstede's (1980) study showed the individualism score and gross national product per capita to be correlated about 0.80. Affluence has a positive effect on SWB (Diener, Diener and Diener 1995). It leads to more control over the environment, more self-determination, and hence more SWB (Lachman and Weaver 1998). However, the correlation between SWB and income is very low in the rich countries (e.g., $r = 0.08$ in the United States and Canada) and high only in the less affluent countries (e.g.,

$r = 0.40$ in India). This suggests that there is a limit in the extent that the SWB of a country can be increased by raising the country's gross national product.

There is considerable evidence (Triandis 1995) that the higher the person's position is in a social structure, the higher is that person's level of idiocentrism. Thus we expect the upper income groups to be more idiocentric and to have higher SWB. Kohn and Slomczynski (1990) reported that in many cultures the higher a person is positioned socially, the more self-determination that person has. That is, the person can decide what to do, when, where, and how. For example, physicians have more say in how to do their job than do ditch diggers. This type of freedom leads to job satisfaction. In fact, in one study, the most job satisfaction among low-level workers was found among garbage collectors, and the attribute used to interpret this findings was that they have high autonomy. In short, high self-determination leads to high SWB. This point is consistent with a vast literature that shows that job satisfaction is higher among professionals than among low-level workers.

However, there can be complications. For example, in Poland during the communist regime, the bureaucrats at the top were the most distressed. Kohn and Slomczynski attribute the distress to insecurity among top managers that were not members of the party. However, I wonder if these top officials were asked to perform according to standards set by the party, and they could not "deliver the goods." It is my impression that in a planned economy, decisions made in the center often do not make sense in the field. Being under the control of a party official in any of the communist countries must have been very stressful.

In terms of individualism-collectivism theory, Kohn and Slomczynski's data support the point that physicians were more idiocentric than the low-level workers, and the high level bureaucrats in communist countries were more allocentric than the workers. They found under communism higher levels of SWB among the workers than among the bureaucrats, but after the fall of communism that the picture reversed itself. The top-level managers became more satisfied than the workers. This is just as we see it in the West (Kohn et al. 1997).

Affluence is associated with busyness. There are myriads ways to spend time, and one has the financial resources to enjoy a great number of activities. As a result there is little time for fantasies. Less time for fantasies leads to a reverse process from the one discussed above in the work of Parducci (1995). Positive life events are seen as more positive in individualist cultures compared to in cultures where by our hypothesis there is much use of fantasies. Consequently there is higher SWB associated with individualism.

Individualism is also associated with high self-esteem and optimism. Kitayama, Markus, Matsumoto, and Norasakkunkit (1997) found that people in the United States show high levels of self-enhancement, an attribute that is related to their self-esteem. Research shows high levels of self-esteem and optimism in individualist cultures. High self-esteem inevitably results in high SWB. Kwan, Bond, and Singelis (1997) found that people in collectivist cultures have high SWB when they have high self-esteem and also get along with members of their ingroups. Kitayama, Markus, and Kurokawa (in press) found that people in Japan feel good when they experience interpersonally engaged emotions, such as close or friendly feelings, while people in the United States feel good when they experience interpersonally disengaged emotions, such as pride or elatedness. This means that well-being is optimized when people adhere to the script (interdependence or independence) that is central to their culture. These authors also found that their U.S. sample reported much higher frequencies of positive than negative emotions, but this phenomenon was not observed in the Japanese sample.

Personality factors are also relevant: The big five factor of openness to experience (high among individualists; see Realo 1999) is related to self-esteem, while the agreeableness factor (high among collectivists; see Realo 1999) is related to harmonious relationships. Self-esteem and good relationships determined life satisfaction in the Kwan et al. study. However, self-esteem was found to be more important in the individualist cultures and agreeableness was more important in the collectivist cultures.

Staudinger, Fleeson, and Baltes (1997) considered personality related to SWB, with neuroticism negatively related and with openness, extroversion, conscientiousness, sense of environmental mastery, personal growth, purpose in life, and self-acceptance positively related to SWB.

Idiocentrism ought to be associated with the freedom to choose comparison others; hence that should lead to high SWB. Idiocentrics tend to be found in complex societies, and complexity results in the need for rules that will simplify the processing of the requests of citizens. Bureaucrats in individualist countries use the principle of universality (deal with all equally) and develop rules that facilitate the satisfaction of the needs of citizens. For example, in the United States I can get my passport renewed by mail, and it takes me about 15 minutes; in Greece my friends tell me that the same activity is likely to take two days, standing in line to see various bureaucrats. Similarly Levine (1997, pp. 104–105) tells of having to spend four days to make an international telephone call in Nepal. Getting a driver's license can take a day in Mexico (Levine 1997, p. 115). These points suggest that Veenhoven's (1995) livability (of permanent residents) score would be higher in many individualist cultures than in less affluent and somewhat collectivist cultures, such as Nepal or Mexico.

Individualist cultures are also dominated by private enterprises, which increase their profits when they provide conveniences. Conveniences may include long hours when stores are open, quick service (e.g., if a long line is formed an additional employee opens another line to expedite payment for groceries), supermarkets that make it possible to buy everything required in one place, payment of bills by mail or e-mail, and the like. All these conveniences increase SWB. By contrast, in the more collectivist countries people spend lots of time on simple tasks such as paying bills or shopping, where they are often not given good service.

I spent several weeks in Austria, a predominantly individualist country but somewhat collectivist (vide the socialist vote). I noticed that in Austria labor unions make sure that employees do not stay up late or work on the weekend. That is good for the employee but not convenient for the general public. Since the general public comprises more than the people who work in stores, this factor reduces well-being overall. Getting things done (e.g., withdrawing money from the bank) is more complicated in Austria; it entails more bureaucracy and is more time-consuming than comparable tasks in the United States. Of course, there are compensating factors, but the high suicide rates in middle-Europe (Austria, Hungary) and certain Scandinavian countries, like Sweden but not Norway, make one wonder if in individualistic cultures extreme bureaucracy leads to low SWB. Individualists are affluent, and have high SWB, so why are there such high rates of suicide in some individualist cultures? Again, that is an interesting topic for research.

Triandis (1995) distinguished two types of individualism and collectivism: horizontal and vertical. Vertical individualism is associated with more competition, stress, and hence lower SWB, and horizontal individualism with more freedom to pursue one's interests, more loneliness, and hence factors that cancel each other in SWB. However, while individualists do not have as many intimate relationships as collectivists (Triandis 1995), they tend to have more acquaintances and friends. Veenhoven (1994) found that the more friends one has, the higher is the SWB ($r = 0.87$). The countries in which people had a large number of friends were individualistic: the United States, Australia, and Scandinavia. The countries in which people reported having a relatively small number of friends were Japan, Mexico, and India, which are mainly collectivist.

Stress can be a big factor in reduced SWB, but it operates more at the individual than at the cultural level. Linsky and Straus (1986) studied stress in different U.S. regions and used the number of business failures, illegitimate births, deaths per 1,000 residents, number of divorces, abortions, and natural disasters to index the social stress within a region. They found stress associated with rapid social change, social instability, little conventional morality, and a "fast buck" mentality. Some states, like Washington, Oregon, and New Jersey, had more business failures than other states; others, like Nevada and Alaska, had more bank failures, and so on. They also found high rates of ulcers, asthma, and respiratory diseases as well as high alcohol abuse in the stressed states. Many of these factors are associated with individualism, but since affluence is also associated with individualism, and affluence is a major factor determining SWB, the effect of social stress on cultural SWB may not be substantial. It is, however, important for individual SWB. These observations reinforce the recommendation that we made earlier for future research to explicitly examine SWB at both the cultural and individual levels.

In individualist cultures unpleasant life events are not faced with sufficient social support. The increase in stress will lead to low SWB at the individual level. However, many people in individualistic societies have high optimism, and this factor can lead to high SWB. On the other hand, pessimism can sometimes be a more powerful predictor of SWB than optimism (Robinson-Whelen, Kim, MacCallum, and Kiecolt-Gleser 1997). If the data point to that finding, further research should be used to study and confirm the effect of pessimism to the culture. While Kitayama's work suggests that there is more pessimism in collectivist cultures than in individualist cultures, this has not been fully established.

Horizontal collectivism fosters in-groups and a sharing of positive and negative life events; hence there is higher SWB. Suh and Diener (1999) found that an exceptionally strong source of SWB for collectivists is the approval they receive from others, such as their parents. The data suggests that approval is much more important for allocentrics than for idiocentrics. Radhakrishnan and Chan (1997) found that Indians were allocentric and did not distinguish between their own goals and the goals of their parents, while Americans, like good idiocentrics, did see their personal goals as quite different from the goals of their parents. Also Americans were found to attach more importance to their own goals than to the goals of their parents. In India low SWB occurred among those who did not view the goals of their parents as important. In America, low SWB occurred when there was a large discrepancy between the goals of the person and the goals of the parents. These complexities call for replication, and the development of a theory about the way cultural context determines which factors result in high SWB.

Vertical collectivism often includes internalization of the norms of the in-group. When one behaves according to norms, often there will be higher SWB. But if one is opposed to the norms of the in-group, there will be low SWB.

There is evidence that collectivism is associated with high levels of social support, which can lead to more collective self-esteem, higher levels of social identify (Tajfel 1982), and thus to high SWB at the individual level. Furthermore collectivism is associated with group consensus, which is related to high SWB (Bliese and Halverson 1998).

People in collectivist cultures are extremely supportive of their ingroup members, but they have cold, and even hostile, relationships with outgroup members. As a result in their interactions with strangers the allocentrics often show little trust. They arrange things so as to make it difficult for strangers to develop interpersonal trust. This can depress SWB at the cultural level. Sagan (1987) further noted the distrust of outgroup members in collectivist cultures reduces SWB for the society as a whole. On the other hand, for people in these cultures who interact mostly with their ingroups, difficult interactions with the outgroup may not have an effect on their SWB. These are relationships that we need to explore in future research.

Ingelhart (1990) reported that postmodern societies, which tend to be individualistic, de-emphasize material and physical security as factors leading to well-being. Interpersonal trust is high among people in the rich countries. Since the rich are individualistic, they may not see much difference between strangers and acquaintances, and they treat all of them with reasonable trust.

Bettecourt and Dorr (1997) examined whether allocentrism was related to SWB. They found that it was but was mediated by collective self-esteem. Collective self-esteem can be private (the extent to which individuals feel positively about their social groups) and public (the extent to which individuals believe that other people feel positively about their social groups). Bettencourt and Dorr (1997) tested American students, and found that those who were allocentric were more satisfied with their lives. Idiocentrism was negatively related to SWB. However, the relationship between allocentrism and SWB was mediated by collective self-esteem. Both private and public collective self-esteem mediated this relationship. It would appear that allocentrics derive some of their life satisfaction from the fact that they like their groups and believe that their groups are liked by others. Note that this relationship is at the individual level, that is, within culture, so it may not generalize to between cultures.

Collectivism is often associated with high power distance (in Hofstede's study the correlation was 0.67). In my travels in both high- and low-power cultures I noted that in high-power cultures petty bureaucrats often make life miserable for members of the society. For instance, they take their time in responding to citizens' requests, require a tip for service, and do little to facilitate these requests. This should result in lower SWB at the cultural level.

In sum, it appears that at the individual level allocentrism is positively related to SWB, but as mentioned above at the cultural level collectivism is negatively related to SWB.

Health   Depression is highest when there is low SWB and high stress. It can lead to an ineffective immune system, hence to more physical illness. Disease obviously decreases SWB, though the effect is short-lived, and people adapt to poor health surprisingly easily (Diener 2000). We can expect therefore that in countries with low SWB there will be more physical illness along with more depression. This relationship is at the cultural level. At the individual level of analysis, allocentrics receive a lot of social support, which reduces the impact of negative life events. Thus it is not likely that depression or physical illness can be associated with allocentrism at the individual level of analysis.

At the cultural level, individualism is related to the frequency of heart attacks (Triandis et al. 1988), but at the individual level SWB depends on day-to-day events. It cannot be correlated well with relatively rare events such as a heart attack. Further research could explore these relationships.

Person-Environment Fit   Each cultural syndrome corresponds to a personality attribute. Tightness is related to compulsive tendencies; complexity is related to cognitive complexity, low authoritarianism, and the like. Individualism is related to idiocentrism; collectivism is related to allocentrism (Triandis et al. 1985). To the extent that a person's attributes match the attributes of the culture, there is a good person-social environment fit, and that should increase SWB. But a mismatch will result in low SWB. For example, students from collectivist cultures experience stress in the United States (Cross 1995), since they are not well suited for the individualistic social environment. Similarly allocentric East Germans who migrated to West Germany before the fall of the wall were less well adjusted than idiocentric East Germans (Schmitz 1994).

It is well known that Mexicans tend to be collectivists (e.g., Marin and Triandis 1985). Kagan and Knight (1979) studied Anglo-American and Mexican-American school children and found that the more competitive Anglo children and the more cooperative Mexican children had the highest levels of self-esteem. In short, when the personality fits the culture, self-esteem is high. Since self-esteem can be related to SWB, we can expect support for the general proposition that when culture and personality are consistent, there is high SWB, and when they are inconsistent there is low SWB.

Conclusions

We must keep the cultural and individual levels of analyses separate, in examining the factors that may affect SWB at different levels. Using the concept of a quasi-stationary equilibrium, we can now identify some forces that increase SWB at the cultural level:

High gross national product per capita
Political freedoms
Social equality
Social security
Satisfactory citizen-bureaucrat relationships
High levels of trust
Efficient public institutions

There are also forces that can lower SWB at the cultural level: Our hypotheses suggest that tight cultures are characterized by fear of criticism, which reduces SWB, high levels of fantasy, which results in perceptual frames that depress SWB, and few opportunities to compare oneself to others in ways that increase self-esteem. Some other forces to consider are as follows:

Civil and international conflict (e.g., war)
Oppression of the political opposition
Undemocratic government
Many vulnerabilities (e.g., floods)

Since tightness is negatively correlated with individualism, we can expect individualism to be positively correlated with SWB at the cultural level. Furthermore many collectivist cultures are high in power distance, which means that petty bureaucrats abuse the citizens, and this decreases cultural SWB. Forces that increase SWB at the individual level include the following:

Good health
Enough education
Fit between personality and culture
Personality open to new experiences
Extroversion
Conscientiousness
Environmental mastery
Personal growth
Purpose in life
Self-acceptance
Sense of self-determination
Opportunities to compare oneself favorably to others
Having many acquaintances
Allocentrism, in terms of receiving social support from many close friends
Less stress (There is some evidence that in traditional societies levels of stress are lower than in modern societies; for example, Henry and Stephens 1977 found that in traditional cultures blood pressure does not increase with age, until age 60.)
Belonging to a liked group

Forces that decrease SWB at the individual level include idiocentrism which is associated with loneliness, social disruption (frequent divorce, job insecurity, high crime rates), and stress. Other factors include the following:

Unemployment
Poor health
Poor personality-to-culture fit

As is evident, at the cultural level, the equilibrium of forces favors individualism, but at the individual level, the equilibrium favors allocentrism. This point is consistent with Triandis's (1995) evaluation of the two cultural patterns. He argued that individualism is a desirable cultural pattern from the point of view of citizen-state relationships and that collectivism is a desirable cultural pattern from the point of view of family relationships and other personal factors, such as receiving social support.

Obviously the picture of the relationship of culture to subjective well-being is complex. Since SWB can be further influenced by age, sex, urban or rural residence, minority status, and other demographics, and there are interactions between culture and demographics, the relationship of culture and SWB is more complicated than the one presented in this chapter. I have proposed numerous areas for further research. In time we can expect the relationships of culture and SWB to become more elucidated.

Acknowledgment

I thank Chansheng Chen for making very useful critical comments on an earlier version of this manuscript.

References

Arrindell, W. A., Hatzichristou, C., Wensink, J., and Rosenberg, E. 1997. Dimensions of national culture as predictors of cross-national differences in subjective well-being. *Personality and Individual Differences* 23: 37–53.

Bettencourt, B. A., and Dorr, N. 1997. Collective self-esteem as a mediator of the relationship between allocentrism and subjective well-being. *Personality and Social Psychology Bulletin* 23: 955–64.

Bliese, P., and Halverson, R. R. 1998. Group consensus and psychological well-being: A large field study. *Journal of Applied Social Psychology* 28: 563–80.

Campbell, A. 1981. *The Sense of Well-being in America: Recent Patterns and Trends*. New York: McGraw-Hill.

Campbell, A., Converse, P. E., and Rodgers, W. L. 1976. *The Quality of American Life: Perceptions, Evaluations, and Satisfactions*. New York: Russell Sage Foundation.

Cross, S. E. 1995. Self-construals, coping, and stress in cross-cultural adaptation. *Journal of Cross-Cultural Psychology* 26: 673–97.

Diener, E. 1984. Subjective well-being. *Psychological Bulletin* 96: 542–75

Diener, E. 1995. A value based index for measuring national quality of life. *Social Indicators Research* 36: 107–27.

Diener, E. 2000. Subjective well-being: The science of happiness and a proposal for a national index. *American Psychologist* 55: 34–43.

Diener, E., and Diener, C. 1995a. The wealth of nations revisited: Income and quality of life. *Social Indicators Research* 36: 275–86.

Diener, E., and Diener, M. 1995b. Cross-cultural correlates of life satisfaction and self-esteem. *Journal of Personality and Social Psychology* 68: 653–63.

Diener, E., and Fujita, F. 1994. Social comparisons and subjective well-being. In B. P. Buunk and F. X. Gibbons, eds., *Health, Coping, and Well-being*. Mahwah, NJ: Lawrence Erlbaum, pp. 329–57.

Diener E., Diener M., and Diener C. 1995. Factors predicting the subjective well being of nations. *Journal of Personality and Social Psychology* 69: 851–64.

Diener, E., Emmons, R. A., Larsen, R. J., and Griffin, S. 1985. The satisfaction with life scale. *Journal of Personality Assessment* 49: 71–75.

Diener, E., Suh, E., Smith, H., and Shao, L. 1995. National differences in reported subjective well-being: Why do they occur? *Social Indicators Research* 34: 7–32.

Fiske, A., Kitayama, S., Markus, H., and Nisbett, R. E. 1997. The cultural matrix of social psychology. In D. T. Gilbert, S. Fiske, and G. Lindzey, eds., *Handbook of Social Psychology*, 4th ed. New York: McGraw-Hill, pp. 915–81.

Henry, J. P., and Stephens, P. M. 1977. *Stress, Health, and Social Environment*. New York: Springer.

Hofstede, G. 1980. *Culture's Consequences*. Beverly Hills, CA: Sage.

Hui, H. C., Yee, C., and Eastman, K. L. 1995. The relationship between individualism-collectivism and job satisfaction. *Applied Psychology: An International Review* 44: 276–82.

Ingelhart, R. 1990. *Culture Shift in Advanced Industrial Society*. Princeton, NJ: Princeton University Press.

Iwao, S. 1993. *Japanese Women: Traditional Image and Changing Reality*. New York: Free Press.

Kagan, S., and Knight, G. P. 1979. Cooperation-competition and self-esteem: A case of cultural relativism. *Journal of Cross-Cultural Psychology* 10: 457–67.

Kitayama, S., Markus, H., and Kurokawa, M. (in press). Does the nature of good feelings depend on culture? A Japan-United States comparison. *Cognition and Emotion*.

Kitayama, S., Markus, H. R., Matsumoto, H., and Norasakkunkit, V. 1997. Individual and collective processes in the construction of the self: Self-enhancement in the United States and self-criticism in Japan. *Journal of Personality and Social Psychology* 72: 1245–67.

Kohn, M. L., and Slomczynski, K. M. (with the collaboration of Carrie Schoenbach). 1990. *Social Structure and Self-direction: A Comparative Analysis of the United States and Poland*. Oxford: Basil Blackwell.

Kohn, M. L., Slomczynski, K. M., Janicka, K., Khmelko, V., Mach, B. W., Paniotto, V., Zaborowski, W., Gutierrez, R., and Heyman, C. 1997. Social structure and personality under conditions of radical social change: A comparative analysis of Poland and Ukraine. *American Sociological Review* 62: 614–38.

Kwan, V. S. Y., Bond, M. H., and Singelis, T. M. 1997. Pancultural explanations of life satisfaction: Adding relationship harmony to self-esteem. *Journal of Personality and Social Psychology* 73: 1038–51.

Lachman, M. E., and Weaver, S. L. 1998. The sense of control as a moderator of social class differences in health and well-being. *Journal of Personality and Social Psychology* 74: 763–73.

Levine, R. 1997. *A Geography of Time: The Temporal Misadventure of a Social Psychologist*. New York: Basic Books.

Levin, R. V., and Norensayan, A. 1999. The pace of life in 31 countries. *Journal of Cross-cultural Psychology* 30: 178–205.

Lewin, K. 1952. Group decision and social change. In G. E. Swanson, T. M. Newcomb, and E. I Hartley, eds., *Readings in Social Psychology*. New York: Holt, pp. 459–73.

Linsky, A. S., and Straus, M. A. 1986. *Social Stress in the U.S.* Dover, MA: Auburn House.

Lyubomirsky, S. 1997. The meaning and expression of happiness: Comparing the United States and Russia. Paper presented at the meetings of the American Psychological Society, in Washington, DC, May 26.

Marin, G., and Triandis, H. C. 1985. Allocentrism as an important characteristic of the behavior of Latin Americans and Hispanics. In R. Diaz-Guerrero, ed., *Cross-cultural and National Studies in Social Psychology*. Amsterdam: North Holland, pp. 85–104.

Moum, T. 1996. Subjective well-being as a short- and long-term predictor of suicide in the general population. World Conference on Quality of Life, University of Northern British Columbia, Prince George, August 22–25.

Oishi, S., Diener, E., Lucas, R. E., and Suh, E. 1999. Cross-cultural variations in predictors of life satisfaction: A goal based approach. *Personality and Social Psychology Bulletin* 25: 980–90.

Parducci, A. 1995. *Happiness, Pleasure, and Judgment. The Contextual Theory and Its Applications*. Mahwah, NJ: Lawrence Erlbaum.

Radhakrishnan, P., and Chan, D. K.-S. 1997. Cultural differences in the relationship between self-discrepancy and life satisfaction: Examining personal and parental goals. *International Journal of Psychology* 32: 387–98.

Realo, A. 1999. *Individualism and Collectivism: An Exploration of Individual and Cultural Differences*. Tartu, Estonia: Tartu University Press.

Robinson-Whelen, S., Kim, C., MacCallum, R. C., and Kiecolt-Glaser, J. K. 1997. Distinguishing optimism from pessimism in older adults: Is it more important to be optimistic or not to be pessimistic? *Journal of Personality and Social Psychology* 73: 1345–53.

Ryff, C. D. 1995. Psychological well-being in adult life. *Current Directions in Psychological Science* 4: 99–104.

Ryff, C. D., and Keyes, C. L. 1995. The structure of psychological well-being revisited. *Journal of Personality and Social Psychology* 69: 719–27.

Sagan, L. L. 1987. *The Health of Nations: True Causes of Sickness and Well-being*. New York: Basic Books.

Schmitz, P. G. 1994. Acculturation and adaptation processes among immigrants in Germany. In A.-M. Bouvy, F. J. R. van de Vijver, P. Boski, and P. G. Schmitz, eds., *Journeys into Cross-cultural Psychology*. Lisse, the Netherlands: Swets and Zeitlinger, pp. 142–57.

Schwartz, S. 1992. Universals in the content and structure of values: Theoretical advances and empirical tests in 20 countries. In M. Zanna, ed., *Advances in Experimental Social Psychology*, vol. 25. New York: Academic Press, pp. 1–66.

Slottje, D. J., Scully, G. W., Hirschberg, J. G., and Hayes, K. J. 1991. *Measuring the Quality of Life across Countries: A Multidimensional Analysis*. Boulder, CO: Westview Press.

Staudinger, U. M., Fleeson, W., and Baltes, P. B. 1997. Predictors of subjective physical health and global well-being during midlife: Similarities and differences between the U.S. and

Germany. Manuscript. Max Planck Institute for Human Development and Education, Berlin, Germany.

Suh, E. M., and Diener, E. 1997. Paper presented to the annual Meeting of the American Psychological Society, Washington DC.

Suh, E. M., and Diener, E. 1999. Self and the use of emotion information: Joining culture, personality, and situational influences. Manuscript submitted for publication.

Suh, E. M., Diener, E., Oishi, S., and Triandis, H. C. 1998. The shifting basis of life satisfaction judgments across cultures: Emotions versus norms. *Journal of Personality and Social Psychology* 74: 482–93.

Tajfel, H. 1982. *Social Identity and Intergroup Relations*. New York: Cambridge University Press.

Triandis, H. C. 1994. *Culture and Social Behavior*. New York: McGraw-Hill.

Triandis, H. C. 1995. *Individualism and Collectivism*. Boulder, CO: Westview Press.

Triandis, H. C., Chen, X. P., and Chan, D. K.-S. 1998. Scenarios for the measurement of collectivism and individualism. *Journal of Cross-Cultural Psychology* 29: 275–89.

Triandis, H. C., Bontempo, R., Villareal, M., Asai, M., and Lucca, N. 1988. Individualism and collectivism: Cross-cultural perspectives on self–in group relationships. *Journal of Personality and Social Psychology* 54: 323–38.

Triandis, H. C., Leung, K., Villareal, M., and Clack, F. L. 1985. Allocentric vs. idiocentric tendencies: Convergent and discriminant validation. *Journal of Research in Personality* 19: 395–415.

United Nations. 1993. *Human Development Report*. New York: Oxford University Press.

Veenhoven, R. 1994. *Correlates of Happiness: 7837 Findings from 603 Studies in 69 Countries 1911–1994*, 3 vols. Rotterdam: Erasmus University Press.

Veenhoven, R. (in association with J. Ehrhardt). 1995. The cross-national pattern of happiness: Test of predictions implied in three theories of happiness. *Social Indicators Research* 34: 33–68.

Verkuyten, M. 1995. Self-esteem, self-concept stability, and aspects of ethnic identity among minority and majority youth in the Netherlands. *Journal of Youth and Adolescence* 24: 155–75.

Verkuyten, M., and Lay, C. 1997. Ethnic minority identity and psychological well-being: The mediating role of collective self-esteem. Paper from Department of General Social Studies, Utrecht University, the Netherlands.

3

Individual Psychological Culture and Subjective Well-being

Charlotte Ratzlaff, David Matsumoto, Natalia Kouznetsova, Jacques Raroque, and Rebecca Ray

In the past twenty-five years there has been a dramatic increase in the number of studies examining the correlates and possible mediators of subjective well-being. While there is not complete consensus on the definition of SWB, it is generally agreed to be more than the absence of negative affect or cognition. Diener (1984), for example, listed three hallmarks of the construct: (1) it resides within the experience of the individual, (2) it includes positive measures, and (3) it involves global assessment of all aspects of a person's life. Later he defined SWB as "a person's evaluative reactions to his or her life—either in terms of life satisfaction (cognitive evaluations) or affect (ongoing emotional reactions)" (Diener and Diener 1995, p. 653). While many researchers take a similarly broad view, others focus on either cognitive or affective aspects; happiness, for example, is often presented as synonymous with SWB.

The impact of culture on SWB has become an important topic of research within the past ten years, as can be witnessed through existence and contents of this entire book. As has been no doubt highlighted elsewhere in this volume, studying SWB across cultures presents its own set of challenges. For example, operationalizing SWB for cultures other than our own is a difficult, though critical, task. Translating existing measures may not be sufficient. Single-item measures are necessarily abstract, and they may reflect a concept that has a very different meaning—or no meaning at all—to members of the target culture. Multiple-item measures may contain more concrete items, but those items may not reflect ways in which SWB manifests itself in a given culture. Because cultures with widely divergent value systems most likely do not define well-being in the same way, it is imperative that we establish equivalence for the concept, as well as for the individual items used to measure the concept (Matsumoto 1994).

Another challenge that faces research examining the relationship between culture and SWB concerns the definition of culture itself. Certainly most people see culture as a social or group construct; thus studies examining cultural differences in SWB often examine differences between cultural groups defined by country, race, or ethnicity. Various approaches to the relationship between ecological culture and SWB, and possible mediators of that relationship, are reviewed elsewhere in this volume, and this work represents by far the majority of research that is done examining the relationship between culture and SWB. To a lesser extent, but of no less importance, is recent work examining the relationship between SWB and culture as represented on the psychological level in individuals. Studies involving culture as an individual psychological construct give us yet another glimpse into the relationship between culture and SWB, aiding in theory construction and method development. Also results are not necessarily similar on the ecological and individual levels. That is, a relationship between national culture and SWB may not necessarily exist on the individual level. The studies that measure individual culture do so primarily through the dimension of individualism-collectivism, but also through other dimensions such as cultural or ethnic identity.

The focus of this chapter is on culture as an individual psychological construct, and on studies examining the relationship between SWB and this definition of culture. In the next section we discuss first culture as an individual psychological construct, contrasting it with culture as an ecological-level construct. Next we examine the dimension of culture that has been most widely studied on the individual level—individualism and collectivism (IC)—and describe recent developments in measurement techniques used to assess IC on the individual level. To show the current status of research in this area, we review studies that examine the relationship between IC or other dimensions of culture on this level and SWB, possible mediators of that relationship, and the effect of discrepancies between individual and ecological culture on SWB. We then provide data from a study in our laboratory that complements the existing literature on this topic, and conclude by providing some recommendations for future research in this area.

Culture as an Individual Psychological Construct

We often speak of the culture of a group as if it were a single, unitary concept true for all members of that group in exactly the same ways. When we speak of a specific culture, we often assume that all the people who have roots in that culture are relatively homogeneous with regard to some psychological trait, characteristic, or behavior. This assumption is also prevalent in cross-cultural research. There is little doubt that on some level, culture is relevant for all members of the group that comprise that culture. In the past decade, however, we have seen increasing awareness that culture exists in individuals as much as it exists as a global social construct. In fact, on any given attribute, the within-culture variance may be as large or larger than the between-culture variance. Culture at the ecological level therefore describes mainstream average tendencies; it cannot describe all behaviors of all people in any culture.

Matsumoto (2000) defines culture as "a dynamic system of rules—explicit and implicit—established by groups in order to ensure their survival, involving attitudes, values, beliefs, norms, and behaviors, shared by a group but harbored differently by each specific unit within the group, communicated across generations, relatively stable but with the potential to change across time." This definition of culture is applicable at multiple levels of analysis. That individuals will, to some degree, differ from societal norms on any given dimension of culture is perhaps intuitively obvious. Few members of a culture will match the prototypical member of that culture on all dimensions. Individual differences in culture can be observed among people in the degree to which they adopt and engage in the attitudes, values, beliefs, and behaviors that, by consensus, constitute their culture. If you are in accord with those shared values or behaviors, then that culture resides in you; if you do not share those values or behaviors, then you do not share that culture. Culture, then, exists on multiple levels, across individuals within groups, and across groups within larger groups (e.g., within an organization).

Triandis, Bontempo, Leung, and Hui (1990) distinguish among three levels of culture: the cultural level, typically measured by nation or other grouping by geographical proximity; the demographic level, measured by ethnicity, race, gender, or other demographic characteristics; and the individual level, which Triandis defines as resulting from "a pattern of construct variation unique to the individual, which cannot be meaningfully interpreted by reference to demographic or cultural membership" (Triandis et al. 1990, p. 303). For the purposes of this chapter, we will use the terms *ecological culture* to refer to the cultural context(s) of the individual (cultural and demographic levels) and *individual culture* to refer to the individual level of participation in the values, beliefs, and traditions of those cultural contexts.

Definitions of individual culture are a bit ambiguous, and perhaps difficult to distinguish from personality. Granted, individual differences in culture can be influenced in part by personality, and personality development may be affected by culture, but there are important differences between individual culture and personality. Culture, whether at the ecological level or the individual level, is learned. It is passed down from generation to generation, through family members, adults outside the family, schools, religious groups, and other institutions. Because each individual comes into contact with a slightly different mix of these socialization and enculturation agents— or even different cultures or subcultures—the degree to which the individual shares in each aspect of the culture or cultures will also differ. The content of individual culture is derived directly from the values, beliefs, norms, traditions, and customs of the larger culture(s). Though there are various theories of personality, it is usually discussed in terms of traits or attributes of individuals within their lifetime and not developed through transmission of shared beliefs, values, attitudes, and behaviors.

Understanding that culture exists at the individual level as well as at the ecological level is important for practical reasons. Our failure in the past to recognize the existence of individual differences in culture has undoubtedly aided in the formation and maintenance of stereotypes. Stereotypes are generalizations about the culture of a group of people that we apply to the individuals within that group. There is often some bit of truth to stereotypes. But they are also often wrong because individuals within a culture may not all harbor those cultural values and norms to the same degree. In addition, given that individuals have their own psychological culture, and that they exist within a larger social or ecological culture, the potential exists for their psychological culture to be either congruent or discrepant with the larger ecological culture in which they live. We can interpret an individual's responses more meaningfully when we know the pattern of responses to the same construct at the broader cultural level. Knowing, for example, that certain individuals value equality and fluidity in gender roles may be useful information. If, however, we know that the culture in which they live values rigid separation in gender roles, we have a context for that information which tells us something more about the individuals.

Individualism and Collectivism on an Individual Level

Possibly the most important, and certainly the most widely used, dimension of psychological culture is individualism-collectivism. To distinguish levels of analysis, Triandis labeled the individual levels of this construct idiocentrism and allocentrism. Generally, idiocentrics are individuals who endorse values, behaviors, and attitudes common to individualistic or independent cultures, and allocentrics are those who endorse values, behaviors, and attitudes common to collectivistic or interdependent cultures. The two levels are likely to be highly correlated, but we cannot assume they represent exactly the same construct. In an early study of allocentric and idiocentric tendencies in the United States, Triandis, Leung, Villareal, and Clack (1985) found factors of allocentrism similar to defining factors of collectivism—subordination of personal to group goals, the ingroup as extension of self, and ingroup identity—within a highly individualistic culture. While these results indicate a high level of correlation between aspects of allocentrism and collectivism, they also hint at the need to discriminate between individual and ecological culture (discussed in more detail in the next section). Some years later, Triandis et al. (1993) reanalyzed earlier data and compared ecological and individual levels of analysis to determine which factors of individualism and collectivism were found at each level, and which existed at both levels. Three of their factors existed at both levels, the remaining six were more related to either individual or ecological culture, but not both. In a chapter on the various consequences of IC for individuals, Triandis (1995) cites several studies that have isolated factors at the individual level markedly similar to those found at the ecological level.

These numerous studies, conducted by different researchers with different purposes, all highlight the relationship between culture as measured by IC and a number of different psychological constructs. More important, they demonstrate the importance of identifying IC as an individual-level construct as well as an ecological-level one. This distinction is important in being able to differentiate individual differences on this cultural dimension within larger cultural groups, and in investigating relationships between it and other psychological constructs on the individual level. The ability to do this well in research, of course, is entirely dependent on the ability to measure IC on the individual level validly and reliably. Fortunately, a number of writers have developed psychometrically appropriate measures of IC on the individual level for use in contemporary research.

Measurement of IC on the Individual Level

Being able to measure IC on the individual level is advantageous for a variety of reasons. First, it allows us to characterize the IC nature of different groups within or across nations or ethnicities and to examine the relative importance of individualism or collectivism in those groups. Triandis and his colleagues, cited below, for example, have administered their measures of IC to samples in different cultures and countries around the world and, on the basis of these data, have been able not only to characterize the cultures as relatively individualistic or collectivistic but also to determine the estimated proportion of the population in each of these samples to carry primarily individualistic or collectivistic tendencies on the individual level. Second, measurement of IC allows for an important methodological check in our research. Using such measures, we would no longer have to assume that the groups in our studies are individualistic or collectivistic; we can demonstrate it empirically. Third, given that there will be individual differences in IC within samples, IC scores can be used as covariates in appropriate analyses. Differences between groups could therefore be tested after the effects of IC were statistically controlled. Ultimately this approach allows researchers to test the degree of contribution of individual-level IC to between group differences on their psychological constructs of interest, which further refines our knowledge about the relationship between IC and psychological variables.

Triandis (1995, app.) and Triandis and Gelfand (1998) reviewed several studies that designed and tested different scales to measure IC on the individual level (we briefly highlight some of these works here; interested readers are directed to Triandis 1995, app., for a comprehensive review and discussion of method, and to Triandis and Gelfand 1998, for additional information and correlations among several measures of IC). By far the most concerted effort has been that of Triandis and his colleagues. These attempts have resulted in the use of different scales across a number of studies. For instance, Hui (1984, 1988) developed the Individualism-Collectivism (INDCOL) Scale to measure an individual's IC tendencies in relation to six collectivities (spouse, parents and children, kin, neighbors, friends, and coworkers and classmates). Triandis, McCusker, and Hui (1990) employed a multimethod approach to measuring IC, which represented an evolution not only in thinking about IC but also in method. These researchers included five methods involving ratings of the social content of the self, perceptions of homogeneity of ingroups and outgroups, attitude and value ratings, and perceptions of social behavior as a function of social distance. Subjects are classified as either individualist or collectivist on the basis of their scores on each method. More recently Triandis and his colleagues (Singelis et al. 1995) developed measures that include items assessing horizontal and vertical individualism and collectivism, representing yet further advances in the conceptual understanding of IC.

The work of other writers (reviewed in Triandis 1995 and Triandis and Gelfand 1998) covers a broad range of psychological constructs in the assessment of IC, including attitudinal, value, and norm ratings; self-perceptions; and independent and interdependent self-construals. Although these works offer researchers a number of alternatives for IC assessment, Triandis's multimethod system and his latest efforts in assessing horizontal and vertical IC are by far the most advanced and sophisticated assessment tools available. These instruments measure IC tendencies in different psychological domains, combining IC tendencies across a wide range of phenomena into a single measurement technique.

Matsumoto (Matsumoto et al. 1997) has developed a nineteen item scale that focuses on interpersonal relationships, one of the facets found in the more broad-based measures discussed above, and incorporates the suggestion by Triandis, Bontempo, Villareal, Asai, and Lucca (1988) that IC differences should vary in different social contexts. The IC Interpersonal Assessment Inventory (ICIAI) measures IC tendencies across four different social relationships (family, close friends, colleagues, and strangers) and two domains (values and behaviors). One of the benefits of being able to assess IC tendencies in different social relationships is the possibility of determining which of the common notions about IC between countries and ethnicities accurately describe differences in specific social relationships.

In summary, there exists today a relatively wide range of measurement tools available for researchers to assess IC on the individual level in their research. These range from the broader-based tools made available by Triandis's multimethod measures, which span attitudes, values, beliefs, opinions, and other psychological domains, to measures specific to context differences (e.g., Hui's work) or interpersonal relationships (Matsumoto's measure). Using these types of measures, researchers can then examine the relationship between individual level culture, as represented by IC, and SWB.

Individual-Level Culture and Subjective Well-being

Given the recent developments in ways to measure culture on an individual level, and the increasing interest in psychological well-being, it is not surprising that some researchers have examined the relationship between the two constructs. As with studies conducted on ecological-level culture and SWB, the various approaches used to study this relationship on an individual level range from simple correlational research to attempts to determine possible mediators of the relationship and the effect of discrepancies between individual and ecological levels of culture. Most of the research to date examines individual levels of IC; a few studies do, however, look at other cultural dimensions.

Research Examining the Relationship between Individual-Level Culture and Subjective Well-being

Most of the studies examining the relationship between IC measured on the individual level and SWB have directly correlated the two constructs. Kasri (1997), for example, attempted to address two of the most fundamental questions in the field: (1) whether or not people of different psychological cultures define and experience well-being in the same way, and (2) whether or not they report the same level of well-being. To analyze differences in the construct of well-being, Kasri compared responses on three measures of individual levels of IC with a multidimensional, open-ended questionnaire about experiences and concept of psychological functioning. She measured IC with Matsumoto's Intercultural Assessment Inventory, a forerunner of the Intercultural Interpersonal Assessment Inventory discussed above; the Individualism-Collectivism scale from Triandis's Multimethod Assessment Techniques; and Hui's INDCOL inventory. The open-ended questionnaire was based on a series of interview questions originated by Ryff (1989; Ryff and Keyes 1995). Responses to the thirteen questions used were coded and compared with responses on the three measures of IC. Of the 240 total comparisons, only 9 were significant, too few to establish a significant overall difference in definition and experience of SWB. Comparisons of the responses on the above three IC measures with two quantitative measures of SWB (Diener's Satisfaction with Life Scale and Neugarten et al.'s Life Satisfaction Index), however, showed significantly higher SWB for individualists.

Florsheim (1997) and Watson, Sherbak, and Morris (1998) also used individual measures of IC to compare with measures related to subjective well-being. These studies attempted to identify factors associated with psychosocial adjustment for each type of individual culture. In a study identifying correlates of adjustment for adolescent Chinese (from the People's Republic of China) immigrants to the United States, Florsheim used items related to individualism and collectivism from the Schwartz Value Survey. He compared these items to three subscales of the Offer Self-image Questionnaire: Coping Self, which covers a range of psychiatrically relevant problems such as depression and suicide ideation; Social Self, which assesses perception of peer relations and friendship patterns, vocational and educational goals, and perceived ability to accomplish those goals; and Psychological Self, which addresses emotions, impulse control, and body image. Collectivism was correlated positively with scores on the Coping Self and Social Self scores, and individualism was correlated with Coping Self scores, though somewhat less strongly than for allocentrics. Overall, participants with higher collectivism were more likely to enjoy higher psychosocial functioning. Knowing the ecological culture of these participants—living in a large, cohesive community of Chinese immigrants and therefore part of a collectivistic society within the United States, or more isolated within this generally individualistic society—would help us interpret these results. Without that knowledge, we are unable to understand the context within which the individual level of culture exists, and any interpretation could be colored by that additional information. One possible interpretation involves maintenance of cultural identity. As studies by Martinez and Dukes and, to some degree, Verkuyten, discussed below, indicate, stronger identification with one's cultural group may be related to SWB. For Chinese immigrants in an individualistic country, maintenance of collectivistic values may be part of a strong cultural identity. Being part of a community fostering both that identity and the values associated with it may further enhance psychosocial functioning for these participants.

Watson et al. (1998), in testing a Rational-Emotive Behavior Therapy model, looked at the interaction among irrational beliefs (Survey of Personal Beliefs and Belief Scale), self-esteem, social responsibility, and IC (Yamaguchi's Collectivism scale plus the Chan Collectivistic and Individualistic Values scale) in American undergraduate students. After partialing out individualistic values, they found that collectivism or collectivist values were related positively to self-worth, social responsibility, social isolation, and all subscales of irrational beliefs but correlated negatively with normlessness. Individualistic values were related to self-esteem and normlessness when collectivistic values were partialed out. These results suggest that collectivistic values are more irrational than individualistic values, at least within a predominantly individualistic culture. At the same time they indicate that both collectivism and individualism have positive as well as negative implications for psychosocial adjustment.

The relationship between SWB and individual culture measured on dimensions not directly related to but suggestive of IC has also been studied. Martinez and Dukes (1997), for example, analyzed the effect of individual ethnic identity on the self-esteem, academic self-confidence, and sense of purpose in life for adolescents, self-identified as Asian, Black, Hispanic, Native American, White, or Mixed, in southern Colorado. Differences among three levels of ethnic identity (unexamined, searching, and achieved) were highly significant for all three measures of well-being, with scores substantially higher for all individuals in the identity achieved category, regardless of ethnic group or gender. White students, generally thought to be the most individualistic, had the lowest ethnic identity, yet scored high on measures of well-being, suggesting that some other level of culture—in this case being part of the dominant ethnic culture—may also affect SWB. For all of the ethnic groups, which range from extremely individualistic to predominantly collectivistic on a demographic level, it is possible to view strong cultural identity as a group-oriented or allocentric tendency. This interpretation would suggest that at least this aspect of collectivism might have positive implications for SWB regardless of IC on a broader level. Still, causal interpretation of these results is difficult. While a strong sense of ethnic identity may lead to increased psychological well-being, high self-esteem, academic self-confidence, and purpose in life may also allow closer identification with one's ethnic group.

Verkuyten (1995) also looked at the relationship between ethnic identity and psychological well-being for adolescents of various ethnic groups. For this study, conducted in the Netherlands, psychological well-being was operationalized as self-esteem and self-stability. All but one of the correlations between ethnic identity and self-esteem were significant. Virtually none of the correlations using self-stability was significant, however. Given that Diener and Diener (1995) have since shown that self-esteem and SWB are different constructs, Verkuyten's study is perhaps best interpreted as showing a correlation between ethnic identity and a possible component or mediator of SWB. Earlier Shek (1992) compared intensity of life meaning with several measures of affective and cognitive status using secondary students in Hong Kong. His results indicate that a more meaningful life is strongly related to psychological well-being. Again, we have insufficient information to determine causality; meaning in life may be part of our value system when we are pleased with our life as easily as the reverse.

Results of the preceding studies suggest that measures of individual levels of IC alone may not be sufficient predictors of subjective well being. The Kasri and Watson et al. studies suggest that on the whole, SWB is more closely related to individualism, while the studies by Florsheim, and perhaps Martinez and Dukes, indicate that collectivism may be more predictive of SWB in some situations. This apparent contradiction could be due to a number of factors, from differences in methodology to possible mediating effects of other variables or of the larger scale cultural context. Given that both Florsheim and Watson et al. found positive as well as negative effects of both types of individual culture, and that Martinez and Dukes were able to link SWB with ethnic identity regardless of ethnic group, we suspect that the relationship between individual culture and SWB may be more complex than can be adequately accounted for in a single-dimension direct relationship study. The correlations between life meaning and SWB found by Shek, and the various correlations of self-esteem to individual culture found by Martinez and Dukes and Verkuyten, suggest that mediating variables such as life meaning or self-esteem may indeed be an important part of the relationship between individual levels of culture and SWB.

Research Examining the Possible Mediators of the Relationship between Individual Level IC and Subjective Well-being

As with comparisons using the ecological level of culture (see Triandis, chapter 2 in this volume), a number of studies have investigated the possible role of mediating variables in the relationship between individual-level culture and SWB. And for good reason, they address basic questions regarding the relationship between IC or other related dimensions and SWB. For example, if mediators exist in these relationships, can we clarify which constructs are truly aspects of affective and cognitive well-being and which are more accurately viewed as mediating the relationship? Do the mediators work in the same way with different cultures?

Research in this area is relatively recent, and consequently many writers are still working to establish the theoretical foundations from which we can develop full models of possible relationships. A few studies, however, have highlighted the role of some variables as possible mediators. Sinha and Verma (1994) and Bettencourt and Dorr (1997), for example, conducted studies to identify mediators of the relationship between allocentrism and SWB. Sinha and Verma measured the levels of individual and ecological IC, social support, and psychological well-being in graduate students at a university in western India. Participants generally rated the society as collectivistic, but on most measures of individual culture, they saw themselves as idiocentric. Allocentrism, where it existed, was correlated with psychological well-being when mediated by high social support but not in conditions of low social support. Though no results were reported for possible correlations between idiocentrism and psychological well-being, the authors did note that social support was not related to level of allocentrism or idiocentrism. Also possible effects of the discrepancy between ecological and individual culture were not explored in the study.

Bettencourt and Dorr studied university students in the United States. Using the Individualism-Collectivism Scale, the Satisfaction with Life Scale, and the Collective Self-esteem (CSE) scale, the authors first established collective self-esteem as a mediator in the relationship between allocentrism and SWB. In this study, idiocentrism was negatively correlated with life satisfaction and with two (Private Collective Self-esteem and Membership Esteem) of the four Collective Self-esteem subscales. For their second study, they added measures of personal self-esteem, life affect (the affective component of subjective well-being), and extroversion. Combining life affect and life satisfaction into a composite score did not significantly affect the relationship between allocentrism and well-being, nor did controlling for personal self-esteem and extroversion eliminate the mediating effect of composite collective self-esteem. The negative correlation between idiocentrism and SWB in an individualistic setting is in direct contrast to the findings by Kasri, discussed above, which found a positive correlation between idiocentrism and SWB. Though both sets of research included similar measures for the two constructs, the authors obtained idiocentrism scores on the Individualism-Collectivism Scale differently. It is possible that using one subscale on the measure to indicate idiocentrism as Bettencourt and Dorr did, rather than Kasri's method of using the overall score, gives sufficiently different results to produce the contradictory findings.

A recent study by Kwan, Bond, and Singelis (1997) examined separate predictors of SWB for individuals with independent and interdependent self-construals. These two types of construals have been linked theoretically to individualistic and collectivistic cultural tendencies (Markus and Kitayama 1991). (Empirical work, however, does not appear to verify this link; Matsumoto, in press.) Participants from an American university in California and a Chinese university in Hong Kong completed measures of personality, self-construal, self-esteem, relationship harmony, collective self-esteem (race-specific form), and life satisfaction. Results indicated that the two self-construals and, at least in part, five personality factors affected life satisfaction for both participants in both locations. While self-esteem and relationship harmony served as mediating factors for independent and interdependent self-construals, respectively, the findings on collective self-esteem (CSE) appeared to contradict results in Bettencourt and Dorr, discussed above. Here, CSE was not a significant mediator for either group after controlling for personal self-esteem and relationship harmony. Perhaps one of the most interesting results is that ecological level culture (U.S. vs. Hong Kong) did not significantly affect the mediating processes of either self-construal or personality, though mean levels of each construct did differ significantly between the two countries.

These findings suggest that a variety of social and personal variables may play an important role in the relationship between individual levels of culture and SWB. Studies by Sinha and Verma and Bettencourt and Dorr both found mediators related to the nature or quality of social relationships. For Sinha and Verma, that mediator was social support; for Bettencourt and Dorr, it was collective self-esteem. Kwan found a more complicated relationship, with personal self-esteem, relationship harmony, and, to some degree, personality factors acting as mediators. Also Kwan's study further adds to the evidence that individual levels of culture, particularly IC, can have both positive and negative implications for SWB. Still, we are a long way from having a clear understanding of these and other possible mediators of the relationship between individual culture and SWB. The studies we have to date are few, and the results are not conclusive. Future research will need to look into how these and other mediators affect the relationship and whether they differ for different types of individual culture. One crucial issue suggested by the existing research is the possibility of multiple mediators. In addition to self-esteem and aspects of social relationships, we also need to ask how factors specifically associated with either individualism (alienation, loneliness) or collectivism (social responsibility) affect SWB for those individuals. The apparent contradictions in the above findings may result from differences in the way each construct was measured, which aspects of the constructs were considered, and the larger cultural contexts of the studies. Until we have all variables in the same study to test against each other, we will not know how they function, in which contexts, with which types of individual culture, or their relative importance to the relationship.

One possible explanation of contradictory findings above—regarding the juxtaposition of individual psychological culture within the larger ecological cultural environment—has received some attention in recent years. As reported above, some studies have shown a positive correlation between IC and SWB, with idiocentric individuals reporting more well-being; other studies, however, have shown a negative correlation between the constructs. There is one way that these seemingly contradictory findings may be related to the specific cultural milieus within which the study is conducted. For example, if the larger cultural milieu is individualistic, idiocentric individuals may find it easier to achieve SWB. If, however, the larger cultural milieu is collectivistic, allocentric individuals may find it easier to achieve SWB. Studies that examine therefore the degree of discrepancy between people's personal, individual-level psychological culture and their perceptions of the larger cultural environment within which they live may shed some light on this important possibility.

Research Examining the Relationship between Self–Culture Discrepancies and Subjective Well-being

A potentially important avenue of research that has not been explored to date involves studies of the discrepancy between individual and ecological cultural values (referred to hereafter as cultural discrepancies), and the relationship between these discrepancies and well-being. While the trend toward measuring individual levels of culture is important, we cannot forget that the individual does not live in isolation. Especially when considering subjective measures of well-being, the individual's attitudes, values, and beliefs and those of the cultural context in which he or she lives should be considered. Triandis (chapter 2 in this volume), long a proponent of distinguishing between individual and ecological levels of a construct, specifically makes a case for considering the ecological context in studies of individual culture and subjective well-being. We speculate that where cultural discrepancies exist, it is reasonable to consider that individual's well-being outcomes may differ depending on the size of this discrepancy. While Martinez and Dukes (1997) and Kwan et al. (1997) included analyses of constructs at the demographic or ecological level, only one of the studies we found explicitly considered the fit of the individual in the societal context—measuring a discrepancy in cultural values—and none directly measured and compared both levels of culture.

To establish preliminary validation of a new, author-created measure of cultural estrangement (the Cultural Estrangement Inventory), Cozzarelli and Karafa (1998) compared responses of American university students on their new measure with those on existing measures of alienation: the Rosenberg Self-esteem Inventory (1965), and the Satisfaction with Life Scale (Diener et al. 1985). The moderate correlations were sufficient to conclude that the new scale was related to these existing measures of alienation but not so strong as to indicate that it was redundant with them. The results also showed that the new Cultural Estrangement Inventory predicted lower levels of self-esteem and life satisfaction. A factor analysis suggested two subscales, Atypicality and Misfit. In the follow-up study the authors also administered measures of depression, anxiety, self-discrepancies (between the perceived real self and ideal self), group membership (e.g., jock, preppie, punk, nerd), and nonconformity. Their purpose here was threefold: (1) to further test the psychological consequences of cultural estrangement; (2) to test the relationship among cultural estrangement, nonconformity, and "fringe" group membership; and (3) to test increased self-discrepancies as a possible mediator of the relationship between cultural estrangement and psychological outcomes. A second factor analysis confirmed the two subscales. Because atypicality was not found to be related to self-discrepancies, that subscale was not included in analyses of possible mediation. Findings indicated that self-discrepancies only partially mediated the relationship and suggest that cultural estrangement is a significant predictor of negative psychological adjustment, both directly and indirectly.

Recently our laboratory conducted a study directly examining the relationship between the discrepancy between one's personal cultural values and perceived societal or ideal values, and a host of variables we considered relevant to predictions of health and SWB. We hypothesized that degree of cultural discrepancies would affect health and well-being outcomes, but through mediating variables rather than directly. Specifically we believed that individuals with greater cultural discrepancies must engage in greater coping strategies to help them manage those discrepancies. Coping strategies, however, should be associated with emotional and mood outcomes; thus greater use of coping processes should result in differential long-term emotional reactions and mood states. Some mood states, particularly anxiety, hostility, or depression, may be detrimental to health and well-being, while others such as vigor, positive affect, and the like, may have positive benefits. Cultural discrepancies therefore influence coping, which in turn affects emotions and moods that have consequences for health and subjective well-being.

We present our initial findings on this project here. In this study, 56 university students (17 male, 39 female, average age = 27.44 years, ethnicities: 35 percent European-American, 31 percent Asian-American, 15 percent Latino/Chicano, 15 percent other) participated in partial fulfillment of class requirements. The participants completed a comprehensive battery of tests in three separate sessions. In the first session, participants were given Matsumoto et al.'s (1997) Individualism-Collectivism Interpersonal Assessment Inventory (ICIAI), the Rokeach Values Survey (RVS), and a short version of Triandis's IC measure limited to attitudes and values. For each, participants rated all items on each scale in relation to themselves, to their perception of society, and then to their perceptions of their ideal. Discrepancy scores were then computed by taking the absolute value of the difference between self and society (PS), and self and ideal (PI) scores on each item. We opted to use multiple measures of psychological culture to examine the robustness of any correlations with SWB and other variables, while at the same time reducing reliance on single measurement methods. While data were analyzed separately for all scales of the ICIAI and RVS, for parsimony we report here only the data aggregated across scales within each measure and across measures.

In a second session, participants completed three mood measures and a coping measure. The mood measures included the Beck Depression Inventory (BDI), the Beck Anxiety Inventory (BAI), and the Multiple Affect Adjective Check List (MAACL). All six scales of the MAACL were scored. (Again, multiple measurements of similar constructs provided considerable internal reliability for our findings.) The participants also completed the Folkman and Lazarus (1988) Ways of

Coping Questionnaire, which scores eight coping styles: confrontive coping, distancing, self-controlling, seeking social support, accepting responsibility, escape-avoidance, planful problem solving, and positive reappraisal.

Finally, in a third session, participants completed a series of measures designed to assess their general physical health and subjective well-being. These measures included the General Health Questionnaire (GHQ), the Health Symptoms Questionnaire (HSQ), and Ryff's Psychological Well-being (PWB) inventory. The overall score and six subscales: autonomy, environmental mastery, personal growth, positive relationships with others, purpose in life, and self-acceptance were computed on the PWB.

We analyzed the data by examining bivariate relationships between sets of variables; while multivariate techniques would be preferred, they are unjustified given the number of variables in relation to the sample size. The order of analysis was determined by the notion that coping and emotion/mood indicators were mediators of the relationship between cultural discrepancy and health. We first computed correlations between the cultural discrepancy scores and each of the eight coping scales of the Ways of Coping Questionnaire. As shown in table 3.1, all eight coping scales were significantly correlated with cultural discrepancy scores. In particular, greater discrepancy scores were associated with higher scores on escape-avoidance, seeking social support, and positive reappraisal coping styles, suggesting that individuals with greater perceived discrepancies between their personal cultural values and their perceptions of societal or ideal values engaged in more of these types of coping processes.

We then computed correlations between each of the eight coping styles and the scores on the BAI, BDI, and MAACL. Seeking social support and positive reappraisal were significantly negatively correlated with BDI scores, indicating that individuals who engaged in these coping styles reported lower depression scores. Escape-avoidance, however, was significantly positively related to both BAI and BDI, indicating that participants who reported more escape-avoidance coping had higher depression and anxiety scores. In addition planful problem solving coping was significantly positively correlated with the positive affect scale on the MAACL.

Finally, to examine the relationship between the emotion/mood scales and the health and well-being scales, we computed correlations between each of these scales as well (table 3.2). BAI and BDI were positively correlated with both measures of physical health, indicating that individuals with higher anxiety or depression scores reported larger number of physical symptoms and health concerns. In addition,

Table 3.1
Correlations between person-culture discrepancy variables and the eight coping styles (decimals omitted)

Discrepancy variable[a]	CC	DI	SC	SSS	AR	EA	PPS	PR
ICIAI PS	370*	416*	533**	436**	378*	351*	426*	339*
ICIAI PI	121	265	128	297	050	038	260	056
ICIAI overall	364*	392*	424*	476*	323	194	431*	277
Rokeach/Triandis PS	407*	302	382*	407*	421*	333*	059	292
Rokeach/Triandis PI	149	031	260	237	109	020	225	158
Rokeach/Triandis overall	540**	344*	552**	390*	489**	382*	276	449**
Composite PS	478**	460**	578**	396*	486**	437*	392*	433*
Composite PI	199	149	288	285	150	020	241	148
Composite overall	498*	393*	643**	401*	439*	329	469**	440**

Note: Asterisks indicate levels of significance: * for $p < 0.05$; ** for $p < 0.01$.
a. Abbreviations are as follows:

ICIAI	Intercultural Interpersonal Assessment Inventory
PS	Person-society discrepancy
PI	Person-ideal discrepancy
CC	Confrontive coping
DI	Distancing
SC	Self-controlling
SSS	Seeking social support
AR	Accepting responsibility
EA	Escape-avoidance
PPS	Planful problem solving
PR	Positive reappraisal

Table 3.2
Correlations between emotion/mood and health/well-being (decimals omitted)

Emotion/mood[a]	GHQ	HSQ	SWB	SWB-AU	SWB-EM	SWB-PG	SWB-PRWO	SWB-PL	SWB-SA
BAI	627**	547**	-498**	-503**	-414*	-459**	-363*	-290	-475**
BDI	544**	605**	-738**	-511**	-657**	-657**	-634**	-520**	-740**
MAACL—anxiety	390**	150	-519**	-481**	-481**	-448**	-397*	-247	-534**
MAACL—depression	248	141	-482**	-345*	-454**	-353*	-472**	-269	-532**
MAACL—hostility	-003	-146	-116	065	-217	-085	-276	037	-144
MAACL—positive affect	-114	-247	463**	194	429**	452**	429**	488**	431**
MAACL—sensation seeking	-049	-114	242	259	200	182	087	179	253
MAACL—dysphoria	215	034	-412*	-256	-430**	-324*	-432--	-170	-448**
MAACL—positive affect/ sensation seeking	-103	-229	431**	233	393*	406**	356*	429**	412**

Notes: Asterisks indicate levels of significance: * for $p < 0.05$; ** for $p < 0.01$.
a. Abbreviations are as follows:

BAI	Beck Anxiety Inventory
BDI	Beck Depression Inventory
MAACL	Multiple affect adjective check list
GHQ	General health questionnaire
HSQ	Health symptoms questionnaire
PWB	Psychological well-being
AU	Autonomy
EM	Environmental mastery
PG	Personal growth
PRWO	Positive relations with others
PL	Purpose in life
SA	Self-acceptance

with only one exception, the BAI and BDI were negatively correlated with all six subscales and the overall scale on the PWB. These findings indicated that those individuals with greater anxiety or depression reported less psychological well-being in all aspects. A number of MAACL scales also produced findings in expected directions. However, since these scales, in general, were not correlated with the coping strategies, it is difficult to interpret their role in mediating the relationship between coping and health.

These findings suggest that increased discrepancies between personal and societal, or personal and ideal, cultural values are associated with greater need for coping, as evidenced in the significant correlations on all coping styles. Different types of coping styles, however, seem to have different effects. Escape-avoidance type of coping is associated with increased depression and anxiety, which in turn are associated with greater physical health concerns and less psychological well-being. Seeking social support, positive reappraisal, and planful problem solving coping strategies, however, are associated with less anxiety and depression, or greater positive affect; these in turn are associated with less physical symptomatology and greater subjective well-being. While these results are preliminary, and need to be replicated with larger sample sizes and more sophisticated analytic methods, they certainly are suggestive of the importance of cultural values discrepancy in predicting health and well-being, and of the potentially large impact of coping and emotion in mediating this relationship.

Conclusion and Recommendations for Further Study

The available literature that examines the association between culture as an individual psychological construct and SWB clearly suggests that an important relationship exists between these two constructs. The most recent of these studies have gone a good way toward establishing a model of this relationship by analyzing several factors; a full model will most likely need to incorporate a variety of possible mediating variables, effects of larger-scale (demographic and ecological) culture, and perceptions of person-environment fit. While none of the existing studies describes a full model, each study is a further step toward a more sophisticated understanding of this important relationship. Still, research in this area of culture and SWB is in its childhood, and there are many more unanswered questions. For example, a number of constructs—self-esteem, purpose in life, affect—are used inconsistently in the above studies, sometimes as a mediator, other times as a measure of SWB or even as a measure of culture. This confusion needs to be cleared, both theoretically and empirically.

Problematic for other reasons is the use of such variables as self-esteem and powerlessness as measures of well-being. Implicit in that use is a value judgment, but by whose definition are they positive or negative? It is critical, as in any cross-cultural study, to ensure that constructs are valid for all cultures being studied. Self-esteem in particular seems to be an especially individualistic construct. Even to use it as a mediator, we need more work on verifying that and on establishing possible collectivistic equivalents (e.g., relationship harmony, social support).

As the studies reviewed here show, the relationship between individual culture and SWB is somewhat complex, and we will need to go beyond extending the consistencies in findings to date and resolving the discrepancies that have arisen. In particular, we look forward to future research in this area focusing on three areas of major concern that now stand before us:

1. The effect of various dimensions of individual level culture, especially further examination of cultural differences other than IC.
2. The effect of various possible mediating variables, focusing on the role of different coping strategies and other possible mediating variables that lead to either positive or negative outcomes in health and well-being.
3. The effect of the larger cultural context examining the relationship between individual and ecological measures of culture, and the degree of contribution of individual level measures to ecological differences in SWB.

Future research then is perhaps best viewed in these three distinct layers. We know that at the layer of individual culture, both individualism and collectivism can act as factors in the relationship, though how, when, and why they each affect SWB is not clear. Ethnic identity, especially for members of ethnic groups outside the dominant culture, also seems to be predictive of SWB, and further studies may well show similar relationships with other dimensions of individual culture. At the second layer, a variety of factors appear to play a mediating role in the relationship between individual levels of culture and SWB. Personal and/or collective self-esteem, the nature and quality of social relationships, coping styles, and personality have all been found to be part of the relationship. We should further investigate these factors, but also look into purpose in life, self- and cultural discrepancies, affect and any other possible mediators. The third layer could be broken into demographic culture and ecological culture. The existing studies indicate that each of these levels

—and certainly any perceived discrepancy between individual and broader levels of culture—is likely to affect the relationship.

Context issues are especially important to the interpretation of results. We need to better understand the role of ecological culture in any relationship between individual culture and SWB. When we find that allocentric individuals are happier than their idiocentric counterparts in a collectivistic culture, we cannot conclude that allocentrism is associated with SWB without considering the importance of person-culture fit in that relationship. If individualistic values are found to be more rational than collectivistic values, we must look at the possibility that this is only true in an individualistic culture. Defining the boundaries of the cultural context is also important. Within a nation the culture of the smaller community, ethnic group, or other subculture may also affect the relationship between individual culture and well-being. Acculturation levels in nations with large immigrant populations may similarly mediate the relationship. A wide variety of cultural contexts should be included in our studies. Certainly more research needs to be done in cultural milieus outside the United States. Broadening our approach in this manner, stepping out of the existing box, may lead to finding new dimensions of individual culture, new mediators, even possibly a different relationship between culture and SWB. Examining new approaches, developing theoretical models, and identifying the central research questions will help guide studies to come.

References

Bettencourt, B. A., and Dorr, N. 1997. Collective self-esteem as a mediator of the relationship between allocentrism and subjective well-being. *Personality and Social Psychology Bulletin* 23: 955–64.

Cozzarelli, C., and Karafa, J. A. 1998. Cultural estrangement and terror management theory. *Personality and Social Psychology Bulletin* 24: 253–67.

Diener, E. 1984. Subjective well-being. *Psychological Bulletin* 95: 542–75.

Diener, E., and Diener, M. 1995. Cross-cultural correlates of life satisfaction and self-esteem. *Journal of Personality and Social Psychology* 68: 653–63.

Diener, E., Emmons, R. A., Larsen, R. J., and Griffin, S. 1985. The Satisfaction with Life Scale. *Journal of Personality Assessment* 49: 71–75.

Florsheim, P. 1997. Chinese adolescent immigrants: Factors related to psychosocial adjustment. *Journal of Youth and Adolescence* 26: 143–63.

Folkman, S., and Lazarus, R. S. 1988. *Ways of Coping Questionniare: Research Edition.* Palo Alto: Consulting Psychologists Press.

Hui, C. H. 1984. Individualism-collectivism: Theory, measurement, and its relation to reward allocation. PhD dissertation. University of Illinois.

Hui, C. H. 1988. Measurement of individualism-collectivism. *Journal of Research in Personality* 22: 17–36.

Kasri, F. 1997. Cross-cultural concepts of subjective well-being. MS thesis. San Francisco State University, San Francisco.

Kwan, V. S. Y., Bond, M. H., and Singelis, T. M., 1997. Pancultural explanations for life satisfaction: Adding relationship harmony to self-esteem. *Journal of Personality and Social Psychology* 73: 1038–51.

Markus, H. R., and Kitayama, S. 1991. Culture and self: Implications for cognition, emotion, and motivation. *Psychological Review* 96: 224–53.

Martinez, R. O., and Dukes, R. L. 1997. The effects of ethnic identity, ethnicity, and gender on adolescent well-being. *Journal of Youth and Adolescence* 26: 503–16.

Matsumoto, D. 2000. *Culture and Psychology*, 2nd ed. Pacific Grove, CA: Brooks Cole.

Matsumoto, D. (in press). Culture and self: An empirical assessment of Markus and Kitayama's theory of independent and interdependent self-construals. *Asian Journal of Social Psychology*.

Matsumoto, D. 1994. *Cultural Influences on Research Methods and Statistics*. Pacific Grove, CA: Brooks Cole.

Matsumoto, D., Weissman, M. D., Preston, K., Brown, B. R., and Kupperbush, C. 1997. Context-specific measurement of individualism-collectivism on the individual level: The Individualism-Collectivism Interpersonal Assessment Inventory. *Journal of Cross-cultural Psychology* 28: 743–67.

Rosenberg, M. 1965. *Society and the Adolescent Self-Image*. Princeton, NJ: Princeton University Press.

Ryff, C. D. 1989. Happiness is everything, or is it? Explorations on the meaning of psychological well-being. *Journal of Personality and Social Psychology* 57: 1069–81.

Ryff, C. D., and Keyes, C. L. M. 1995. The structure of psychological well-being revisited. *Journal of Personality and Social Psychology* 69: 719–27.

Shek, D. T. 1992. Meaning of life and psychological well-being: An empirical study using the Chinese version of the Purpose in Life questionnaire. *Journal of Genetic Psychology* 153: 185–200.

Singelis, T. M., Triandis, H. C., Bhawuk, D. S., and Gelfand, M. 1995. Horizontal and vertical dimensions of individualism and collectivism: A theoretical and measurement refinement. *Cross-cultural Research* 29: 240–75.

Sinha, J. P., and Verma, J. 1994. Social support as a moderator of the relationship between allocentrism and psychological well-being. In U. Kim, H. C. Triandis, and G. Yoon., eds., *Cross-cultural Research and Methodology: Individualism and Collectivism: Theory, Method, and Applications*, vol. 18. Thousand Oaks, CA: Sage.

Triandis, H. C. 1995. *Individualism and Collectivism*. Boulder, CO: Westview Press.

Triandis, H. C., Bontempo, R., Leung, K., and Hui, C. H. 1990. A method for determining cultural, demographic, and personal constructs. *Journal of Cross-cultural Psychology* 21: 302–18.

Triandis, H. C., Bontempo, R., Villareal, M. J., Asai, M., and Lucca, N. 1988. Individualism and collectivism: Cross-cultural perspectives on self-ingroup relationships. *Journal of Personality and Social Psychology* 4: 323–38.

Triandis, H. C., and Gelfand, M. J. 1998. Converging measurement of horizontal and vertical individualism and collectivism. *Journal of Personality and Social Psychology* 74: 118–28.

Triandis, H. C., Leung, K., Villareal, M. J., and Clack, F. L. 1985. Allocentric versus idiocentric tendencies: Convergent and discriminant validation. *Journal of Research in Personality* 19: 395–415.

Triandis, H. C., McCusker, C., and Hui, C. H. 1990. Multimethod probes of individualism and collectivism. *Journal of Personality and Social Psychology* 59: 1006–20.

Triandis, H. C., McCusker, C., Betancourt, H., Iwao, S., Leung, K., Salazar, J. M., Setiadi, B., Sinha, J. P. B., Touzard, H., and Zaleski, Z. 1993. An etic-emic analysis of individualism and collectivism. *Journal of Cross-cultural Psychology* 24: 366–83.

Verkuyten, M. 1995. Self-esteem, self-concept stability, and aspects of ethnic identity among minority and majority youth in the Netherlands. *Journal of Youth and Adolescence* 24: 155–75.

Watson, P. J., Sherbak, J., and Morris, R. J. 1998. Irrational beliefs, individualism-collectivism, and adjustment. *Personality and Individual Differences* 24: 173–79.

II

Cultural Differences in the Definition and Causes of Well-being

4

Self, the Hyphen between Culture and Subjective Well-being

Eunkook M. Suh

The self stands at the junction of subjective well-being and culture. Culture provides form and shape to the self, which in turn influences how individuals feel and think about various aspects of their lives—the central research issue of SWB. Given its overlapping intersections with both culture and subjective experience, the self holds a key in unraveling the complex relation between culture and SWB. Most of the existing studies on culture and SWB, however, have used aggregated cultural variables, such as individualism and power distance, in their analyses (Arindell et al. 1997; Diener, Diener, and Diener 1995; Veenhoven 1993). Although important advances are made from this approach, the psychological mechanisms involved in the experience and judgment of SWB among different cultural members remain rather poorly understood. In order to fill in this theoretical vacuum, the present chapter contends that the field needs to carefully observe the various ways in which the self mediates the influence of culture on SWB.

Western theories of psychological well-being are firmly established on a highly individuated self concept; individuals are believed to be metaphysically discrete and separate from others just as their physical bodies are. Psychological characteristics commonly associated with mental health in North America (e.g., self-actualization, autonomy) portray the personal qualities of a highly independent, self-reliant individual who is capable of transcending the influences of others and of the society. Such ideals, to borrow Geertz's (1984, p. 126) expression, are "rather peculiar idea(s) within the context of the world's cultures." East Asian notions of selfhood, in particular, are antithetical to the typical North American understanding of the person. The East Asian discussion of the individual starts with the Confucian assumption that the person exists in relationship to others (King and Bond 1985). The individual is viewed as being fundamentally socially oriented (Yang 1984), situation centered (Hsu 1953), interdependent (Markus and Kitayama 1991), and inextricably bonded with others through emotional ties (Choi and Choi 1994). Such cultural assumptions of selfhood are inevitably incorporated in concepts of psychological well-being. Accordingly, the list of Western psychological virtues associated with the individuated self model appears to have far less importance in determining the SWB of East Asian cultural members. The first section of the chapter is focused on this issue.

The second section discusses the important role played by the self in the judgment of SWB. For instance, individualist cultures that advocate the primacy of individual experience chronically direct the attention of their members to their internal psychological attributes. In contrast, in East Asian cultures where salient cultural tasks constitute others, individuals are constantly drawn to external social cues. The basis of life satisfaction judgment seems to differ between these two cultures, depending on what types of information are chronically accessible to the individual. Finally, the chapter concludes by addressing an issue that is attracting increasing attention among cross-cultural researchers. Namely, why are North Americans happier and more self-positive than East Asians? In addition to motivational reasons, the chapter proposes that cultural differences in mean levels of SWB and positive self-judgments could partly arise from the diverging ways in which North Americans and East Asians evaluate themselves.

Correlates of Subjective Well-being

A common expression used by a Korean wife when introducing her husband to a stranger is "This is our father." Although the exact origin of this expression is not clear, it appears to be related to the general East Asian tendency to restrain the self from becoming uncomfortably salient in a social context. By referring to her husband from the perspective of her children ("our father") rather than from her own ("my husband"), the wife may draw less attention to the self in the social context. Although this interpretation is speculative, what is unambiguously clear is that East Asian cultural members constantly tone down their individuality by avoiding overly self-promoting and self-assertive self-presentations. The central motives of the self in these cultures, accordingly, are quite different from those of the North Americans who are encouraged, if not obliged, to discover and assert their distinct positive inner qualities (Fiske et al. 1998; Markus and Kitayama 1991).

Self-enhancement and self-consistency are two motives of the self that hold prominent positions in Western psychology (Brown 1998; Jones 1973; Sedikides and Strube 1997; Swann et al. 1987). In this light, it is not surprising that high self-esteem and self-congruence have been long regarded as quintessential markers of mental health in the West (Allport 1961; Lecky 1945; Maslow 1954; Rogers 1965). Self-esteem and self-congruence, respectively, represent the crystallized fulfillment of the needs of self-enhancement and self-consistency. A growing number of cross-cultural psychologists, however, find that the motive of self-enhancement (Kashima and Triandis 1986; Kitayama et al. 1997; Heine et al. 1999) as well as the motive of self-consistency (Bachnik 1992; Heine and Lehman 1997; Kashima et al. 1992; Rosenberger 1989) are weaker in East Asian than in Western cultures. In line with this cultural difference, recent findings further suggest that both self-esteem and level of identity consistency are less powerful predictors of SWB in collectivist than in individualist cultures.

Self-esteem

Liking oneself appears to be the panacea for most psychological problems in North American cultures. People who possess high self-esteem are able to find more meaning in their lives and ward off anxiety more successfully (Greenberg et al. 1992), are less prone to substance abuse (Hawkins, Catalano, and Miller 1992), and are less affected by negative moods (Brown and Mankowski 1993) than those who have negative views of themselves. Not surprisingly, self-esteem is a strong predictor of SWB among North Americans (Campbell 1981; Lucas, Diener, and Suh 1996).

Recent cross-cultural findings indicate, however, that the strength of the relation between self-esteem and SWB varies considerably across cultures. Although Diener and Diener (1995) found that life satisfaction correlated positively with self-esteem across all of the 31 nations they examined, the size of this correlation differed substantially across nations. For instance, self-esteem and life satisfaction correlated 0.60 in samples from the United States and from Canada, whereas they correlated only 0.08 among Indian and 0.27 among Bahrain women. Across the entire pool of nations, the individualism of the nations correlated 0.53 with the size of the self-esteem and life satisfaction relation. Thus self-esteem predicts life satisfaction more strongly in individualist than in collectivist societies.

In addition to self-esteem, Kwan, Bond, and Singelis (1997) hypothesized that maintaining a harmonious relationship with others may be a particularly important source of life satisfaction in collectivist cultures. When the SWB responses of U.S. and Hong Kong college students were analyzed through structural equation models, self-esteem and relationship harmony each had an additive effect on life satisfaction and were separable in both cultures. However, as predicted, relationship harmony turned out to be as important as self-esteem in predicting the life satisfaction of Hong Kong respondents. In contrast, the standardized path coefficient of self-esteem (0.63) was significantly larger than the coefficient of relationship harmony (0.23) in the United States. In addition to replicating the findings of Diener and Diener (1995), Kwan et al. found an indigenous collectivist factor (relationship harmony) that importantly predicts SWB in a collectivist cultural setting.

If self-esteem is indeed less central to East Asian individuals, they should be less disturbed by threats to their self-esteem than individualists. A study by Brockner and Chen (1996) supports this idea. They examined how college students from the United States and the People's Republic of China (PRC) react to a negative feedback about the self after completing a test that purportedly measures the individual's cognitive ability. In the United States, but not among the PRC sample, individuals with high self-esteem engaged in greater self-protective response (e.g., less internal attribution) to negative feedback than those with low self-esteem.

A further analysis by Brockner and Chen (1996) revealed that the pattern of self-protective behavior observed at the cultural level also exists at the individual level. Even among the PRC respondents, those with a more independent self-construal resembled the general self-protective behavior of the U.S. participants. Conversely, within the United States, those with a less independent self-construal resembled the self-protective patterns exhibited by the PRC sample. In other words, in both cultures, individuals whose self-system "mismatched" the cultural prototype engaged in a self-protective style that was consonant with the typical pattern of the "opposite" culture. This finding suggests that a psychological phenomenon observed at the cultural level tends to occur also at the individual level. It highlights the fact that a large amount of individual variance exists within a culture and also that there is considerable overlap in the psychological behaviors of different cultural members.

The above studies suggest that having a positive self-view is beneficial to SWB in most cultures. As Diener and Diener (1995) found, self-esteem was correlated positively with SWB in all of the 31 nations they observed. However, the degree of importance varies substantially across cultures. Self-esteem is a very important element of life satisfaction in individualist cultures because their members are "taught to like themselves, and doing so is a sign of mental adjustment" (Diener and Diener 1995, p. 653). In cultures where the collective takes precedence over the individual, however, positive feelings about the self appear to constitute a smaller part of one's overall life satisfaction. In fact the term "self-esteem" does not even exist in the common vocabulary of Koreans. Furthermore, at this point it is unclear whether the exact origin of this positive self-feeling is similar across cultures. That is, even though self-esteem relates positively with SWB across cultures, we need to gain a more refined understanding of what types of experience cause the positive self-feelings of collectivist versus individualist cultural members. Overall, although recent studies indicate that self-esteem is positively related to SWB across cultures, its intrinsic importance has been overestimated by traditional Western theories of psychological well-being.

Identity Consistency

Possessing an internally coherent self-identity is considered to be another integral ingredient of mental health in Western theories. Despite the multifaceted nature of the self, the prevailing view in psychology asserts that the person should coherently integrate the various components of the self and be consistent across situations. Lecky (1945), one of the earliest proponents of this idea, claimed that people seek to understand who they are by integrating various self-perceptions into an organized knowledge structure. Because information that is inconsistent with the existing self-view must go through a strenuous "repair work," Lecky argued that people are strongly motivated to act in manners consistent with their self-views. The psychological importance of having a consistent identity has been reiterated in the writings of prominent personality theorists, such as Maslow (1968), Rogers (1965), Erikson (1950), and Jourard (1974), and is supported by contemporary research (Donahue et al. 1993.)

The above-mentioned theoretical position fits well with the North American cultural ethos that heralds the autonomy of the individual: the self, not the situation, should be the "anchor" of personal behavior. The decontextualized Western self derives its meaning, purpose, and behavioral guidance primarily from its internal sources. Thus it follows quite naturally that establishing a well-organized, internally and cross-situationally consistent self-structure is a prerequisite condition of mental health in the West. The question is whether this idea holds equally true in East Asian cultures where the focus is more often on the social context than on the person. Being rigidly self-consistent by insisting the principles of the internal self rather than those of the interpersonal context, for instance, could be construed as a reflection of personal immaturity or arrogance in East Asian cultures.

With this question in mind, Suh (2000) recently investigated the consistency of Korean and American college students' self-views across social roles in relation to their SWB. Participants in both cultures were asked to rate how accurately twenty different personality traits (e.g., emotional, impulsive) described themselves in general, and also when they were engaging in five different social roles (e.g., son/daughter, friend). A number of interesting findings emerged. First, the self-views of Korean students were significantly more flexible across roles than those of the Americans. For instance, the personality profile of the general self, on average, correlated 0.32 across the five different social selves among the Koreans, whereas the mean of this within-person correlation was 0.58 in the U.S. sample. Thus the overall self-views of the Korean participants changed to a greater degree across social contexts than those of the Americans, implying that self-consistency needs are weaker in collectivist than in individualist cultures.

More important, Suh (2000) found that the degree of identity consistency was a significantly stronger predictor of SWB in the United States than in Korea. Based on a method developed by Block (1961), an index of identity consistency was obtained for each individual by factor analyzing his or her trait-role matrix (20 traits × 6 roles). This index of identity consistency, which reflects the degree to which an individual's ordering of the traits from the most to least self-descriptive is consistent across roles, correlated with SWB measures in a similar direction between the two samples. However, a significant cultural difference was observed in the strength of these relations. The correlation between the level of identity consistency and life satisfaction, for instance, was 0.49 among the Americans and 0.22 among the Koreans. Also the relation between identity consistency and unpleasant affect was significantly stronger among the American ($r = -0.50$) than the Korean ($r = -0.23$) respondents ($p < 0.05$).

One intriguing cultural difference emerged from the informant reports. According to the informant reports, highly self-consistent individuals were viewed by others to be socially more skilled ($r = 0.37, p < 0.01$) and more likable ($r = 0.33, p < 0.05$) than inconsistent individuals in the United States. Interestingly, however, Korean informants showed no such sign of preference between consistent versus inconsistent individuals. In short, in contrast to the situation in the United States, highly self-consistent people were not more popular than inconsistent people in Korea. Compared to the United States, the contingency between self-consistent behavior and social reward appears to be significantly weaker, or even absent in East Asian cultures. Although this conclusion needs more extensive examination, it may offer illuminating insights to understanding why the motive of self-consistency is weaker and why identity consistency is less predictive of SWB in East Asian cultures.

As in the case of self-esteem, maintaining a coherently organized personal identity does relate to SWB in both individualist and collectivist cultures. However, a similar caveat should be added. Unlike the traditional assumptions held in mainstream psychology, the need of self-consistency does not appear to be a universally strong psychological motive. Furthermore the psychological benefits accrued by maintaining a consistent identity across different social settings seem to be smaller in East Asian cultures than in North America. An impending task is to better understand the primary motives of the collectivist self and to uncover the concrete psychological constructs arising from these needs that contribute to SWB in East Asian societies.

Basis of Life Satisfaction Judgments

Subjective well-being, as the term indicates, is primarily concerned with the person's subjective judgment of his or her well-being (Diener et al. 1999). Because the standards of self-evaluation are deferred to the individual, evaluating whether one's life as a whole is satisfying or not can be a challenging cognitive task to the respondent. Theoretically, after retrieving, weighing, and appraising a wide variety of personal information, the person will need to translate his or her judgment into a numeric response. In reality, however, individuals rarely go through this exhausting mental process. Rather, as Schwarz, Strack, and their colleagues demonstrate, individuals tend to reduce their cognitive efforts by relying on cues that are readily accessible and salient at the time of their life satisfaction judgments (Schwarz and Strack 1999).

Cultures, by emphasizing different elements of experience and by giving priority to different types of information, play a key role in determining what types of information are chronically salient among their cultural members (Triandis 1989). This leads to the idea that the judgment of life satisfaction could be based on different sources of information across cultures. For instance, the North American culture strongly encourages its members to attend to, cultivate, and express their unique inner qualities. One consequence of this is that individuals tend to attach great value and validity to their internal, phenomenological experiences. Private emotions, in particular, are believed to reflect the most genuine aspects of the self (Andersen and Ross 1984). As a result individuals frequently use emotions as a piece of information in various self-judgments (e.g., Batson et al. 1995; Schwarz and Clore 1988). Even when explicitly asked to ignore, individualists tend to find it quite difficult to dismiss emotion-laden information (Edwards and Bryan 1997).

A recent study by Gilovich, Savitsky, and Medvec (1998) illustrates how strongly internal experience affects the psychological judgments made in individualist cultures. They found that North American college students tend to overestimate the extent to which others can discern their internal states, a phenomenon the authors labeled as the *illusion of transparency*. For instance, people believe that their feelings of disgust are more apparent than they actually are and overestimate how well others can detect their lies. After disproving a number of potential explanations, the authors conclude that this bias stems primarily from the powerful impact of the phenomenological experience on self-judgment. When individuals judge how apparent their internal states are to others, they begin the process by examining their subjective phenomenological experience. However, the internal experience is usually so salient that the adjustments individuals make to this phenomenological "anchor" tend to be insufficient. As a result people erroneously conclude that their internal states "leak out" more than they actually do. This study exemplifies how strongly internal experiences affect the self-inference processes of individualist cultural members.

A growing body of evidence suggests, however, that internal phenomenological states, such as emotions, are less central to the psychological behaviors of collectivist cultural members (Levenson et al. 1992; Levine et al. 1995; Miller and Bersoff 1998; Potter 1988). Such a cultural difference, regarding the significance of internal experience, seems to emerge at a relatively early age. A recent study by Han, Leichtman, and Wang (1998) is illuminating. They presented an identical children's story to 4- and 6-year-old Korean, Chinese, and American children and asked them to recall the story the next day. Content analysis indicated that compared to the Asians, American children used more internal emotion words and more frequently mentioned themselves relative to others when they recalled the story. Interestingly the American children used more internal qualifiers even though the story that was presented in the experiment was originally published in Korea. Thus, even at a relatively early age, North American children seem to schematize experience more in reference to internal referents of the self than East Asian peers.

If the primary source of self-knowledge differs across cultures, the judgment of life satisfaction may also be based on different cues across cultures. A recent study by Suh, Diener, Oishi, and Triandis (1998) supports this idea. When the relation between emotions and life satisfaction was compared across 41 nations, significantly stronger correlations were found in individualist than in collectivist societies. For instance, life satisfaction correlated 0.48 with affect balance (frequency of positive minus negative affect) in the United States, but 0.22 in India, and 0.32 in Japan. Across nations the strength of the life satisfaction and emotion correlation was related significantly to the nations' degree of individualism ($r = 0.52$). Thus the more individualist the nation, the more heavily life satisfaction judgments tended to be based on internal emotions.

Considering that collectivists view external factors, such as norms, roles, and obligations as prime determinants of behavior (Fiske et al., 1998; Triandis 1995), Suh et al. (1998) further hypothesized that collectivists will pay considerable attention to normative concerns ("Is it culturally desirable to feel personally satisfied?") when they evaluate their overall lives. To test this idea, Suh et al. compared the relative weight of emotions and norms in life satisfaction judgments at the individual level using another international sample. As predicted, individuals of collectivist cultures based their judgments equally strongly on norms and emotions. On the other hand, norms played a negligible role in the life satisfaction judgment of individualists. As found earlier, individualists' judgments of life satisfaction were based predominantly on their internal emotions.

What crucial factor causes the divergent self-evaluation pattern between individualist and collectivist cultures? Suh et al. (1998) proposed that the cultural difference was primarily due to the relative salience of the autonomous versus the relational aspects of the self. According to this perspective, individualists' global self-evaluations tend to be based chiefly on private experiences (e.g., emotions) because the culture constantly directs the person's attention to the unique, individuated aspects of his or her identity. Collectivists, on the other hand, base their self-judgments heavily on external referents (e.g., norms) because diverse cultural mechanisms perpetually highlight the relational and interdependent aspects of the self.

Theoretically, then, an analogous self-judgment process may take place between individuals *within* a culture. For instance, the "idiocentric" mode of life satisfaction judgment (i.e., reliance on emotion) should be pronounced among individuals whose distinct individuality from others is salient. Conversely, life satisfaction judgments may be based more heavily on social information (e.g., social appraisal) when the relational aspects of the self are highly accessible. A recent within-culture study supports this idea. Compared to European-American participants, Suh and Diener (1999) found that Asian-Americans downplayed the importance of emotions but heavily emphasized social appraisal (i.e., significant other's evaluation of one's life) in their life satisfaction judgments. This ethnic group difference was replicated not only at the individual level between allocentric versus idiocentric respondents, but also between experimental priming conditions. Regardless of the respondent's stable personal characteristics, internal emotions served as a principal source of self-evaluation when the person's distinct individuality was primed. However, when the person's attention was directed toward the relational aspects of the self, life satisfaction judgments were strongly based on how s/he thought significant others might view her or his life (social appraisal).

In sum, the multilevel research conducted among cultures (Suh et al. 1998), ethnic groups, individual differences in personality, and priming conditions (Suh and Diener 1999) converge to demonstrate that the self plays a pivotal role in determining the relative weight of internal versus external information in judgments of life satisfaction. Since the time of Wundt, psychology traditionally believed that the best way to evaluate ourselves is to "look inward" to our internal feelings and thoughts. In general, the life satisfaction judgment styles of those who highly endorse the independent elements of the self seem to match this traditional assumption. However, regardless of the specific cause, when individuals view themselves primarily in relational terms, self-evaluation appears to be based to a significant degree on external, social information. These findings not only highlight the pervasive influence of the self on the process of SWB judgments, but as we will discuss in the following section, they may also provide important clues to understanding why cultural differences in levels of SWB occur.

Why Are North Americans Happier Than East Asians?

"I feel very confident and very proud of what I've done" was the comment the U.S. national team coach offered to the press moments after losing a highly publicized match against Iran in the 1998 World Cup soccer tournament (Associated Press 1998). Although such flattering self-appraisal baffles many East Asians, research shows that such positive attitudes about the self are held prevalently among North American cultural members. For instance, individuals typically take credit for success, but detach themselves from failure (Miller and Ross 1975), feel quite invulnerable to negative future events (Perloff and Fetzer 1986; Weinstein 1980), and rate themselves "above average" on various positive personal qualities (Dunning, Meyerowitz, and Holzberg 1989). Such self-serving tendencies are so widespread and robust among the "normal" population that they are believed to be the typical way the North Americans think of themselves (Armor and Taylor 1998; Taylor and Brown 1988).

The self-views of East Asian cultural members are comparably less positive. In comparison to North Americans, for example, East Asians are less optimistic about their future (Heine and Lehman 1995), have more moderate levels of self-esteem (Diener and Diener 1995), exhibit less self-serving bias (Kashima and Triandis 1986), and engage in less self-enhancement (Bond, Leung, and Wan 1982; Kitayama et al. 1997; Yik, Bond, and Paulus 1998). An interesting cultural effect was found when Lee and Seligman (1997) studied the attribution styles of White Americans, Chinese Americans, and mainland Chinese participants. The level of optimism displayed by the American Chinese was stronger than the mainland Chinese group but weaker than the White Americans, suggesting that the degree of optimism is related with the amount of exposure to individualist cultural values. Heine et al. (1999) also provide evidence that engagement in North American culture fosters the development of self-esteem.

Not surprisingly, North Americans report significantly higher levels of SWB than East Asians (Diener, Diener, and Diener 1995; Diener and Suh 1999; Diener et al. 1995). For instance, compared to 36 percent of Japanese and 49 percent of Korean men, 83 percent of American men and 78 percent of Canadian men reported above neutral levels of life satisfaction in Diener and Diener's study (1995). The majority of North Americans not only say that they are happy in an absolute sense (by reporting above neutral points on SWB measures), but also believe that their current age is the happiest time of life (*USA Weekend* 1998).

Why are North Americans so happy and self-positive? This is one of the most perplexing questions that have emerged from recent cross-cultural studies. Although a number of hypotheses have been considered, including possible cultural differences in emotion norms (Diener et al. 1996), response styles (Diener et al. 1995), and self-effacing motives (Kitayama et al. 1997), our understanding of this issue remains rudimentary. Because most of the current studies in this area rely on self-report measures, some may raise the possibility that self-presentational motives (e.g., to appear modest) lower the SWB reports of East Asians. Although this is a valid concern that warrants constant attention in comparing cross-cultural means, recent studies fail to lend a strong support for this interpretation (e.g., see Chen, Lee, and Stevenson 1995; Diener et al. 1995; Heine et al. 1999). In the following section we focus on some of the potential motivational and cognitive reasons that might lead to mean cultural differences in SWB and positive self-views.

Motivational Factors

Our self-understanding depends to a great extent on how we *wish* to view ourselves (e.g., Brown 1993). Motivation has a ubiquitous influence on our reasoning by affecting the cognitive strategies for accessing, constructing, and evaluating information

(Kunda 1990). Because people have a strong propensity to seek or interpret evidence in ways that confirm their expectations (Nickerson 1998), people are more likely to evaluate their lives and experiences positively when they have a strong incentive to do so. Thus, in attempting to understand why North Americans and East Asians differ so much in their mean levels of SWB, we should first consider the issue from a motivational perspective. In particular, whether the culture believes SWB hinges primarily on personal abilities or on less controllable external factors could affect how strongly its members try to view themselves in a positive tone.

The pursuit of happiness, in individualist North American cultures, is an inviolable individual right. In a culture that offers great amounts of opportunity and freedom to each cultural member, happiness is considered to be the ultimate culmination of one's labor and effort. Perhaps this is why happiness is not only one of the foremost concerns of Americans, but has such a enormous positive "halo" effect. For instance, Americans even believe that happy people are more likely to go to heaven than unhappy people (King and Napa 1998). The downside of individualism, at least from a personal perspective, however, is that each individual is highly accountable for his or her unhappiness and low self-regard. The psychological "pressure" to be happy and self-confident thus is strong in North American cultures. As the prevalent use of self-serving cognitive strategies implies (Greenwald 1980; Taylor and Brown 1988; Tesser 1988), individualist cultural members invest a considerable amount of effort to convince both the self and others that they are happy, self-confident, and in full control of their lives. It seems quite probable that such motivational reasons, to some degree, implicitly elevate the SWB reports of North American cultural members.

East Asian cultural perspectives on happiness are quite different from those of the West (e.g., Lee 1992; Minami 1971; D. Suh 1994). According to the Japanese social psychologist Hiroshi Minami (1971), for instance, a "habit of hesitation" (p. 34) toward happiness exists in traditional Japanese culture. This hesitant Eastern attitude toward happiness may partly originate from the Confucian idea that both happiness and unhappiness stem from a common "root" (Lee 1992). Unhappiness is believed to arrive on the heel of happiness, and vice versa. It is therefore taught that happiness should not be embraced with excessive joy. The upside of this logic is that the unhappiness of the moment should be endured with hope because happiness is imminent. Because the ebb and flow of happiness in life are believed to be essentially determined by heavenly forces, the individual is advised to find ways to be satisfied with his or her allotted amount of bliss. Traces of these traditional ideas, although becoming weaker among younger generations, are still found in various East Asian customs, habits, and beliefs. An important consequence of these lay beliefs is that East Asian individuals feel personally less obliged to be happy and satisfied with their lives than North American cultural members do.

There is some evidence suggesting that SWB is a more central motive of North Americans than of East Asians. For instance, Chinese college students value happiness less strongly than Americans (Diener et al. 1995) or Australians (Feather 1986). Diener, Suh, Smith, and Shao also found that Chinese respondents think less frequently than Americans about whether their life is happy, satisfying, or joyful. More interestingly, when American and Korean students were asked to complete a life satisfaction scale as a culturally ideal person would, Korean students reported significantly lower scores. Not only is the ideal level of life satisfaction lower in East Asian cultures, but positive emotions, such as joy and happiness, are also not as highly valued by East Asians as they are by Americans (Diener et al. 1996). The cultural value placed on the concept of SWB as a whole, thus, seems to vary between individualist and collectivist cultures.

To return to the main argument, cultural attributions concerning the determinants of happiness should affect how strongly cultural members strive to achieve SWB. North Americans are likely to try to be happier and more positive about their lives than East Asians because SWB is tightly linked with individual effort in the former culture. Such differences in motivation level can lead to actual mean differences in SWB. The involvement of self-deceptive mechanisms cannot be completely ruled out (e.g., Shedler, Mayman, and Manis 1993). The more crucial reason, however, might be related to people's self-confirming information-processing tendencies. As mentioned earlier, people rarely seek or interpret evidence impartially. Rather, the norm is to selectively "see" what we desire to see and overweight the evidence that positively confirms our expectations (Greenwald 1980; Kulik, Sledge, and Mahler 1986; Nickerson 1998). For instance, American and Japanese tend to weigh positive and negative information differently to promote their different self-enhancing versus self-effacing needs (Kitayama et al. 1997). Similarly SWB reports, which are based on highly flexible criteria, are likely to be influenced by the degree to which cultural members desire to portray themselves as a person who is happy and satisfied with his life.

In sum, cultural perceptions concerning the nature and the meaning of personal happiness seem to differ between North American and East Asian societies. Global success in life is often measured by the individual's level of happiness in Western cultures that is founded on the moral visions of personal freedom and liberty. Personal happiness occupies a less salient position in Eastern cultures that frequently expect their members to subordinate their personal desires, goals, and aspirations to those of the collective. Therefore members of these two respective cultures are likely to differ in terms of how much they center their personal goals, interests, and efforts on the attainment of SWB. Such cultural difference in the motive to be happy, through various intangible ways, could influence the SWB level reported by the members of these two cultures.

A motivational account of SWB highlights an important psychological dimension underlying cultural variations in SWB. Nonetheless, it is quite obvious that cultural differences in SWB cannot be caused by motivational reasons alone. Above all, given the constraints of reality, there is a clear limit as to how much motivation can influence the level of SWB. Another weakness of the motivational model of SWB is that it understates the psychological mechanisms underlying this cultural phenomenon. Although it suggests that motivational factors affect the direction and the amount of bias involved in SWB reports, the question of *how* cultural variations in SWB level arise is not explicitly addressed in motivational explanations.

In this regard the possibility that cognitive factors collaborate with motivational factors in creating cultural differences in SWB and positive self-views warrants consideration. For instance, is there an important difference in how North Americans and East Asians typically evaluate themselves? If so, are different cultural patterns of self-evaluation associated with different levels of SWB? Drawing evidence from recent developments in the self-judgment literature, the variance of SWB across cultures is discussed from a cognitive perspective in the following section. The idea that cultural difference in egocentric self-evaluation tendencies might partly cause mean differences in SWB and positive self-view is proposed.

Cognitive Factors

No matter how positively we wish (or need) to see ourselves, self-evaluations are constrained by reality (Armor and Taylor 1998; Kunda 1990). People may overestimate their chances of winning a poker game on a given night, but few believe that they can win the lottery every week. Desired conclusions about the self are difficult to maintain unless the individual can muster reasonable evidence to support them. That is, although motivation may provide the spark for the positive illusions about the self, cognitive mechanisms keep them afloat. In order to understand why cultural differences in happiness and positive self-view occur, it is therefore imperative to consider the cognitive strategies that might work in concert with the motivational factors.

One prominent self-judgmental characteristic of North Americans is the tendency to process information in reference to the self. Such egocentric, self-referent information-processing tendencies are found consistently across a wide variety of judgmental contexts (Beuhler, Griffin, and Ross 1994; Fenigstein and Abrams 1993; Griffin and Ross 1991; Ross and Sicoly 1979; Weinstein and Lachendro 1982; Zuckerman et al. 1983). Although the details vary across studies, the core of this phenomenon is that individuals are strongly inclined to pay greater amount of attention to the self than to others, external standards, or objective information when they make judgments about themselves.

Importantly, such egocentric self-judgment tendencies are found to significantly contribute to the overly positive self-views of North Americans. According to a series of studies conducted by Dunning and his colleagues (Dunning 1993; Dunning and McElwee 1995; Dunning and Hayes 1996), most people are able to view themselves "above average" on many dimensions because their self-evaluative standards are constructed fundamentally in reference to the self. For example, an exceptional golfer who plays tennis terribly tends to define "athleticism" primarily in terms of his golf rather than his tennis skills. As a result, even though other tennis players may find it outrageous, this seasoned golfer is likely to say that he is above average in terms of athletic talent. Put differently, most people tend to score unduly highly on various "self-evaluation exams" primarily because the "test items" are integrated to put themselves in a highly favorable light.

One of Dunning, Meyerowitz, and Holzberg's (1989) studies eloquently demonstrates the relation between this egocentric tendency and positive self-view. An interesting result emerged when Dunning et al. asked Cornell University students to evaluate their artistic and athletic talents on a set of criteria generated by either themselves ("own-criteria" group) or by another person ("yoked" group). The underlying idea was that if people self-enhance by selectively choosing self-serving standards of evaluation, self-appraisal will deflate when they are forced to evaluate themselves on criteria generated by another person. This is what precisely happened. Compared to the pretest level, the self-evaluation of the "own-criteria" group remained unchanged, whereas the self-evaluation of the "yoked" group dropped considerably.

If positive self-illusions are based in part on egocentric judgment tendencies, increasing the salience of other people's qualities may diminish the positive illusions about the self. A number of studies support this idea. For instance, Alicke et al.

(1995) found that even a minimal contact with a concrete comparison target attenuated the above-than-average bias to a significant degree. Also, simply asking individuals to compare others to themselves (other-focused), rather than themselves to others (self-focused), weakens illusory superiority biases (Hoorens 1995). Overly positive projections about one's future are also partly caused by egocentric self-judgment tendencies. Weinstein (1980; Weinstein and Lachendro 1982) argued that unrealistic optimism stems from the fact that individuals focus on factors that improve their own chances of experiencing positive events while failing to consider that other people also have equally good, but different reasons to be optimistic. As predicted, Weinstein found that the sense of relative superiority drops when individuals are given a chance to read other people's list of optimistic reasons.

In addition to experimental studies, findings obtained from individual difference studies further support the notion that the use of internal, subjective criteria is a key ingredient of positive self-view. For instance, compared to unhappy people, Lyubomirsky and Ross (1997) found that happy individuals relied more heavily on internal, subjective standards than on external social comparison information in self-evaluation processes. Wayment and Taylor (1995) drew similar conclusions from their comparative study of high versus low self-esteem individuals. On the other hand, a significant volume of evidence suggests that being excessively sensitive to external, social sources of self-evaluation leads to depression and unhappiness among North Americans (e.g., Butler, Hokanson, and Flynn 1994; Fritz and Helgeson 1998; Kernis and Waschull 1995; Lyubomirsky and Ross 1997).

These studies collectively suggest that there is a strong tendency among North Americans to tailor the evaluations about the self in order to protect or bolster positive views of them. For this purpose, evaluating the self on the basis of subjective, internal standards rather than on external, objective information appears to be an effective cognitive strategy. In some cases, North Americans may not engage in any systematic self-evaluation at all. Individualist cultural members who are told throughout their lives that they are "special" in one way or another seem to routinely apply an "I am a great person" heuristic in various self-judgments (see Alicke et al. 1995). Unless situational forces demand them to, they seem to have minimal interest in "objectively" verifying their positive self-views. For instance, how the self objectively stands in comparison to one's roommate in various domains (e.g., academic achievement, physical attractiveness) has no significant impact on college students' SWB (Diener and Fujita 1997). Instead, Diener and Fujita found that preexisting information about the self have a more notable influence on SWB than objective social comparison information in natural settings. Hence the possibility that SWB reports of North Americans may be based more frequently on preexisting positive self-feelings, rather than on objective external information deserves careful scrutiny. Brown (1993) raises a similar point concerning the nature of self-esteem in North America.

In short, a wealth of evidence indicates not only that egocentric self-evaluation strategies are widely used by North Americans, but also that they play a crucial role in prompting overly positive views about the self (e.g., Beauregard and Dunning 1998; Conway and Howell 1989; Fenigstein and Abrams 1993; Ross and Sicoly 1979; Weinstein and Lachendro 1983; Wood and Taylor 1991). However, we are now discovering that the self-understandings of collectivist individuals are less governed by internal standards (Lu and Shih 1997; Suh and Diener 1999; Suh et al. 1998). As a Korean social psychologist described, the question, "How am I viewed by others?" is a more salient concern than "This is what I think" in East Asian cultures (Yoon 1994). Because the *social* rather than the subjective images of the self are of central concern, evaluating the self primarily in terms of subjective, idiosyncratic criteria proves to be less meaningful for the central purposes of collectivist cultural members. Consequently the self-appraisals of East Asians are based relatively heavily on more visible external standards, such as norms and other's expectations, which are, unfortunately, more difficult to revise, change, or dismiss than subjective standards.

To conclude by using Dunning et al.'s (1989) earlier experiment as an analogy, the typical East Asian style of self-judgment in some sense resembles the "yoked" condition in that culturally established self-appraisal criteria are imposed on the individual through the explicit forms of social expectations, duties, and obligations. The highly self-focused North American mode of self-appraisal, on the other hand, resembles the "own-criteria" condition in that the assessment is essentially based on subjective, internal standards that are easier to tailor in service to the self. As we have seen, the two conditions lead to different levels of self-evaluation; evaluations about the self are much more likely to be positive when they are based on internal than on external criteria.

A crucial question that calls for a systematic future research is whether such culturally divergent cognitive strategies of self-appraisal play a role in causing the dramatic difference between North Americans and East Asians in their levels of SWB and positive self-views. East Asian culture's emphasis on objective, detailed referents of the self may restrict how positively individuals can view themselves. On the other hand, the North American culture socializes its members to focus more on private reasons for why they should feel positive about themselves than on the various external, social "tags" attached to the self. The highly favorable self-views of North Americans could partly stem from the fact that their self-judgments are more often geared toward confirming preexisting positive beliefs about the self than toward drawing a conclusion based on objective details of the self. The cognitive model of SWB raises refreshing questions that need to be explored and answered by future research.

Concluding Comment

The field of SWB as a whole has made significant strides during the past three decades (Diener et al. 1999). Its theories and methodologies have become more sophisticated and the disciplinary emphasis has shifted from finding descriptive characteristics of happy people to understanding the psychological principles that make people happy and satisfied with their lives. Although the cross-cultural investigation of SWB has just begun, it is hoped that similar methodological and theoretical advances can be made in this young field in the ensuing decades. One general goal for future research is to gradually move on from identifying cultural differences in SWB to seeking more proximal explanations for why and how cultural differences in SWB occur. The study of self, although it is only one of the diverse approaches that will be required to achieve this goal, has embarked on a promising note.

References

Alicke, M. D., Klotz, M. L., Breitenbecher, D. L., Turak, T. J., and Vredenburg, D. S. 1995. Personal contact, individuation, and the better-than-average effect. *Journal of Personality and Social Psychology* 68: 804–25.

Allport, G. 1961. *Pattern and Growth in Personality*. New York: Holt, Rinehart, and Winston.

Andersen, S. M., and Ross, L. 1984. Self-knowledge and social inference: I. The impact of cognitive/affective and behavioral data. *Journal of Personality and Social Psychology* 46: 280–93.

Armor, D. A., and Taylor, S. E. 1998. Situated optimism: Specific outcome expectancies and self-regulation. In M. P. Zanna, ed., *Advances in Experimental Social Psychology*, vol. 30. San Diego, CA: Academic Press, pp. 309–79.

Arrindell, W. A., Hatzichristou, C., Wensink, J., Rosenberg, E., Twillert, B. V., Stedema, J., and Meijer, D. 1997. Dimensions of national culture as predictors of cross-cultural differences in subjective well-being. *Personality and Individual Differences* 23: 37–53.

Associated Press. 1998 (June 24). *U.S. coach might pay for losses.*

Bachnik, J. 1992. The two "faces" of self and society in Japan. *Ethos* 20: 3–32.

Batson, C. D., Turk, C. L., Shaw, L. L., and Klein, T. R. 1995. Information function of empathic emotion: Learning that we value the other's welfare. *Journal of Personality and Social Psychology* 68: 300–13.

Beauregard, K. S., and Dunning, D. 1998. Turning up the contrast: Self-enhancement motives prompt egocentric contrast effects in social judgments. *Journal of Personality and Social Psychology* 74: 606–21.

Beuhler, R., Griffin, D., and Ross, M. 1994. Exploring the "planning fallacy": Why people underestimate their task completion times. *Journal of Personality and Social Psychology* 67: 366–81.

Block, J. 1961. Ego identity, role variability, and adjustment. *Journal of Consulting Psychology* 25: 392–97.

Bond, M. H., Leung, K., and Wan, K.-C. 1982. The social impact of self-effacing attributions: The Chinese case. *Journal of Social Psychology* 118: 157–66.

Brockner, J., and Chen, Y. 1996. The moderating roles of self-esteem and self-construal in reaction to a threat to the self: Evidence from the People's Republic of China and the United States. *Journal of Personality and Social Psychology* 71: 603–15.

Brown, J. D. 1993. Self-esteem and self-evaluation: Feeling is believing. In J. Suls, ed., *Psychological Perspectives on the Self*, vol. 4. Hillsdale, NJ: Lawrence Erlbaum, pp. 27–58.

Brown, J. D. 1998. *The Self*. New York: McGraw-Hill.

Brown, J. D., and Mankowski, T. A. 1993. Self-esteem, mood, and self-evaluation: Changes in mood and the way you see you. *Journal of Personality and Social Psychology* 64: 421–30.

Butler, A. C., Hokanson, J. E., and Flynn, H. A. 1994. A comparison of self-esteem liability and low trait self-esteem as vulnerability factors for depression. *Journal of Personality and Social Psychology* 66: 166–77.

Campbell, A. 1981. *The Sense of Well-being in America: Recent Patterns and Trends*. New York: McGraw-Hill.

Chen, C., Lee, S., and Stevenson, H. W. 1995. Response style and cross-cultural comparisons of rating scales among East Asian and North American students. *Psychological Science* 6: 170–75.

Choi, S. C., and Choi, S. H. 1994. We-ness: A Korean discourse of collectivism. In G. Yoon and S. C. Choi, eds., *Psychology of the Korean People: Collectivism and Individualism*. Seoul, Korea: Dong-A, pp. 57–84.

Conway, M., and Howell, A. 1989. Ego-involvement leads to positive self-schema activation and to a positivity bias in information processing. *Motivation and Emotion* 13: 159–77.

Diener, E., and Diener, M. 1995. Cross-cultural correlates of life satisfaction and self-esteem. *Journal of Personality and Social Psychology* 68: 653–63.

Diener, E., Diener, M., and Diener, C. 1995. Factors predicting the subjective well-being of nations. *Journal of Personality and Social Psychology* 69: 851–64.

Diener, E., and Fujita, F. 1997. Social comparison and subjective well-being. In B. Buunk and R. Gibbons, eds., *Health, Coping, and Social Comparison*. Mahwah, NJ: Lawrence Erlbaum.

Diener, E., and Suh, E. M. 1999. National differences in subjective well-being. In D. Kahneman, E. Diener, and N. Schwarz, eds., *Well-being: The Foundations of Hedonic Psychology*. New York: Russell-Sage.

Diener, E., Suh, E. M., Lucas, R., and Smith, H. 1999. Subjective well-being: Three decades of progress. *Psychological Bulletin* 125: 276–302.

Diener, E., Suh, E., Oishi, S., and Shao, L. 1996. *Norms for Affect: National Comparisons*. Paper presented at the Ninth Conference of International Society for Research on Emotions. Toronto, Canada.

Diener, E., Suh, E. M., Smith, H., and Shao, L. 1995. National differences in subjective well-being: Why do they occur? *Social Indicators Research* 34: 7–32.

Donahue, E. M., Robins, R. W., Roberts, B. W., and John, O. P. 1993. The divided self: Concurrent and longitudinal effects of psychological adjustment and social roles on self-concept differentiation. *Journal of Personality and Social Psychology* 64: 834–46.

Dunning, D. 1993. Words to live by: The self and definition of social concepts and categories. In J. Suls, ed., *Psychological Perspectives on the Self*, vol. 4. Englewood Cliffs, NJ: Lawrence Erlbaum, pp. 99–126.

Dunning, D., and McElwee, R. O. 1995. Idiosyncratic trait definitions: Implications for self-description and social judgment. *Journal of Personality and Social Psychology* 68: 936–46.

Dunning, D., Meyerowitz, J. A., and Holzberg, A. 1989. Ambiguity and self-evaluation: The role of idiosyncratic trait definitions in self-serving assessments of ability. *Journal of Personality and Social Psychology* 57: 1082–90.

Dunning, D., and Hayes, A. F. 1996. Evidence for egocentric comparison in social judgment. *Journal of Personality and Social Psychology* 71: 213–19.

Edwards, K., and Bryan, T. S. 1997. Judgmental biases produced by instructions to disregard: The (paradoxical) case of emotional information. *Personality and Social Psychology Bulletin* 23: 849–64.

Erikson, E. 1950. *Childhood and Society*. New York: Norton.

Feather, N. T. 1986. Value systems across cultures: Australia and China. *International Journal of Psychology* 21: 697–715.

Fenigstein, A., and Abrams, D. 1993. Self-attention and the egocentric assumption of shared perspectives. *Journal of Experimental Social Psychology* 29: 287–303.

Fiske, A. P., Kitayama, S., Markus, H. R., and Nisbett, R. E. 1998. The cultural matrix of social psychology. In D. Gilbert, S. Fiske, and G. Lindsey, eds., *Handbook of Social Psychology*. New York: McGraw-Hill, pp. 915–81.

Fritz, H. L., and Helgeson, V. S. 1998. Distinctions of unmitigated communion from communion: Self-neglect and overinvolvement with others. *Journal of Personality and Social Psychology* 75: 121–40.

Geertz, C. 1984. "From the native's point of view": On the nature of anthropological understanding. In R. A. Shweder and R. A. LeVine, eds., *Culture Theory: Essays on Mind, Self, and Emotion*. Cambridge: Cambridge University Press, pp. 123–36.

Gilovich, T., Savitsky, K., and Medvec, V. H. 1998. The illusion of transparency: Biased assessment of others' ability to read one's emotional states. *Journal of Personality and Social Psychology* 75: 332–46.

Greenberg, J., Solomon, S., Pyszczynski, T., Rosenblatt, A., Burling, J., Lyon, D., Simon, L., and Pinel, E. 1992. Why do people need self-esteem? Converging evidence that self-esteem serves an anxiety-buffering function. *Journal of Personality and Social Psychology* 63: 913–22.

Greenwald. A. G. 1980. The totalitarian ego: Fabrication and revision of personal history. *American Psychologist* 35: 603–18.

Griffin, D. W., and Ross, L. 1991. Subjective construal, social inference, and human misunderstanding. In M. P. Zanna, ed., *Advances in Experimental Social Psychology*, vol. 24. San Diego, CA: Academic Press, pp. 319–59.

Han, J. J., Leichtman, M. D., and Wang, Q. 1998. Autobiographical memory in Korean, Chinese, and American children. *Developmental Psychology* 34: 701–13.

Hawkins, J. D., Catalano, R. F., and Miller, J. Y. 1992. Risk and protective factors for alcohol and other drug problems in adolescence and early adulthood: Implications for substance abuse programs. *Psychological Bulletin* 112: 64–105.

Heine, S. J., and Lehman, D. R. 1995. Cultural variation in unrealistic optimism: Does the West feel more invulnerable than the East? *Journal of Personality and Social Psychology* 68: 595–607.

Heine, S. J., and Lehman, D. R. 1997. Culture, dissonance, and self-affirmation. *Personality and Social Psychology Bulletin* 23: 389–400.

Heine, S. J., Lehman, D. R., Markus, H. R., and Kitayama, S. 1999. Culture and the need for positive self-regard. *Psychological Review* 106: 766–94.

Hoorens, V. 1995. Self-favoring biases, self-presentation, and the self-other asymmetry in social comparison. *Journal of Personality* 63: 793–817.

Hsu, F. L. K. 1953. *Americans and Chinese: Two Ways of Life*. New York: Schuman.

Jones, S. C. 1973. Self and interpersonal evaluations: Esteem theories versus consistency theories. *Psychological Bulletin* 79: 185–99.

Jourard, S. M. 1974. *Healthy Personality: An Approach from the Viewpoint of Humanistic Psychology*. New York: Macmillan.

Kashima, Y., and Triandis, H. C. 1986. The self-serving bias in attributions as a coping strategy: A cross-cultural study. *Journal of Cross-cultural Psychology* 17: 83–97.

Kashima, Y., Siegal, M., Tanaka, K., and Kashima, E. S. 1992. Do people believe behaviours are consistent with attitudes? Towards a cultural psychology of attribution processes. *British Journal of Social Psychology* 31: 111–24.

Kernis, M. H., and Waschull, S. B. 1995. The interactive role of stability and level of self-esteem: Research and theory. In M. P. Zanna, ed., *Advances in Experimental Social Psychology*, vol. 27. San Diego, CA: Academic Press, pp. 93–141.

King, A. Y. C., and Bond, M. H. 1985. The Confucian paradigm of man: A sociological view. In W. S. Tseng and D. Y. H. Wu, eds., *Chinese Culture and Mental Health*. New York: Academic Press, pp. 29–46.

King, L. A., and Napa, C. K. 1998. What makes a good life? *Journal of Personality and Social Psychology* 75: 156–65.

Kitayama, S., Markus, H. R., Matsumoto, H., and Norasakkunkit, V. 1997. Individual and collective processes in the construction of the self: Self-enhancement tendencies in the United States and self-criticism in Japan. *Journal of Personality and Social Psychology* 72: 1245–67.

Kulik, J. A., Sledge, P., and Mahler, H. I. M. 1986. Self-confirmatory attribution, egocentrism, and the perpetuation of self-beliefs. *Journal of Personality and Social Psychology* 50: 587–94.

Kunda, Z. 1990. The case for motivated reasoning. *Psychological Bulletin* 108: 480–98.

Kwan, V. S. Y. , Bond, M. H., and Singelis, T. M. 1997. Pancultural explanations for life satisfaction: Adding relational harmony to self-esteem. *Journal of Personality and Social Psychology* 73: 1038–51.

Lecky, P. 1945. *Self-consistency: A Theory of Personality*. New York: Island.

Lee, K. T. 1992. *The Mental Structure of Koreans* (in Korean) Seoul: Shinwon Cultural Press.

Lee, Y-T., and Seligman, M. E. P. 1997. Are Americans more optimistic than the Chinese? *Personality and Social Psychological Bulletin* 23: 32–40.

Levenson, R. W., Ekman, P., Heider, K., and Friesen, W. V. 1992. Emotion and automatic nervous system activity in the Minangkabau of West Sumatra. *Journal of Personality and Social Psychology* 62: 972–88.

Levine, R., Sato, S., Hashimoto, T., and Verma, J. 1995. Love and marriage in eleven cultures. *Journal of Cross-cultural Psychology* 26: 554–71.

Lu, L., and Shih, J. B. 1997. Sources of happiness: A qualitative approach. *Journal of Social Psychology* 137: 181–87.

Lucas, R., Diener, E., and Suh, E. 1996. Discriminant validity of subjective well-being measures. *Journal of Personality and Social Psychology* 71: 616–28.

Lyubomirsky, S., and Ross, L. 1997. Hedonic consequences of social comparison: Happy and unhappy people. *Journal of Personality and Social Psychology* 73: 1141–57.

Markus, H., and Kitayama, S. 1991. Culture and self: Implications for cognition, emotion, and motivation. *Psychological Review* 98: 224–53.

Maslow, A. H. 1954. *Motivation and Personality*. New York: Harper and Brothers.

Maslow, A. H. 1968. *Toward a Psychology of Being*. New York: Van Nostrand.

Miller, J. G., and Bersoff, D. M. 1998. The role of liking in perceptions of the moral responsibility to help: A cultural perspective. *Journal of Experimental Social Psychology* 34: 443–69.

Miller, D. T., and Ross, M. 1975. Self-serving biases in the attribution of causality: Fact or fiction? *Psychological Bulletin* 82: 213–35.

Minami, H. 1971. *Psychology of the Japanese People*. Toronto University of Toronto Press.

Nickerson, R. S. 1998. Confirmation bias: A ubiquitous phenomenon in many guises. *Review of General Psychology* 2: 175–220.

Perloff, L. S., and Fetzer, B. K. 1986. Self-other judgments and perceived invulnerability of victimization. *Journal of Personality and Social Psychology* 50: 502–10.

Potter, S. H. 1988. The cultural construction of emotion in rural Chinese social life. *Ethos* 16: 181–208.

Rogers, C. 1965. *Client-Centered Therapy: Its Current Practice, Implication, and Theory.* Boston: Houghton Mifflin.

Rosenberger, N. 1989. Dialectic balance in the polar model of self: The Japan case. *Ethos* 17: 88–113.

Ross, M., and Sicoly, F. 1979. Egocentric biases in availability and attribution. *Journal of Personality and Social Psychology* 37: 322–36.

Schwarz, N., and Clore, G. L. 1988. How do I feel about it? Informative functions of affective states. In K. Fiedler and J. Forgas, eds., *Affect, Cognition, and Social Behavior.* Toronto: Hogrefe, pp. 44–62.

Schwarz, N., and Strack, F. 1999. Reports of subjective well-being: Judgmental processes and their methodological implications. In D. Kahneman, E. Diener, and N. Schwarz, eds., *Well-being: The Foundations of Hedonic Psychology.* New York: Russell Sage, pp. 61–84.

Sedikides, C., and Strube, M. J. 1997. Self-evaluation: To thine own self be good, to thine own self be sure, to thine own self be true, and to thine own self be better. In M. P. Zanna, ed., *Advances in Experimental Social Psychology*, vol. 29. San Diego, CA: Academic Press, pp. 209–69.

Shedler, J., Mayman, M., and Manis, M. 1993. The illusion of mental health. *American Psychologist* 48: 1117–31.

Sheldon, K. M., Ryan, R. M., Rawsthorne, L. J., and Ilardi, B. 1997. Trait self and true self: Cross-role variation in the big-five personality traits and its relations with psychological authenticity and subjective well-being. *Journal of Personality and Social Psychology* 73: 1380–93.

Suh, D. S. 1994. The Korean attitude towards happiness in classical literature. In *Comparative Analysis of Eastern and Western Thinking* (in Korean). Seoul: Sungkyunkwan University Press, pp. 25–55.

Suh, E. M. 2000. *Culture, identity consistency, and subjective well-being.* Manuscript submitted for publication. University of Illinois at Urbana-Champaign.

Suh, E. M., and Diener, E. 1999. The use of emotion and social appraisal information in life satisfaction judgments: Joining culture, personality, and situational influences. Manuscript in preparation. University of Illinois at Urbana-Champaign.

Suh, E., Diener, E., Oishi, S., and Triandis, H. C. 1998. The shifting basis of life satisfaction judgments across cultures: Emotions versus norms. *Journal of Personality and Social Psychology* 74: 482–93.

Swann, W. B., Griffin, J. J., Predmore, S. C., and Gaines, B. 1987. The cognitive-affective crossfire: When self-consistency confronts self-enhancement. *Journal of Personality and Social Psychology* 52: 881–89.

Taylor, S. E., and Brown, J. D. 1988. Illusion and well-being: A social psychological perspective on mental health. *Psychological Bulletin* 103: 193–210.

Tesser, A. 1988. Toward a self-evaluation maintenance model of social behavior. In L. Berkowitz, ed., *Advances in Experimental Social Psychology*, vol. 21. New York: Academic Press, pp. 181–227.

Triandis, H. C. 1989. The self and social behavior in different cultural contexts. *Psychological Review* 96: 506–20.

Triandis, H. C. 1995. *Individualism and Collectivism*. Boulder, CO: Westview Press.

USA Weekend. 1998. The age of contentment. July 3–5.

Veenhoven, R. 1993. *Happiness in Nations: Subjective Interpretation of Life in 56 Nations 1946–1992*. Rotterdam: Risbo.

Wayment, H., and Taylor, S. E. 1995. Self-evaluation processes: Motives, information use, and self-esteem. *Journal of Personality* 63: 729–57.

Weinstein, N. D. 1980. Unrealistic optimism about future life events. *Journal of Personality and Social Psychology* 39: 806–20.

Weinstein, N. D., and Lachendro, E. 1982. Egocentrism as a source of unrealistic optimism. *Personality and Social Psychology Bulletin* 8: 195–200.

Wood, J. V., and Taylor, K. L. 1991. Serving self-relevant goals through social comparison. In J. Suls and T. A. Wills, eds., *Social Comparison: Contemporary Theory and Research*. Hillsdale, NJ: Lawrence Erlbaum, pp. 23–50.

Yang, K. S. 1981. Social orientation and individual modernity among Chinese students in Taiwan. *Journal of Social Psychology* 113: 159–70.

Yik, M. S. M., Bond, M. H., and Paulhus, D. L. 1998. Do Chinese self-enhance or self-efface? It's a matter of domain. *Personality and Social Psychology Bulletin* 24: 399–406.

Yoon, T. R. 1994. The Koreans, their culture and personality. In G. Yoon and S. C. Choi, eds., *Psychology of the Korean People: Collectivism and Individualism*. Seoul: Dong-A, pp. 15–26.

Zuckerman, M., Kernis, M. H., Guarnera, S. M., Murphy, J. F., and Rappoport, L. 1983. The egocentric bias: Seeing oneself as cause and target of others' behavior. *Journal of Personality* 51: 621–30.

5

Goals as Cornerstones of Subjective Well-being: Linking Individuals and Cultures

Shigehiro Oishi

What is "the good life"? American TV commercials constantly send an implicit message that life is good to the degree that one works hard, plays hard, and has a lot of fun. Gatorade had Michael Jordan say "Life is sport." Reebok had Roger Clemens say "Life is short. Play hard." Miller Lite had twenty something men say "Life is good" (as long as they are drinking beer with attractive women?). Do these prescriptions outline the universal form of a "good life"? Or is this set of norms specific to American culture? In this chapter I will attempt to explore cultural variation in descriptors of well-being and analyze the role of culture. I will first review two universalist models of psychological well-being, followed by a discussion of a relativist approach, or the goal as a moderator model. These three models of well-being will be tested in the data collected from 39 nations.

Self-determination Theory of Psychological Well-being

Based on the literature on intrinsic motivation, Ryan, Sheldon, Kasser, and Deci (1996) proposed a self-determination model of well-being. This model postulates that there are three universal psychological needs, namely autonomy, competence, and relatedness, and that the gratification of these needs is a key predictor of psychological well-being (see also Ryan 1995). More specifically, this model predicts that the pursuit of intrinsic goals (e.g., personal growth, autonomy, enhancement of others and communities) will provide people with a deep sense of satisfaction, whereas the pursuit of extrinsic goals (e.g., financial success, physical attractiveness, and social reputation) would not provide people with such satisfaction (see Ryan 1995; Sheldon and Kasser 1995; Sheldon et al. 1997 for elaboration on psychological authenticity, integrity, consistency, and coherence).

Consistent with the self-determination model of well-being, Kasser and Ryan (1993) found that the importance of self-acceptance, community feeling, and affiliation was positively associated with self-actualization and vitality, whereas it was negatively associated with behavioral problems. In addition they found that the importance of financial success was negatively correlated with self-actualization and vitality, whereas it was positively associated with behavioral problems. Furthermore, in a community sample, Kasser and Ryan (1996) extended the previous findings to depression, anxiety, and physical symptoms. That is, they found that importance placed on financial success, fame, and physical attractiveness was positively associated with depression, anxiety, and more physical symptoms, whereas importance placed on community feeling, self-acceptance, and affiliation was negatively associated with these psychological ill-being indexes. More recently Kasser and Ryan (in press) found that the relative importance of extrinsic goals was associated with lower self-esteem, more television consumption, greater drug use, and a lower quality of relationships with friends and romantic partners.

In addition to the content of goals, research based on the self-determination model showed that the types of activities in which individuals engaged (e.g., Sheldon et al. 1996), the reasons for the engagement (e.g., Elliot and Sheldon 1997; Elliot, Sheldon, and Church 1997), and progress toward goals (e.g., Sheldon and Kasser 1998) have a profound impact on individuals' well-being. For example, Sheldon et al. (1996) found that college students tended to be happier on days when they engaged in activities for intrinsic reasons. Furthermore Sheldon and Kasser (1998) found that progress toward intrinsic goals was positively associated with increase in life satisfaction, whereas progress toward extrinsic goals (e.g., making good grades) was not associated with positive changes in life satisfaction. Summarizing these findings, Ryan et al. (1996) argued that the only way in which individuals enhance their well-being is to value personal growth, autonomy, meaningful relationships, and community service, and to make progress toward these so-called intrinsic goals. In other words, according to the self-determination theory, the "good life" is the life in which an individual strives for personal growth, independence, meaningful relationships with others, and community service.

Ryff's Multidimensional Model of Psychological Well-being

Ryff (1989a, 1989b; Ryff and Keyes 1995; Schmutte and Ryff 1997) proposed another universalist model of well-being based on the literature on human development. She criticized that traditional well-being research was exclusively focused on emotional well-being, and that the assessment of affect would not provide a clear answer to what it means to be psychologically well; people can experience positive emotions, and yet consider their lives to be meaningless. Ryff insists that psychological functioning should be assessed in terms of self-acceptance, personal growth, purpose in life, positive relations with others, environmental mastery, and autonomy. Ryff and Keyes (1995) showed that the six-factor structure of well-being fit the data, and that although the overall score did not differ across age groups, specific scale scores did differ across age groups. For example, purpose in life and personal growth declined over time, whereas environmental mastery and autonomy increased over time. The developmental shift in the mean level of respective well-being indexes suggests that salient aspects of well-being could vary across life span. More specifically, the above finding suggests that active pursuit of goals and self-improvement characterize young adulthood, whereas a sense of control over one's life characterizes later life. Ryff (1989b) also found via interviews that middle-aged and older adults, both men and women, mentioned having good relationships with others as one of the most important aspect of being well.

Although empirical findings indicate a qualitative shift in the definition of "good life" across life span, Ryff seems to emphasize a universal significance of purpose in life and quality relationships with others. In fact Ryff and Singer (1998) note that they targeted purpose in life and quality relations with others as primary features of positive human health "partly because of their pervasiveness—indeed *universality* —across philosophical, ethical, and social scientific formulations, but in addition, because of their capacity to engage the mind and body" (p. 9, italic added by the author).

The Goal Approach to Well-being

Whereas the previous two models focus on the universality of positive self-regard, community service, purpose in life, and positive relationships with others, goal researchers take into account individual differences and developmental shifts in markers of well-being (e.g., Brunstein 1993; Cantor et al. 1991; Diener and Fujita 1995; Emmons 1986, 1991; Harlow and Cantor 1996; Palys and Litte 1983; Sanderson and Cantor 1997). In this chapter I broadly define goals as desired states internalized by individuals (see Austin and Vancouver 1996 for a review on goal constructs). Values, which are defined as guiding principles in life (Schwartz and

Sagiv 1995), can be considered as higher-order goals, whereas personal strivings, which are defined as what individuals are characteristically trying to do in daily life (Emmons 1986), can be conceptualized as lower-order goals. Basically the goal as a moderator model of well-being (Oishi et al. 1999) assumes that markers of well-being vary across individuals, depending on their goals and values. For instance, this model posits that an individual whose goal is getting into medical school (and therefore getting A's) is satisfied with his or her life to the extent that this individual does well in school. On the other hand, an individual whose goal is having a rewarding romantic relationship is satisfied with his or her life to the extent that this individual has such a relationship. The premise of the goal as a moderator model is that people gain and maintain their well-being mostly from the area on which they place special importance, and that to the extent that individuals differ in their goals and values, they differ in their sources of satisfaction.

The moderating role of personal strivings in types of daily events and emotional experiences was first tested by Emmons (1991) in a 21-day daily diary study among college students. Intra-individual analyses revealed that individuals who were striving for achievement reported more intense positive emotions when they experienced positive events related to achievement than when they experienced positive events unrelated to achievement. Likewise individuals who were striving for affiliation and intimacy reported experiencing more intense positive emotions when they experienced positive events relevant to interpersonal relationships than when they experienced positive events aside from interpersonal issues. In a similar daily diary study, Oishi, Diener, Suh et al. (1999) replicated Emmons's findings in daily life satisfaction. That is, the degree to which daily achievement satisfaction predicted daily life satisfaction was significantly stronger among those who valued Achievement than those who did not. Likewise the degree to which daily social life satisfaction predicted daily life satisfaction was significantly stronger among those who valued Benevolence than among those who did not. Furthermore these researchers found that global life satisfaction was predicted from value-congruent domain satisfactions. Namely general satisfaction with their achievements predicted global life satisfaction of Achievement-oriented individuals, whereas general satisfaction with social relationships predicted global life satisfaction of individuals who valued Benevolence.

In line with the above conceptualization, Brunstein, Schultheiss, and Grassmann (1998) tested the moderating role of needs in the link between personal goals and emotional well-being. Similar to Sheldon and Kasser (1998), Brunstein et al. assessed progress toward goals and changes in emotional well-being over time. Unlike Sheldon and Kasser, however, Brunstein et al. also measured participants' needs using a picture-story method similar to the Thematic Apperception Test. These researchers found in two studies that progress toward need-congruent goals predicted positive changes in emotional well-being over time. That is, for those who had a high need for Power and Achievement, progress toward Power- and Achievement-related goals was conducive to enhancement of their emotional well-being, whereas progress toward relationships was not as conducive to enhancement of emotional well-being for these individuals.

Furthermore several researchers found evidence that the processes through which people experience and recall emotional experiences differs across individuals, depending on their personality (e.g., Bolger and Schilling 1991; Bolger and Zuckerman 1995; Cote and Moskowitz 1998; Feldman Barrett 1997; Feldmann Barrett and Pietromonaco 1997; Moskowitz and Cote 1995; Schimmack and Hartmann 1997; Suls, Green, and Hillis 1998; Suls, Martin, and David 1998). Moskowitz and Cote (1995), for instance, examined whether the trait "agreeableness" would moderate the link between behavior and affect. Using the event-contingent recording method for 20 days, Moskowitz and Cote found that agreeableness was positively associated with the degree to which participants experienced positive emotions while engaging in agreeable behaviors. Likewise, in a 8-day daily diary study, Suls, Martin, and David (1998) found that the trait "agreeableness" predicted the extent to which interpersonal conflicts generated emotional distress. That is, the more agreeable individuals were, the more psychological distress they experienced from interpersonal conflicts in daily lives. Given that agreeableness is positively related to needs such as nurturance and abasement, and negatively related to needs such as dominance and aggression (Costa and McCrae 1988), it is possible to view the results of Moskowitz and Cote (1995) and Suls, Martin, and David (1998) as evidence for the idea that needs determine the types of behaviors and events that generate emotional reactions.

In addition to the various determinants of life satisfaction and emotional well-being investigated above, Oishi, Schimmack, and Diener (1999) explored specific types of positive emotions that made individuals feel good about their lives in general. Based on the goal as a moderator model, these authors postulated that specific emotional experiences that make people feel positive about their lives would differ, depending on their needs and values. Specifically, they assumed that highly arousing emotional experience would be a marker of "good life" for sensation seekers. As expected, two daily diary studies revealed that the degree of correlation between highly arousing physical pleasure and daily satisfaction was significantly stronger among high sensation seekers than among low sensation seekers. These results indicate that the link between emotions and perceptions of life is not uniform across individuals. Rather, the "if ... then ..." patterns of relations (Mischel and Shoda 1995) of emotions and life satisfaction differ, depending on individuals' needs and values: *if* high sensation seekers experienced highly arousing emotions, *then* they would feel good about their lives.

The Goal Approach to Cultural Variation in SWB

The three individual-level models of well-being summarized above give rise to two interesting hypotheses about the determinants of SWB across cultures. The self-determination model (Ryan et al. 1996) and the multidimensional model of psychological well-being (Ryff and Keyes 1995) posit that well-being should be universally predicted from the degree of positive self-regard, quality relationships, and purpose in life. On the other hand, the goal approach posits that predictors should differ across cultures, depending on salient needs and values. Before testing these hypotheses, I review relevant cross-cultural studies.

Positive Self-regard and Well-being

Ample evidence indicates that positive self-regard is positively associated with life satisfaction across cultures (e.g., Diener and Diener 1995; Grob et al. 1996; Kwan, Bond, and Singelis 1997; Leelakulthanit and Day 1993; Majumdar and Dasgupta 1997; Oishi et al. 1999). However, the centrality of positive self-regard to well-being appears to vary across cultures, notably between individualist and collectivist countries. Based on data collected from 49 universities in 31 countries, Diener and Diener (1995) examined the relations between domain satisfactions and global life satisfaction. Consistent with Triandis's (1995) individualism-collectivism theory and Markus and Kitayama's (1991) cultural theory of the self, self-esteem was a stronger predictor of global life satisfaction in individualist nations than in collectivist nations. For instance, the correlation between self-esteem and life satisfaction in India was 0.08 among Indian women, whereas it was 0.60 among American women. Similarly, in a large international study, Oishi, Diener, Lucas et al. (1999, study 2) tested the role of individualism-collectivism in the relations between domain and global life satisfaction, controlling for the effect of economy. Based on college student samples from 39 nations, these researchers found that satisfaction with self was a stronger predictor of life satisfaction in individualist nations than in collectivist nations, even after controlling for national income.

Relationship Satisfaction and Well-being

Another axis of psychological well-being in the self-determination theory (Ryan et al. 1996) and the multidimensional model of well-being (Ryff and Singer 1998) is positive relationships with others. Previous evidence on the relative importance of relationship satisfaction in predicting overall life satisfaction is mixed. Studies using a single-item scale (e.g., Diener and Diener 1995; Leelakulthanit and Day 1993) found equally significant correlations between family satisfaction and life satisfaction in individualist and collectivist countries. On the other hand, Kwan et al. (1997) found that relationship harmony, or the degree to which individuals have harmonious relationships with others, had a significant predictive power, above and beyond self-esteem in Hong Kong, but not in the United States.

Norms, Parental Expectations, and Well-being

The aforementioned studies on relationship satisfaction essentially assessed the degree of association between the evaluation of family as an external entity and the evaluation of one's own life. The question "how satisfied are you with your family?" is vastly different from "When you evaluate your life, how much do you consider expectations from your parents and family as criteria?" Thus the findings above do not exclude the possibility that quality relationships with others, particularly an internalized form of relationships (e.g., fulfilling expectations), plays a more central role in collectivist cultures than in individualist cultures. In fact, using the goal construct as a framework, Radhakrishnan and Chan (1997) found support for this view. Participants (54 Indian and 55 American college students) in this study listed 10 goals they had in their life (self-set goals) and 10 goals they perceived their parents as having for them (parental goals). For each goal, participants rated importance from their perspective and their parents' perspective, and discrepancy score was computed by taking the difference between self-rated importance and parent-rated importance. A regression analysis revealed that the degree of discrepancy between importance given by the self and parents on the self-set goals was a significant predictor only for Americans, whereas the degree of discrepancy from parental goals was a significant predictor only for Indians. In other words, self-set goals play a central role in the evaluation of life among Americans, whereas parental goals play a primary role in the evaluation of life among Indians. As suggested by Markus and

Kitayama (1991), people in collectivist cultures internalize family's and friends' expectations, whereas people in individualist cultures set up their own expectations for themselves. Therefore, although the degree to which satisfaction with family is related to global life satisfaction is similar across cultures, parental expectations seem to play a more critical role as a standard for life satisfaction judgments among people in collectivist cultures than in individualist cultures.

Additional evidence for the importance of external standards in collectivist cultures is provided by the two large international studies conducted by Suh, Diener, Oishi, and Triandis (1998). These researchers investigated the relative importance of internal versus external standards in life satisfaction judgments across cultures. Suh et al. (1998, study 2) assessed the frequency of emotional experiences and norms for life satisfaction (i.e., how much one should be satisfied with his or her life) among college students from 39 countries. Suh et al. expected that emotions would be a reliable indicator of life satisfaction for people in individualist nations, whereas they would not be a reliable standard for life satisfaction for people in collectivist nations. Instead, the researchers postulated that norms would be a predictor of life satisfaction in collectivist nations. Consistent with their predictions and results from Radhakrishnan and Chan (1997), life satisfaction of people in individualist nations was primarily predicted from emotional experiences, whereas that of people in collectivist nations was equally predicted from emotional experiences and norms for life satisfaction. These findings suggest that the degree to which one is living a life close to external standards is a better indicator of life satisfaction in collectivist nations. Such external standards present a sharp contrast with the self-determination model of psychological well-being (Ryan et al. 1996) which posits that individuals are "well" to the extent that they live a life congruent with their internal standards. In sum, cultural variation in the correlates of SWB reviewed above highlights the fact that the way in which individuals attain and maintain their well-being might differ across cultures. At the same time it highlights the importance of re-examining extant SWB models from the perspective of cultural constructionism (e.g., Markus, Kitayama, and Heiman 1996).

The Present Study

Although previous cross-cultural studies (e.g., Diener and Diener 1995; Kwan et al. 1997; Radhakrishnan and Chan 1997; Suh et al. 1998) as a whole provide a rough picture of "who is happy" and "who is satisfied" in different cultures, the picture is far from complete. Moreover previous research did not examine systematic variation in descriptions of psychologically well-functioning individuals across cultures. The present study was conducted to identify lawful variation in the personhood of psychologically well-functioning individuals in diverse cultures, as well as to test the universality of the self-determination theory (Ryan et al. 1996). More specifically, I tested the following questions: Are individuals who pursue goals related to financial success and social reputation lower in psychological well-being across cultures? Are people who pursue goals related to community services and relationships healthier psychologically across cultures? Do autonomous individuals perceive their lives as better than dependent individuals in all culture? The universalist models of well-being predict that autonomy and quality relationships will be indexes of well-being across cultures. On the other hand, the goal as a moderator model predicts that autonomy will be a stronger predictor of well-being in individualist cultures, whereas quality relationships with others will be a stronger predictor in collectivist cultures.

To examine the aforementioned questions, I assessed the importance of intrinsic goals (i.e., self-acceptance and relationship-orientation) and extrinsic goals (i.e., power-orientation and conformity) by Triandis's (1995) individualism-collectivism scale in the data collected from 39 nations. This scale consists of four subscales: vertical individualism (VI; emphasis on competition and power), horizontal individualism (HI; emphasis on autonomy of individuals), vertical collectivism (VC; emphasis on duty and sacrifice of individual's desires), and horizontal collectivism (HC; emphasis on amicable relationships with others). According to Kasser and Ryan (1993, 1995) and Ryff (1989a; Ryff and Singer 1998), vertical individualism and vertical collectivism should be associated with negative well-being, whereas horizontal individualism and horizontal collectivism should be associated with positive well-being.

Method

Participants
Participants were 6,782 college students from 39 countries (2,625 males and 4,118 females). These nations represent a diverse selection: 2 nations from North America, 4 nations from South America, 14 nations from Asia, 13 from Europe, and 5 from Africa. Eighty-four percent of the participants were between 18 and 25 years of age, and 10 percent of the participants were between 26 and 35 years old. Because of missing items, the number of participants differed slightly across analyses.

Measures and Ratings

Global Life Satisfaction   Global life satisfaction, or cognitive assessment of life as a whole, was measured by the Satisfaction with Life Scale (SWLS; Diener et al. 1985). The SWLS consists of five statements, to which respondents are asked to indicate their degree of agreement, using a 7-point scale, ranging from 1 (*strongly disagree*) to 7 (*strongly agree*). The total SWLS score ranges from 7 to 35. The SWLS has adequate psychometric properties (see Pavot and Diener 1993), and it has demonstrated validity among Korean (Suh 1994), mainland Chinese (Shao 1993), and Russian samples (Balatsky and Diener 1993). Cronbach's alpha of the SWLS ranged from 0.41 to 0.94 with the mean of 0.78 (SD = 0.09).

Individualism-Collectivism Scale (ICS)   We assessed 4 facets of the individualism-collectivism construct by the individualism-collectivism scale (Triandis 1995), which consists of 8 items per facet and 32 in total. Vertical individualism (VI) is defined as self-interest and competition. VI includes items such as "Winning is everything," and "It is important for me that I do my job better than others." Cronbach's alpha for the VI subscale ranged from 0.36 to 0.86 with the mean of 0.70 (SD = 0.11). Horizontal individualism (HI) is characterized by independence and autonomy. Representative items include "I enjoy being unique and different from others in many ways," "I prefer to be direct and forthright when discussing with people," and "What happens to me is my own doing." Cronbach's alpha for the HI subscale ranged from 0.44 to 0.75 with the mean of 0.63 (SD = 0.08). Vertical collectivism (VC) is defined as the priority of group goals over individual's goal and respect for elders and persons in authority. Sample items include "I would do what would please my family, even if I detested that activity," and "Children should be taught to place duty before pleasure." Cronbach's alpha for the VC ranged from 0.24 to 0.80 with the mean of 0.57 (SD = 0.13). Horizontal collectivism (HC) is characterized by relationship-orientation and harmony. Items include "It is important for me to maintain harmony within my group," and "I feel good when I cooperate with others." Cronbach's alpha ranged from 0.49 to 0.86 with the mean of 0.70 (SD = 0.10). The participants answered how strongly they agree or disagree with each statement on a 9-point scale, ranging from 1 (*strongly disagree*) to 9 (*strongly agree*).

Individualism-Collectivism (IC) Ratings   We obtained the IC rating for each nation, when possible, by averaging Hofstede's (1980) individualism-collectivism scores, which were based on the data provided by individuals working for a multi-national organization and Harry Triandis's personal ratings (personal communication, February 1996). Triandis rated the degree of individualism-collectivism of the 39 nations on a scale ranging from 1 (*most collectivist*) to 10 (*most individualist*). Hofstede's individualism-collectivism scores were converted to a 10-point scale compatible with Triandis's ratings.

Procedure   The original questionnaire was constructed in English by Ed Diener. This questionnaire was then translated into Spanish, Japanese, Korean, and Chinese by bilingual individuals. Bilingual individuals other than those who engaged in the initial translation subsequently translated the non-English versions of the questionnaire back to English. Ratings made of the back translations indicated that they showed an excellent fit to the original English version (Shao 1997). In other nations, local collaborators translated the English version to the local language. The data were collected in university classrooms by local collaborators.

Results

First, we computed zero-order correlation coefficients between each of the four facets of the Individualism-Collectivism Scale and the Satisfaction with Life Scale for each nation, which are shown in the parentheses in table 5.1. Replicating the findings of Kasser and Ryan (1993, 1996), horizontal individualism, or autonomy, was significantly positively related to life satisfaction in many of the highly individualistic nations such as the United States, Australia, Germany, and Finland. Inconsistent with the findings of Kasser and Ryan, however, horizontal individualism was not associated with life satisfaction in most of the collectivist nations, including China, Columbia, Pakistan, Korea, Peru, Ghana, Tanzania, Bahrain, Singapore, Turkey, Taiwan, and Japan. Horizontal collectivism, or relationship-orientation, was not related to overall life satisfaction in most of the highly individualist nations. On the other hand, the degree of horizontal collectivism was positively associated with life satisfaction in some of the collectivist nations such as China, Columbia, Portugal, and Taiwan. Though mostly nonsignificant, vertical individualism, or competitiveness, was negatively related to life satisfaction in most countries. Vertical collectivism, or conformity, was positively related to life satisfaction in Columbia, Spain, and Hungary, whereas it was negatively related to life satisfaction in Indonesia, Taiwan, South Africa, Puerto Rico, and Denmark.

To examine the relation between each facet of the Individualism-Collectivism Scale and life satisfaction, controlling for the other facets, we performed simultaneous regression analyses within each nation, predicting life satisfaction from four facets of the Individualism-Collectivism Scale. Unstandardized regression coefficients for each facet of the ICS for each nation are shown in table 5.1. On average, the unstandardized regression coefficients for horizontal individualism (M = 0.75, SD = 0.24) and horizontal collectivism (M = 0.17, SD = 0.53) were positive, whereas those for vertical individualism (M = −0.18, SD = 0.27) and vertical collectivism (M = −0.37, SD = 0.34) were negative. That is, horizontal individualism and horizontal collectivism were, on average, positively associated with life satisfaction, whereas vertical individualism and vertical collectivism were negatively related to life satisfaction. The patterns of association were mostly consistent with those of correlations described in the parentheses. In other words, horizontal individualism, or autonomy, was again positively associated with life satisfaction in most of the highly individualist nations such as the United States, Australia, and Germany, whereas it was not related to life satisfaction in most of the collectivist nations such as China, Columbia, and Taiwan. Consistent with the previous correlational analyses, horizontal collectivism, or relationship-orientation, was positively associated with life satisfaction in some of the collectivist nations such as China, Pakistan, and Taiwan, whereas it was mostly irrelevant to life satisfaction in highly individualist nations such as Australia, Denmark, and Finland. Vertical individualism was almost uniformly negatively associated with life satisfaction across nations. Consistent with the self-determination theory (Ryan et al. 1996), vertical collectivism, or conformity, was negatively associated with life satisfaction in the United States and Denmark. However, the negative relation between conformity and life satisfaction was not replicated in highly hierarchical societies such as China, Korea, and Japan.

Hypothesis Testing   Although the correlation and regression analyses described above revealed general trends in the size of association between each facet of individualism-collectivism and life satisfaction, they did not yield a formal test of the multi-level interaction between the size of within-nation association and nation level characteristics. To test our hypothesis that being autonomous will be associated with higher well-being in countries where autonomy is highly valued, we performed hierarchical linear modelings (HLM; Bryk and Raudenbush 1992). The present HLM involves two levels of regression analysis. As in the within-nation regression analyses, at level 1, participant's life satisfaction was predicted from the subscale scores of the Individualism-Collectivism Scale for each nation. Level 1 analysis yielded 39 regression analyses. At level 2, regression slopes obtained from level 1 analyses were predicted from the expert ratings of individualism-collectivism. As seen in table 5.2, the HLM analysis revealed that the degree to which horizontal individualism, or being independent, is related to positive life satisfaction varied across countries, depending on the level of individualism. Specifically, being autonomous was more strongly associated with positive life satisfaction in individualist nations than in collectivist nations. The proportion of variance explained by the IC ratings at level 2 can be computed by comparing error variance of the slope for horizontal individualism in the model without the IC as a level 2 predictor with error variance in the full model (see Bryk and Raudenbush 1992, ch. 4). Error variance of the slopes in the simple model was 0.087, whereas it was reduced to 0.058 in the full model: $(0.087 - 0.058)/0.087 = 0.33$. Thus 33 percent of the variance in the slopes for horizontal individualism (i.e., 33 percent of the cross-national difference in the slope for HI) was explained by the IC ratings. On the other hand, the degree to which horizontal collectivism (relationship-orientation), vertical individualism (competitiveness), and vertical collectivism (dutifulness) are related to life satisfaction did not differ across countries along the level of the IC ratings.

Discussion

The present investigation was undertaken with two goals in mind: (1) to identify the descriptors of psychologically well-functioning individuals in different cultures and (2) to examine the universality of the self-determination theory (Ryan et al. 1996) and the multidimensional model of well-being (Ryff 1989a). Several interesting findings emerged from the present analysis. First, replicating previous findings (e.g., Kasser and Ryan 1993, 1996), the present study revealed that autonomous individuals were more satisfied with their lives than those who were less autonomous in highly individualist nations such as the United States, Australia, Germany, and Finland. Also consistent with previous findings (Kasser and Ryan 1993; 1996), power-orientation was negatively associated with life satisfaction in individualist nations such as Norway and Finland. Also, consistent with previous findings (Kasser and Ryan 1993, 1996; Ryff and Keyes 1995), relationship-orientation was marginally significantly related to life satisfaction in the United States. Nevertheless,

Table 5.1
Unstandardized regression coefficients of within-nation regression analyses

Nation	N	IC	HI		HC		VI		VC	
			B	r	B	r	B	r	B	r
China	558	2.00	−0.02	(0.02)	0.52*	(0.09*)	−0.23	(−0.01)	0.02	(0.05)
Columbia	100	2.15	0.31	(0.07)	0.86	(0.25**)	−0.34	(−0.05)	0.62	(0.19+)
Indonesia	90	2.20	1.03*	(0.15)	0.65	(−0.05)	0.44	(0.07)	−1.65**	(−0.22*)
Pakistan	155	2.20	0.21	(0.11)	1.37**	(0.23**)	0.15	(0.04)	−0.84*	(−0.04)
Korea	277	2.40	0.01	(−0.01)	−0.13	(−0.01)	−0.31	(−0.04)	0.21	(0.02)
Peru	129	2.80	0.50	(0.09)	0.17	(0.10)	−0.65+	(−0.10)	0.38	(0.08)
Ghana	118	3.00	0.77	(0.05)	−0.81+	(−0.19*)	−0.61	(−0.11)	0.06	(−0.11)
Nepal	99	3.00	0.56	(0.23*)	0.33	(0.19+)	0.28	(0.18+)	−0.04	(0.13)
Nigeria	244	3.00	0.58+	(0.15*)	0.27	(0.07)	0.21	(0.09)	−0.31	(0.03)
Tanzania	96	3.00	1.10	(0.03)	−0.11	(−0.14)	−1.01	(−0.10)	−0.62	(−0.19+)
Zimbabwe	109	3.00	0.95*	(0.14)	0.11	(0.00)	−1.05*	(−0.17+)	−0.10	(−0.00)
Bahrain	124	3.00	0.04	(0.03)	−0.02	(−0.03)	0.26	(0.04)	−0.35	(−0.07)
Singapore	131	3.50	0.31	(−0.01)	0.15	(−0.00)	−1.20**	(−0.25**)	−0.28	(−0.06)
Turkey	100	3.85	0.31	(0.09)	−0.34	(−0.14)	0.34	(0.13)	−0.39	(−0.14)
Portugal	139	3.85	0.53	(0.11)	0.74	(0.18*)	0.03	(0.02)	0.48	(0.13)
Taiwan	533	3.85	0.37	(−0.07)	1.81**	(0.29**)	−1.14**	(−0.33**)	−0.66	(−0.13**)
Brazil	112	3.90	−0.17	(−0.09)	−0.26	(−0.11)	−0.32	(−0.07)	−0.25	(−0.10)
Lithuania	101	4.00	0.96	(0.14)	1.06*	(0.15)	−0.45	(−0.08)	−1.36**	(−0.16)
Estonia	119	4.00	−0.07	(−0.02)	0.35	(0.06)	−0.19	(−0.05)	−0.69	(−0.09)
India	93	4.00	1.01	(0.11)	−0.61	(−0.05)	−0.19	(0.01)	0.25	(−0.01)
Japan	200	4.30	0.47	(0.08)	0.33	(0.10)	−0.37	(−0.06)	0.05	(0.07)
Egypt	120	4.40	3.28**	(0.28**)	−2.13**	(−0.31**)	−2.43**	(−0.08)	1.14+	(−0.10)
Hong Kong	142	4.75	0.41	(0.03)	−0.21	(0.01)	−0.80+	(−0.13)	0.38	(0.06)
Argentina	90	4.80	0.37	(0.12)	0.70	(0.18+)	−0.03	(−0.08)	−0.45	(−0.06)
Guam	186	5.00	1.15**	(0.23**)	−0.24	(−0.02)	0.46	(0.16*)	−0.04	(0.01)

Slovenia	50	5.00	1.69+	(0.32*)	0.54	(0.26+)	−0.49	(−0.14)	0.51	(0.26+)
Greece	129	5.25	1.80**	(0.29**)	−0.09	(0.08)	0.12	(0.04)	−0.04	(0.07)
Spain	327	5.55	−0.01	(0.02)	−0.24	(−0.03)	0.39	(0.10+)	0.78*	(0.12*)
South Africa	373	5.75	0.75*	(0.08)	−0.37+	(−0.12*)	−0.32	(−0.06)	−0.37	(−0.10*)
Hungary	74	6.00	0.40	(0.05)	0.13	(0.17)	−0.71	(−0.16)	1.36	(0.25*)
Austria	164	6.75	0.64	(0.09)	0.77*	(0.16*)	−0.87	(−0.04)	−0.87+	(−0.05)
Italy	289	6.80	0.62	(0.12*)	1.17**	(0.24**)	0.08	(0.03)	0.24	(0.13*)
Norway	99	6.95	0.46	(0.03)	−0.38	(−0.09)	−0.88+	(−0.14)	−0.41	(−0.06)
Puerto Rico	87	7.00	1.27+	(0.18+)	0.21	(0.24*)	−1.16*	(−0.21+)	0.56	(−0.25*)
Finland	91	7.15	1.40*	(0.21*)	0.03	(0.03)	−0.95+	(−0.15)	−0.97	(−0.04)
Germany	108	7.35	2.51**	(0.31**)	−0.20	(−0.01)	−0.54	(−0.08)	−0.59	(−0.00)
Denmark	91	7.70	0.63	(0.11)	−0.05	(−0.06)	−0.13	(−0.05)	−1.66*	(−0.26**)
Australia	292	9.00	1.04*	(0.15*)	0.26	(0.05)	−0.16	(−0.01)	−0.42	(−0.02)
United States	443	9.55	1.09**	(0.16**)	0.39+	(0.07)	0.06	(0.05)	−0.69*	(−0.01)
Mean			0.75		0.17		−0.18		−0.37	

Note: Zero-order correlation coefficients in parenthesis. Predicting life satisfaction from horizontal individualism (HI), horizontal collectivism (HC), vertical individualism (VI), and vertical collectivism (VC). Levels of significance indicated as $+p < 0.10$, $*p < 0.05$, $**p < 0.01$.

Table 5.2
Hierarchical linear modeling (HLM): Predicting within-nation slopes from individualism-collectivism (IC) ratings

	Coefficient (G)	SE	T ratio
Model for Intercept (B0)			
Intercept	21.49	0.27	79.14**
IC	0.48	0.14	3.41**
Model for HI slope (B1)			
Intercept	0.70	0.08	8.38**
IC	0.11	0.04	2.69**
Model for HC slope (B2)			
Intercept	0.20	0.10	1.89
IC	−0.01	0.05	−0.28
Model for VI slope (B3)			
Intercept	−0.19	0.09	−2.32*
IC	−0.03	0.04	−0.82
Model for VC slope (B4)			
Intercept	−0.35	0.09	−4.07**
IC	0.02	0.04	0.39

Notes: Levels of significance indicated as $*p < 0.05$, $**p < 0.01$.
Model specification was as follows:

Level 1 model

$SWLS = B0 + B1*(HI) + B2*(HC) + B3*(VI) + B4*(VC) + Error$

Level 2 model

$B0 = G00 + G01*(IC) + U0$
$B1 = G10 + G11*(IC) + U1$
$B2 = G20 + G21*(IC) + U2$
$B3 = G30 + G31*(IC) + U3$
$B4 = G40 + G41*(IC) + U4$

it was not related to life satisfaction in many of the other individualist nations (see table 5.1). Overall, it appears that the present results provide general support for the two universalist models of well-being in Western nations. That is, the gratification of psychological needs such as autonomy and relatedness seems to be an important indicator of life satisfaction in Western nations.

In many of the non-Western nations, however, autonomous individuals were no more satisfied with their lives than those who were less autonomous. This point deserves serious attention in light of the fact that out of the 39 nations, only five (the United States, Australia, Denmark, Germany, and Finland) nations were given the IC ratings greater than 7 in a 10-point scale, and showed clearly individualistic patterns of results (see table 5.1). In other words, individualist nations are rather a minority in the world. Nevertheless, as pointed out by Triandis (1995), most psychological models are generated based on research conducted in individualist nations. Cultural differences in descriptors of well-being found in this study suggest that future psychological models of well-being should account for not only Western individuals but also non-Western people.

In addition to cultural differences observed from visual inspection of table 5.1, the HLM analyses identified systematic patterns of cultural differences in descriptors of well-being. As predicted from the goal as a moderator model of SWB, the degree to which autonomy was related to well-being differed across cultures, depending on the salient values in cultures. Specifically, the degree of association between autonomy and life satisfaction was significantly stronger in individualist nations than in collectivist nations. The degree of association between relationship-orientation and life satisfaction was not, however, stronger in collectivist nations than in individualist nations based on the expert ratings (see Diener and Diener 1995 for similar findings concerning satisfaction with family and friends).

Finally, cultural differences in the attributes of well-being found in the present study raise some caution to the universality of two psychological well-being models (Ryan et al. 1996; Ryff and Singer 1998). Systematic cultural variation in descriptors of well-functioning individuals indicates that different cultures and social environments have different modes of behaviors, values, and attitudes that are suited for adjustment in particular societies. Furthermore these findings call for new ways of conceptualizing well-being that account for social contexts in which people live. To form social contextual theories of well-being, however, first the role of culture in individuals' well-being should be clearly understood. In this regard, key questions that have emerged from the present study are the following: Are individuals satisfied with their lives to the extent that they behave in accordance with cultural norms? Or, are they satisfied with their lives to the extent that they are moving toward personal goals that are consistent with cultural norms? Although the present study does not directly answer these questions, these issues are critical in understanding the interplay between culture and individuals' well-being in the future. Thus I will next analyze the possible ways in which the future research can investigate the role of cultures in well-being, by comparing Markus and Kitayama's (1994) cultural norm model of well-being with our goal as a moderator model.

Congruence with Social Norms or Personal Goals?

From the perspective of cultural psychology, Markus and Kitayama (1994) maintain that the very nature of "good feelings" is different from culture to culture, depending on the construction of the self. Kitayama, Markus, Kurokawa, and Negishi (1993, cited in Markus and Kitayama 1994) found that good feelings typically involved friendliness and fulfillment of obligations and expectations in Japan, whereas they typically involved pride and attainment of personal goals in the United States. Accordingly, they concluded that "Normative behavior typically feels 'good' or 'right' (Markus and Kitayama 1994, p. 91). In the present context this suggests that the degree to which individuals engage in normative behaviors determines their life satisfaction (see figure 5.1).

Alternatively, however, the present findings can be explained from another perspective. Individuals' goals are often influenced by cultural norms. Children living in individualist cultures learn that being independent is good, and being dependent is bad. Adults in the individualist cultures therefore tend to strive for independence. Similarly children in collectivist cultures learn that being cooperative with others and being responsible for their roles are crucial. Consequently people in collectivist cultures tend to strive for being responsible and cooperative with group members. To the extent that societal goals and individuals' goals are congruent, striving for individuals' goals manifest itself as normative behavior. As long as personal goals are congruent with cultural norms, Markus and Kitayama's (1994) model and our goal model both predict the same if–then pattern of relations between behavior (goal attainment) and satisfaction. However, the specific role of culture in the process is different. Markus and Kitayama's model posits that culture determines what appropriate behaviors are, and that individuals feel good about themselves when they are engaging in these behaviors and following cultural norms. On the other hand, we posit that culture influences the types of goals individuals pursue, and that they feel good when they are moving toward their personal goals (e.g., Brunstein et al. 1998; Oishi et al. 1999). For instance, suppose that Toru, a Japanese college student, feels good about his life when he does a good job at work as an assistant to his senior editor. According to Markus and Kitayama (1994), Toru feels good in this situation because he is fulfilling his role. If Toru's personal goal is to help the senior editor as much as possible, however, it could be said that he feels good in this situation because it meets his personal goal.

The difference in the two models is perhaps clearer when an individual's goal is incongruent with cultural norms. Suppose that Aki, a Japanese consultant, does not

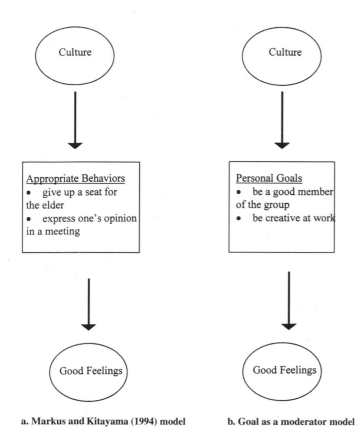

a. Markus and Kitayama (1994) model   **b. Goal as a moderator model**

Figure 5.1
Role of culture in Markus and Kitayama's (1994) model and the goal as a moderator model. Both models assume cultural variations in the sources of well-being, so both models assume a moderating role of culture. The specific role of culture in this process, however, is different. In Markus and Kitayama's model (a) cultural influences lead to appropriate behavior, and engagement in such behavior leads to good feelings. In the goal as the moderator model (b) culture affects the selection of goals, and the pursuit of that goal and its attainment lead to good feelings.

value helping others at all. The only thing she cares about is getting her job done. As a Japanese, however, she is well aware that helping colleagues is highly regarded in her company. Does she feel good about herself when she helps her colleagues? Or does she feel better when she gets things done? Put another way, is it following social norms that provides a sense of "good feelings" or is it following personal standards? According to Markus and Kitayama (1994), Aki should experience "good feelings" when she helps her colleagues rather than when she gets things done. On the other hand, the goal as a moderator model predicts that Aki should experience "good feelings" when she gets things done at work rather than when she helps others. Although both Markus and Kitayama's social norm theory and our goal as a moderator model of well-being predict cultural variations in the determinants of SWB, there are important differences in the role of culture. Markus and Kitayama conceptualize that culture prescribes acceptable behaviors, and that to the extent individuals follow this behavioral prescription, they feel satisfied. Because cultural norms are by definition shared by members of a particular culture, this model does not posit much individual difference within the same culture in the way in which they feel well. On the other hand, the goal as a moderator model posits that culture influences the types of goals individuals pursue, and that they are satisfied with their lives to the extent they are moving toward their goals. Although people in the same culture tend to pursue similar goals, the goal as a moderator allows for individual differences in the sources of well-being within a culture.

How can we test these two competing models of well-being across cultures? To answer this question, it is instructive to first ponder why the current data, as well as previous cross-cultural studies, do not provide a direct test of this question. The statement cited earlier "Normative behavior typically feels "good" or "right" (Markus and Kitayama 1994, p. 91) mostly concerns the intra-individual level. That is, this statement can be elaborated as follows: individuals should feel "good" or "right" when they engage in normative behaviors more than when engaging in nonnormative behaviors. Similarly the goal as a moderator model concerns the intra-individual level. For instance, one of the central postulates of this model is that individuals should feel good about their lives when they are moving toward their goals more than when they are not. In short, it is essential to assess individuals' behaviors and well-being repeatedly over time to test the models described above. Unfortunately, the current data set as well as most previous cross-cultural data, accessed participants' well-being only once. Once the repeatedly measured data are collected, however, a three-level analysis is available: within-individual data points as level 1 (e.g., specific behavior and emotion that followed the behavior), inter-individual data as level 2 (e.g., personal goals, attitudes, and values), and inter-cultural level data as level 3 (e.g., the level of individualism-collectivism, national means of certain values and attitudes). As shown by Mischel and Shoda (1995; Shoda, Mischel, and Wright 1994), this type of data provides if–then patterns of relations between antecedent events or behaviors and consequent feeling and sense of satisfaction for each individual. Then individuals' profiles can be predicted either from culture level variables (e.g., norms) or from person level variables (e.g., personal goals, attitudes, and values). The cultural norm model (Markus and Kitayama 1994) predicts that inter-individual differences in the if–then patterns will be explained from culture level variables, whereas the goal model predicts that they will be explained from person level variables. The test of these competing models in the future should bring a clearer understanding of the role of culture in sources and processes of SWB.

Theoretical Implications for the Distinction of Emotional Well-being and Meaning in Life

Markus and Kitayama's (1994) contention about normative behaviors and "good feelings" poses another intriguing question about the distinction between emotional well-being and meaning of life. Although Markus and Kitayama's argument is exclusive to the realm of emotional well-being, normative behaviors seem to be closely related to a sense of meaning in life. When individuals achieve their personal goals, they typically feel good (McGregor and Little 1998). However, the attainment of personal goals may not necessarily evoke a deep sense of meaning in life if the goal is strictly meeting one's selfish desires (e.g., getting out of a boring meeting; see Sheldon and Kasser 1998). On the other hand, fulfilling social norms and parental expectations (e.g., recycling, writing to parents) may not always elicit "good feelings." However, it may be these normative behaviors that are most likely to elicit a sense of meaning in life, for they tend to cast light on one's place in the world and relationship with larger entities (e.g., family, community, and society). In the case of Aki whose personal goals are inconsistent with cultural norms, when she gets a lot of things done, she may feel "happy." However, when she achieves her personal goals, she may not necessarily feel a deep sense of satisfaction. When she helps her colleagues, on the other hand, she may feel meaning in her life but may not necessarily feel happy. In a sense, I believe that the contention of the self-determination theory (Ryan et al. 1996) and the multidimensional well-being theory (Ryff 1989a;

Ryff and Singer 1998) bears on these prosocial and moral components of normative behaviors discussed here. That is, prosocial and moral behaviors may not necessarily elicit "joy," but they are more likely to endow individuals with a sense of meaning in life.

Alternatively, however, the experience of or the lack of meaning in life can be conceptualized as a function of congruence between personal goals and cultural norms. To the extent that personal goals are congruent with social norms, individuals may experience both a sense of happiness and meaning in life. Conversely, to the degree that personal goals are incongruent with cultural norms, individuals may feel either lack of happiness or meaning in life. In Japan, where a cultural norm is to be cooperative with other group members, Aki may not feel a sense of meaning in life because she may not feel like a valuable member of the society. On the other hand, in the United States, where a cultural norm is to take care of oneself, Aki might feel a sense of meaning more easily because she could feel that she is a good independent member of the society. To recapitulate, the above analysis yields two different hypotheses regarding "joy" and meaning in life: (1) personal goals will be linked with emotional well-being, whereas normative behavior will be linked with a sense of meaning, or alternatively (2) congruence between personal goals and cultural norms will generate both happiness and meaning, whereas the discrepancy will result in the lack of meaning in life. To increase our understanding of short-term emotional well-being and a long-term sense of fulfillment, more research is needed concerning the link of personal and societal goals to happiness and meaning of life.

Conclusion

Recent cross-cultural research on SWB (e.g., Diener and Diener 1995; Kwan et al. 1997; Oishi et al. 1999; Radhakrishnan and Chan 1997; Suh et al. 1998) has revealed large cultural differences in the correlates of well-being. These studies, including the present one, delineated "who is happy?" in various nations, and explored how the descriptions of satisfied persons differed across cultures. They did not, however, provide insight into other fundamental questions in SWB research: namely, "what makes people happy?" and "what is the role of culture in individuals' well-being?" As the SWB research expands its scope, answers to the latter questions are needed not only to grasp the processes influencing well-being in general, but also to advance our understanding of the precise role of culture in happiness and meaning in life. Future cross-cultural research should move from the investigation on descriptive aspects of SWB to functions and processes of SWB. To this end, the goal as a moderator model in combination with the existing models provides a promising framework.

References

Austin, J. T., and Vancouver, J. B. 1996. Goal constructs in psychology: Structure, process, and content. *Psychological Bulletin* 120: 338–75.

Balatsky, G., and Diener, E. 1993. Subjective well-being among Russian students. *Social Indicators Research* 28: 225–43.

Bolger, N., and Schilling, E. 1991. Personality and the problems of everyday life: The role of neuroticism in exposure and reactivity to daily stressors. *Journal of Personality* 59: 355–86.

Bolger, N., and Zuckerman, A. 1995. A framework for studying personality in the stress process. *Journal of Personality and Social Psychology* 69: 890–902.

Brunstein, J. C. 1993. Personal goals and subjective well-being: A longitudinal study. *Journal of Personality and Social Psychology* 65: 1061–70.

Brunstein, J. C., Schultheiss, O. C., and Grassmann, R. 1998. Personal goals and emotional well-being: The moderating role of motive dispositions. *Journal of Personality and Social Psychology* 75: 494–508.

Bryk, A. S., and Raudenbush, S. W. 1992. *Hierarchical Linear Models: Applications and Data Analysis Methods*. Newburry Park, CA: Sage.

Cantor, N., Norem, J., Langston, C., Zirkel, S., Fleeson, W., and Cook-Flannagan, C. 1991. Life tasks and daily life experience. *Journal of Personality* 59: 425–51.

Costa, P. T., Jr., and McCrae, R. R. 1988. From catalog to classification: Murray's needs and the five-factor model. *Journal of Personality and Social Psychology* 55: 258–65.

Cote, S., and Moskowitz, D. S. 1998. On the dynamic covariation between interpersonal behavior and affect: Prediction from neuroticism, extraversion, and agreeableness. *Journal of Personality and Social Psychology* 75: 1032 46.

Deci, E. L., and Ryan, R. M. 1990. A motivational approach to self: Integration in personality. In R. A. Dienstbier, ed., *Perspectives on Motivation*. Lincoln: University of Nebraska Press, pp. 237–88.

Diener, E., and Diener, M. 1995. Cross-cultural correlates of life satisfaction and self-esteem. *Journal of Personality and Social Psychology* 68: 653–63.

Diener, E., Emmons, R. A., Larsen, R. J., and Griffin, S. 1985. The Satisfaction with Life Scale. *Journal of Personality Assessment* 49: 71–75.

Diener, E., and Fujita, F. 1995. Resources, personal strivings, and subjective well-being: A nomothetic and ideographic approach. *Journal of Personality and Social Psychology* 68: 926–35.

Elliot, A. J., and Sheldon, K. M. 1997. Avoidance achievement motivation: A personal goals analysis. *Journal of Personality and Social Psychology* 73: 171–85.

Elliot, A. J., Sheldon, K. M., and Church, M. A. 1997. Avoidance personal goals and subjective well-being. *Personality and Social Psychology Bulletin* 23: 915–27.

Emmons, R. A. 1986. Personal strivings: An approach to personality and subjective well-being. *Journal of Personality and Social Psychology* 51: 1058–68.

Emmons, R. A. 1991. Personal strivings, daily life events, and psychological and physical well-being. *Journal of Personality* 59: 453–72.

Feldman Barrett, L. 1997. The relationships among momentary emotion experiences, personality descriptions, and retrospective ratings of emotion. *Personality and Social Psychology Bulletin* 23: 1100–10.

Feldman Barrett, L., and Pietromonaco, P. R. 1997. Accuracy of the five-factor model in predicting perceptions of daily social interactions. *Personality and Social Psychology Bulletin* 23: 1173–87.

Grob, A., Little, T. D., Wanner, B., Wearing, A. J., and Euronet. 1996. Adolescents' well-being and perceived control across 14 sociocultural contexts. *Journal of Personality and Social Psychology* 71: 785–95.

Harlow, R. E., and Cantor, N. 1996. Still participating after all these years: A study of life task participation in later life. *Journal of Personality and Social Psychology* 71: 1235–49.

Kasser, T., and Ryan, R. M. 1993. A dark side of the American dream: Correlates of financial success as a central life aspiration. *Journal of Personality and Social Psychology* 65: 410–22.

Kasser, T., and Ryan, R. M. 1996. Further examining the American dream: Differential correlates of intrinsic and extrinsic goals. *Personality and Social Psychology Bulletin* 22: 280–87.

Kasser, T., and Ryan, R. M. (in press). Be careful what you wish for: Optimal functioning and the relative attainment of intrinsic and extrinsic goals. In P. Schmuck and K. M. Sheldon, eds., *Life Goals and Well-being*. Lengerich, Germany: Pabst Science Publishers.

Kwan, V. S. Y., Bond, M. H., and Singelis, T. M. 1997. Pancultural explanations for life satisfaction: Adding relationship harmony to self-esteem. *Journal of Personality and Social Psychology* 73: 1038–51.

Leeakulthanit, O., and Day, R. 1993. Cross-cultural comparisons of quality of life of Thais and Americans. *Social Indicators Research* 30: 49–70.

Majumdar, S., and Dasgupta, S. K. 1997. Sense of well-being and perceived quality of life in Calcutta. Paper presented at the conference of the International Society of Quality of Life Studies in Charlotte, NC.

Markus, H. R., and Kitayama, S. 1991. Culture and the self: Implications for cognition, emotion, and motivation. *Psychological Review* 98: 224–53.

Markus, H. R., and Kitayama, S. 1994. The cultural construction of self and emotion: Implications for social behavior. In S. Kitayama, and H. R. Markus, eds., *Emotion and Culture: Empirical Studies of Mutual Influence*. Washington, DC: American Psychological Association, pp. 89–130.

Markus, H. R., Kitayama, S., and Heiman, R. J. 1996. Culture and "basic" psychological principles. In E. T. Higgns and A. W. Kruglanski, eds., *Social Psychology: Handbook of Basic Principles*. New York: Guilford, pp. 857–913.

McGregor, I., and Little, B. R. 1998. Personal projects, happiness, and meaning: On doing well and being yourself. *Journal of Personality and Social Psychology* 74: 494–512.

Mischel, W., and Shoda, Y. 1995. A cognitive-affective system theory of personality: Reconceptualizing situations, dispositions, dynamics, and invariance in personality structure. *Psychological Review* 102: 246–68.

Moskowitz, D. S. and Cote, S. 1995. Do interpersonal traits predict affect? A comparison of three models. *Journal of Personality and Social Psychology* 69: 915–24.

Oishi, S., Diener, E., Suh, E. M., and Lucas, R. E. 1999. Value as a moderator in subjective well-being. *Journal of Personality* 67: 157–84.

Oishi, S., Diener, E., Lucas, R. E., and Suh, E. M. 1999. Cross-cultural variations in predictors of life satisfaction: Perspectives from needs and values. *Personality and Social Psychology Bulletin* 25: 980–90.

Oishi, S., Schimmack, U., and Diener, E. 1999. Emotional experience and life satisfaction: Beyond the nomothetic approach to subjective well-being. Manuscript submitted for publication. University of Illinois, Champaign.

Palys, T. S., and Little, B. R. 1983. Perceived life satisfaction and the organization of personal project systems. *Journal of Personality and Social Psychology* 44: 1221–30.

Pavot, W., and Diener, E. 1993. Review of the Satisfaction with Life Scale. *Psychological Assessment* 5: 164–72.

Radhakrishnan, P., and Chan, D. K. S. 1997. Cultural differences in the relation between self-discrepancy and life satisfaction. *International Journal of Psychology* 32: 387–98.

Ryan, R. M. 1995. Psychological needs and the facilitation of integrative processes. *Journal of Personality* 63: 397–427.

Ryan, R. M., Sheldon, K. M., Kasser, T., and Deci, E. L. 1996. All goals are not created equal. In P. M. Gollwitzer and J. A. Bargh, eds., *The Psychology of Action: Linking Cognition and Motivation to Behavior.* New York: Guilford, pp. 7–26.

Ryff, C. D. (1989a). Happiness is everything, or is it? Exploration on the meaning of psychological well-being. *Journal of Personality and Social Psychology* 57: 1069–81.

Ryff, C. D. (1989b). In the eye of the beholder: Views of psychological well-being in middle and old-aged adults. *Psychology and Aging* 4: 195–210.

Ryff, C. D., and Keyes, L. M. (1995). The structure of psychological well-being revisited. *Journal of Personality and Social Psychology* 69: 719–27.

Ryff, C. D., and Singer, B. (1998). The contours of positive human health. *Psychological Inquiry* 9: 1–28.

Sanderson, C. A., and Cantor, N. (1997). Creating satisfaction in steady dating relationships: The role of personal goals and situational affordances. *Journal of Personality and Social Psychology* 73: 1424–33.

Schimmack, U., and Hartmann, K. 1997. Individual differences in the memory representation of emotional episodes: Exploring the cognitive processes in repression. *Journal of Personality and Social Psychology* 73: 1064–79.

Schwartz, S. H. 1994. Beyond individualism-collectivism: New cultural dimensions of values. In U. Kim, H. C. Triandis, C. Kagitcibasi, S.-C. Choi and G. Yoon, eds., *Individualism-Collectivism: Theory, Method, and Application*. Newbury Park, CA: Sage, pp. 85–119.

Schwartz, S. H., and Sagiv, L. 1995. Identifying culture-specifics in the content and structure of values. *Journal of Cross-Cultural Psychology* 26: 92–116.

Shao, L. 1993. Multilanguage comparability of life satisfaction and happiness measures in mainland Chinese and American students. Unpublished maser's thesis. University of Illinois, Urbana-Champaign.

Shao, L. 1997. Extraversion and positive affect. PhD dissertation. University of Illinois, Urbana-Champaign.

Sheldon, K. M., and Kasser, T. 1995. Coherence and congruence: Two aspects of personality integration. *Journal of Personality and Social Psychology* 68: 531–43.

Sheldon, K. M., and Kasser, T. 1998. Pursuing personal goals: Skills enable progress, but not all progress is beneficial. *Personality and Social Psychology Bulletin* 24: 1319–31.

Sheldon, K. M., Ryan, R. M., Rawsthorne, L. J., and Ilardi, B. 1997. Trait self and true self: Cross-role variation in the big-five personality traits and its relations with psychological authenticity and subjective well-being. *Journal of Personality and Social Psychology* 73: 1380–93.

Sheldon, K. M., Ryan, R. M., and Reis, H. 1996. What makes for a good day? Competence and autonomy in the day, and in the person. *Personality and Social Psychology Bulletin* 22: 1270–79.

Shoda, Y., Mischel, W., and Wright, J. C. 1994. Intra-individual stability in the organization and patterning of behavior: Incorporating psychological situations into the idiographic analysis of personality. *Journal of Personality and Social Psychology* 67: 674–87.

Suh, E. 1994. Emotion norms, values, familiarity, and subjective well-being: A cross-cultural examination. Master's thesis. University of Illinois, Urbana-Champaign.

Suh, E., Diener, E., Oishi, S., and Triandis, H. C. 1998. The shifting basis of life satisfaction judgments across cultures: Emotion versus norms. *Journal of Personality and Social Psychology* 74: 482–93.

Suls, J. Green, P., and Hillis, S. 1998. Emotional reactivity to everyday problems, affective inertia, and neuroticism. *Personality and Social Psychology Bulletin* 24: 127–36.

Suls, J., Martin, R., and David, J. P. 1998. Person-environment fit and its limits: Agreeableness, neuroticism, and emotional reactivity to interpersonal conflicts. *Personality and Social Psychology Bulletin* 24: 88–98.

Triandis, H. C. 1995. *Individualism and Collectivism*. Boulder, CO: Westview.

6

The Pursuit of Happiness and the Realization of Sympathy: Cultural Patterns of Self, Social Relations, and Well-being

Shinobu Kitayama and Hazel Rose Markus

The brutish pursuit of individual ends is harmful to the ends and the peace of all, to the rhythm of their work and joys—and rebounds on the individual himself.
(Mauss 1925, *The Gift: The Form and Reason for Exchange in Archaic Societies*, trans. by W. D. Halls, p. 77)

Introduction

A review of research on well-being conducted in 1967 by Wilson concluded that the happy person is a "young, healthy, well-educated, well-paid, extroverted, optimistic, worry-free, religious, married person with high self-esteem, job morale, modest aspirations, of either sex and of a wide range of intelligence" (p. 294). Recent approaches (Cantor and Sanderson 1998) have added a few other qualities such as personal goals to the list, but still the picture of the happy person remains largely unchanged (Diener et al. 1999). Can we now be reasonably satisfied with the conclusion that optimism, self-esteem, and positive affectivity are requirements for human happiness and well-being?

Recent work from a cultural perspective suggests that the answer may be yes as long as the humans are engaged in social worlds that are arranged and practiced like those of middle-class North America. Should these worlds be otherwise arranged and engaged, however, the answer may well be no. The purpose of this chapter is to examine two distinct models of the self and well-being. We will argue that as exemplified in many American cultural contexts, the personal pursuit of happiness and the recognition of this pursuit by the self and others are defining of the happiness itself (Myers 1992). However, as exemplified in many East Asian cultures, happiness assumes a different subjective form—it is a state that emerges when taking a critical and disciplined stance to the personal self and thus engaging the sympathy of others (Lewis 1995; Kitayama and Markus 1999; Menon and Shweder 1998).

In both cases the respective attitude toward happiness and well-being is recognized to be a central aspect of the self, and further it characterizes the self-relevant psychological tendencies or processes of the people who engage in these divergent cultural worlds. Moreover the appropriate attitude toward well-being is necessary to be a legitimate member of the cultural community of which one is part. It is this interpersonal consequence of cultural adaptation that is a significant contributor to happiness and subjective well-being. Our theoretical perspective assumes that the self and the social relations of a given community are mutually constitutive and that being a self amounts to being part of the attendant social relations. To "be well" requires an attunement between the self and the social relations that are organized and maintained by the cultural practices and meanings of a community.

Well-being as a Collaborative Project
The self is the topic of central significance in social and personality psychology. Yet it is only recently that the field has recognized considerable cultural and ethnic variations in the ways in which the self is construed and practiced (e.g., Fiske et al. 1998; Kitayama 1998; Markus, Kitayama, and Heiman 1996; Triandis 1989, 1995). Furthermore it is becoming increasingly clear that the construction of the self is socially mediated, meaning that it occurs in conjunction with the construction of social relationships (e.g., Baumeister and Leary 1996; Baldwin 1999; Gergen and Gergen 1988; Leary et al. 1995; Markus and Cross 1990). Thus we are now rediscovering, affirming, and beginning to explore broader and deeper implications of ideas originally proposed by G. H. Mead (1934) and C. H. Cooley (1902). These theorists argued, well before the advent of the modern personality and social psychology, that the self is a social product, inseparable from the construction of the attendant social relationships. Although these theorists never explicitly examined culture, their ideas may be pushed a step forward to suggest that the co-construction of the self and social relations can take a variety of different forms depending on the cultural resources—the ideas, images, icons, assumptions, behavioral routines, scripts, etc.—that are invoked in the history of the culture.

Just as people cannot live in a general way and must of necessity live in some set of culture-specific ways, a person cannot just "be well" in a general way. The very nature of what it means to be well or to experience well-being takes culture-specific forms (Shweder 1998). What it means to feel good or to live a good life requires being able to realize culturally mandated ways of being. Well-being then is very much a collaborative project, one can't experience well-being by one's self; it requires engaging a system of consensual understandings and practices and depends on the nature of one's connections and relations to others. Seemingly individual attributes like optimism, extroversion, efficacy, mastery, or self-esteem believed to be essential for individual happiness may require a North American social world or a cultural complex that is organized in specific ways, and that depends on a specific knot of shared understandings and assumptions and on the particular consensual reactions and actions of others. Well-being, even for individualists, requires interdependence among people who tacitly agree to approve of and support each other in particular ways that have been shaped by culture and history. The interpersonal and collective sources of well-being are often not evident because in North American social worlds, social relations are patterned in a way that brings the reality of the bounded, "nonsocial" self to the fore of individual conscious experience, while obscuring the reality of the very relations that give rise to it (Kitayama and Markus 1999).

To the extent that the relevant social world is arranged and practiced differently, incorporating different cultural models of what is good, what is moral, or what is self, well-being may assume forms other than those currently described and documented in the psychological literature. What counts as "well-being" depends on how the concepts of "well" and "being" are defined and practiced. And these variations can make a difference not only for the content or the meaning of well-being, but in the very processes that create and maintain well-being. It is not just that different things make people happy in different cultural contexts—this is obviously the case. More significantly it is the ways of "being well" and the experience of well-being that are different.

The Role of Cross-cultural Comparison

Cultural practices and meanings define the most natural and ordinary ways of acting in a variety of mundane everyday situations such as saying hello and goodbye, having conversations, exchanging gossip, eating lunch and dinner, and playing sports (Cole 1996; Miller and Goodnow 1995). No matter how natural or ordinary they might seem at first glance, a closer scrutiny reveals that these everyday situations are in fact regulated and constituted by an intricate, although often haphazard collection of socially shared cognitions, beliefs, images, and behavioral patterns, beneath which one can sometimes discern implicit cultural assumptions and premises about what is the person and the self and how it is related to other people and objects in the world (Durkheim 1964; Farr 1988; Fiske et al. 1998; Kitayama and Markus 1999; Markus et al. 1997; Markus, Mullally, and Kitayama 1997; Moscovici 1984; Shweder 1998).

The web of cultural practices and meanings are often invisible to those who are accustomed to them and whose mode of thinking, feeling, and acting is well-coordinated and attuned to the requirements they invite, the opportunities they afford, and the constraints they impose. To the degree that this attunement is attained, cultural practices and meanings are taken for granted, undoubted and often even undoubtable. The challenge is to make explicit the nature of the typically invisible organization of cultural practices and meanings and to use this analysis to inform our understanding of subjectively natural psychological processes and structures.

One way to do this, which has proved to be quite useful and often extremely powerful, is to draw a comparison between two divergent broadly defined cultural groups (Berry et al. 1992; Gergen et al. 1996; Greenfield 1997a; Markus and Kitayama 1991a; Siegel, Lonner, and Berry 1998; but see also Hermans and Kempen 1998, for a critical view on this approach). The purpose is not so much to describe regional variations, but to bring to the fore the assumptions, premises, and narratives that are hidden underneath, "behind" what people think, feel and do. These assumptions have generated, over history, the predominant mode of being that is collectively shared in a given cultural region. Only when researchers find that what appears to be so natural and is thus so taken for granted in their own cultural contexts does not hold somewhere else, do they begin to notice the culture-specific grounding of the natural and ordinary.

In this chapter we will draw on an expanding literature on cultural and psychological differences between European-American populations and East Asian populations (Fiske et al. 1998; Kitayama and Markus 1999; Markus et al. 1997; Triandis 1995). Specifically, we will argue that in European-American cultural contexts, the self and social relations are simultaneously constructed on the basis of the model of the person as an active, independent agent that influences other people. Well-being in this cultural context is associated with self-esteem and the pursuit of one's own happiness. These optimistic stances to the self give rise to constructions of an independent agent. Accordingly well-being in this cultural context is bound to be subjective, personal, or individual in scope. By contrast, in East Asian cultural contexts, happiness and well-being are constructed in accordance with the model of the person as an active, interdependent agent who adjusts to other people. Well-being in this context is thus related not so much to self-esteem, optimism, and efficacy, but rather, more to self-criticism and discipline. These critical stances to the self give rise to sympathy both to and from others, and therefore they may be crucial for constructions of an interdependent agent. Accordingly well-being is bound to be more relational, intersubjective, communal, and collective in scope.

Self, Social Relations, and Well-being

Independent and Interdependent Modes of "Being" a Self in a Relationship

European-American Constructions   To understand the precise nature of the cultural variation in the constructions of the self and social relations, we have suggested that many social situations in North America have been historically constructed on the basis of the model of the self as an independent, autonomous entity. The independent model of the person incorporates the following ideas: (1) a person is an autonomous entity defined by a distinctive set of attributes, qualities, or processes; (2) this configuration of internal attributes or processes determines or causes behavior; (3) interpersonal relations are established through each other's prosocial, mutually beneficial influences. In other words, American social relations emerge out of each other's prosocial influences, such as praising, advising, and encouraging. Social situations constructed in this way are in turn likely to afford the corresponding sense of the self as efficacious, in control, and capable. But equally important, these very social situations that afford a strong sense of self-esteem should also afford a strong sense of interpersonal connectedness, insofar as the model of the self as an independent agent that influences others in the surrounding is a blueprint by which both the self and social relationships are simultaneously constructed.

It is the fundamental insight of G. H. Mead (1934) that meaning of one's act (and thus, eventually one's self and being) is complete only if the act (or gesture in his terminology) is answered by others' acts (e.g., see Bourdieu 1972; Bruner 1990; Giddens 1984; Goffman 1959, 1967; Shore 1997, for similar analyses). As a consequence the intention of the first person is often underdetermined until or unless it is placed in a proper interpersonal context. In this process of meaning making, culturally conventionalized scripts play essential roles. Thus one's action that conforms to an appropriate script is likely to be answered by others' affirmative responses and feedback, which will in turn symbolically complete the act initiated by the first person.

For example, in North American cultural context, an assertive behavior initiated by one person may be answered by others in such a way that a friendly, yet adversarial discussion ensues whereby the first person's assertive act is interpersonally affirmed and made fully meaningful. Although never determined in full beforehand, such unfolding of the event is facilitated and, to a large extent, ascertained by the fact that there are great many cultural scripts for the self's independence in this cultural context. In this sense the self's autonomy and independence may best be seen as a culturally scripted way to participate in social relationships and to be a member of the community in the North American cultural context. In the absence of cultural scripts that encompass such behaviors, others may feel embarrassed or feel at ill-ease, and in any event, they may know little by way of properly responding to such an action. Hence the person's behavior will be left less than fully meaningful (by inviting different, unwelcome meaning such as embarrassment) and, correspondingly, symbolic affirmation or completion of the self will be exceedingly difficult.

The independent model of the self and social relations is schematically illustrated in figure 6.1a. Three central features of this model are of note:

1. In this model the idea of prosocial interpersonal influence is used as the glue of the relationship. Thus people in a relationship are expected to exert prosocial influences on others. In many cases these influences take the form of praising and admiring, namely to find something good in the other person and say to the person something good because of it.

2. In this model individuals who participate in the relationship are conceptualized as carrying high self-esteem, being composed of desirable, praiseworthy attributes, and willing to express these positive internal attributes.

3. The prosocial influences assumed to connect people and the high self-esteem of the people to be connected are mutually interdependent. One exists and is promoted because of the other.

There are two interrelated reasons for the interdependency between the person characteristic and the relational characteristic. First, in order for someone to praise someone else, this second person has to demonstrate to the first person a certain reason for the praise. Hence the psychological characteristics of each person assumed here (i.e., having and willing to express positive and desirable features of the self) invite the prosocial influences such as praising and admiring from others in the relationship. The second reason stems from the fact that the prosocial influencing mode of interpersonal connection is likely to promote an enhanced sense of the efficaciousness and esteem of the self. For one thing, praising and admiring con-

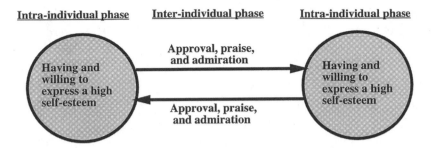

Figure 6.1a
Cultural complex of self-esteem and mutually approving relationship common in Europe and America.

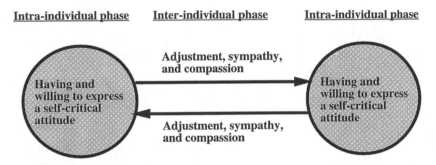

Figure 6.1b
Cultural complex of self-criticism and mutually sympathetic relationship common in East Asia.

veyed to the self from others in a relationship may directly contribute to the self-enhancement. For the other, the very act of praising and admiring others can carry a self-affirming quality, insofar as it is interpreted as a sign of certain desirable characteristics of the self such as generosity, honesty, and friendliness.

At the outset it should be made clear that situational scripts that encourage the development of independent selves are unevenly distributed in North America. They may be most available among middle-class, well-educated, and well-paid white males. As we will see below, this is an important source of within-culture variability. Yet we maintain that the focus on the predominant mode of being enables us to recognize its historical and collective groundings and thus culture-boundedness of any psychological processes associated with it.

East Asian Constructions   By contrast, many social situations in East Asia have been historically constructed on the basis of the model of the self as interdependent entity (e.g., Ames, Dissanayake, and Kasulis 1994; DeVos 1985; Kondo 1990; Nakamura 1964, 1989; Rosenberger 1992; Menon and Shweder 1998; Plath 1980; Shweder and Bourne 1985; Triandis 1995; Weisz, Rothbaum, and Blackburn 1984). The interdependent model of the person incorporates a different set of ideas; they include the following: (1) a person is part of an encompassing set of social relationships, (2) behavior is a consequence of being responsive to the others with whom one is interdependent, and (3) interpersonal relations therefore are established through active acts of adjustment of the self to the requirements of the surrounding social situations. In other words, East Asian social relations are maintained by individuals who engage actively in an effort for mutual adjustment. Social situations constructed in this way are in turn likely to afford the corresponding sense of the self.

The interdependent model of the self and social relations is schematically illustrated in figure 6.1b. Again there are three central features in this model:

1. The idea of interpersonal adjustment is used as the glue of the relationship. Thus people in a relationship are expected to take the perspective of others in the relationship, feel empathically with them, and act accordingly, often altruistically, on others' behalf. Thinking and feeling for and with another person and behaving on his behalf presupposes that the other person is less than perfect, often worthy of and requiring some help or support in many cases.
2. Individuals who participate in the relationship are conceptualized as carrying deficits, shortcomings, or at least attitudes to the self that are attuned to their own potentially negative features.
3. The sympathetic adjustments assumed to connect people and the self-critical attitudes of the people to be connected are mutually interdependent. One is a necessary element for the other.

Again, there are two interrelated reasons for the interdependency between the person characteristic and the relational characteristic. First, in order for someone to give sympathy to someone else, this second person has to demonstrate to the first person a certain reason for the sympathy. Hence the psychological characteristics of each person assumed here (i.e., having and willing to express a self-critical attitude) invite the prosocial adjustments such as sympathy and compassion from others in the relationship. Second, the prosocial adjustment mode of interpersonal connection would promote a sense of security and assurance with which to continue to exercise self-critical appraisals of the self. For one thing, sympathy and compassion conveyed to the self from others in a relationship may directly contribute to the sense of security. For the other, the very act of sympathy and compassion can affirm the image of the self as an interdependent entity, insofar as it is a clear sign of his own commitment to the social relationship.

In short, within each model of interpersonal relationship the person characteristics and the relationship characteristics are coordinated with each other, with one serving necessary, reinforcing or otherwise, compensating roles for the other. Thus, in the independent case, the person characteristic of high self-esteem is both a consequence and a prerequisite for participating in the independent, mutually approving relationship. Likewise, in the interdependent case, the person characteristic of self-critical attitude is both a consequence and a prerequisite for participating in the interdependent, mutually sympathetic relationship.

These two forms of relationships are likely to exist in all cultures and societies (Fiske 1993; Clark and Mills 1979; Mills and Clark 1994). Nevertheless, the prevalence of these two types of relationships may vary, so does the degree to which these two types of relationships are conventionalized and reinforced by available cultural resources. Hence, to the extent that many, if not most, interpersonal relations in one's social life are constructed in accordance with the respective cultural model, the correlated characteristics of the person as highly esteemed, capable, in control, and efficacious in the independent case or as both critical to the self and warm-hearted to others may most properly be conceptualized as the intrapersonal phase of the cultural complex depicted in each of the two figures. Furthermore the characteristics of the interpersonal communications as mutually admiring and praising in the independent case and mutually sympathizing in the interdependent case may be best seen as the interpersonal phase of the same complex. The two elements are inseparable, and thus any analysis of one would be incomplete without taking into account the other.

Cultural Models of the Self and Individual Self-systems

In the present analysis we distinguish between cultural models of the self as independent or interdependent and forms of each individual self as independent or interdependent. Once this distinction is made explicit, it becomes crucial to begin specifying the relationship between the two constructs. Numerous cross-cultural studies have indicated that cultural models of the self are associated with analogous psychological forms and functions of selves in the respective community (Markus and Kitayama 1991a). Nevertheless, this association may be much more dynamic than has been appreciated so far in the literature. For example, when beliefs about independence or interdependence, or correlated values, are examined cross-culturally, the distribution of endorsement responses to these beliefs and values has considerable overlap across different cultures (e.g., Hofstede 1980; Smith and Schwartz 1997; Triandis 1995). Clearly, many individuals in any given culture resist and disapprove of the dominant ideologies and values of their own culture, although, as is often, a majority may tend to approve them.

Typically in the literature, it is assumed that people in different cultural contexts tend to internalize and thus to believe the respective models of the self and that, by virtue of this internalizing of the cultural models, psychological systems show cross-culturally divergent characteristics. The several notable attempts to measure self-construals at the individual level, and then to relate the individual differences in self-construal to differences in psychological functions in other domains (e.g., Kwan, Bond, and Singelis 1997; Kiuchi 1995; Takata and Matsumoto 1995; Okazaki 1997; Singelis 1994) are all grounded in the assumption that cultural views of the self have to be internalized in order for them to have any significant influences on psychological processes. The same assumption can be found in analyses on influences of lay theories in social thinking and social behavior (e.g., Dweck 1993).

In contrast to this "standard view" of cultural influences, we suggest that the transformation of cultural models to individual psychological and interpersonal systems is mediated collectively by the way in which situational scripts are accumulated and thus available in the respective cultural context. This by no means denies the involvement of internalized cognitive models of the self in mediating psychological responses. Nevertheless, it emphasizes the role of collectively constructed social situations in the analysis of culture's influences on psychological processes. Although the historical process involved in the making of the cultural reservoir of meanings and ideas is inherently difficult to study directly, it is still possible to examine some implications of such an analysis (e.g., Kitayama et al. 1997, 1999).

According to our analysis the collectively mediated cultural influences should be largely unconscious, operating outside of the conscious recognition of each participating individual. The unconscious nature of collective mediation, however, is due neither to Freudian repression nor to mere benign failure in memory retrieval. It instead results because the collective processes of producing, preserving, or otherwise terminating various meanings and practices (which enter the definitions and constructions of every contemporaneous social situation) operate over generations while each individual is interacting with other members of their own community with totally different, personally much more relevant goals, intents, or concerns in mind.

Although psychological processes are certainly involved in the collective processes of transmission and selection of ideas, meanings, and practices (Sperber 1996), this involvement is partial at best, and in fact no individual can be in the privileged position of perfect sight or control over the collective processes. Precisely because the collectively mediated cultural influences are unconscious in principle and uncontrollable in practice, they are very difficult to identify, let alone to resist. And this should be the case for both lay people and researchers alike. For this reason these cultural influences may be quite pervasive, widespread, and powerful in forming the basis of "being" for ordinary people and, yet, remain elusive for those researchers who have sought to understand them. The theoretical frameworks presented in figures 6.1a and b represent our initial attempt to characterize the "collective landscape" of the social situations in the respective cultural contexts, within which each individual self-system, every concrete social transaction, and therefore wellness or badness of the "being" are shaped and held in place.

Cultural Participation and Subjective Well-being

Subjective well-being can be influenced by a number of factors (Diener and Diener 1998; Ryff and Singer 1998). Although the theoretical framework suggested above is not intended to encompass all such factors, it does highlight one significant cluster of factors that has been relatively neglected in the contemporary literature on the topic. According to our theoretical framework, a subjective assessment of wellness or badness of "being" may not purely be an individual, psychological product. It is often afforded and invited by a number of social and cultural processes. We assume that psychological processes brought to bear on cultural and social adaptation are best conceptualized as the intra-individual phase of the pertinent cultural complex. These processes are sustained, reinforced, or compensated by the interpersonal and sociocultural phase of the same complex. In turn, the latter processes are also sustained by the proper, "natural," active, and well-coordinated workings of the intra-individual processes. Thus these two phases are mutually constitutive, and further they define necessary elements of the entire cultural complex.

There are two related, but theoretically distinct reasons why attunement with a dominant cultural complex of a given society can be expected to lead to an enhanced sense of well-being. One is symbolic. Culturally sanctioned forms of social relationship, called here the cultural complexes, are associated with predominant ideologies, important values and norms, and many other associated ideas, images, lay theories, and common sense. Hence, by being part of such a cultural complex, one should be able to locate him or herself within the rich array of meanings provided by the cultural symbolic systems, thereby affirming the self as a meaningful, stable, and largely respectable cultural entity. The thick layer of meanings associated with the cultural complex of self-esteem and mutually approving relationship in European American cultures and those associated with the cultural complex of self-criticism and mutually sympathetic relationship in East Asian, particularly Japanese culture, are illustrated in figures 6.2a and b, respectively.

These figures are not intended to be exhaustive of all the supportive meanings and local knowledge, but the purpose is to indicate that the respective cultural complex is associated with a redundant, mutually related set of ideas, theories, ideologies, values, and norms that as a whole provides a convincing rationale about why the practices involved in the complex are justified or at least justifiable. The point here is not so much that these meanings are all available to any single individual, but rather, to note that they are widely distributed and embodied in the practices and meanings of the respective societies so that they feel "natural"—seemingly overdetermined by laws or orders of prehuman, or suprahuman kind (e.g., freedom or human rights as God-given in contemporary North American culture)—and furthermore that when necessary, individuals can readily justify the pertinent cultural complex in which they participate.

The second reason why an attunement of one's psychological systems with the pertinent cultural complex is associated with well-being is socioemotional. There is reason to believe that any cultural complex used to regulate social relationships such as the ones illustrated in figures 6.1a and b assures a degree of reciprocal social exchange of resources, which can be materialistic, symbolic, psychological, or most likely, a combination thereof. Any cultural complexes that are existent today are the ones that were invented or otherwise incorporated from other cultural groups at some point in the history of the respective cultural group and have since been used by an increasingly greater number of people in the group so that, over time, they have become conventional. It is likely that many other systems of social relationships

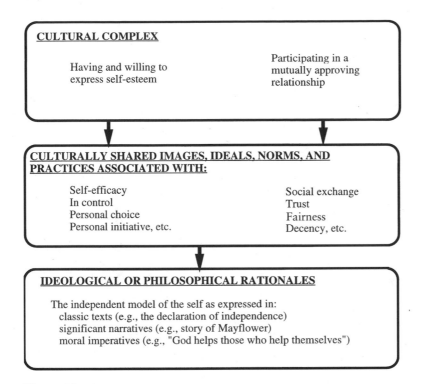

CULTURAL COMPLEX

Having and willing to
express self-esteem

Participating in a
mutually approving
relationship

**CULTURALLY SHARED IMAGES, IDEALS, NORMS, AND
PRACTICES ASSOCIATED WITH:**

Self-efficacy
In control
Personal choice
Personal initiative, etc.

Social exchange
Trust
Fairness
Decency, etc.

IDEOLOGICAL OR PHILOSOPHICAL RATIONALES

The independent model of the self as expressed in:
classic texts (e.g., the declaration of independence)
significant narratives (e.g., story of Mayflower)
moral imperatives (e.g., "God helps those who help themselves")

Figure 6.2a
Meanings associated with the cultural complex of self-esteem and mutually approving
relationship.

were also invented, but they were "weeded out" for one reason or another. One
important class of factors that leads eventually to the disappearance of any cultural
practice is the properties of the practice that do not meet requirements imposed by
the species-specific characteristics of any human social group (Durham 1991).

It is safe to assume that humans as a species have evolved to cooperate with one
another to attain necessary resources for living (Fiske 1992). These resources can be
material. Thus, for example, food exchange among members of any group would
often be necessary for the survival of the group as a whole. Equally often and, perhaps, more important in a world where basic biological needs of the organisms are
unlikely to be severely threatened, more significant resources may be socioemotional. Hence it is likely that any cultural complexes assure some minimal reciprocity, as highlighted by the bidirectional arrows in figures 6.1a and b. Thus the

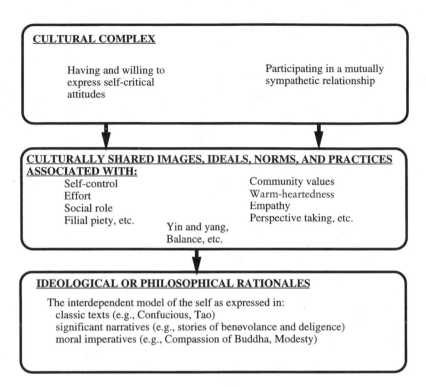

Figure 6.2b
Meanings associated with the cultural complex of self-criticism and mutually sympathetic relationship.

cultural complexes in European American groups are characterized by mutually approving social relationship, whereas those in East Asian groups are noted for their mutually sympathetic property. This analysis implies that participating in any predominant form of cultural complex for social relationship often assures that each person will receive resources of various kinds from other participants. These resources are often impossible to attain without interacting with others, and therefore cultural participation is likely to enhance both objective and subjective well-being.

Review of Empirical Research

Well-being—American Style
Our theoretical analysis to this point suggests that well-being results from the pursuit of happiness and living according to middle-class American meanings and

practices. This pursuit is related to the experience of happiness as well as to an independent, active, outgoing self. Americans, for example, are exceptionally happy (Diener and Diener 1995). The percentage of Americans reporting happiness is above 80 percent. Even people with objectively challenging life circumstances (i.e., economic hardship) report being happy (Smith 1979; Freeman 1978; Diener et al. 1995). Moreover, in a recent representative sample of 1,500 U.S. adults, Herzog, Franks, Markus, and Holmberg (1998) found that the terms "happy," "outgoing," "active," and also "independent" were the most frequently generated personality attributes in an open-ended self-description tasks. Fewer than 2 percent of all self-descriptions were negative. In a close-ended task which required rating themselves on various attributes, 69 percent said that the term "independent" described them extremely well, 60 percent said "active" described them extremely well, 51 percent said "content" described them extremely well, and 48 percent of these respondents reported that "outgoing" described them "extremely well."

A number of studies have shown that in North America people with more complex or more elaborated selves are less likely to be depressed and more likely to have higher self-esteem and better physical health (Herzog et al. 1998; Linville 1987). Another large body of research demonstrates a strong, positive relationship between a sense of control (also called self-efficacy, mastery, self-directedness, or agency) and both health and well-being (Ross and Wu 1995; Marmot et al. 1997). Moreover people with higher levels of education are likely to experience greater well-being, particularly in the form of self-esteem, purpose in life, and physical health. And it is people with more education who are the ones most likely to show evidence of an agentic, independent self (House et al. 1994, Herzog et al. 1998; Ross and Wu 1995), to display high levels of individualism (Triandis 1995) and high levels of control (Lachman and Weaver 1998), and to reveal relatively more false uniqueness and high self-esteem. (Josephs, Markus, and Tafarodi 1992). The ways of life typically associated with completing a college education (e.g., performing a role that is relatively esteemed or powerful) are likely to result in the self in line with the American cultural imperative—an autonomous, free, in-control self. People with lower levels of education often report high levels of happiness and life satisfaction, but they are less likely to manifest many of the other features of the independent self; they show relatively lower levels of control, self-esteem, optimism, and are less likely to have elaborated self-concepts.

In a recent in-depth study of everyday well-being, Markus, Ryff, Connor, Pudberry, and Barnett (1998) asked middle-class adults at midlife to describe in their own terms what it meant to have their lives go well and what well-being meant to them. The analysis of their open-ended answers to these questions found that college-educated respondents in American cultural contexts see themselves as active, independent agents who influence others. When describing why they thought they were responsible, for example, college-educated respondents described themselves as "taking initiative" and as "juggling and balancing" their responsibilities. One college-educated respondent claimed "I am good at juggling multiple tasks. I have a family life that demands that, and I have a professional life that demands that." Another said, "I seek out responsibility, and I believe in a person being responsible for his or her own actions." High school-educated respondents, however, were significantly less likely to describe themselves in this way and more likely to describe themselves as "adjusting to circumstances," and as "being dependable." One high school-educated respondent said "Life is a big responsibility. And it's not going to always go the way that we want it to go, and so there's just sometimes where you got to go with the flow." Another high school-educated respondent claimed "People know they can count on me; that's being responsible." Across a variety of questions relevant to well-being, college-educated respondents' way of interacting with the world implied a sense of self as independent of, acting on, and controlling situations while high school-educated respondents portrayed a sense of the self as embedded in and adapting to situations.

In an analysis performed on these narratives of well-being, all of the sentences generated during the interview were coded for whether the focus of the sentence was the self (e.g., "I am very responsible even when its something I really don't like to do") or on the other (e.g., "If my family is counting on me, I try not to let them down"). The number of sentences generated by the high school-educated and college-educated respondents did not differ, and all respondents had more self-focus than other focus sentences. College-educated respondents, however, focused on the self 3.9 times more often than they focused on others, while high school-educated respondents focused on the self only 1.8 times more than they focused on others. These data suggest that for those respondents with a college level education behavior is understood as individuals expressing themselves and selves are experienced as active, independent agents who influence each other.

Self-enhancement and Self-criticism

In the backdrop of what is known about well-being–American style, it is significant to note that well-being in many non-Western cultural contexts may not include being extroverted, optimistic, worry free, or having high self-esteem. In some East Asian contexts, for example, well-being requires not personal feelings of happiness but self-criticism, failure, and suffering—these are necessary experiences before one can find the path and "be well." Elsewhere we have argued with initial evidence that in Japanese cultural context this attitude is often necessary for personal achievement because it leads to a recognition of one's shortcomings and, therefore, to hard work (Heine et al. 1999; Kitayama and Karasawa 1995). Furthermore, as we will see, the self-critical attitude enables the person to fully participate in mutually sympathetic social relations.

By now, there exists considerable evidence that self-relevant psychological tendencies associated with the normative mode of cultural participation are quite diverse across cultures. A strong emphasis on self-esteem is barely heard of in East Asia, where a much stronger value is attached to self-criticism, discipline, and improvement (e.g., Heine, et al. 1999; Kitayama, Markus, and Lieberman 1995).

Self-descriptions   Kanagawa, Cross, and Markus (in press), for example, examined self-descriptions of both American and Japanese college students and found that American descriptions are predominantly positive in evaluative connotation, but a majority of Japanese descriptions are negative. This remarkable cross-cultural divergence in the ratio of positive to negative descriptions has been repeatedly found in North America–East Asian comparisons (Bond 1991; Markus et al. 1998; Karasawa 1998).

Self and Other Ratings   A similar cross-cultural difference has been reported between Canadians and Chinese. Yik, Bond, and Paulhus (1998) had college students in both Canada and Hong Kong interact with each other in small groups over an extended period of time. Afterward, the respondents rated the self (self-ratings) as well as the other members of their own group (other ratings) on a number of personality dimensions. Overall, in the Chinese sample the self-ratings were evaluatively less positive than the other ratings, suggesting the presence of a tendency to be critical to the self among East Asians. A very similar result is also reported by Isaka (1996) in a study with a virtually identical method in Japan. By contrast, in the Canadian sample the self-ratings were evaluatively more positive than the other-ratings, suggesting the presence of an opposite, self-enhancing tendency.

It is important that self-criticism in China and self-enhancement in Canada varied across different domains of personality. In terms of the big-five classificatory scheme, in China self-criticism was remarkably strong for emotional stability, agreeableness, and conscientiousness, virtually nonexistent for surgency, and somewhat reversed for openness to experience. By contrast, in Canada self-enhancement was strongest for surgency and openness to experience, moderate for agreeableness and conscientiousness, and virtually nonexistent for emotional stability. The authors suggest that agentic domains such as surgency and openness to experience lend themselves to self-enhancement while domains of communion, such as agreeableness and conscientiousness, to self-criticism.

"Better-Than-Average" Effects   One important class of tasks used in contemporary personality and social psychology to demonstrate self-enhancement is to ask respondents to make a comparative judgment between the self and others in a given population and show that the "average" respondent thinks that he or she is better than the average other (Taylor and Brown 1988). In one of these tasks subjects are asked to judge the proportion of others in a given group who are better than themselves in a given domain. If the subjects make this estimate without any bias toward enhancement or criticism, the overall mean of all the subjects should converge to 50 percent. Curiously North American subjects typically underestimate this proportion. This judgmental bias, called the false uniqueness effect, may be taken to suggest that individuals in North America are bound to judge the self in a self-enhancing fashion, to be better than what it "really" is. Another task of the same type involves asking subjects to make a judgment of how vulnerable they think they are to a variety of risks as compared to average others in a given population (Weinstein 1979). Again, in the absence of any psychological bias, the perceived vulnerabilities of all the subjects should converge to the vulnerability rating for average others. Yet in North America the self is judged to be less vulnerable than average others, hence suggesting an illusorily optimistic tendency, which in turn may well have resulted from the operation of self-enhancing tendencies.

Neither of these two effects, however, happens in any clear-cut fashion in Japan. Thus Markus and Kitayama (1991b) showed that a false uniqueness bias was quite pronounced in a North American sample but virtually nonexistent in a comparable Japanese sample. Likewise Heine and Lehman (1995) found a quite robust illusory optimism in Canada but virtually no similar effect in Japan. In both cases the absence of the bias cannot be accounted for by positing that the Japanese rated themselves to be moderate, around right in the middle of the population. In fact the average variance of responses does not typically differ across cultures.

In this class of tasks, very little evidence exists for self-criticism among East Asians. These findings are in sharp contrast with other types of tasks where evidence for self-criticism is much more marked. At present it is not clear why this is the case. A recent study by Matsumoto and Kitayama (1998) suggests that a more careful analysis on domains or contents of judgment may lead to a fuller understanding of the cross-cultural differences in these tasks. Focusing on the false-uniqueness effect, these researchers asked both Japanese and American respondents to judge what proportion of others in their own colleges were better than themselves in each of 20 different domains. When the 20 domains were combined, a quite reliable self-enhancing bias was found for Americans, who on average judged only 32.4 percent of others to be better than themselves. This effect was entirely disappeared for Japanese with the overall mean of 50.2 percent.

As in the Yik et al. study reviewed above, however, Matsumoto and Kitayama also found considerable variations among the 20 domains of judgment. The results for each domain are summarized in figure 6.3 separately for Japan and the United States. The average ratings greater than 50 indicate self-enhancement and those smaller than 50 show self-criticism. As can be seen, self-enhancement was found across the board for all the 20 domains in the United States. At the same time, however, the magnitude of the effect varied considerably. Thus it was strongest for sympathy, trustworthiness, sincerity, and sensitivity and weakest on decision-making ability, "brain," confidence, and diligence. Japanese results showed an analogous variation. Thus, for domains of sympathy, creativity, sincerity, and sensitivity, reliable self-enhancing effects were evident. But for domains of diligence, interpersonal skills, attractiveness, and confidence, there was a reliable self-critical tendency. Overall, then, self-enhancement in North America and self-criticism in Japan depend in part on the domains being assessed.

The pattern observed by Matsumoto and Kitayama conforms only partially to Yik et al's (1998) suggestion that self-criticism in Asia is most pronounced in the domains of communion and self-enhancement is most pronounced in the domains of autonomy. It is more in line with the findings by Markus and Kitayama (1991b), which indicated that self-enhancement is strongest in the domain of interdependence, weakest in the domain of abilities, with the domain of independence falling in-between. More research is required to determine which are the exact domains or properties of domains that invite the respective psychological tendencies. Nevertheless, it is clear that these psychological tendencies are not static psychological markers of different cultural groups. To the contrary, they are collectively constructed and held

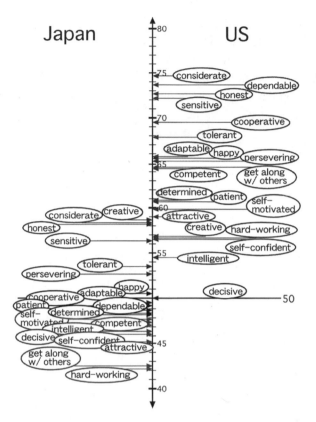

Figure 6.3
False uniqueness effect (or the absence thereof) in Japan and the United States.

in place in conjunction with the ways in which different domains or facets of social life are constructed in the respective cultural contexts. Thus these psychological tendencies may not be purely psychological, but instead, they may be sustained by the ways in which pertinent social realities are constructed in each cultural context.

Collective Construction of Self-relevant Psychological Tendencies   Kitayama et al. (1997) have found evidence that above psychological tendencies are collectively constructed in that they are both afforded and sustained by ways in which mundane self-relevant social situations are defined. These researchers prepared 400 social situations, described in sentences, that were randomly sampled from a larger set of situations that had been generated by Japanese college undergraduates and those generated by their American counterparts. Both Japanese and American college undergraduates were asked to read each of these situations and to judge whether and to what extent their own self-esteem would increase or decrease in each situation if they were in it. The American group responded with a strong self-enhancing tendency. Thus they judged that their self-esteem would increase more in the success situations than it would decrease in the failure situations. By contrast, the Japanese group showed a marked tendency for self-criticism; they judged that their self-esteem would decrease more in the failure situations than it would increase in the success situations.

Critical perceptions and appraisals of the self prevalent in Japan and self-enhancing perceptions and appraisals of the self in the United States are not only psychological phenomena. They are also collective and socially shared in that they are afforded, encouraged, and invited by the very ways in which social situations that are common in each cultural context are constructed. Half of the situations used by the aforementioned study by Kitayama and colleagues (Kitayama et al. 1997) had been sampled from the Japanese cultural context and the remaining half, from the American cultural context. In addition to the self-critical appraisal in Japan and the self-enhancing appraisal in the United States, described above, we found that the situations sampled from Japan and those sampled from the United States had unique influences on these appraisals. Thus the American success situations were judged by both Japanese and American respondents to increase their self-esteem more than the American failure situations were to decrease it. Hence the American self-enhancement was produced in part because the social situations that were common in this cultural context encouraged or invited this tendency. Conversely, the Japanese failure situations were judged by both Japanese and American respondents to decrease their self-esteem more than the Japanese success situations were to increase it. Hence self-criticism in Japan was a response tendency that was resonant with and in fact invited by the very social situations prevalent in this cultural context. Together, American respondents were most self-enhancing when responding to American situations and Japanese respondents, most self-critical when responding to Japanese situations.

What is it about American and Japanese situations that encourage the divergent psychological tendencies? In our re-analysis of the situations in the above study, we found first that the situations generated by the Japanese focused on the other (e.g., my self-esteem increases when my family members praise me) 2.3 times as often as they focused on the self (e.g., my self-esteem increases when I have a girlfriend).

However, for Americans the number of situations focusing on the self and those focusing on the other was the same.

Further, in support of the idea that the American self is constructed within a system that is characterized by mutual approval, praise, and admiration, we found that 35 percent of the success situations generated by the Americans involved being praised or approved. Of these situation a third involved self-approval and another 45 percent involved approval from romantic partners, friends, or family members. In almost half of the cases the approval or praise was nonspecific such that no mention was made of what the praise or approval was about (e.g., "my self-esteem increases when someone tells me she loves me"). In almost half of the American approval or praise situations, no mention was made of what the praise or approval was about—they were nonspecific (e.g., "my self-esteem increases when someone tells me she loves me"). For the Japanese, we found that 26 percent of the success situations generated involved being praised or approved. But only 12 percent involved self-approval and only 20 percent involved approval from romantic partners, friends, or family members. In over half of these situations, the person providing the praise or the support was not mentioned (e.g., "when I am told my cooking is good"). Further the most common reason for the approval or appraise was a specific talent.

With respect to the failure situations, we found that 39 percent of the situations generated by the Japanese and 41 percent of the situations generated by the Americans involved criticism or social disapproval. For the Americans most criticism came from the self and peers. For the Japanese the source of the majority of the criticism was unspecified (e.g., when I realize that people have been saying bad things behind my back). For the Japanese the next most common failure situation was being excluded from the group, while for the Americans it was individual failure.

Although still preliminary, the foregoing analysis suggests that American success situations are characterized by those elements that make both Japanese and Americans feel good, while Japanese failure situations are configured with those elements that afford relatively negative feelings about the self for both Americans and Japanese. These social situations constitute the "collective landscape" of the respective cultural context. This "landscape" is often invisible and therefore difficult to capture in self-report measures of cultural values or beliefs. Nonetheless, it defines the semiotic frame for every psychological action and reaction. It is the social or interpersonal field or the mundane informal structure (as opposed to formal structure, e.g., institutionalized socioeconomic hierarchy) that has the potential of evoking certain meanings, inviting responses in their all modalities—cognitive, emotional, motivational, or behavioral, and thus affording psychological systems of some kinds—not of all kinds. Put differently, all these psychological processes are collectively constructed by each individual's active participation and engagement in each distinct cultural world. This implies that the "collective landscape" of each cultural region should also be fully taken into account in any analysis of subjective and objective well-being across cultures.

Good Feelings across Cultures

Correlates of Subjective Well-being   One important element of subjective well-being is to experience good feelings. Although it might seem innocuous to assume that good feelings are good feelings for any peoples, what in fact constitutes the good feelings may well depend on culture. We have noted above that self-enhancement, involving personal success, promotion, and pursuit of happiness, is a significant element in the mode of being in European-American cultural contexts. But it is self-criticism, relative focus on negative aspects and own sufferings that constitute the mode of being in East Asian cultural groups. This of course should not be taken to imply that people in East Asia never feel good. They do experience good feelings, but these good feelings may not be associated with self-promotion or enhancement, or more or less explicit pursuit of such feelings. Instead, general good feelings, or a sense of well-being, is something that can emerge out of a self-critical stance sustained on the self and thus an ensuing interpersonal engagement of the self with others in a social relationship. As illustrated in figures 6.1a and b, in European-American cultures good feelings are associated with participating in some form of mutually approving relationship, but in East Asian cultures it may be participation in a certain form of mutually sympathetic relationship that is most closely associated with good feelings.

Some initial evidence has been obtained by Kitayama, Markus, and Kurokawa (2000). These researchers asked both American and Japanese college students to report a frequency with which they experienced each of many emotions. Five types of emotions were included (see Kitayama, Markus, and Matsumoto 1995). First is a set of positive emotions that typically result from an affirmation of the self as independent, efficacious, and competent, such as pride and feelings of superiority. Second are those that typically result from an affirmation of the self as interdependent, connected to others, and relational, such as close feelings, friendly feelings, and feelings of respect. Third are those that typically result from a threat on the self's independence and competence and that thus typically motivates the person to resist the threat such as anger and disgust. Fourth are those that typically result from a threat on the self's interdependence and relationality and that thus typically motivate the person to restore it, such as shame and guilt. The final set of emotions is also positive but relatively general "elated," "calm," and "happy." They are not contingent on any specific types of antecedents. These general good feelings provide the best proxy for subjective well-being.

Kitayama and colleagues first ascertained that the reported frequencies of the emotions within each set were highly correlated. They then went on to examine the correlations among the three types of positive emotions. The results were consistent with the idea that general good feelings are associated with participation in the respective cultural complexes of either self-esteem and mutually approving relationships in the United States or self-criticism and mutually sympathetic relationships. Thus, for American data, the reported frequency for the general good feelings was highly correlated with the reported frequency for the interpersonally disengaged, independent emotions ($r = 0.54$). The corresponding correlation was significantly lower for the interpersonally engaged, interdependent emotions ($r = 0.30$). By contrast, for Japanese data the pattern was completely reversed. Thus the correlation with the general good feelings was much higher for the interdependent emotions than for the independent emotions ($rs = 0.58$ and 0.20, respectively).

Notice that positive disengaging emotions (e.g., pride) are more arousing than equally positive but engaging emotions (e.g., close feelings). Therefore it might be the case that the cross-cultural difference observed above was mediated by arousal such that Americans are more likely than Japanese to experience general good feelings when they are stimulated and aroused. Extensive value surveys conducted by Schwartz and colleagues have shown that values of individualism and independence are closely associated with emotional stimulation (see Smith and Schwartz 1997 for a review). If so, however, the cross-cultural difference observed above would take different forms for general feelings that vary in the associated levels of arousal. The American result should be evident mostly for highly arousing general good feelings, but the Japanese result should be observed largely for less arousing ones. Fortunately, Kitayama et al. used three terms for general good feelings that differed in their levels of arousal. Thus one (i.e., elated) was clearly more arousing than the remaining two (i.e., calm, relaxed). Hence we computed correlations between each of these general feeling terms and the two more specific types of good feelings, that is, engaged and disengaged. Relevant correlations are summarized in table 6.1 sep-

Table 6.1
Correlations between each of the general feeling terms used in the present research and the two more specific types of good feelings (engaged or disengaged) in Japan and the United States

	Japanese		American	
	Men	Women	Men	Women
Correlation between the positive disengaged emotions and				
Elated feelings	0.39	0.30	0.58	0.62
Relaxed feelings	0.25	0.06	0.66	0.68
Calm feelings	0.15	0.10	0.61	0.59
Happiness	0.34	0.27	—	—
Correlation between the positive engaged emotions and				
Elated feelings	0.80	0.81	0.06	0.30
Relaxed feelings	0.71	0.68	0.33	0.30
Calm feelings	0.54	0.46	0.38	0.29
Happiness	0.81	0.79	—	—

arately for males and females. The pattern of association between the two specific types of good feelings and the general good feelings was similar regardless of the levels of arousal associated with the terms used to designate general good feelings. Hence it is unlikely that the current finding was an artifact generated by a supposedly strong preference of Americans for arousing experiences.

These data are consistent with the current framework in that with a cultural premise and imperative of the self as independent, social motivations are bound to be centered around the culturally sanctioned concern for discovering and confirming desirable internal attributes of the self. Such internal attributes may include, although they by no means are limited to, positive subjective feelings (Suh et al. 1998). By contrast, with a cultural premise and imperative of the self as interdependent, social motivations may tend to be anchored around the culturally authorized concern for fitting in or adjusting oneself to interpersonal context and for maintaining mutually engaging social relationships. In further support of the current analysis, Kwan et al. (1997) have shown that one's engagement in a harmonious relationship contributes to life satisfaction, and this association is stronger in Hong Kong than in the United

States. Although the current findings are derived from only two cultural groups, they resonate with the results from a large cross-national study on self-esteem and subjective well-being. Thus Diener and Diener (1995) found that self-esteem (analogous to disengaged positive emotions, e.g., pride) is strongly related to subjective well-being (analogous to generalized positive emotions, e.g., happy) in individualist cultures such as the United States but only moderately so in collectivist cultures such as Japan (see also Suh, Diener, and Triandis 1998).

Maximization of Positivity versus Balancing of Positivity and Negativity—Two Viable Strategies?   Another striking cross-cultural difference observed in the Kitayama et al. (2000) study concerns the correlations between positive and negative emotions. As shown in figure 6.4, these correlations were largely negative in the United States. This finding is consistent with the proposal in the current social psychological literature that negative emotions can be reduced by positive events or ideations about them even in totally unrelated domains (e.g., Steele 1988). Further this proposition is predicated on the assumption that many Americans focus pri-

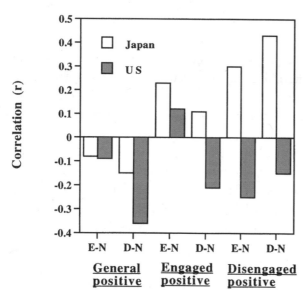

Figure 6.4
Correlations of three positive emotion types (general, engaged, and disengaged) with two negative emotion types (engaged [E–N] and disengaged [D–E]) on Japan, and the United States (based on Kitayama, Markus, and Kurokawa 2000).

marily on pleasantness when experiencing emotions (see Feldman 1995). Given this sociopsychological dynamic of emotional experience, a reasonable recommendation for well-being is to maximize positive feelings and minimize negative feelings—the one often advocated in media and daily discourses in the contemporary American popular culture. The only exception to the antagonistic relationship between positive and negative emotions was the correlation between positive engaged emotions (e.g., friendly feelings) and negative engaged emotions (e.g., guilt), which was marginally positive ($p < 0.10$). This is consistent with the hypothesis that interpersonally positive events are not truly good and thus are not associated with general good feelings.

By contrast, in Japan the correlations between good feelings and negative were mostly positive. If nothing else, this finding suggests that good events in Japan may often fail to carry unequivocally positive connotations. For example, interpersonally engaging experiences may often carry negative repercussions such as ensuing obligations and worries. Likewise personally successful experiences may also result in certain negative consequences such as envy by others or concerns about "standing out" too much. Conversely, negative events may not be perceived to be totally bad and devastating, as long as these events are perceived to invite positive experiences such as sympathy from others or additional opportunities for learning and improvement. As a consequence many Japanese may be primed relatively more to an arousal dimension than to a pleasantness dimension when experiencing emotions (see Feldman 1995). In such a cultural context, the recommendation of choice for attaining well-being is not to maximize positivity or to minimize negativity, but to keep a good balance between them so as to stay "calm," "undisturbed," "unaroused," and thus "healthy." Indeed, traditional medicine in Eastern cultures, especially in China and associated areas including Japan, has emphasized such a balance of bodily substances and spirits, or that of yin and yang (Kitayama and Markus 1999; Ohnuki-Tierney 1984).

One striking consequence of the cross-culturally divergent, socially and collectively sustained strategies of emotion management—maximization of positivity/minimization of negativity in North America and balancing of positivity and negativity in Japan—was revealed in the reported frequencies of experiencing positive and negative emotions. In the United States the reported frequency of emotional experience was much higher for positive emotions than for negative emotions. Consistent with the strong focus and emphasis on positivity—happiness, esteem, efficacy, and control—of American selves as reviewed earlier, the finding here indicates that

Americans do pursue, with a good deal of success at least at the level of subjective experience, positive affectivity in life. But the effect is entirely absent in Japan. Although predicted by our analysis, this contrast between the American and the Japanese data proved quite notable in its magnitude. Whereas in the American data nearly half of the entire variation among the 31 emotions (67 percent for males and 38 percent for females) was accounted for in terms of their evaluative connotations as positive or negative, the corresponding proportion in Japan was nearly zero.

Perhaps, given the lay theories of yin and yang, the cultural ideal of balancing of competing forces in life, and a closely knit web of interpersonal relations where positive interpersonal feedback of sympathy is often contingent upon self-critical attitudes, suffering, and difficulties, negative emotions and positive emotions may likely be perceived to be both bad in their excess, and thus to be avoided. Only when the person detaches him or herself from a seemingly natural desire for good feelings and an aversion against bad feelings can he or she most effectively immerse him or herself in the web of mutually sympathetic relations, which in turn may well ensure the emergence of subjective well-being, life satisfaction, and thus happiness. In East Asia, therefore, happiness may not be what one wishes to pursue. If one does, it will go away—if one doesn't, it may come.

Overall, then, in East Asia subjective well-being may be moderate by its very nature. This is in stark contrast to the predominantly American middle-class ethos of maximization of individual happiness as the criterion of subjective well-being. This consideration raises one important methodological issue. The scale of subjective well-being that is most frequently used in the literature mostly consists of items that solicit an agreement with unqualified positivity and idealness of one's own life, such as "The conditions of my life are excellent" or "So far I have gotten the important things I want in life" (Diener and Diener 1998). The degree of positivity implied here may fit well to the American ethos of pursuit of happiness; however, it may seem somewhat excessive given the East Asian sensibility for balance and moderacy. It is a future challenge of this field to develop a measure of subjective well-being that has a better ethnographic and cultural validity as applied to cultural contexts other than the contemporary North America.

Sympathy and Implicit Self-attachment in Japan

A seemingly curious dialectic of well-being in East Asian cultural context has to be examined more fully and thoroughly before grasping the entire scope of subjective and objective well-being as constructed in this cultural region. Self-critical attitudes seem to be prerequisites for well-being, and especially for good feelings associated with the self. Yet, once one has incorporated these feelings into him or herself to elevate his or her own self-evaluations, the self-critical attitudes will go away and so will the good feelings. The nature of this dialectic may be pursued at least in two directions. First, the other-orientedness or sympathetic tendencies to others may well be reciprocated as long as these orientations and tendencies are perceived to be "genuine"—that is, if they are not perceived to be motivated by self-related concerns such as the wish to be reciprocated by others to whom one extends sympathy. Second, well-being within the scheme of self-criticism and mutually sympathetic relationships is likely to be intersubjective—not neatly fitted into each individual participant in the relationship. A consideration of these two points follows.

Sympathy and Interpersonal Reciprocity   To begin with, our analysis implies that the psychological tendency of sympathy is the intra-individual phase of participating in the cultural complex of a mutually sympathetic relationship (see figure 6.1b). If so, sympathetic people should be both givers and receivers of support and help. The reciprocity is ensured between sympathetic people, in part because the psychological tendency of sympathy helps them to participate in mutually sympathetic cultural complexes. It is also possible that the sympathetic psychological tendency is a consequence of participating in such relationships. It may thus be predicted that with sympathetic tendency, not only the reported frequency of helping others but also the reported frequency of being helped by others would increase.

To examine this possibility, Uchida and Kitayama (1998) developed a scale of interpersonal sympathy that is grounded in the Japanese cultural practices and meanings. We first asked a group of 12 Japanese college students to describe both people who are sympathetic and those who lack sympathy. Drawing on the descriptions, a tentative set of 56 items designed to measure sympathy were written. Another group of 126 college students were subsequently asked to report the degree to which each item would apply to themselves. A factor analysis showed a single-factor structure in the data; thus the researchers chose 22 items that had relatively high factor loadings to yield a sympathy scale, such that half (10) were reverse-coded items, and that the content domains described were as diverse as possible. Sample items are given in table 6.2. In several samples the scale has proved to be quite reliable ($\alpha > 0.80$). Further the scale had a systematic relationship with other existent scales, thus positively correlating with emotional empathy (Mehrabian and Epstein 1972, $r = 0.72$), interdependent construal of the self (Singelis 1994,

Table 6.2
Sample items of the sympathy scale developed by Uchida and Kitayama (1998)

Sometimes I feel like praying for someone who is going through hardship.

I don't think I am easily moved to tears.*

While everything is going well with me, but think about my friend who is in trouble, I feel sorry for him/her.

When someone is outcast from a group, it must be his/her own fault.*

Even if someone does their best, it means nothing if they are not successful.*

When I see a person who is doing their best, I feel like I want to cheer them up.

Note: Asterisk indicates reversely worded items.

$r = 0.55$), self-monitoring (Snyder 1974, $r = 0.30$), and general trust (Yamagishi, Cook, and Watabe 1998, $r = 0.33$), but largely independent of independent construal of the self (Singelis 1994, $r = 0.02$) and self-esteem (Rosenberg 1965, $r = 0.05$).

In order to test the notion that sympathy is mutual, Kitayama and Uchida (1998, Study 1) asked Japanese college undergraduates ($N = 125$) to report how frequently they engaged in each of 16 helping acts preselected by Kikuchi (1988) to be fairly common in daily life of the Japanese cultural context. Because there were substantial inter-item correlations, the responses for them were averaged to form a single index of the perceived frequency of giving help. The respondents were also asked to report how frequently they received each of 20 kinds of support and help from someone they knew. These 20 kinds of support had also been preselected by Hisada, Senda, and Minoguchi (1989) to be fairly common among Japanese college students. Again, since the responses were mutually correlated, they were combined to yield a single index of the perceived frequency of receiving help. In addition to these measures of interpersonal reciprocity, the respondents completed the sympathy scale, Snyder's self-monitoring scale, and Rosenberg's self-esteem scale. These three scales were used to predict the degree of reciprocity.

The results are summarized in figure 6.5. As predicted, with sympathy not only the perceived frequency of offering help, but also that of receiving help increased ($\beta s = 0.40, 0.35$, $ps < 0.001$). The other two personality measures predicted only one of the two frequency measures. Thus self-monitoring was related to the perceived frequency of offering help but not to that of receiving help ($\beta = 0.30$, $p < 0.001$, $\beta = 0.10$, n.s.), whereas self-esteem was related to the perceived frequency of receiving help ($\beta = 0.26$, $p < 0.001$) but not to that of offering help ($\beta = 0.12$,

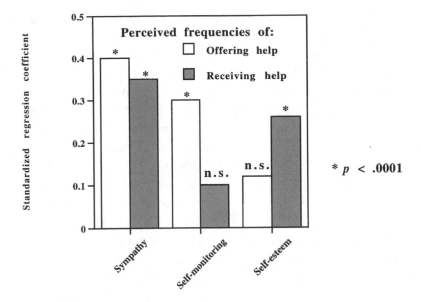

Figure 6.5
Predicting the perceived frequencies of offering and receiving help as a function of sympathy,
self-monitoring, and self-esteem (Kitayama and Uchida 1998).

n.s.). Among the three personality measures examined here, it was only sympathy
that was related with both offering ($\beta = 0.43$, $p < 0.001$) and receiving help ($\beta = 0.56$, $p < 0.001$). In their second study Kitayama and Uchida (1998) replicated the
association between sympathy and the perceived frequencies of both offering and
receiving help. In addition they found that the general belief that people are trust-
worthy (Yamagishi, Cook, and Watabe 1998) is correlated with the perceived frequencies of both offering and receiving help, but these effects are entirely vanished
once the effect of sympathy is statistically controlled. On the basis of these data,
Kitayama and Uchida concluded that at least in Japanese cultural contexts general
trust is a consequence of participating in mutually sympathetic relationships.

The effects of self-monitoring deserves a comment. Self-monitoring is a tendency
to act deliberately and strategically to conform to expectations of others and to
manipulate impressions they may have of the self. Hence it is to be anticipated that
those with a greater self-monitoring tendency often offer help. But the underlying
motivation for the helping behavior is not intrinsic. Rather than feeling compelled
to help because of the personal need in a relationship, they may well be motivated

to offer help because of impression management concerns. Hence they may feel most strongly motivated to help someone to the extent that doing so is an effective means for impression management. Consistent with this analysis, Kitayama and Uchida find that with self-monitoring tendencies, one is more likely to offer help. Importantly, however, those high in self-monitoring do not receive any more help than those low in self-monitoring. Supposedly, within a tightly knit interdependent relationship, one's ulterior motive is likely to be noticed by others, and once this is so noticed, it is likely to nullify any tendencies to reciprocate any items in return in the form of sympathy. Thus the intentional pursuit of getting help from the others by offering help is unlikely to produce any desired outcome within the social relationships grounded in the model of mutual sympathy. In other words, the strategy of tit-for-tat, if exercised intentionally and strategically, may not work.

Could the role of sympathy in giving and receiving help be generalized across cultures? Our preliminary data suggest that the answer is likely to be no. Kitayama and Uchida (1999a) asked 79 Japanese undergraduates and 76 American undergraduates to fill out several scales including the ones of the perceived frequencies of offering and receiving help. The results are summarized in table 6.3. In Japan, sympathy was reliably associated with the reported frequencies of both offering and receiving help, but in the United States, such an association was found only for the reported frequency of receiving help. Furthermore the data provided initial support for the contention that getting interpersonal support is associated with the cultural mandates of either independence in the United States or interdependence in Japan. Thus, in Japan, the reported frequency of receiving help increased with other interdependence-related variables (self-sympathy and interdependent construal of self) but decreased with independent construal of self. By contrast, in the United States, it reliably increased with self-esteem.

In this study we also asked the respondents to report the frequency of experiencing several general good feelings such as happy, relaxed, elated, and calm. The aforementioned study by Kitayama et al. (2000) had shown that these general good feelings are associated with interpersonal engagement and interdependence in Japan. We suggest that in the Japanese cultural context sympathetic psychological tendencies invite socioemotional support from others in a relationship. Because the recognition of such support affirms the sense of the self as interdependent, it should conduce to a higher frequency of feeling generally good. By contrast, Kitayama et al. (2000) had found that in American cultural context, the general good feelings are associated primarily with interpersonal disengagement and independence. We

Table 6.3
Predicting the reported frequencies of offering and receiving help as a function of sympathy, self-esteem, and several other variables in Japan and the United States

	Japanese respondents		American respondents	
	Offer	Receive	Offer	Receive
Sympathy[a]	0.31*	0.39***	0.11	0.32**
Self-sympathy[b]	−0.01	0.24*	−0.02	−0.05
Self-esteem[c]	−0.03	0.15	−0.06	0.26*
Independent construal of self[d]	0.09	−0.26**	0.17	0.09
Interdependent construal of self[d]	0.18	0.21*	−0.07	0.16
General trust[e]	0.02	0.02	0.16	0.13

Note: Levels of significance indicated as $+p < 0.10$, $*p < 0.05$, $**p < 0.01$, $***p < 0.001$.
a. Sympathy was measured by the scale developed by Uchida and Kitayama (1998; see table 6.2).
b. Self-sympathy refers to the tendency to hold sympathetic attitudes to the self. This tendency is assumed to be a source for positive self-attachment of Japanese selves who maintain self-critical attitudes (Kitayama and Markus 1999). It was measured by statements such as "When I achieve something like passing an entrance examination or getting a license, I sometimes look back on my hardship and think, 'I did a good job'" and "If I get hurt or become ill, I feel sympathetic toward myself."
c. Self-esteem was measured by a scale developed by Rosenberg (1965).
d. Both independent and interdependent construals of the self were measured by a scale developed by Singelis (1994).
e. General trust was measured by a scale developed by Yamagishi, Cook, and Watabe (1998).

suggest that in this cultural context the esteem of the self that is detached from the surrounding is the major focus in affirming the self, and as a consequence increased self-esteem should lead to a higher frequency of feeling generally good.

To examine these possibilities, Kitayama and Uchida (1999a) regressed the perceived frequency of experiencing the general good feelings on both the perceived frequency of receiving help and self-esteem. The results are summarized in table 6.4. As predicted, the perceived frequency of experiencing the general good feelings were best predicted by self-esteem in the United States, but it was predicted equally well or even better by the perceived frequency of receiving help than by self-esteem in Japan. Thus, in the Japanese cultural context interdependent orientations, especially sympathetic tendencies, enable one to participate in mutually benefiting interpersonal relations (table 6.3), which in turn leads to general good feelings and thus to a sense of well-being. By contrast, in the United States it is mostly self-esteem and the

Table 6.4

Contribution of self-esteem and the reported frequency of receiving help in predicting the reported frequency of experiencing four general positive feelings

	Japanese respondents		American respondents	
	Self-esteem	Frequency of receiving help	Self-esteem	Frequency of receiving help
Happy	0.29**	0.40***	0.35***	0.20+
Relaxed	0.12	0.25*	0.41***	0.14
Elated	0.22*	0.24*	0.21+	0.06
Calm	0.18	0.10	0.37***	0.08
Combined	0.30**	0.37***	0.49***	0.18+

Note: Levels of significance indicated as $+p < 0.10$, $*p < 0.05$, $**p < 0.01$, $***p < 0.001$.

predisposition toward positivity that leads to a frequent experience of these general good feelings. The recognition of relatedness, as represented here in terms of the perceived frequency of receiving help, had only a marginal effect on the frequency of experiencing general good feelings.

Good Feelings as an Intersubjective State   Typically, in the current social science literature, emotions are conceptualized to be purely psychological, subjective experience both rooted in and animated by internal programs of affect (Ekman 1984). Social factors are subsequently brought back in to the theoretical framework in the forms of either antecedents (i.e., cognitive appraisals) or consequences of the operation of the affect programs (see Kitayama and Markus 1994; Kitayama and Masuda 1995; White 1994, for critical appraisals of this literature). Good feelings, well-being, and happiness are no exception. They are conceptualized as properties of an individual, a subjective state well bounded in him or herself (see figure 6.6a). This construal of well-being is in accordance with European-American lay theories and practices of the self and emotion in general and those of well-being and life satisfaction in particular. Thus subjective well-being may well be a summary of affective values attached to concrete and discrete personal experiences one had in the past (Kahneman 1999).

By contrast, our analysis implies that the good feelings in Japan may be much more interpersonal and communal. They are not possessed or owned by the self; rather they are shared in a relationship, and, by virtue of this sharedness, the good

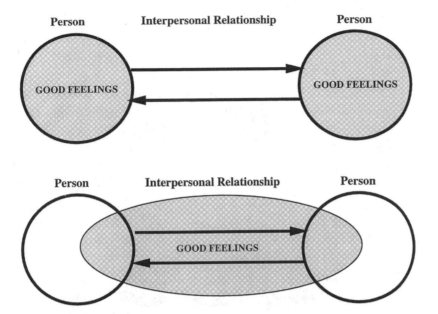

Figure 6.6
Two construals of good feelings: (a) Happiness as a subjective state that "belongs to" an individual person and thus experienced as a personal property (common in European-American cultural contexts) and (b) happiness as an intersubjective state that is "shared" with others and thus experienced as a property of the interpersonal atmosphere (common in East Asian cultural contexts).

feelings are associated with the self (see Mesquita 1993 for an important analysis on sharedness of emotions). Many researchers of emotion in Asian communities have commented that emotions in Asian cultural contexts are construed to be much more social and communal, serving as an index of the nature of the attendant social relationship, as much as (or even rather than) they reveal inner affective states (e.g., Lutz 1988). Likewise Menon and Shweder (1998) suggest that well-being of Indian women is immersed in the notions of social harmony, cyclic continuity of the extended household and lineage, and associated duties and obligations (see LeVine and LeVine 1998, for an East African case, and Shore 1998, for a Samoan case).

A dramatic consequence of the cross-culturally divergent construals of inner sensations has been shown in a cross-cultural investigation of facial feedback processes. Levenson and colleagues (Levenson et al. 1992) have shown that once the face is posed to mimic expressions of different emotions, there typically result both systematic changes in different aspects of autonomic activation, such as blood pressure, galvanic skin response, and heart rate, and corresponding changes in subjective experience of emotions in North America. Consistent with a large body of studies on facial feedback hypothesis (Matsumoto 1987), this work indicates that inner sensations caused by contraction of facial musculature of, say, grimace or smile, are often enough to generate an emotional state, albeit a slight and perhaps diminished one, of anger or happiness. Yet, in a Sumatran village where the researchers conducted the same study, they failed to find comparable changes in the subjective experience of emotional states, though they replicated the physiological changes that were contingent on posed facial expressions. The researchers commented that in Asian cultural contexts interpersonal context serves as an important element of emotional experience, so much so that without an appropriate interpersonal context provided, the inner sensations are not sufficient to produce any distinct emotional experience.

In Japan as well, emotional states are acknowledged to be constituted significantly by the nature of interpersonal relationships, and this may well apply to well-being, good feelings, and happiness. As shown in figure 6.6b, good feelings are likely to be contingent on mutually sympathetic interpersonal relationships involving mutual adjustment, sympathy, and the giving and taking of care and help. These feelings are likely to go away once one leaves, even temporarily, the relationship. Therefore they are not perceived to be owned by the self, but instead they are categorized to be in the "space" between the self and his or her partner in the relationship or in the atmosphere.

One important consequence of this is that Japanese individuals are unlikely to report good feelings once they explicitly focus on themselves and make self-evaluations. As noted earlier, the Japanese do not reportedly experience good feelings any more frequently than bad feelings. In fact they often draw negative, self-critical inferences when asked to evaluate themselves. Yet the Japanese mode of being a self in a social relationship is grounded in the cultural ideas of sympathy, compassion, and adjustment, and therefore the negative, critical, and at best ambivalent attitudes or evaluations of the self toward itself invites the interpersonal sharing of good feelings. These good feelings in turn are likely to contribute to the sense of well-being and general life satisfaction. In short, Japanese selves are critical and disciplined, and thus do not show any obvious tendency to elevate self-evaluation. Yet these disciplined selves should be associated with interpersonally shared good feelings.

Initial evidence has been obtained in a series of studies conducted in Japan with implicit self-attachment tasks. For example, Kitayama and Karasawa (1997) asked Japanese subjects to report their preferences of letters in the Japanese alphabet and showed that any single letter was liked by those who possessed it in their names more than the remaining letters (e.g., see also Greenwald and Banaji 1995; Hoorens et al. 1990; Nuttin 1985). In addition to this name letter effect, Uchida and Kitayama (1999) have also obtained evidence for implicit self-attachment in Japan with a version of the "implicit association test" developed by Greenwald and colleagues (Greenwald, McGhee, and Schwartz 1998). On half of the experimental trials subjects were to indicate whether a handwriting was their own or someone else's, whereas on the remaining half they were to judge the evaluative meaning of an emotional word. These two types of trials were randomly ordered. In the self-good condition, the subjects were to tap their left knee with their left hand either if the handwriting was their own or if the word was positive. If, however, the handwriting was someone else's or if the word was negative, they were to tap their right knee with their right hand. In the self-bad condition, the response combination was reversed so that the self (or other) judgment for handwritings was combined with the bad (or good) judgment for words. Uchida and Kitayama observed that the time required to complete all the trials was considerably shorter in the self-good condition than in the self-bad condition, thus demonstrating the presence of implicit association between self and positive evaluation.

Importantly, in a recent series of studies Kitayama and Uchida (1999b) have shown that the implicit self-attachment as measured by the name letter effect is correlated with sympathy as measured by a personality inventory once an interpersonal context is reinstated. To reinstate interpersonal contexts, we sometimes asked subjects to think how they are blessed or not blessed (most Japanese mention events of interpersonal nature), and at other times we had subjects indicate whether or not each of many interpersonally relevant traits (caring, helpful, honest, etc.) were descriptive of themselves. Regardless of the methods used to reinstate interpersonal contexts, we have consistently found a moderate, but reliable correlation between the implicit self-attachment effect and sympathy ($0.28 < r < 0.45$). Curiously this correlation vanishes if no interpersonal context is reinstated. These data are consistent with the hypothesis that good feelings associated implicitly with the self in Japanese cultural contexts are quite contingent on habitual and constant participation in a mutually sympathetic relationship (as revealed by one's level of sympathetic tendency).

Conclusions

Well-being or happiness is an amorphous concept. It refers to something good about one's mode of being. But what it is that is thought or felt to be good, where and how such thoughts, evaluations, or feelings come about, and the degree to which this assessment is monitored, made focal in conscious experience, reified as an indicator of goodness or badness of one's own state of being, and thus incorporated into the very notion of well-being or happiness itself, vary considerably across cultures. This chapter is just a beginning of deconstructing the notion of happiness as typically used and taken for granted in the contemporary Western social science literature on the topic. We did so by drawing a comparison between contemporary North American culture and contemporary Japanese culture.

Happiness American Style: Pursuit and Expression

According to the independent model of the self that characterizes many, although certainly not all, American cultural contexts, the self is rooted in a set of internal attributes such as personality attributes, preferences, subjective feeling states, and attitudes. A major cultural task, one that is often mutually pursued by caretakers, friends, and teachers in the relevant contexts, is to continually identify these attributes and then to ensure that they are consistently expressed in behavior, recognized, and affirmed. Most American children through ideas and practices repeatedly amplified in the media, in the home, and on the playground seem to quickly develop habits of identifying the positive features of their own and their friends' behaviors, while holding on to the idea that they are just slightly better than their peers. They also develop articulated selves that are distinctly positive and attribute-based and are encouraged to express themselves and take control (Fiske et al. 1998; Markus et al. 1996; Lewis 1995). Moreover, being happy is a dominant concern and a basic value for most North Americans. The Declaration of Independence, for example, proclaims that the pursuit of happiness is an inalienable right. Failing to be happy implies that one is shirking one's responsibility and failing to realize the American cultural mandate. So together Americans construct a world in which they can be happy—they accentuate the positive, affirm each other's selves, and arrange situations that showcase successes and achievements and that allow them to experience themselves as influencing and being in control rather being controlled or influenced (see figure 6.1a).

Bellah, Madsen, Sullivan, Swindler, and Tipton (1985) describe America as a culture of expressive individualism. People who find a way or who are afforded an opportunity to express themselves are those most likely to receive assurances that they are realizing the culturally mandated task, and these are the people who will receive the positive feedback and reassurances from others that will underscore their sense of self. The self reveals itself through actions, and actions in turn serve to actualize, validate, and maintain the self. The best way of laying claim to a particular aspect of the self is to behave in accordance with it. Consequently those who are expressive, outgoing, and active have the greatest likelihood of expressing and affirming the self. Similarly conveying a sense of optimism underscores the sense that one feels positively about the self. Further, expressing one's feelings (particularly one's positive feelings) which are often believed to be unique and defining of the person, fosters the idea of a distinct self that is not like other selves.

Happiness Japanese Style: Dialectic of Well-being

We began this chapter by suggesting that in many cultures outside of contemporary North America, especially in East Asia, well-being or happiness may emerge from sustained attitudes toward the self that are critical, disciplined, and negative. This dynamic is essentially sociocultural in that these attitudes enable the cultural complex of interdependent, mutually sympathetic relationships to sustain itself (see figure 6.1b). From an American perspective, the notion that nonpursuit of happiness invites happiness might be too passive. By itself this is enough to deter or otherwise, pollute the state of happiness. Even worse, if this notion were interpreted within a Machiavellian mindset to imply that nonpursuit of happiness is the best means to strategically pursue happiness, or more specifically, if it were to be taken to suggest that East Asians pretend self-criticism or effacement so as to maximize their self-interest in general and their happiness in particular, then the overwhelming impression would be that of denigration of human integrity or loss of personal dignity.

We maintain that the Machiavellian interpretation is grounded in an independent model of the self, and therefore not revealing but rather distorting the nature of East Asian sensibility and moral commitment (see similar analyses by Menon and Shweder 1998, for an Indian case, and Greenfield 1997b, for ethnicity and intelligence testing). Indeed, a closer scrutiny of the system of mutually sympathetic relationship suggests that happiness can arise from nonpursuit of happiness precisely because of, rather than despite, the fact that one refrains from pursuing it.

For example, suppose that one pretends to be critical to him or herself or to be in difficulty in order to solicit sympathy or support from others. No matter how good an actor the person might be, this pretension might be detected by others in a relationship. And to the extent that this happens, as is likely according to the closeness of the interdependence, the others will stop providing sympathy to the person. We recall the Kitayama and Uchida finding that with self-monitoring tendencies one may offer more help but not receive any more help. And this finding reflects the insight of Marcel Mauss (1925), quoted at the beginning of this chapter, which was based on his study of customs involving gift exchange in non-Western, "archaic" societies. Others' benevolence or good intention, and thus devotion to a relationship, will be felt to be all the more meaningful and genuine if the receiver of the benevolence remains self-disciplined, not expecting these others to extend the support to him or herself. Hence, given the view of the self as socially connected, embedded, and interdependent, a full engagement of the self in a social relationship—and thus happiness, life satisfaction, and well-being, can arise only through actively refraining from the pursuit of happiness or well-being for the personal self and instead maintaining a critical attitude toward the self.

Future Directions

For some time psychologists have been concerned exclusively with negative emotional states such as frustration, aggression, stress, burnout, anxiety, shame, and guilt. Recently they have focused on health and well-being. As psychology broadens to include an analysis of well-being and the meaning of a good life, it will be important to move beyond the cultural commitments that have been inherent in psychological theorizing on illness and disorders and to appreciate from the beginning that contrary to what is typically assumed (e.g., see Seligman 1998), well-being will not always involve the pursuit of positivity. A culturally grounded approach to the nature of well-being, satisfaction, and happiness can nicely supplement earlier research on emotion to produce a fuller account of human emotional experience—its sociocultural and individual dynamics (Ryff and Singer 1998). As we have tried to illuminate in this chapter, many puzzles and unknowns will be clarified in the years to come. In our studies we found that the cultural perspective offers a number of useful directions for future research in this area.

First, it should be recognized that well-being is best conceptualized as an attunement between an individual and his or her sociocultural context. This should be taken more seriously in studies on well-being. While initially the North American mode of well-being appears to be entirely individual and interpersonally detached, upon closer scrutiny it becomes clear that this socially detached mode of being is actually a culturally constructed way of participation in the social and interpersonal context. The same conclusion could be made if the analysis is extended to other cultural contexts where well-being is more explicitly and inseparably contingent on interpersonal and societal structures, relations, and processes (see Menon and Shweder 1998).

Second, the notion that it is good to increase the good and to decrease the bad may be cultural; it is rooted in the European-American ideology of linear progress. Many ideas of Asian origins, such as life cycle (rather than life course), karmic transmigration of souls (rather than fateful decline and eventual death), and yin and yang (rather than maximal happiness for maximal number of people), are grounded in different ideological bases, which, diverse as they might be at first glance, are all rooted in a wholistic conception of the universe and a world where everything is connected with everything else. It is these interdependencies that determine what has happened, what does happen, and what will, in an ever contingent and thus virtually unpredictable fashion. Despite the initial attempt presented in this chapter, implications of the cross-cultural differences in the ideologies of well-being have been left largely unexplored. Often as innocuous and well-intended as they are, various attempts to apply theories of happiness that are implicitly grounded in Western ideas of progress, liberalism, egalitarianism, and freedom to other cultural contexts may not reveal but distort lived experiences of the people in those cultures.

Finally, the literature on well-being has so far been based on large surveys. Although useful in revealing general descriptions, this methodology has inherent limitations. The cultural perspective presented here suggests that cultural meanings are often tacit—they are not recognized by the person who engages in them, and they therefore are unlikely to be revealed in any survey data. A variety of reasons underlie this problem of survey methodology. The most important is that cultural meanings are embodied in patterns of cultural practices and conventions. Such practices and conventions are often tacit, normative, carrying little, if any, subjective significance. Yet they are a significant contributor to subjective well-being. They provide the framework within which individuals, singly or collectively, seek to achieve cultural adaptation in order to attain a state of well-being. Research can benefit from thorough and dense descriptions of the lived world of the peoples under study, and then by bringing this cultural knowledge to bear on the theories and methods developed to test those theories.

Notes

1. "Praise," or "approval," is an act of providing positive feedback to someone who has acted on his own good qualities. Therefore the act of praising cannot be treated as independent of the good act of the other person. Although the qualities of a person are frequently taken as the basis for the act, upon closer examination it should be clear that they are constitutive of the praise itself. That is to say, just as the good qualities are symbolically affirmed and completed by the act of the praise itself, the intention to praise is symbolically affirmed and completed provided that there are reasons for the praise. Therefore concepts like "good character" and "worthy of praise or approval" are constructed interpersonally and collaboratively, and they reflect the entire cultural structure as shown in figure 6.1. While these concepts are understandable in the absence of a cultural context, the psychological and interpersonal correlates can be different depending on the extent to which they are embedded in the cultural structure.

2. As in the independent case, the reason for the sympathy is a necessary element in constituting the expression of sympathy, just as sympathy is necessary in maintaining the meaning of self-criticism. Again, concepts like "sympathy" and "self-criticism" should be regarded as characteristic of an entire cultural structure as is shown in figure 6.2. This is not to deny the obvious fact that sympathy is understandable in the absence of a cultural context. Nevertheless, we suggest that sympathy entails different psychological and interpersonal effects depending on the extent to which it is embedded in the cultural structure.

References

Ames, P. T., Dissanayake, W., and Kasulis, T. P. 1994. *Self as Person in Asian Theory and Practice*. Albany: State University of New York Press.

Baumeister, R. F., and Leary, M. R. 1995. The need to belong: Desire for interpersonal attachments as a fundamental human motivation. *Psychological Bulletin* 117: 497–529.

Berry, J. W., Poortinga, Y. H., Segall, M. H., and Dasen, P. R. 1992. *Cross-cultural Psychology: Research and Applications*. New York: Cambridge University Press.

Bellah, R. N., Madsen, R., Sullivan, W. M., Swindler, A., and Tipton, S. M. 1985. *Habits of the Heart: Individualism and Commitment in American Life*. Berkeley: University of California Press.

Bourdieu, P. 1972. *Outline of a Theory of Practice*. Cambridge: Cambridge University Press.

Bruner, J. 1990. *Acts of Meaning*. Cambridge: Harvard University Press.

Cantor, N., and Sanderson, C. A. 1999. Life task participation and well-being: The importance of taking part in daily life. In D. Kahneman, E. Diener, and N. Schwartz, eds., *Well-being: The Foundations of Hedonic Psychology*. New York: Russell-Sage.

Clark, M. S., and Mills, J. 1979. Interpersonal attraction in exchange and communal relationships. *Journal of Personality and Social Psychology* 37: 12–24.

Cole, M. 1996. *Cultural Psychology*. Cambridge: Harvard University Press.

Cooley, C. H. 1902. *Human Nature and the Social Order.* New York: Scribners.

DeVos, G. A. 1985. Dimensions of the self in Japanese culture. In A. J. Marsella, G. De Vos, and F. L. K. Hsu, eds., *Culture and Self: Asian and Western Perspectives.* New York: Tavistock Publications, pp. 141–82.

Diener, E., and Diener, M. B. 1995. Cross-cultural correlates of life satisfaction and self-esteem. *Journal of Personality and Social Psychology* 68: 653–63.

Diener, E., and Diener, M. B. 1998. Happiness: subjective well-being. In H. S. Friedman, ed., *Encyclopedia of Mental Health*, vol. 2. pp. 311–21.

Diener, E., Suh. E., Lucas, R. E., and Smith, H. L. 1999. Subjective well-being: Three decades of progress. *Psychological Bulletin* 125: 276–302.

Diener, E., Suh, E. M., Smith, H, and Shao, L. 1995. National differences in subjective well-being: Why do they occur? *Social Indicators Research* 34: 7–32.

Durham, W. H. 1991. *Coevolution: Genes, Cultures, and Human Diversity.* Stanford, CA: Stanford University Press.

Durkheim 1964. *The Rules of Sociological Method.* New York: Free Press of Glencoe. (Original work published in 1938.)

Dweck, C. S. 1993. Implicit theories: Individual differences in the likelihood and meaning of dispositional inference. *Personality and Social Psychology Bulletin* 19: 644–56.

Ekman, P. 1984. Expression and the nature of emotion. In K. Scherer and P. Ekman, eds., *Approaches to Emotion.* Lawrence Erlbaum.

Farr, R. 1988. From collective to social representations: Aller et retour. *Culture and Psychology* 4: 275–96.

Feldman, L. A. 1995. Valence-focus and arousal-focus: Individual differences in the structure of affective experience. *Journal of Personality and Social Psychology* 69: 153–66.

Fiske, A. P. 1992. The four elementary forms of sociality: Framework for a unified theory of social relations. *Psychological Review* 99: 689–723.

Fiske, A. P., Kitayama, S., Markus, H. R., and Nisbett, R. E. 1997. The cultural matrix of social psychology. In D. T. Gilbert, S. Fiske, and G. Lindzey, eds., *Handbook of Social Psychology*, 4th ed. New York: McGraw-Hill.

Gergen, K. J., and Gergen, M. M. 1988. Narrative and the self as relationship. In L. Berkowitz, ed., *Advances in Experimental Social Psychology*, vol. 21. pp. 17–56.

Gergen, K., J., Gulerce, A., Lock, A., and Misra, G. 1996. Psychological science in cultural context. *American Psychologist* 51: 496–503.

Giddens, A. 1984. *The Constitution of Society.* Oxford, UK: Polity Press.

Goffman, E. 1959. *The Presentation of Self in Everyday Life.* Garden City, NY: Doubleday.

Goffman, E. 1967. *Interaction Ritual.* New York: Doubleday Anchor.

Greenfield, P. M. 1997a. Culture as process: Empirical methods for cultural psychology. In J. W. Berry, Y. H. Poortinga, and J. Pandey, eds., *Handbook of Cross-cultural Psychology*, vol. 1. Boston: Allyn and Bacon, pp. 301–46.

Greenfield, P. M. 1997b. You can't take it with you. Testing across cultures. *American Psychologist* 52: 1115–24.

Greenwald, A. G., and Banaji, M. R. 1995. Implicit social cognition: Attitudes, self-esteem, and stereotypes. *Psychological Review* 102: 4–27.

Greenwald, A. G., McGhee, D. E., and Schwartz, J. L. K. 1998. Measuring individual difference in implicit cognition: The implicit association test. *Journal of Personality and Social Psychology* 74: 1464–80.

Heine, S., Kitayama, S., Takata, T., Lehman, D. R., and Ide, E. 1999. Divergent consequences of success and failure in Japan and North America. Unpublished manuscript. University of Pennsylvania.

Heine, S. J., and Lehman, D. R. 1995. Cultural variation in unrealistic optimism: Is the West more invulnerable than the East? *Journal of Personality and Social Psychology.*

Heine, S. J., Lehman, D. R., Markus, H. R., and Kitayama, S. 1999. Culture and the need for positive self-regard. *Psychological Review* 106: 766–94.

Hermans, H. J. M., and Kempen, H. J. G. 1998. Moving cultures: The perilous problems of cultural dichotomies in a globalizing society. *American Psychologist* 53: 1111–20.

Herzog, A. R., Franks, M. M., Markus, H. R., and Holmberg, D. 1998. Activities and well-being in older age: Effects of self-concept and educational attainment. *Psychology and Aging* 13: 179–85.

Hisada, M., Senda, S., and Minoguchi, M. 1989. Development of social support scale. Paper presented at the 30th meeting of the Japanese Psychological Association.

Hofstede, G. 1980. *Culture's Consequences: International Differences in Work-Related Values.* Beverly Hills, CA: Sage.

Hoorens, V., Nuttin, J. M., Herman, I. E., and Pavakanun, U. 1990. Mastery pleasure versus mere ownership: A quasi-experimental cross-cultural and cross-alphabetical test of the name letter effect. *European Journal of Social Psychology* 20: 181–205.

House, J. S., Lepowski, J. M., Kinney, A. M., Mero, R. P., Kesler, R. C., and Herzog, A. R. 1994. The social stratification of aging and health. *Journal of Health and Behavior* 35: 213–34.

Josephs, R. A., Markus, H. R., and Tafarodi, R. W. 1992. Gender and self-esteem. *Journal of Personality and Social Psychology* 63: 391–402.

Kahneman, D. 1999. Objective happiness. In D. Kahneman, E. Diener, and N. Schwartz, eds., *Well-being: The Foundations of Hedonic Psychology.* New York: Russell-Sage.

Isaka, Y. 1996. Paper presented at the Japanese Psychological Association meeting.

Kanagawa, C., Cross, S., and Markus, H. R. (in press). Who am I?: The Psychology of the Conceptual Self. *Personality and Social Psychology Bulletin.*

Karasawa, M. 1998. The cultural basis of self- and other-perceptions: Self-criticism and other-enhancement in Japan. PhD dissertation. Shirayuri College, Tokyo, Japan.

Kikuchi, A. 1988. *Science of Sympathy: Psychology and Skills of Prosocial Behaviors* (in Japanese). Kawashima Shoten, Japan.

Kitayama, S. 1998. *Cultural Psychology of Self and Emotion* (in Japanese). Tokyo: Kyoritsu Shuppan.

Kitayama, S., and Karasawa, M. 1995. Self: A cultural psychological perspective (in Japanese). *Japanese Journal of Experimental Social Psychology* 35: 133–62.

Kitayama, S., and Karasawa, M. 1997. Implicit self-esteem in Japan: Name letters and birthday numbers. *Personality and Social Psychology Bulletin* 23: 736–42.

Kitayama, S., and Markus, H. R. 1994. *Emotion and Culture: Empirical Investigations of Mutual Influence.* Washington, DC: American Psychological Association.

Kitayama, S., and Markus, H. R. 1999. Yin and yang of the Japanese self: The cultural psychology of personality coherence. In D. Cervone and Y. Shoda, eds., *The Coherence of Personality: Social Cognitive Bases of Personality Consistency, Variability, and Organization.* New York: Guilford Press.

Kitayama, S., Markus, H. R., and Lieberman, C. 1995. The collective construction of self-esteem: Implications for culture, self, and emotion. In J. Russell, J. Fernandez-Dols, T. Manstead, and J. Wellenkamp, eds., *Everyday Conceptions of Emotion: An Introduction to the Psychology, Anthropology, and Linguistics of Emotion.* Dordrecht: Kluwer Academic.

Kitayama, S., Markus, H. R., and Kurokawa, M. 2000. Culture, emotion, and well-being: Good feelings in Japan and the United States. *Cognition and Emotion* 14: 93–124.

Kitayama, S., Markus, H. R., and Matsumoto, H. 1995. A cultural perspective on self-conscious emotions. In J. P. Tangney, and K. W. Fisher, eds., *Self-conscious Emotions: The Psychology of Shame, Guilt, Embarrassment, and Pride.* New York: Guilford Press.

Kitayama, S., Markus, H. R., Matsumoto, H., and Norasakkunkit, V. 1997. Individual and collective processes of self-esteem management: Self-enhancement in the United States and self-depreciation in Japan. *Journal of Personality and Social Psychology* 72: 1245–67.

Kitayama, S., and Masuda, T. 1995. Reappraising cognitive appraisal from a cultural perspective. *Psychological Inquiry* 6: 217–23.

Kitayama, S., Matsumoto, H., Takagi, H., and Markus, H. R. 1999. Collective construction of the self in two cultures: Evaluative ego-centricity and positivity. Under review.

Kitayama, S., and Uchida, Y. 1998. The Japanese self and mutually sympathetic relationship: II. Sympathy and interpersonal reciprocity. Under review.

Kitayama, S., and Uchida, Y. 1999a. Implicit self-attachment as sympathy to the self: Japanese constructions of the self. Paper presented at the 3rd conference of the Asian Association of Social Psychology, August 4–7, Taipei, Taiwan.

Kitayama, S., and Uchida, Y. 1999b. Divergent correlates of good feelings in Japan and the United States. Unpublished data. Kyoto University.

Kiuchi, A. 1995. Construction of a scale for independent and interdependent construal of the self and its reliability and validity. *Japanese Journal of Psychology* 66: 100–106.

Kondo, D. K. 1990. *Crafting Selves: Power, Gender, and Discourses of Identity in a Japanese Workplace.* Chicago: University of Chicago Press.

Kwan, V. S. Y., Bond, M. H., and Singelis, T. M. 1997. Pancultural explanations for life satisfaction: Adding relationship harmony to self-esteem. *Journal of Personality and Social Psychology* 73: 1038–51.

Lachman, M. E., and Weaver, S. L. 1998. The sense of control as a moderator of social class differences in health and well-being. *Journal of Personality and Social Psychology* 74: 763–73.

Leary, M. R., Tambor, E. S., Terdal, S. K., and Downs, D. L. 1995. Self-esteem as an interpersonal monitor: The sociometer hypothesis. *Journal of Personality and Social Psychology* 68: 518–30.

Lebra, T. S. 1976. *Japanese Patterns of Behavior*. Honolulu: University of Hawaii Press.

Levenson, R. W., Ekman, P., Heider, K., and Friesen, W. V. 1992. Emotion and autonomic nervous system activity in the Minangkabau of West Sumatra. *Journal of Personality and Social Psychology* 62: 972–88.

LeVine, R. A., and LeVine, S. 1998. Fertility and maturity in Africa: Gusii parents in middle adulthood. In R. A. Shweder, ed., *Welcome to Middle Age! (and Other Cultural Fictions)*. Chicago: University of Chicago Press, pp. 189–210.

Lewis, C. C. 1995. *Educating Hearts and Minds*. Cambridge: Cambridge University Press.

Linville, P. W. 1987. Self-complexity as a cognitive buffer against stress-related illness and depression. *Journal of Personality and Social Psychology* 52: 663–76.

Lutz, C. 1988. Unnatural emotions: Everyday sentiments on a Micronesian atoll and their challenges to Western theory. Chicago: University of Chicago Press.

Markus, H. R., and Cross, S. 1990. The interpersonal self. In L. A. Pervin, ed. *Handbook of Personality: Theory and Research*. New York: Guilford Press.

Markus, H. R., and Kitayama, S. 1991a. Culture and the self: Implications for cognition, emotion, and motivation. *Psychological Review* 98: 224–53.

Markus, H. R., and Kitayama, S. 1991b. Cultural variation in self-concept. In G. R. Goethals and J. Strauss, eds., *Multidisciplinary Perspectives on the Self*. New York: Springer.

Markus, H. R., Kitayama, S., and Heiman, R. J. 1996. Culture and basic psychological principles. In E. T. Higgins and A. W. Kruglanski, eds., *Social Psychology: Handbook of Basic Principles*. New York: Guilford Press, pp. 857–913.

Markus, H. R., Kitayama, S., Mullally, P., Masuda, T., and Fryberg, S. 1997. Of selves and selfways: Patterns of individuality and uniformity in identity. Unpublished manuscript. Stanford University.

Markus, H. R., Mullally, P. R., and Kitayama, S. 1997. Selfways: Diversity in modes of cultural participation. In U. Neisser and D. Jopling, eds., *The Conceptual Self in Context*. New York: Cambridge University Press, pp. 13–60.

Markus, H. R., Ryff, C. D., Connor, A., Pudberry, E. K., and Barnett, K. L. (in press). "I am responsible": Themes and variations in American understanding of responsibility. In A. S. Rossi, ed., *Caring and Doing for Others: Social Responsibility in the Domains of Family, Work, and Community*.

Marmot, M. G., Ryff, C. D., Bumpass, L. L., and Shipley, M. 1997. Social inequalities in health: Next questions and converging evidence. *Social Science and Medicine* 44: 901–10.

Matsumoto, D. 1987. The role of facial response in the experience of emotion: Methodological problems and meta-analysis. *Journal of Personality and Social Psychology* 52: 769–74.

Matsumoto, H., and Kitayama, S. 1998. False uniqueness effect in Japan and the United States: Effects of culture and domains. Unpublished manuscript. Kyoto University.

Mauss, M. 1925. *The Gift: The Form and Reason for Exchange in Archaic Societies*. Trans. W. D. Halls. New York: Norton, 1990.

Mead, G. H. 1934. *Mind, Self, and Society*. University of Chicago Press.

Mehrabian, A., and Epstein, N. 1972 A measure of emotional empathy. *Journal of Personality* 40: 523–43.

Menon, U., and Shweder, R. A. 1998. The return of the "white man's burden": The moral discourse of anthropology and the domestic life of Hindu women. In R. A. Shweder, ed., *Welcome to Middle Age! (and Other Cultural Fictions)*. Chicago: University of Chicago Press, pp. 139–88.

Mesquita, B. C. 1993. Cultural variations in emotions: A comparative study of Dutch, Surinamese and Turkish people in the Netherlands. PhD thesis. University of Amsterdam.

Miller, P. J., and Goodnow, J. J. 1995. Cultural practices: Toward an integration of culture and development. In J. J. Goodnow, P. J. Miller, and F. Kessel, eds., *Cultural Practices as Contexts for Development*. New Directions for Child Development, vol. 67. San Francisco: Jossey-Bass.

Mills, J., and Clark, M. S. 1994. Communal and exchange relationships: Controversies and research. In R. Erber and R. Gilmour, eds., *Theoretical Frameworks for Personal Relationships*. Hillsdale, NJ: Lawrence Erlbaum, pp. 29–42.

Moscovici, S. 1984. The phenomena of social representation. In R. M. Farr and S. Moscovici, eds., *Social Representation*. Cambridge, England: Cambridge University Press, pp. 3–69.

Myers, D. G. 1992. *The Pursuit of Happiness: Who Is Happy—and Why?* New York: William Morrow.

Nakamura, H. 1964. *Ways of Thinking of Eastern Peoples*. Honolulu: University of Hawaii Press.

Nakamura, H. 1989. *Ways of Thinking of Japanese People* (in Japanese). Tokyo: Shunjyu-sha.

Nuttin, J. M., Jr. 1985. Narcissism beyond Gestalt and awareness: The name letter effect. *European Journal of Social Psychology* 15: 353–61.

Ohnuki-Tierney, E. 1984. *Illness and Culture in Contemporary Japan*. Cambridge: Cambridge University Press.

Okazaki, S. 1997. Sources of ethic differences between Asian American and White American college students on measures of depression and social anxiety. *Journal of Abnormal Psychology* 106: 52–60.

Plath, D. W. 1980. *Long Engagement: Maturity in Modern Japan*. Stanford: Stanford University Press.

Rogers, C. 1951. *Client-Centered Therapy: Its Current Practice, Implications and Theory*. Boston: Houghton Mifflin.

Rosenberg, M. 1965. *Society and Adolescent Self-image*. Princeton: Princeton University Press.

Rosenberger, N. R. 1992. *Japanese Sense of Self*. Cambridge: Cambridge University Press.

Ross, C. E., and Wu, C. U. 1995. The links between education and health. *American Sociological Review* 60: 719–45.

Ryff, C. D., and Singer, B. 1998. The contours of positive human health. *Psychological Inquiry* 9: 1–28.

Segall, M. H., Lonner, W. J., and Berry, J. W. 1998. Cross-cultural psychology as a scholarly discipline: On the flowering of culture in behavioral research. *American Psychologist* 53: 1101–10.

Seligman, M. 1998. *APA Monitor*, vol. 29, no, 10, p. 2.

Shore, B. 1997. *Culture in Mind: Cognition, Culture and the Problem of Meaning*. Oxford: Oxford University Press.

Shore, B. 1998. Status reversal: The coming of aging in Samoa. In R. A. Shweder, ed., *Welcome to Middle Age! (and Other Cultural Fictions)*. Chicago: University of Chicago Press, pp. 101–38.

Sperber, D. 1996. *Explaining Culture: A Naturalistic Approach*. Oxford: Blackwell.

Shweder, R. A. 1998. *Welcome to Middle Age! (and Other Cultural Fictions)*. Chicago: University of Chicago Press.

Shweder, R. A., and Bourne, E. J. 1984. Does the concept of the person vary cross-culturally? In R. A. Shweder and R. A LeVine, eds., *Culture Theory: Essays on Mind, Self, and Emotion*. Cambridge: Cambridge University Press, pp. 158–99.

Singelis, T. M. 1994. The measurement of independent and interdependent self-construals. *Personality and Social Psychology Bulletin* 20: 580–91.

Smith, P. B., and Schwartz, S. H. 1997. Values. In J. W. Berry, M. H. Segall, C. Kagitcibasi, eds., *Handbook of Cross-cultural Psychology*, vol. 3. Boston: Allyn and Bacon.

Snyder, M. 1974. The self-monitoring of expressive behavior. *Journal of Personality and Social Psychology* 30: 526–37.

Steele, C. 1988. The psychology of self-affirmation: Sustaining the integrity of the self. In L. Berkowitz, ed., *Advances in Experimental Social Psychology*, vol. 21. San Diego: Academic Press, pp. 181–227.

Suh, E., Diener, E., and Triandis, H. 1998. The shifting basis of life satisfaction judgments across cultures: Emotions versus norms. *Journal of Personality and Social Psychology* 74: 482–93.

Takata, T., and Matsumoto, Y. 1995. The structure of self in Japanese culture: Aspects and age differences. *Japanese Journal of Psychology* 66: 213–18.

Taylor, S. E., and Brown, J. D. 1988. Illusion and well-being: A social psychological perspective on mental health. *Psychological Bulletin* 103: 193–210.

Triandis, H. C. 1989. The self and social behavior in differing cultural contexts. *Psychological Review* 96: 506–20.

Triandis, H. C. 1995. *Individualism and Collectivism*. Boulder, CO: Westview Press.

Uchida, Y., and Kitayama, S. 1998. The Japanese self and mutually sympathetic relationship: I. Measurement of sympathetic tendencies. Under review.

Uchida, Y., and Kitayama, S. 1999. Implicit self-attachment in Japan: An examination with an implicit association test. Paper presented at the Japanese Psychological Association meeting.

Weinstein, N. D. 1979. Unrealistic optimism about illness susceptibility: Conclusions from a community-wide sample. *Journal of Behavioral Medicine* 10: 481–500.

Weisz, J. R., Rothbaum, F. M., and Blackburn, T. C. 1984. Standing out and standing in: The psychology of control in America and Japan. *American Psychologist* 39: 955–69.

White, G. M. 1994. Affecting culture: Emotion and morality in everyday life. In S. Kitayama and H. R. Markus, eds., *Emotion and culture: Empirical studies of mutual influence*. Washington, DC: American Psychological Association.

Wilson, W. 1967. Correlates of avowed happiness. *Psychological Bulletin* 67: 294–306.

Yamagishi, T., Cook, K., and Watabe, M. 1998. Uncertainty, trust, and commitment formation in the United States and Japan. *American Journal of Sociology* 104: 165–94.

Yik, M. S. M., Bond, M. H., and Paulhus, D. L. 1998. Do Chinese self-enhance or self-efface? It's a matter of domain. *Personality and Social Psychology Bulletin* 24: 399–406.

III
Societal Conditions

7

Genes, Culture, Democracy, and Happiness

Ronald Inglehart and Hans-Dieter Klingemann

Growing evidence that an individual's happiness level is largely shaped by genetic factors has aroused widespread interest. Neuroscientists have found close linkages between reported happiness and dopamine and serotonin levels in the brain, and they have found that genes seem to play a major role in regulating these levels (Ebstein et al. 1996; Hamer 1996). Furthermore, a recent study of over 3,000 identical and fraternal twins (some raised together and some apart) found that genetically identical twins reported similar levels of happiness even when they had different life experiences—but fraternal twins did not (Lykken and Tellegen 1996). Evidence of genetic influences on well-being is powerful.

These findings are especially significant because previous studies have found that differences in income, education, occupation, gender, marital status and other demographic characteristics explain surprisingly little of the variation in people's levels of subjective well-being. As one would expect, those with higher incomes report somewhat higher levels of happiness and life satisfaction than those with lower incomes, but the differences are small, generally explaining no more than 4 percent of the variation—and education, occupation, age, religiosity, and gender explain even less (Andrews and Withey 1976; Inglehart 1990; Myers and Diener 1995). This persistent finding has been explained in term of "aspiration adjustment" and "set-point" models, both of which postulate as follows: (1) Recent changes, such as receiving a raise or losing one's job, can have a major impact on an individual's well-being—but that people's aspirations adjust to their level of achievement. After a year or so, they report about the same level of well-being as they did before the change, returning to the individual's normal "set-point." (2) Different individuals have different set-points. Year after year, some people display higher levels of well-being than others (Costa, McCrae, and Zonderman 1987).

As in earlier studies, Lykkens and Tellegen (1996) find only modest variation in well-being across standard social background variables, but they find strong evidence of genetic effects. They conclude that the differences in individuals' "set points" reflect genetic influences. Among the twins they studied, socioeconomic status, educational attainment, family income, marital status, or religious commitment could not explain more than about 3 percent of the variance in well-being—but they found that from 44 to 52 percent of the variance in well-being was linked with genetic variation. "The reported well-being of one's identical twin, either now or 10 years earlier, is a far better predictor of one's self-rated happiness than is one's own educational achievement, income, or status" (Lykkens and Tellegen 1996, p. 189). Press reports of these findings suggested that happiness is almost entirely determined by one's genes.[1]

We find the evidence of genetic effects convincing. But this article demonstrates that cultural and historical factors also play powerful roles. These factors have received little attention in this discussion because cultural variation is—as the very concept implies—relatively constant *within* a given society but shows relatively great variation *between* different societies. Virtually all of the research on genetic influences on subjective well-being (including the research on twins) has been carried out within single societies where subjective well-being varies within a relatively narrow range. Only a small minority of Americans, for example, describe themselves as unhappy or dissatisfied with their lives. However, as we will demonstrate, this is not the case in some societies. Similarly the U.S. public's mean life satisfaction rating is 7.7, near the top of a ten-point scale, but among the 64 societies examined here, the means range from 3.7 to 8.2. Because its relatively high baseline is a constant within the United States, it plays no part in any analysis based on U.S. data alone. Within the relatively narrow range of variation inside any given country, genetic factors may, indeed, account for most of the variance. But across the much broader range of cross-national variation, cultural differences seem to explain at least as much of the variance in well-being as do genetic factors. Let us examine the evidence.

Since 1973 the European Union has surveyed representative national samples of its member-countries' publics, asking questions about subjective well-being as well as other topics. Previous research indicates that a very effective measure of one's overall subjective well-being is provided by the question, How satisfied are you with your life as a whole? Would you say that you are very satisfied, reasonably satisfied, not very satisfied, or not at all satisfied with your life as a whole? Figure 7.1 shows

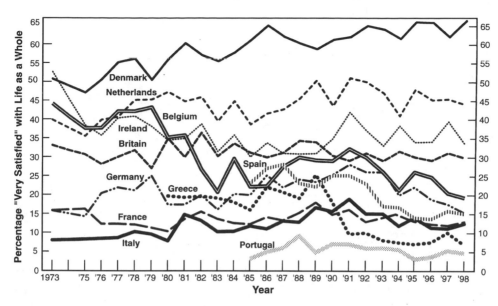

Figure 7.1
Cross-national differences in satisfaction with one's life as a whole, 1973–1998. Source: Euro-Barometer surveys carried out in each respective year.

the large and stable differences that exist in the life satisfaction levels of different societies. In the 1998 survey, for example, more than 65 percent of the Danish public described themselves as "very satisfied" with their lives as a whole; at the other end of the scale, only 5 percent of the Portuguese public said they were "very satisfied." Year after year, the Danes are about five times as likely to report high levels of life satisfaction as the French or Italians, and about twelve times as likely to do so as the Portuguese.

Can these cross-national differences be attributed to translation problems? Perhaps the word "satisfied" in English is not equivalent to *satisfait* in French, or *sodisfatto* in Italian, or *zufrieden* in German, or *tilfreds* in Danish. If so, the French and Italians might show much lower levels of subjective well-being than the Danes simply because *satisfait* and *sodisfatto* imply a higher level of well-being than does *tilfreds*. This interpretation does not hold up under closer examination. As we will see shortly (see figure 7.2), the Swiss rank substantially higher than their counterparts speaking the same languages in France, Germany, and Italy—indeed, they rank as high as the Danes. The Swiss historical experience has been quite different from that

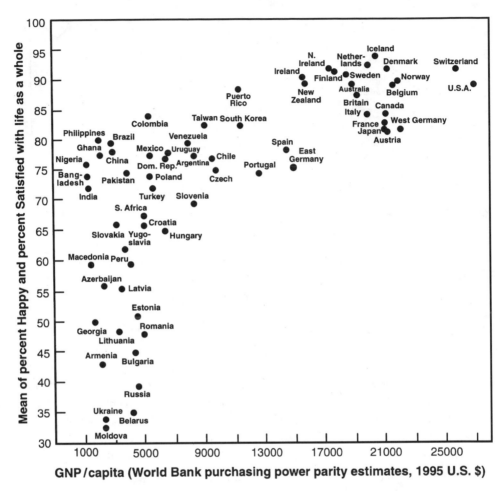

Figure 7.2
Subjective well-being by level of economic development ($R = 0.70$, $N = 65$, $p < 0.0000$).
Source: World Values Surveys; GNP/capita purchasing power estimates from World Bank,
World Development Report, 1997.

of their neighbors, and it seems to have shaped the Swiss culture's baseline level of well-being. Other comparisons point to similar conclusions: these cross-cultural differences are not artifacts of translation; they seem to reflect given societies' historical experiences.

Moreover these differences are relatively stable characteristics of given cultures: they don't simply reflect transient influences that have temporarily inflated or depressed the life-satisfaction levels of given societies. Throughout the twenty-five-year period covered by these surveys, the Danes have virtually always ranked highest in life satisfaction (and in happiness and other measures of subjective well-being): for the past twenty-five years from 50 to 65 percent of the Danish public has always described themselves as "very satisfied" with their lives as a whole. We find similar stability at the opposite end of the scale. Portugal was not included in these surveys until it joined the European Union. From that point on, her public has always manifested the lowest level of subjective well-being of any European Union society, with the percentage describing themselves as "very satisfied" never rising above 9 percent. Similarly throughout this twenty-five-year period the French and the Italians have always ranked relatively low: in both countries the percentage describing themselves as "very satisfied" virtually never rose above 15 percent but never fell to the Portuguese level. At the other end of the scale, the Dutch almost always rank as the second most satisfied public, immediately after the Danes, with 40 to 50 percent describing themselves as "very satisfied" with their lives throughout this twenty-five-year period. The Irish and the British generally come next, followed by the Germans and Spaniards who show lower levels of well-being, though never quite as low as the French or Italians. One of the eleven countries in figure 7.1 shows a significant and enduring decline: the Belgians consistently fell in the 35 to 45 point range in the 1970s, but in the early 1980s they dropped to the 20 to 30 point range and have remained there ever since. Nevertheless, the overall stability is impressive. Most publics show about the same level of well-being at the end of this twenty-five-year period as they did at the start: the correlation between each country's satisfaction level in the earliest available survey, and in the latest (1998) survey is 0.80. Even with only eleven cases, this is significant at the 0.003 level. The happiness levels of these societies show a similar pattern (among the 64 societies included in the World Values Survey, the correlation between happiness and life satisfaction is 0.81).

It seems that cultures, as well as individuals, have a normal baseline level of well-being that varies only moderately in response to current events. Do these cross-national differences reflect genetic differences? It seems unlikely. For one thing, we observe a substantial and enduring decline in the set point of the Belgians, which is difficult to reconcile with a genetic interpretation: it implies that a sudden change in the Belgian gene pool must have taken place between 1979 and 1983. We find it far more plausible to attribute this decline to historic factors such as the pervasive malaise linked with interethnic conflicts that have afflicted Belgian society, leading to Belgium being divided into a federation organized along ethnic lines in 1993.

It is even more difficult to reconcile a genetic interpretation with the evidence shown in table 7.1, which shows the cross-national variation in subjective well-being levels among a much broader range of societies than the eleven West European countries just examined.[2] Table 7.1 shows the mean levels of happiness and life satisfaction in 64 societies on all six inhabited continents, as measured in the World Values Surveys (Inglehart, 1997). These 64 societies contain over 75 percent of the world's population, and they have nominal per capita incomes ranging from $300 to about $30,000. As this table shows, their happiness and life satisfaction levels differ tremendously. Even Portugal, which ranked lowest among the 11 societies in figure 7.1, ranks relatively high in this broader context. Although only about 5 percent of the Portuguese consider themselves "very satisfied" with their lives as a whole, about 75 percent of the Portuguese are at least fairly satisfied with their lives. This holds true of the publics of virtually all advanced industrial societies: at least three-quarters of their people consider themselves either "very happy" or "fairly happy," and at least three-quarters place themselves on the upper half of a ten-point scale, indicating that they are reasonably satisfied with their lives as a whole. In Denmark, Iceland, Finland, the Netherlands, and Switzerland, more than 90 percent of the public describe themselves as happy and satisfied with their lives as a whole.

But this does *not* hold true of the entire world. Previous research, mainly limited to advanced industrial societies, led to the conclusion that happiness is the norm throughout the world. It is not. In several of these societies, over half of the public described themselves as either unhappy or very unhappy, and over half described themselves as dissatisfied with their lives as a whole.

Cross-national variation in subjective well-being is strongly linked with the society's level of economic development, as figure 7.2 demonstrates. The global correlation between well-being and GNP in figure 7.2 is 0.70, which is significant at the 0.0000 level. This suggests that economic development has an important impact on human happiness. A genetic interpretation would require us to assume that the peoples of rich countries differ genetically from those of poor countries—*and* that the peoples of recently rich societies such as Japan, South Korea, and Taiwan have experienced sudden genetic changes. Another view would be to assume that happiness causes a society to become rich. Few people would accept these assumptions. It is more plausible to conclude that the move from extreme poverty to prosperity has an effect on human happiness. This process is not linear, however. The correlation weakens as one moves up the economic scale. Above $13,000 in 1995 purchasing power parity, there is no significant linkage between wealth and subjective well-being. The transition from a subsistence economy to moderate economic security has a large impact on happiness and life satisfaction, but above the level of Portugal or Spain, economic growth no longer makes a difference. Inglehart (1990) has argued that this reflects the change of values connected with economic growth.

Economic development is not the only factor shaping a society's baseline level of subjective well-being. This baseline or "set point" may reflect a society's historical past. Figure 7.3 singles out two historical factors that may be significant for a society's economic development. Virtually all societies that experienced communist rule show relatively low levels of subjective well-being, even when compared with societies at a much lower economic level, such as India, Bangladesh, and Nigeria. Those societies that experienced communist rule for a relatively long time show lower levels than those that experienced it only since World War II. Note in the figure that seven of the eight lowest-ranking societies are former members of the USSR.

In contrast, virtually all historically Protestant societies show relatively high levels of subjective well-being. A similar effect persists today in countries (the United States being an exception) where only small minority of the public regularly attends church. As Max Weber pointed out, Protestant societies were the first to industrialize, and although economic development now has spread throughout the world, Protestant societies still are relatively wealthy in large part because of this early lead. Interestingly societies that were shaped by *both* Protestantism and communism tend to show higher levels of subjective well-being than other formerly communist countries. Latvia and Estonia rank above other Soviet successor states, as does the former East Germany above the other formerly communist societies of Central and Eastern Europe.

Are the very low levels of well-being found in former USSR countries a permanent, possibly genetic feature of their societies, or are they a relatively recent characteristic linked with economic instability after the collapse of communism? Data from two recent World Values Surveys indicate that the peoples of these societies maintained low levels of well-being throughout the 1990s. Although it was extremely difficult to carry out cross-national surveys in most state socialist societies before the

Table 7.1
Happiness, life satisfaction, and subjective well-being in 65 countries (percentages "Happy," "Satisfied," and mean of the two)

	Latest survey	Happiness	Life satisfaction	Subjective well-being
Iceland	1990	97	91	94.0
Netherlands	1990	93	92	92.5
Denmark	1990	94	90	92.0
Northern Ireland	1990	93	91	92.0
Switzerland	1996	95	89	92.0
Finland	1996	92	91	91.5
Sweden	1996	95	87	91.0
Ireland	1990	93	88	90.5
Norway	1996	94	86	90.0
Belgium	1990	93	86	89.5
United States	1995	94	85	89.5
Australia	1995	94	85	89.5
New Zealand	1998	95	84	89.5
Puerto Rico	1995	91	86	88.5
Britain	1998	90	85	87.5
Italy	1990	86	83	84.5
Canada	1990	79	90	84.5
Colombia	1997	90	77*	83.5
West Germany	1997	84	82	83.0
Taiwan	1995	89	76	82.5
South Korea	1996	89	76*	82.5
France	1990	92	72	82.0
Japan	1995	90	74	82.0
Austria	1990	91	72	81.5
Ghana	1995	72	88	80.0
Venezuela	1995	93	66	79.5
Philippines	1996	93	66	79.5
Spain	1996	87	70	78.5
China	1995	84	72	78.0
Uruguay	1996	81	75	78.0
Argentina	1995	83	72	77.5
Brazil	1996	83	72	77.5
Pakistan	1997	83	72*	77.5
Mexico	1996	71	83	77.0
Chile	1996	80	74	77.0
Nigeria	1995	81	71	76.0
East Germany	1997	79	72	75.5

Table 7.1 (continued)

	Latest survey	Happiness	Life satisfaction	Subjective well-being
Hungary	**1981**	78	71	**74.5**
Portugal	1990	73	76	74.5
Dominican Republic	1996	74	75	74.5
Poland	1996	86	62	74.0
Bangladesh	1997	85	63	74.0
India	1996	77	67	72.0
Turkey	1996	90	54	72.0
Tambov (Russia)	**1981**	64	76	**70.0**
Czech Republic	1990	73	66	69.5
Slovenia	1995	74	65	69.5
South Africa	1996	79	56	67.5
Croatia	1995	70	62	66.0
Hungary	**1998**	78	52	**65.0**
Hungary	**1990**	68	56	**62.0**
Peru	1996	63	61	62.0
Bosnia	1997	76	47	61.5
Yugoslavia	1996	71	51	61.0
Romania	1990	62	57	59.5
Azerbaijan	1995	78	41	59.5
Macedonia	1996	63	49	56.0
Slovakia	1990	52	59	55.5
Latvia	1996	71	36	53.5
Estonia	1996	65	37	51.0
Georgia	1996	65	35	50.0
Lithuania	1996	57	40	48.5
Russia	**1990**	52	44	**48.0**
Bulgaria	1998	57	33	45.0
Armenia	1995	57	29	43.0
Russia	**1995**	51	28	**39.5**
Tambov (Russia)	**1995**	47	25	**36.0**
Belarus	1996	46	24	35.0
Ukraine	1996	48	20	34.0
Moldova	1996	44	21	32.5

Source: World Values Surveys.
Notes: SWB obtained as the mean of happiness and life satisfaction. An * indicates that the score is estimated from the ranking of the other variable. Hungary and Russia in bold type show the effect of the collapse of communism in data from 1981, 1990–91, and 1995–98. (Tambov oblast in 1981) Clearly there was much more change there than in the noncommunist countries.

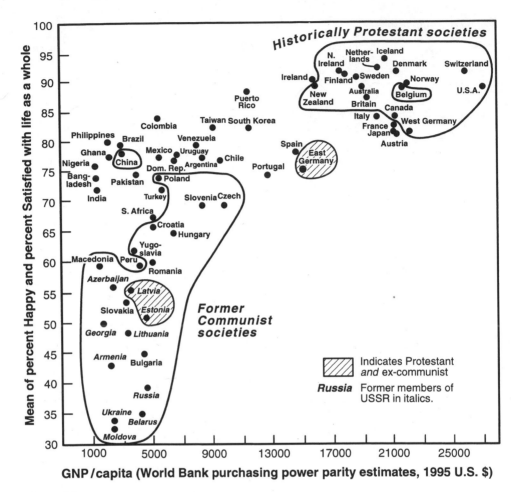

Figure 7.3
Subjective well-being by level of economic development and historical heritage of given societies.

collapse of communism between 1989 and 1991, the World Values Survey group was able to carry out two such surveys in the 1981: one in Hungary, and one in Tambov oblast, which our Soviet colleagues selected as a region that was reasonably representative of the Russian republic as a whole. The Hungarian data place that country's public at 74.5 on our well-being axis in 1981—a level comparable to that of Bangladesh or Turkey (see table 7.1). In the 1990 survey the Hungarian level of well-being dropped to 62.5, which is below the level of any noncommunist society except Peru (table 7.1). In short, the Hungarians already ranked lower than other industrial societies in 1981, seven years before the end of communist rule. By 1990 subjective well-being in Hungary had fallen even lower, but a low level was present well before the collapse of communism.

The only other formerly communist society for which our time series reaches back before the collapse of communism is Russia, and that series depends on our willingness to accept the 1981 survey in Tambov oblast as representative of Russia. It was not possible to perform the 1981 World Values Survey throughout Russia, but our Soviet colleagues did carry it out in Tambov oblast, a region that they considered representative of Russia as a whole. In order to verify this assumption, we surveyed Tambov oblast again in 1995, along with a separate survey of the Russian republic. The results from Tambov and Russia in 1995 are similar: Russia ranks 61st and Tambov ranks 62nd among the societies surveyed, with only Belarus, Ukraine, and Moldova ranking lower in well-being. Our Russian colleagues' belief that Tambov was reasonably representative of Russia as a whole seems justified.

Figure 7.4 plots the trajectory of subjective well-being in Russia from 1981 to 1995, using Tambov oblast as a stand-in for Russia in 1981. The results indicate that the subjective well-being of the Russian people was even lower than that of the Hungarians in 1981, and below that of Nigeria, Bangladesh, Turkey, and India. We suspect that twenty years earlier Russia's level of well-being probably was higher, but by 1981 she was experiencing rising alcoholism, absenteeism, and other symptoms of demoralization. The subjective well-being of its people was lower than that of countries with a fraction of the income. From this already low level, Russian subjective well-being fell sharply, so that by 1990 the Russians manifested extreme malaise. Over half the population said they were dissatisfied with their lives as a whole. Within a year the communist system had collapsed, and the Soviet Union had broken up into fifteen successor states. Well-being continued to fall after the collapse, and in 1995 the overwhelming majority of the population said they were dissatisfied with their lives. As we have seen, life satisfaction is normally very stable

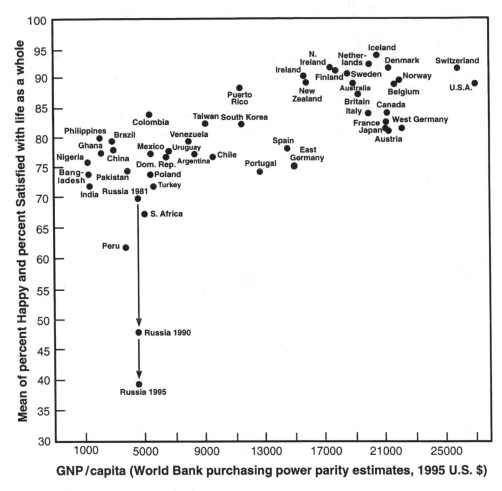

Figure 7.4
Collapse of communism and the decline of subjective well-being in Russia. The correlation between GDP/capita and subjective well-being, omitting the former communist societies, is $r = 0.74$. Source: World Values Surveys. Data for Russia in 1981 from Tambov oblast, 1981.

in advanced industrial societies. But it can and does show sharp declines—and it seems significant that in the Belgian case, a comparatively mild decline was followed by splitting the state into a federation. In the case of the formerly communist societies, a much sharper decline was followed by the collapse of the political and economic systems, and the breakup of the Soviet Union, Czechoslovakia, and Yugoslavia into separate countries. The sharp decline in subjective well-being experienced by the Russian people since 1981 is impossible to reconcile with a genetic interpretation of the cross-national differences: it must reflect historical events. Diener, Suh, Lucas, and Smith (1999) also mention the existence of cross-national differences as indicating the presence of environmental effects that cannot be genetic.

Subjective Well-being and Democracy

It is significant that in both the Belgian and the Soviet cases, sharp declines in subjective well-being *preceded* major constitutional changes, rather than following them. Changes in a society's level of well-being are not merely the result of institutional factors: they can lead to institutional changes. A society's level of subjective well-being is of more than merely academic interest: it is intimately related to the legitimacy of the socioeconomic and political system, as we have argued elsewhere (Inglehart 1997, pp. 160–215). In the long run, if people feel that their lives have gone well under a given regime, it helps endow those institutions with legitimacy. But conversely, if the subjective well-being of an entire society falls sharply below its normal baseline, it can destabilize the entire sociopolitical order. Major changes like this are rare. Apart from the Belgian and Soviet cases, all the evidence points to continuity over time. But it seems that a sharp change in subjective well-being can have important societal-level consequences.

Historical evidence suggests that a sharp decline in subjective well-being can undermine a society's most basic institutions. But conversely, high levels of subjective well-being are conducive to the survival of democratic institutions. Thus deep malaise in Weimar Germany led to the collapse of democracy, but a rising sense of well-being linked with West Germany's postwar economic miracle helped legitimize her newly established democratic institutions.

New evidence from the World Values Surveys supports the hypothesis that a society's prevailing level of subjective well-being is closely linked with the flourishing of democratic institutions. Figure 7.5 shows the relationship between our index

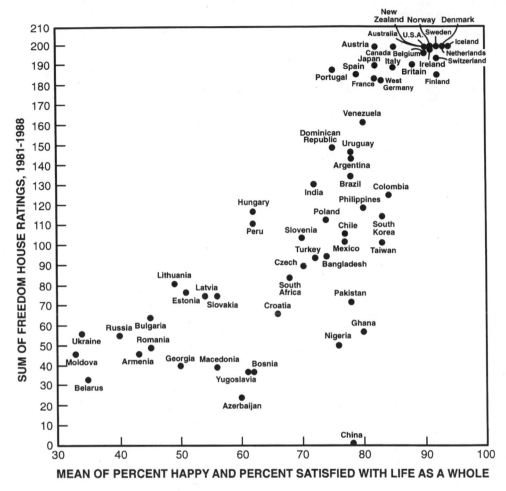

Figure 7.5
Subjective well-being and democratic institutions ($r = 0.78$, $N = 62$, $p = 0.0000$). The vertical axis shows the sum of the Freedom House ratings for civil liberties and political rights. Since these ratings give high scores for low levels of democracy, we reversed polarity by subtracting these sums from 236 (China, which had the maximum score of 235, has a score of 1 after this transformation). The horizontal axis reflects each public's mean factor score on happiness and overall life satisfaction and subjective well-being. Source: Freedom House surveys reported in successive editions of *Freedom in the World*; survey data from the 1990 and 1995 World Values Surveys.

of subjective well-being and the extent to which that society has democratic institutions, as indicated by the Freedom House annual ratings of political rights and civil liberties (Freedom House 1982–1999). The vertical axis reflects the sum of each society's scores from 1981 to 1998, transformed so that high scores reflect high levels of political rights and civil liberties.

A society's level of subjective well-being is closely linked with the flourishing of democratic institutions. The correlation is 0.78, which is a remarkably powerful relationship considering that the two variables are measured at different levels and come from completely different sources. But what is the causal direction? It is implausible that certain nationalities are genetically predisposed to be happy and democratic; it seems more likely that these differences reflect the fact that the nation is a key unit of shared historical, political, and economic experiences. But what specific factors shape these cross-cultural differences?

One interpretation of figure 7.5 may be that democratic institutions cause a society to have high levels of subjective well-being. This interpretation is attractive because it provides a strong advertisement for democracy: "Adopt democratic institutions and live happily ever after."

Unfortunately, reality does not seem to be quite that simple. Democratic institutions do not necessarily make a people happy: history furnishes compelling examples. · Democratic institutions did not make the people of Weimar Germany happy—quite the contrary, there is ample evidence that they experienced desperation. Similarly subjective well-being has not risen since Russia adopted free elections in 1991, but has fallen sharply: economic decline, ideological disillusionment, and high crime rates seem to have had more impact on the well-being of the Russian people than the move toward democracy. The same holds true of most other postcommunist societies: they have experienced *declining* subjective well-being during the 1990s, despite democratization. Conversely, Freedom House ranks China as the most authoritarian society among the 64 countries included in the World Values Surveys, but the Chinese public shows a higher level of subjective well-being than any other society that has experienced communist rule. China, unlike other formerly communist states, has moved toward a market economy without liberalizing her political system. If democratic institutions determined happiness, China should have the unhappiest public of all. But in fact, the Chinese show higher levels of well-being than less authoritarian societies, and they rank above some democracies. Although the lack of democracy has given rise to frustration and resistance, China's remarkably high levels of economic growth since 1978 seem to have more than offset the lack

Table 7.2
Regression analysis: Subjective well-being

Independent variables	Model 1	Model 2	Model 3	Model 4
1995 GNP/capita, PPP estimates (1,000s)	.459* (.223)	.429* (.214)	.738**** (.135)	.921**** (.120)
Number of years under communist rule	−.200**** (.048)	−.224**** (.046)	−.269**** (.040)	−.253**** (.040)
Percentage of workforce in industrial sector	−.373*** (.110)	−.358*** (.105)	−.356** (.107)	−.380*** (.109)
Historically Protestant dummy variable (1 = Protestant)	4.48* (1.80)	4.23* (1.77)	4.60** (1.77)	—
Freedom House democracy scores (1972–1998)	−.053* (.026)	−.046 (.025)	—	—
Educational enrollment, percentage in 1st, 2nd, and 3rd levels	−.041 (.091)	—	—	—
Adjusted R^2	.801	.807	.792	.780
N	102	105	105	105

Sources: World Values Survey; GNP/capita and percentage of workforce in industry from World Bank, *World Development Report, 1997*; educational enrollment from United Nations, *Human Development Report*.
Notes: The dependent variable is the mean obtained for the SWB in table 7.2. Levels of significance are **** at 0.000 level, *** at 0.001, ** at 0.01, * at 0.05.

of democracy. These findings undermine any simplistic assumption that democratic institutions are the main determinant of human happiness (or, more broadly, that institutions determine culture). Democracy is a good thing, and it probably makes some contribution to human happiness, but it does not seem to have nearly as much impact as other aspects of people's experience.

In order to measure the relative importance of these causal factors, we performed an OLS multiple regression analysis, using each society's subjective well-being level as the dependent variable. Table 7.2 shows the results.

Model 1 includes three indicators of economic development: GNP per capita, the percentage of the work force employed in the industrial sector, and the society's educational enrollment at primary, secondary, and tertiary levels. It also includes the number of years of communist rule experienced by the society (ranging from 0 to 74) and a dummy variable that taps whether or not the society was historically dominated by Protestant elites. Finally, it includes the sum of each country's Freedom House democracy scores from 1981 through 1998 in order to measure the extent to which democratic institutions contribute to subjective well-being. For the sake of readability, this chapter's graphs show only the results from the latest survey available for each country, but our regression analyses utilize the broadest possible database, employing all available surveys from 1981 through 1997.

The variables included in model 1 explain fully 80 percent of the cross-national variance in subjective well-being, and all but one of these variables shows a significant effect. Somewhat surprisingly, a society's level of education does not seem to have a significant impact on well-being. When we drop education from the analysis in model 2, the amount of explained variance actually rises slightly, to 81 percent. The society's level of democracy (as indicated by the Freedom House scores) was only marginally significant in model 1 and now drops below significance. Although democracy and well-being are strongly linked, the interpretation that democracy determines well-being does not stand up: other factors—particularly the number of years of communist rule and the society's level of economic development—seem to play much more powerful roles. When we drop the Freedom House indicator from the equation (model 3) the percentage of explained variance falls slightly, suggesting that although democracy is not the decisive factor, it does contribute to well-being. Its powerful zero-order correlation with well-being reflects the fact that both democracy and well-being are closely linked with economic development. Thus, when the Freedom House indicator is dropped from the regression, the impact of per capita GNP jumps to a 0.001 level of significance. Our other indicator of development, the percentage of the work force in the industrial sector, is also important, and its impact is negative: having a large proportion employed in the service sector has a positive impact on well-being, but countries with large industrial sectors tend to rank low on well-being. The number of years of communist rule experienced by a society shows a major negative impact on well-being in all of our models: even controlling for the fact that the formerly communist societies tend to be poorer and have larger industrial sectors than other industrial societies, the historical experience of communist rule seems to have depressed the happiness and life satisfaction levels of the peoples who experienced it. This legacy was still clearly visible in surveys carried out several years after the collapse of communism in Europe.

A Protestant heritage consistently shows a significantly positive linkage with well-being, but its effect is modest. When we drop that variable from the equation, in model 4, the percentage of explained variance falls by about 1 percent: the striking linkage between Protestantism and well-being shown in figure 7.3 is mainly (but not entirely) due to the fact that historically Protestant societies tend to be relatively wealthy. The key influences shaping cross-cultural differences in baseline levels of subjective well-being seem to be the society's level of economic development and whether or not it experienced communist rule.

These findings in no way refute the evidence that genetic factors play an important role in subjective well-being; we find that evidence compelling. But these findings do indicate that genetic factors are only part of the story. Happiness levels vary cross-culturally. Since cultures are constructed by human beings, this suggests that the pursuit of happiness is not completely futile. Genes may play a crucial role, but beliefs and values also are important.

Our findings also indicate that varying levels of well-being are closely linked with a society's political institutions: sharp declines in a society's level of well-being can lead to the collapse of the social and political system; while high levels of well-being contribute to the survival and flourishing of democratic institutions.

Notes

1. This is clearly an overstatement. Both Lykken and Tellegen (1996) and Diener, Suh, Lucas, and Smith (1999) point out that only 40 percent of the variance in subjective well-being is stable over 10 years, and it is this variance that is 80 percent heritable.

2. The data for the 51 following societies are from the 1995–1997 World Values Survey: United States, Australia, New Zealand, China, Japan, Taiwan, South Korea, Turkey, Pakistan, Bangladesh, India, the Philippines, Armenia, Azerbaijan, Georgia, Great Britain, East Germany, West Germany, Switzerland, Norway, Sweden, Finland, Spain, Russia, Ukraine, Belarus, Estonia, Latvia, Lithuania, Moldova, Poland, Hungary, Bulgaria, Slovenia, Croatia, Yugoslavia, Bosnia, Macedonia, Nigeria, South Africa, Ghana, Argentina, Brazil, Chile, Colombia, Dominican Republic, Mexico, Peru, Puerto Rico, Uruguay, Venezuela. Data for Canada, France, Italy, Portugal, Netherlands, Belgium, Denmark, Iceland, Ireland, Northern Ireland, Austria, Czech Republic, Slovakia, and Romania are from the 1990 World Values Survey. The data from the European Values Survey, the 1990 World Values Surveys, and the Eurobarometer surveys are available from the ICPSR survey data archive.

References

Andrews, F. M. and Withey, S. B. 1976. *Social Indicators of Well-being: Americans' Perceptions of Life Quality*. New York: Plenum.

Costa, P. T., McCrae, R. R., and Zonderman, A. B. 1987. *British Journal of Psychology* 78: 299–306.

Diener, E., Suh, E. M., Lucas, R. E., and Smith, H. E. 1999. Subjective well-being: Three decades of progress. *Psychological Bulletin* 125: 276–302.

Ebstein, R. P., et al. 1996. Dopamine D4 receptor (D4DR) exon III polymorphism associated with the human personality trait of Novelty Seeking. *Nature Genetics* 12: 78–80.

Hamer, D. H. 1996. The Heritability of Happiness. *Nature Genetics* 14: 125–26.

Freedom House. 1982–1999. *Freedom in the World: The Annual Survey of Political Rights and Civil Liberties*. New York.

Inglehart, R. F. 1990. *Culture Shift in Advanced Industrial Society*. Princeton: Princeton University Press.

Inglehart, R. F. 1997. *Modernization and Postmodernization: Cultural, Economic and Political Change in 43 Societies*. Princeton: Princeton University Press.

Lykken, D., and Tellegen, A. 1996. Happiness is a stochastic phenomenon. *Psychological Science* 7: 186–89.

Myers, D. G. and Diener, E. 1995. Who is happy? *Psychological Science* 6: 10–19.

8

Money and Happiness: Income and Subjective Well-being across Nations

Ed Diener and Shigehiro Oishi

Throughout the world most people now desire a high level of material wealth. The policies of most governments are focused on increasing material prosperity, and most individuals throughout the world desire homes, appliances, universal education, a varied diet, sophisticated medical treatment, and amenities that are available in the wealthiest nations. Although people have many goals, one is struck by the degree to which material prosperity has become an important aim in most societies. For example, dictatorships and economic systems alike have fallen in the last decades when they failed to provide economic prosperity. It is not surprising then that national governments now focus on economic growth as their first goal. Therefore it is important to ask whether increases in material prosperity will be accompanied by increases in subjective well-being (SWB). Krugman wrote, "in the end, economics is not about wealth, it's about the pursuit of happiness" (1998, p. 24). Will greater wealth produce greater happiness?

In light of the widespread attention now afforded to material prosperity, it should not be surprising that dramatic increases in wealth characterize many nations. North America, Western Europe, and Australia have traditionally been prosperous, but many countries are joining their ranks. Nations in the Pacific Rim and Latin America are equalling or exceeding the wealth of western nations. The most populous countries, China and India, have recently exhibited high economic growth rates, albeit from a low initial level of wealth. Although most of the nations of sub–Sahara Africa and certain Asian countries such as Afghanistan still lag far behind the rest of the world and exhibit little or no economic growth, a large number of societies show unprecedented prosperity. Thus people's increasing material desires are matched by heightened productivity in many countries.

Although material prosperity is now a possibility for much of the globe, there are potential problems with a wealthy world. Scholars have expressed a number of reservations about the accumulation of wealth (e.g., see Droge et al. 1993; Wachtel 1983). One concern about economic development is the potential for ruining the environment. Not only does wealth production require the use of natural resources such as trees, minerals, and oil, it also produces byproducts that can pollute water, air, and land. Another concern with material prosperity as a major goal is that it might redirect attention from more important aims such as love, self-development, and spirituality. Perhaps the pursuit of money will distract us from endeavors that are essential to human well-being. Yet another concern with wealth is that its pursuit might be frustrating and endless because feeling satisfied with one's wealth may be a zero-sum game between the members of a society. In other words, feeling that one's income is adequate may depend on being in the upper distribution of income, leaving some segments of society to always feel dissatisfied, no matter how wealthy they are in absolute terms. On the other hand, it might be that material prosperity will help people meet a number of their inherent needs and therefore will produce heightened well-being. In light of the huge importance now placed on material prosperity, and on the economic development occurring throughout much of the world, we need to inquire as to whether increasing income will produce high levels of subjective well-being.

One standard against which to judge the outcomes of economic prosperity is subjective well-being—how people themselves evaluate their lives. Subjective well-being includes several key components such as life satisfaction, financial satisfaction, pleasant affect, and the absence of unpleasant affect. Each of these components reflects people's evaluations, both affective and cognitive, of their own lives. Subjective well-being is a particularly democratic outcome variable because it allows people to judge their own lives, instead of focusing on quality of life assessments made by "experts." In this chapter we emphasize life satisfaction as the key outcome variable for our analyses because this is the most widely available SWB measure across cultures. However, we will also present evidence on financial satisfaction when it is available, especially because the effects of income might vary for the different types of subjective well-being. The effects of money on other social indicators such as health and crime will not be covered in this paper (see, for example, Diener 1995).

In this chapter we describe the empirical evidence on the relation of income and SWB. One goal of this chapter is to review the existing evidence on money and happiness across cultures. A second goal is to examine several theories about why money relates to happiness.

Models of Income and SWB

There are several conceptual models that purport to explain the relation between income and happiness. Livability theory was proposed by Veenhoven (1991, 1995) and is based on the idea that income increases SWB only insofar as it allows people to meet their inborn needs. In this model, income should have large effects on SWB in poor countries, and at lower levels of income within wealthy nations, because it is here that income influences whether a person can meet needs such as for food, shelter, and clothing. According to Veenhoven's model, however, SWB should not differ between most income groups in affluent countries, or between the most affluent groups in poor nations, because above a certain level of income all individuals will have met the needs for which money can buy fulfillment.

An extension of Veenhoven's model is based on Maslow's (1954) theory of needs. In this approach, meeting needs is also seen as causing increased SWB, but self-actualization needs open up a vast array of rewarding activities at the upper levels of income. For example, wealth might allow participation in foreign travel, challenging hobbies such as sailing or mountaineering, intellectual exploration and artistic creativity, and philanthropy that might be most available at high levels of income. Thus in this approach needs are seen as explaining the income-SWB relation, but this relation is not necessarily limited to increases in income at the lower levels. In this theory increases in income above the basic needs level would only produce increases in SWB to the extent that people used their income for self-actualizing activities. If instead people used their higher incomes to pursue status, or frivolous material goods, no increase in SWB would occur. Thus a more "livable" society might depend on how money is spent, not just how much money people have.

In contrast to theories based on needs, relativistic judgment models suggest that people assess the adequacy of their incomes in relation to variable standards. Easterlin (1974) hypothesized that people use social comparison to decide whether their income is satisfying. For example, if a person of moderate means lived next-door to a wealthy family, he or she would tend to be dissatisfied. In contrast, if this middle-class individual lived next-door to a poor family, he or she would be more satisfied because of the favorable comparison standard provided by the neighbor. Easterlin reasoned that people are likely to compare with other nearby people within their own countries but are unlikely to compare to distant individuals in other nations. Based on this reasoning, he argued that within-nation correlations between income and SWB ought to be substantial, whereas differences in SWB across nations differing in wealth ought to be minimal. Unfortunately for Easterlin's hypothesis, as we will see, the data are often opposite of that pattern.

Another variable standard on which people might judge their income is their past riches. Parducci (1995) proposed in his range-frequency theory that people's reactions to current events are based on the context provided by past events happening to that person. Because circumstances in the person's past life provide the context against which new events are judged, events that are better than this context will be judged positively. In this general approach, one would be satisfied with one's material standing if it were higher than one's past income. Similarly one would be dissatisfied with one's income, no matter how high in absolute terms, if it were lower than one's past income. For example, a billionaire might be dissatisfied in a year in which she earned "only" two million dollars. In the range-frequency theory, as in the hedonic treadmill theory of Brickman and Campbell (1971), people tend toward hedonic neutrality, at least if their event distribution is normally distributed.

The culture approach provides yet another explanation for national differences in SWB relative to income. Within this general model there are a number of specific explanations for why societies differ overall in SWB. In this tradition, differences in happiness are likely to be partly due to what people value. If people highly value money, they will be more likely to earn more of it. Furthermore SWB would result from an interaction between values and money, with high income producing high happiness only in those societies (or individuals) where money is highly prized. Thus a key in the culture approach to explaining the relation between income and SWB is to understand the value people in different cultures place on material prosperity, since this is likely to moderate the effects of income on SWB.

An approach that combines elements of each of the other approaches is the material desires concept. In this model, people will be happy to the extent that they can obtain the things they desire, or at least make progress toward those aims. For instance, in the material domain, if people want a sailboat, they will be happier if they have one, or at least make progress toward obtaining one. If there is no possibility of ever obtaining something that is highly desired, it is predicted that dissatisfaction will result. However, desires can change, and therefore a person may adjust her goals to cope with a situation in which an aim cannot be reached. If it is apparent that a woman may never be able to afford a sailboat, for instance, she may switch her goal to obtaining a canoe. Similarly a person might raise her aspirations if she has been very successful in an area. In our example, the person might obtain a sailboat, and yet still grow dissatisfied as she comes to desire an even speedier one. The goal model can accommodate the needs approach because it is recognized that a person's physical needs usually have a strong influence on his or her desires. People usually want good food, appliances, clothes, and protective housing, for example, because of the needs they fulfill and comfort they provide. The goal approach can also subsume the relativistic approach because it is recognized that what others possess sometimes influences what a person desires, and that a person's former possessions often will influence what one currently desires. However, a person may desire to give up some of the goods of the past, and in this case having fewer material possessions might be related to higher SWB. Finally, the material desires approach can subsume the aspects of the culture approach related to people's values and goals for material goods and services. In sum, the material desires approach predicts that the relation between income and happiness will depend on the number of people's material desires that can be met, and this approach predicts that needs, social comparisons, and past income are relevant insofar as they influence current desires.

In analyzing these different models, there are a number of types of evidence that are relevant. First, there are the correlations within nations between income and SWB, and these correlations can also be compared across nations differing in wealth. Similarly there are differences in SWB within nations between the poorest and wealthiest individuals, thus giving the effect size for the extreme income categories. We can compare the wealthiest group to the next-most wealthy group. We can also examine across nations the correlation between the average per capita wealth of countries and the mean levels of SWB in them. We can then assess changes in SWB over time, and this type of analysis can be particularly informative because of the rapid increase in income in the last decades in many societies. Finally, we can examine a small number of experimental or quasi-experimental studies because they might give us a clue about the causal role of income on happiness.

Each type of evidence helps us to evaluate the various models of income and SWB. For example, Parducci's model suggests that growth in income ought to be accompanied by higher SWB, and Easterlin's social comparison model predicts that there will be little difference between nations in SWB. The basic needs model predicts that there should be no difference in SWB between the wealthiest and next-most wealthy individuals in the richer nations. As we will see, the extant data allow us to reject some models.

The Evidence

Methodological Concerns in Measuring SWB across Cultures

One of the problems with past analyses of income and SWB is that they were usually based on small samples, or on a relatively narrow range of nations. For example, past analyses based on the first World Value Survey included over 150,000 respondents, but virtually all of the nations were highly westernized wealthy countries. Thus analyses at the nation level can be misleading due to the restriction of range of important variables such as national income. In this chapter we focus on studies that include a broad sampling of countries as well as relatively large samples within each society. For example, we present data from the World Value Survey II (World Values Study Group 1994) that include large probability samples from many diverse nations. In addition we examine our own international study of college students. Although the number of respondents within nations was smaller in this data set, it includes a more diverse set of countries and therefore is complementary to the World Value Survey II. By focusing on these surveys, we hope to achieve firmer conclusions that are broadly representative and do not suffer from problems in restriction of range on key variables that hampered most earlier analyses.

One can inquire about the validity of the SWB measures, especially when the researcher is making comparisons across cultures. Self-report measures of SWB converge adequately with other measures of SWB in the United States (e.g., Sandvik, Diener, and Seidlitz 1993). However, researchers have not made comparisons across cultures or nations using measures in addition to self-report. We need multimeasure studies in order to achieve greater confidence in our conclusions across societies. Although self-report measures provide interesting conclusions, we would be more comfortable if the findings could be replicated using measures of memory, experience sampling, informant reports, physiology, and facial expression.

Veenhoven (1993; Ouweneel and Veenhoven 1991) discussed the issue of comparing surveys across different languages, one problem being that words denoting SWB might not translate exactly between languages. Therefore different SWB values might be due to variations in the nuances of language rather than to true differences in SWB. Veenhoven approached this question by examining SWB values in multilingual nations such as Belgium and Canada where the SWB surveys have been administered in different regions in different languages. He concluded that translation problems are not a major impediment in comparing different societies in SWB. Shao (1993) arrived at a similar conclusion using a different methodology. Shao compared the life satisfaction scores of bilingual individuals who responded to a survey in English or in Mandarin Chinese, and then later responded to the same survey in the other language. Shao found very similar mean values for the two formats, and also found that the pattern of correlations of the two administrations of the scales with other variables was quite similar. Thus earlier findings on language differences tend to be reassuring but by no means definitive in indicating that there are no problems in this area.

One way of examining the issue of response validity across cultures is to examine the degree to which surveys using different questions and response formats versus those using the exact same items produce more or less similar results. This approach is interesting because it can suggest whether the self-report scale used for measuring SWB can influence the results. We compared correlations for international surveys that used identical questions versus those in which different questions were used. In both cases we identified surveys that were given in the same year within the same nation, chosen from Veenhoven's (1993) list of surveys, and randomly selected 100 nation-year pairs using the same survey instrument and 100 nation-year pairs in which different measures were used. We compared the values of identical and different surveys after they had been transformed using a sophisticated scaling technique to calibrate scales for equivalence. Veenhoven (1993) relied on expert raters to transform the responses of various scales onto the same metric by having each response option rated for intensity, and then recalculating SWB scores from various surveys based on these scaled response values (see Torgerson 1958).

We used Veenhoven's transformed scores and evaluated the degree to which surveys converged when identical survey versus different survey instruments were used. We found across nations and years that 100 identical survey pairs (conducted in the same nations in the same years with the same measure) correlated 0.95, whereas alternative surveys (different measuring instruments used, but 100 survey pairs within the same nations and same years) correlated 0.60, a significant difference in correlations ($p < 0.001$). This is a strong indication that the method used has some influence on the outcome, although the substantial correlation even when different survey instruments were used does suggest a degree of convergent validity for the measures. The difference between the correlations for identical versus different surveys points to two conclusions. First, we should not make comparisons using different survey instruments, even using sophisticated scaling methods to transform the values. It is for this reason that in this chapter we do not move across survey instruments in analyzing data. For example, we compute time trends for nations only when data over years using the same instrument are available. The concern we have with comparing different scales across cultures also applies if we examine time trends within one nation, if different measures are used.

Second, and more fundamentally, the differences in correlations across identical and different survey instruments indicates that the method of measurement can influence SWB estimates for nations. Although we do not understand why or how this occurs, we must use caution in interpreting cross-cultural comparisons. We need more work on how people in different cultures respond to different types of scales because there is virtually no work on this question.

Response artifacts across cultures have been studied by Diener, Suh, Smith, and Shao (1995). Although the findings are beyond the scope of this chapter, Diener et al. concluded that the artifacts they assessed could not account completely for the differences between nations they found. They concluded that artifacts such as differences in humility between nations probably had little effect on their cross-nation findings. Despite these encouraging findings, much more research is needed to examine the influence of artifacts across cultures, and how the meaning of the measures varies across cultures. For example, a positivity bias might influence global measures of SWB more than it influences more concrete, specific types of satisfaction.

Cross-sectional Within-nation Data

The simplest type of data we can examine regarding the relation of wealth to SWB is the correlation of income and well-being measures within nations at one point in time. This cross-sectional type of data reveals the degree to which within the same nation richer people are happier than poorer individuals. In table 8.1 we show the relation between reported life satisfaction and family income in 19 nations. The nations we show in the table are those for whom we have results from both a large, representative survey (the World Value Survey II) and from our international college student survey.

As can be seen, the relation between life satisfaction and income is positive in most nations. Although values are shown only for nations where both data sets are available, the means at the bottom of the table are for 40 nations in both surveys. The Netherlands was dropped from the college survey because of the small sample size, and the data for Kuwait arrived after these analyses were completed. Because of concerns about whether the SWB scales have interval scale properties, we also present the Spearman rank-order correlation for income and life satisfaction for the World Value Survey. As can be seen, the values are close to those for the Pearson

Table 8.1
Relation between income and satisfaction across nations

| Nation | Financial satisfaction and income correlations | | Life satisfaction and income correlations | | | Effect size |
	WVS II	College	WVS	WVS Spearman	College	
Argentina	0.12	0.02	0.11	0.09	0.13	
Austria	0.05	0.05	0.07	0.09	0.05	0.22
Brazil	0.13	0.10	−0.02	−0.05	0.06	
China	0.09	0.21	0.04	0.03	0.18	
Denmark	0.12	0.35	0.21	0.17	−0.04	0.48
Estonia	0.34	0.29	0.08	0.07	0.24	
Finland	0.11	0.39	−0.02	−0.02	0.16	
Hungary	0.22	0.41	0.19	0.18	−0.01	
Italy	0.20	0.34	0.07	0.04	0.04	
India	0.28	0.11	0.17	0.18	0.09	
Japan	0.28	−0.07	0.18	0.19	−0.01	0.94
Nigeria	0.36	0.26	0.21	0.21	0.12	0.53
Norway	0.14	0.07	0.14	0.13	0.13	0.55
Portugal	0.26	0.31	0.08	0.08	0.19	0.63
Slovenia	0.52	−0.05	0.29	0.28	−0.08	
South Africa	0.50	0.44	0.38	0.34	0.29	1.18
Spain	0.28	0.14	0.13	0.11	0.20	0.62
Turkey	0.39	0.23	0.17	0.16	0.22	
United States	0.22	0.19	0.15	0.10	0.10	
Mean	0.25	0.18	0.13	0.12	0.10	0.46

Note: Effect size is for the lowest versus highest income categories in the World Value Survey II.

correlations. What is striking about all of these correlations is that SWB shows a relatively low relation to life satisfaction. As might be expected, because it is closer to income in the causal chain, financial satisfaction is more strongly related to income than is life satisfaction. Nevertheless, even the correlations for financial satisfaction tend to be modest. One might anticipate a very strong correlation between financial satisfaction and income if this relation were highly dependent on an objective assessment of one's wealth. Thus satisfaction with income depends on factors other than objective income. One hypothesis is that financial satisfaction depends more on comparison factors, whereas life satisfaction depends more on needs and desires.

In light of the relatively small correlations between income and financial satisfaction, we used regression with the college student sample to predict financial satisfaction from objective income and from general life satisfaction. Whereas income produced a standardized beta of 0.09 ($p < 0.001$), life satisfaction produced a beta of 0.39 ($p < 0.001$). This finding suggests that financial satisfaction is predicted to some degree by people's objective income, but factors such as personality and other life circumstances appear to more strongly predict financial satisfaction. In other words, people's global feelings about their lives sometimes might be more important predictors of whether they will be satisfied with their income than is their objective income!

Comparing the Lowest and Highest Income Groups   Another way that we can examine the relation of income to SWB is to compare the lowest and highest income groups in each nation. By examining the effect size for this comparison, we can gain a sense of the size of influence on SWB of being poor versus well off. In the rightmost column of table 8.1 are shown the effect sizes for those nations where there were at least 20 respondents in both the richest and poorest groups in the World Value Survey II. As can be seen, the effect sizes range from small (e.g., Austria) to medium (e.g., Norway) to very large (e.g., South Africa). The mean effect size across all 22 nations for which there were adequate numbers of respondents was 0.46, a figure that would be classified as moderate by Cohen (1977). In terms of scale units, this effect size would amount to 0.98 units on a scale with a range of 9 points. The richest and poorest groups on average differed by about one scale unit on the 1 to 10 life satisfaction scale, or about 11 percent of the total range of the scale. Thus it would be an error to claim that income has no relation to SWB but also a mistake to suppose that the relation is immense.

Comparing the Top Income Groups   If meeting basic physical needs is the reason that income has some correlation with SWB, we would expect that the top two income groups would not differ because the second highest group certainly possesses adequate money to meet their biological needs. The comparison of these two income groups was most straightforward in the international college survey because identical income categories were used in all nations, making computations across countries simpler. For life satisfaction, the highest income group's mean of 23.91 was significantly higher (t (1,855) $=$ 3.48, $p < 0.001$) than the penultimate income group's mean of 22.36, in an analysis in which we controlled for satisfaction differences between nations. For financial satisfaction, the means of 4.59 versus 4.29 were also significantly different (t (1,817) $=$ 4.03, $p < 0.001$). In the World Value Survey, different income categories were used in each nation; we therefore compared whatever the top two income categories were across all the nations. The difference in life satisfaction of the top two income groups in the World Value Survey II was very small, 7.69 versus 7.63, but significant, t (4,109) $=$ 2.25, $p < 0.05$, controlling for satisfaction differences between nations. For financial satisfaction in the World Value Survey II, the means were 7.62 and 7.15, t (3,965) $=$ 7.26, $p < 0.001$. These analyses reveal that the effects of income on SWB are not confined to the levels of income where basic needs are at issue.

Differences between Income Effects across Nations   Veenhoven (1991) reported that the correlation between income and SWB was stronger in poorer nations, and concluded from this finding that income is important to satisfaction when it helps basic human needs. In our analyses of our international college survey, there was a tendency for the correlation of income and satisfaction to be higher in poorer nations, but this trend was not statistically significant. However, in figure 8.1 we show data for the nine poorest and nine richest nations for both life satisfaction and financial satisfaction. As can be seen in the upper graph, money has more effect on life satisfaction in poor nations—because of the low well-being of poorer students in the more impoverished nations. The life satisfaction of students in the wealthy nations seems to be not much affected by their family income. Surprisingly the lower graph shows that higher-income students are less satisfied with their incomes in wealthy versus poorer nations, suggesting an effect of material desires and perhaps social comparison on their financial satisfaction. Figure 8.1 indicates that types of subjective well-being, for example financial satisfaction versus life satisfaction,

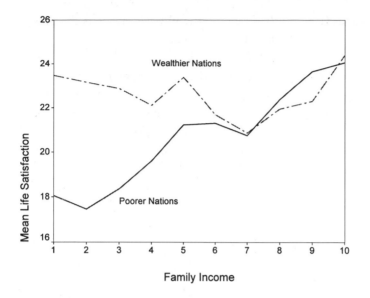

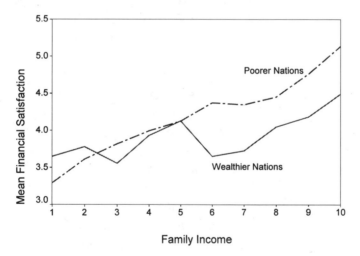

Figure 8.1
Life and financial satisfaction in relation to family income in poor and wealthy societies.
Cross-national data from college students in nine countries.

may follow different patterns and be affected by different processes. Further the figure points to a smaller effect of income on SWB in wealthy compared to poor nations. In the World Value Survey II, Oishi, Diener, Lucas, and Suh (1999) report that financial satisfaction is more strongly related to life satisfaction in poor nations than in rich ones.

Causal Direction   Based on the cross-sectional data reviewed above, we cannot be certain whether income causes higher SWB or whether higher SWB causes income. However, evidence is available that suggests that a causal path goes from income to SWB. Smith and Razzell (1975) studied lottery pool winners in England and found that on average they were happier than controls who bought tickets but did not win. Because lotteries are inherently random, this finding of Smith and Razzell suggests that higher income can raise one's SWB. Similarly Brickman, Coates, and Janoff-Bulman (1978) found that lottery winners were somewhat happier than a comparison group (but this effect was not significant owing to the small sample size of winners). A potential problem with the lottery studies, however, is that differential rates of responding and different characteristics of responders in the lottery winner versus comparison groups could lead to the results. Furthermore the measurement might have been reactive because the winners know why they were selected. A large experiment with welfare recipients gave certain randomly selected people a much larger amount of money than the standard welfare payments (Thoits and Hannon 1979). In these "negative income tax" studies, recipients of more money actually reported greater levels of stress. Perhaps money can increase pleasant emotions, but it also increase stress if it requires lifestyle changes or sets a person apart from his or her friends.

We can also examine the opposite causal direction—that happy people are more likely to grow richer over time. In this case we of course do not have experimental data, but we can gain hints about the question of causality with longitudinal studies. In an analysis of the 10-year longitudinal NHANES data set (Cornoni-Huntley et al. 1983), we found that people who were happier at time 1 did not increase more in income over the ensuing decade than people who were less happy at time 1. Indeed, we found that unhappy people in the poorest group tended to become happier over time (affect balance) than happy individuals in the poorest group. In a large longitudinal study of college students, we found a small effect of subjective well-being (pleasant and unpleasant affect) on income 18 years later. Thus, although the evidence is by no means definitive, it appears that happiness on average does not have a large effect on wealth.

Between-Nation Differences

Ouweneel and Veenhoven (1991) reported that the correlation of mean income in 28 nations and the average SWB in them was 0.62, and Diener, Diener, and Diener (1995) reported this correlation to be 0.59 in another sample. In table 8.2 are presented the mean life satisfaction figures for 42 nations, as well as the wealth of these nations. These figures are based on two types of surveys: the World Value Survey II, and numbers on life satisfaction presented in Veenhoven (1993) which used a similar life satisfaction scale to the World Value Survey life satisfaction item. In order to average the two surveys when both were available for a country, we standardized the scores within them. Across these nations the correlation between mean life satisfaction and mean income was 0.69 ($p < 0.001$). Thus earlier findings that the average SWB in nations correlates with the wealth of nations is strongly supported. When one examines individual nations, there is a clear tendency for wealthier nations such as Norway, Austria, and Switzerland to have high life satisfaction, and poor nations such as Bulgaria, South Africa, and India to have lower life satisfaction. Inglehart and Klingemann (chapter 7 in this volume) also found a very strong relation between the wealth of societies and their level of subjective well-being.

The question sometimes arises as to why the national income and average SWB correlations are high, whereas the correlations of income and SWB within nations are modest. Part of the explanation lies in aggregation, and in what gets averaged out of the "error term" when mean values by nations are considered. For example, personality may have a substantial influence on SWB, but individual differences in temperament are averaged out when only the mean level of SWB is considered for a nation. National values of SWB reflect only mean between-country differences. Thus the error term (which includes deviations from a linear relation due to factors such as culture or the meaning of the SWB scales across nations) for nation-level correlations will be much different than the error term for correlations based on individuals within nations (which includes measurement error as well as all the myriad of personal factors in addition to income that can influence SWB). Therefore the absence of individual differences in the between-nation correlations gives the figures a different interpretation than within-nation correlations. An example of the

Table 8.2
National income and mean life satisfaction by nation

Nation	Income[a]	Life satisfaction[b]	Nation	Income[a]	Life satisfaction[b]
India	$1,290	−1.88	Greece	$11,400	−1.05
Nigeria	1,430	−0.42	Portugal	12,400	0.17
China	2,510	0.43	Ireland	13,550	0.94
Estonia	2,820	−1.13	Spain	14,040	−0.23
South Africa	3,010	−0.39	Finland	16,390	0.77
Latvia	3,220	−1.49	Sweden	17,130	1.15
Lithuania	3,240	−1.12	Britain	17,970	0.40
Belarus	4,320	−1.71	Netherlands	18,080	0.87
Bulgaria	4,380	−2.31	Italy	18,610	−0.05
Romania	4,090	−1.28	Australia	19,000	0.94
Turkey	4,610	−0.63	France	19,670	−0.25
Russia	4,610	−0.95	Canada	19,960	0.95
Poland	5,480	−0.36	Austria	20,230	−0.19
Brazil	5,630	0.30	Belgium	20,270	0.70
Hungary	6,310	−1.07	Denmark	20,800	1.28
Mexico	7,040	0.29	Norway	21,120	0.80
Slovenia	7,140	−0.78	Iceland	21,150	0.97
Chile	8,890	0.75	Japan	21,350	−0.90
Czech Republic	8,900	−0.77	Switzerland	25,150	1.38
Argentina	8,920	0.38	United States	25,860	0.78
South Korea	10,540	−0.87	Luxembourg	28,770	0.68

a. Income is purchasing power parity in U.S. dollars where available, and GNP per capita in a few nations where the former number could not be located.
b. Mean of World Value Survey II Life Satisfaction and Veenhoven's (1993) list of nations using a 1–10 life satisfaction scale. When only one survey was conducted, our life satisfaction figure represents that single survey. Life satisfaction values are standard scores.

effects of aggregation can be seen when we aggregate individuals within income categories, and examine the mean levels of SWB for the categories. For our international college student sample, the correlation of the 10 income categories and the mean financial satisfaction for the categories is 0.96, although the correlation of income and financial satisfaction is only 0.18 based on the exact same data at the individual level. This example is based on aggregation of data within income categories instead of within nations, but it makes apparent the dramatic differences that can occur when considering correlations based on different levels of analyses.

For the World Value Survey II, the correlation between the 1 to 10 income categories and mean life satisfaction within those categories is 0.99, although the average correlation within nations between income and life satisfaction is only 0.24 in this sample! The effects of income are of course not any stronger, but instead are being considered in light of deviations from linearity of the mean SWB for each income group. The correlation within nations between income and SWB is based on individual variability, whereas the between-nation correlations represent the departure from linearity for the average income in a nation and the average SWB in a nation, with the effects of other within-nation variables aggregated out.

Another way to compare the size of effects of income within societies versus between countries is to examine both between and within countries the unstandardized betas in predicting life satisfaction with linear regression. The unstandardized beta indicates the slope of the regression line, either between countries or within them, depending on the analysis. The unstandardized beta between nations was 0.70, almost twice the average unstandardized beta within nations (0.36). Due to the limited number of nations, however, the confidence interval for the between nations weight includes the within-nations beta. Between countries there is an increase of about 0.7 scale units (on the 30-point Satisfaction with Life Scale) or about 7 units from the poorest of nations to the richest of nations, suggesting that income on average can move a nation across about 1/4 of the entire life satisfaction scale. The within-nation mean slope indicates that the richest and poorest people within countries on average differ by about $3\frac{1}{2}$ points on the 30-point SWLS. Note that the sample was college students, and it therefore might underestimate the effects of income because college students are likely to be spared the worst effects of poverty, and may not fully reap the rewards of wealth. Nonetheless, the comparison of the unstandardized betas suggests that between-nation effects may be stronger regardless of the error term being used. It might be, for example, that factors that covary with national income such as human rights may enhance the SWB of richer nations. Furthermore poor people may receive some benefits of national wealth (e.g., parks and better health care) if they live in a wealthy nation, and even rich people may find it difficult to avoid certain problems if they live in a poor society (e.g., poor roads). Thus the effects of national wealth may be stronger than the effects of individual wealth because all people in a wealthy society profit in some ways, and poor people and rich people within a society may be leveled to some degree by shared community resources, or lack thereof. Furthermore wealthy nations have better health, more freedom and human rights, and greater political stability than poor nations, and these factors may contribute to well-being beyond the fact that the average person has more money in wealthy nations. Note that the nation-resource argument made here is exactly opposite of the social comparison hypothesis advanced by Easterlin (1974), in which he suggested that poor people living in wealthy nations would suffer the most because of the unfavorable social comparisons forced on them. Our analysis suggests that moving to a wealthier nation is more likely to increase happiness than making more money within one's own nation.

If we compare the *standardized* betas between nations with the average occurring within nations (0.51 vs. 0.12), we find a value about four times as large. This influence is much larger than the unstandardized beta difference, and it therefore suggests that the aggregation argument advanced earlier also has some validity because there is relatively more variation due to other sources occurring within nations. Thus it appears that between nation differences in income may be larger than within-nation differences both because of the greater impact of additional factors affecting the SWB of individuals with societies, but also because of the broad effects of national wealth on most individuals in a country.

National Income and Other Variables

It is difficult to conclude with certainty why respondents in wealthier nations report higher levels of SWB on average. The wealth of nations correlates, often strongly, with a variety of desirable characteristics: greater human rights, the fulfillment of basic human needs, and social equality (Diener, Diener, and Diener 1995), for example. In addition the wealth of nations correlates inversely with the amount of sunny days in a country (Diener 1996). Schyns (1998) found that after controlling for income, the correlations of human rights, gender equality, and individualism with SWB fell to virtually zero. Similarly Diener, Diener, and Diener found that human rights and equality had a near zero correlation with SWB when income was controlled. However, because our samples of nations are not large, it is difficult to separate the influence of the various intercorrelated characteristics of nations. The high multicollinearity between predictors exacerbates the difficulty. For example, Diener, Diener, and Diener reported that individualism predicted the SWB of nations even when holding national income constant, but Schyns failed to replicate this finding. This lack of replicability indicates that we cannot accurately tease apart these highly correlated influences with the available data.

Diener, Diener, and Diener found that income predicted the SWB of nations even when basic need fulfillment was controlled. Basic need fulfillment within nations was assessed by health indices, sanitary drinking water, and food calories available. The fact that income predicted beyond the effects of basic needs suggests that income is not simply related to SWB to the extent that people are able to purchase physiological necessities. Once again, however, we need larger and more diverse samples of nations to reach definitive conclusions.

National Income Growth and SWB

During the past decades a number of nations have sustained dramatic increases in wealth, whereas others have remained relatively stagnant. For example, during the span of the surveys, over a period from 1946 to 1992, real income (after taxes and inflation are controlled) in the Unites States grew about 22 times. Individuals at the 50th percentile in 1947 would be at the 20th percentile in 1996, close to the poverty line (Krugman 1998). Similarly nations such as Japan, South Korea, China, and Singapore have experienced rapid economic growth. In contrast, nations such as Kuwait and Argentina had much slower economic growth.

Based on an analysis of the U.S. General Social Surveys, Oswald (1997) reports a very slight increase in the United States in happiness from 1972 to 1990. Diener and Suh (1997) show longitudinal data from the United States, Japan, and France that indicates that SWB in these nations has been virtually flat since World War II. In order to extend this longitudinal analysis to other nations, as well as to relate it to growth in income, we examined the compilation of surveys collected by Veenhoven (1993). Table 8.3 presents the slope between income and SWB over years for 14 nations. We elected to analyze the slopes for SWB only for those nations where there was a minimum of at least 4 surveys on which to base our analyses. In addition we desired to analyze the slopes only in nations where the same survey instrument was used repeatedly. Thus the nations all are highly economically developed. As can be seen, the slopes across these societies are on average virtually flat, despite steep economic growth in most of these countries. The economic growth rates in the neighborhood of 2 or 3 percent are more dramatic than they may seem. For instance, a growth rate of 2 percent will in the course of 20 years lead to about 50 percent more real income (after controlling inflation) per person, and a growth rate of 4 percent will lead to more than a 50 percent increase in real incomes in only 10 years. Considered against the backdrop of world history, these economic growth rates are virtually unprecedented. Thus, despite many more goods and services over time, people on average did not report being happier.

Table 8.3
Economic growth and change in life satisfaction over time

Nation	Slope of SWB	Number of years of surveys	Average percent economic growth, 1965–1990
Belgium	−0.04**	19	2.6
Denmark	0.02**	19	2.1
England	−0.04*	11	2.0
France	0.01	19	2.4
West Germany	0.02**	19	2.4
Greece	−0.01	12	2.8
Ireland	−0.03**	19	3.0
Italy	0.04**	19	3.0
Japan	0.01*	22	4.1
Luxembourg	0.03**	19	
Netherlands	0.00	19	1.8
Norway	−0.03	4	3.4
Portugal	0.09**	8	3.0
Spain	0.03	8	2.4
United States	0.00	18	1.7
Mean	0.007	15.7	2.4

Sources: Percent growth is based on the World Bank's (1992) *World Development Report*. The life satisfaction figures used are based on Veenhoven's (1993).
Notes: Nations listed for which at least four surveys were included. The life satisfaction scale used in England and the United States was a three-point scale, whereas the scale used in the other nations was a four-point scale.

Data reported by Hagerty and Veenhoven (1999) suggest that life satisfaction in many nations has been increasing over time. They examined fewer early surveys and more surveys in the 1990s than we covered and arrived at slightly different conclusions. Nevertheless, life satisfaction in some of the industrialized nations they examined went down, leaving us with the question of why SWB might either increase or decrease, despite economic growth. When they analyzed the correlation between growth in GDP per person and growth in life satisfaction, Hagerty and Veenhoven found a positive, but nonsignificant, correlation of 0.21.

One explanation for the lack of a clear rise in SWB in all nations experiencing economic growth is that there was also an increase in negative variables such as crime in these countries, which tended to offset the increased income. It should be noted, however, that homicide levels across countries do not correlate with SWB (Diener 1994). Furthermore Michalos and Zumbo (1998) reported that victims of crime were not less happy than others. Nonetheless, a breakdown of intimate relationships, or an increase in stress, might be variables that could counterbalance the influence of income gains. However, increases in negative factors over time could be offset by other positive things which have also occurred. For example, longevity has increased during this period. Birth control came into widespread use, as did computers. Cures for childhood leukemia became commonplace, and viagra was invented. The point is that although some negative factors increased during this period, there were other positive trends as well. Thus the idea that the effects of increased income were offset by a general degradation in society must be proved rather than asserted.

The alternative explanation of the relatively flat slopes for SWB is that desires increased in the richest nations as income increased, leading to no net psychological effect. Another alternative explanation is that only a very sharp increase in income will produce a rise in SWB, and that rise will last only a short period of time before people adapt. Finally, judging from the inconsistencies reported here and by Hagerty and Veenhoven, it may be that we simply have not possessed the statistical power to definitely identify an upward trend that is occurring due to rising incomes, because of the noise introduced by other factors. Although we do not know the reason, we can say that dramatic increases in national productivity were not accompanied on average by invariant increases in SWB. What is sorely lacking in all longitudinal nation studies to date is the inclusion of nations where economic growth is flat or declining. Without the inclusion of such societies, we are in a weak position to make inferences about how economic change increases SWB because we are experiencing only nations where growth is occurring.

Unfortunately, there were no poor nations that met the criterion of having at least four surveys over time using the same scale. However, there were three poorer nations where three surveys were administered, and the slopes in all three are positive: India, 0.09; Mexico, 0.06, and Philippines, 0.01. This is suggestive evidence that growth in the poorest nations can increase SWB, although slope lines based on only 3 points are highly unreliable. Survey data from different years are also available from nations such as Brazil and South Korea, suggesting increases in SWB. But because these data come from different surveys and rely on few time points, they must be accepted with extreme caution. Therefore it may be that rapid growth in poorer nations leads to heightened SWB, although the evidence on this issue is preliminary.

If we examine the slopes of SWB, we can see that SWB in some nations such as Portugal tended up, and SWB in other nations such as Belgium tended down. In light of these differences, we correlated the SWB slope changes with economic aspects of the countries. The correlation between the slope and inflation was -0.30, which became a significant -0.47 ($p < 0.05$) when we controlled for GNP. This is suggestive evidence that rapid inflation can lead to reductions in SWB. Because of the small sample size of nations, however, this conclusion needs to be replicated on a larger sample of nations when sufficient data are available. The correlation between the SWB slopes and the economic growth rate was -0.11, indicating that among this sample of wealthier nations, higher levels of growth were not related to increasing levels of SWB.

We can also examine the effects of growth in static analyses, where single surveys of SWB in nations are correlated with the level of growth that is occurring in those societies. The advantage here is that we can use more nations and a broader range of nations because we are not restricted to countries where surveys have been conducted repeatedly with the same instrument. This approach produces mixed results across surveys. Economic growth of countries and the mean level of SWB in those nations correlated at the following levels: World Value Survey II, r $(31) = 0.49$, $p < 0.01$; our international college sample, r $(36) = -0.16$ n.s.; life satisfaction in Michalos's (1991) college sample, r $(28) = -0.21$; N.S.; Ouweneel and Veenhoven's (1991) sample of nations using a 3-point happiness scale, r $(26) = -0.15$ n.s.; Veenhoven's (1993) sample of nations using a 10- or 11-point life satisfaction measure, r $(23) = -0.24$ n.s. When income (purchasing power parity) was controlled, the correlations tended to become stronger—in both the positive and negative directions. These conflicting findings are not surprising when one realizes that economic growth can be beneficial in some ways but also be accompanied by both rapidly rising expectations and undesirable concomitants such as rapid urbanization. It seems that without larger samples of nations and longitudinal data we will not be able to fully understand the effects of economic growth on SWB.

Equality

It could be that the manner in which income is divided in a nation is more important than the mean level of income there. For instance, it might be that a nation with nearly equal incomes is happier than a country where some people are very rich and many are very poor. Scandinavian nations approximate the former condition and Latin American societies more nearly approximate the latter. It should be noted, however, that richer countries also tend to be more equal, as indicated by lower Gini coefficients (Diener, Diener, and Diener 1995), and as a result studying the effects of equality separate from income is not straightforward. Ouweneel and Veenhoven (1991) found that income equality correlated 0.40 with the reported happiness in nations, and that this rose to 0.70 when economic prosperity was controlled. However, Diener, Diener, and Diener discovered that the income of nations and equality was correlated 0.84, and that controlling for income lowered the prediction of SWB by equality to 0.04. Schyns (1998) reported that gender equality correlated 0.52 ($p < 0.001$) with the happiness question in the World Value Survey II, but she also found that gender equality correlated 0.74 with the gross domestic product per capita of nations. Thus gender equality correlated a nonsignificant 0.10 with SWB when income was controlled.

In the present study we used the ratio of the income in the highest income group to the lowest income group (World Development Report 1994) to estimate income equality in nations, a high number thus indicating greater inequality. Income *inequality* did not correlate significantly with the World Value Survey II life satisfaction measure ($r = 0.20$), with life satisfaction in our college sample ($r = -0.03$), or in the combined life satisfaction surveys using similar scales ($r = 0.21$). However, higher inequality was *positively* and significantly related to higher SWB in two surveys when income of the nations was controlled! In the World Value Survey II, inequality and life satisfaction correlated 0.52 ($p < 0.05$) across nations, with income controlled, and this figure was 0.54 in the combined life satisfaction survey ($p < 0.01$). This unexpected finding probably occurred because equality is relatively high in Eastern European nations, but SWB is low, and equality is low in the Latin American nations where SWB is higher than would be predicted based on income. For instance, Colombia and Brazil had two of the most unequal income distributions of the nations we examined, and yet their life satisfaction scores were relatively high on the surveys we examined.

We very much doubt that inequality produces higher SWB. Instead, the findings seem to be due to particular historical and cultural characteristics that happen to covary with equality in this relatively small number of nations. Nonetheless, the results do suggest that equality of incomes within nations is not necessarily a prerequisite to high mean SWB. These findings also cast further doubt on Easterlin's

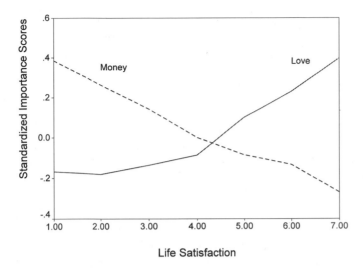

Figure 8.2
Relation of the rated importance of love and money to life satisfaction controlled for societal differences.

version of the social comparison hypothesis because societies with a small wealthy class and many poor people can be as high or higher in SWB than nations with relative income equality between persons. However, Veenhoven (1993) reported that nations with more equality had a greater standard deviation for SWB. When we controlled for income in the World Value Survey II nations, we replicated this finding (partial r (20) = 0.64, $p < 0.001$). Thus, although mean levels of life satisfaction can be high in nations with more income inequality, there is also a greater dispersion of SWB in these societies.

Materialism

Related to the question of the effects of money on SWB is the question of materialism: How happy are people who place great importance on money? In figure 8.2 we show the importance students placed on money in relation to their life satisfaction —respondents who rated money as less important were most satisfied. For comparison purposes we also show the importance students placed on love, in which case greater importance is accompanied by greater life satisfaction. The trends shown are controlled for differences between nations, but when we also controlled for individual income, virtually the same results were evident. This gives cross-national support to the idea of Ryan et al. (1996) and Kasser (2000) that strongly being motivated by money relates to less happiness, although we are uncertain of the psychological process causing this.

Discussion

In the data we analyzed, several conclusions are clear. First, income within nations correlated with SWB, and this trend was true even for comparisons between the wealthiest income categories. Further we found a large correlation between the wealth of nations and the level of SWB reported in them. Despite these positive findings, we also found that the average industrialized nation has not experienced large increases in SWB over the years since WW II, even as wealth has increased dramatically. However, there was suggestive evidence that SWB in poorer nations has increased as their economies have prospered. Despite this finding, the effects of rapid income growth are not uniform, suggesting that perhaps desires can outstrip even rapid economic development. We found that financial satisfaction is due to more than objective income; general life satisfaction predicts it as well. This finding indicates that people's global feelings of well-being make them more satisfied with their incomes, controlling for actual income. Income inequality in nations did not inevitably produce negative effects. For example, the poorest groups in some relatively poor nations were quite satisfied with their lives.

Evaluating the Theories

The extant findings on income and SWB are consistent with the desires/goals approach, but other models such as that based on Maslow's theory can also explain the findings. If we examine additional evidence, greater credence can be placed on the desires/goals theory. For example, Diener, Crawford, Oishi, and Wirtz (1998) manipulated the desirability of goods available to wealthy people in a hypothetical future society. It was found that subjects were less satisfied with a mid-level income in that society if wealthy people were said to possess goods that were extremely desirable as opposed to goods that were moderately desirable. In another experiment, Diener et al. manipulated beliefs about how much income would be required to purchase certain goods. They found that subjects' satisfaction with their predicted future income depended on the experimental manipulation of how many desired goods could be purchased with that income. In yet a third study Diener et al. found that people's personal goals influenced whether they were satisfied with particular levels of income. Thus other evidence corroborates the idea that whether people are satisfied with their income depends on whether people can meet their material desires and goals.

The existing evidence does not support an interpretation of the income-SWB link that is based on one's past income. If a person's income has gone up, this model suggests that people are more likely to be happy. The data on income growth suggest that this model cannot fully account for the link between income and SWB, and Diener, Sandvik, Seidlitz, and Diener (1993) also present evidence that is inconsistent with this model. Similarly the data cast doubt on social comparison as a primary way to understand the SWB-income connection. There are large mean differences across nations in SWB that are not consistent with Easterlin's (1974) social comparison model, and again, Diener, Sandvik, Seidlitz, and Diener also report evidence that is inconsistent with this approach. One reason that social comparison is not a simple process influencing SWB is that people use much discretion in the comparison targets they choose, and base their social comparison perceptions on their own feelings about themselves instead of on actual comparison calculations (e.g., Diener and Fujita 1997). Thus social comparison and comparison to one's past do not appear to be the major girders shoring up the SWB-income relation.

The idea that culture can influence one's satisfaction with income does receive some support in the data we analyzed. Certain nations are happier than one might expect based on their incomes, and the Latin American nations fall uniformly in this group. It is particularly noteworthy that poor individuals in the Latin American nations do not report very low levels of SWB, as they often do elsewhere. Culture may influence the importance placed on material wealth and thereby dampen the ill effects of poverty in some societies, although this moderating influence on the SWB-income relation has not been explored in depth.

Veenhoven (1995) reviewed evidence and concluded that livability theory, the idea that objective conditions that serve human nature produce happiness, fits the data best. He suggests that characteristics of societies are related to the degree to which they meet universal human needs, and in turn achieve high SWB. The reason that SWB has not increased appreciably in wealthier societies, according to this approach, is that increased material wealth beyond a certain point has not helped these societies better meet human needs. Veenhoven reviews evidence on cultural approaches and relativistic approaches and concludes that these models are incorrect. Veenhoven's approach is consistent with humanistic theories such as that of Maslow (1954), and the emphasis of the "Rochester school" (e.g., Ryan et al. 1996) on intrinsic values.

Veenhoven's model based solely on basic physiological needs does not seem tenable based on the evidence we review. Our finding that the highest income group is more satisfied than the second-highest income group is inconsistent with the basic needs model because both groups can fully meet their physical needs. Nevertheless, Veenhoven's livability model remains tenable if one accepts the notion that even large amounts of income might be used to meet self-actualization needs. At this point it appears that both the material desires model and the Maslowian extension of Veenhoven's needs model can explain the existing data. One difference between these two models is the prediction of the Maslow model that income at higher levels will increase SWB only if it is used in ways to promote self-growth, whereas the material desires model predicts that the lack of fulfillment of a wide range of desires, no matter how frivolous they may appear, can harm SWB if the goods and services are strongly wanted by the individual. A major task for future research is to obtain data that can test these two models in a comparative fashion.

Subjective Influences on Satisfaction

Ravaillion and Lokshin (1998) are economists studying Russian's utility function for money. They asked respondents to rate their income on a nine-step ladder on which the lowest step represents the poorest people and the top step represents rich people, and label this "welfare." In other words, people are asked to subjectively evaluate their income on a poor-rich continuum. Although objective income significantly predicts this measure, it explains only a small part of the variance in it. Healthier, married, and better-educated people rate their economic welfare higher, and unemployed people rate it lower, than their objective incomes would predict. People in richer geographic areas had lower perceived welfare, controlling for income and other variables. Growth rates in real income predict only a small part of changes over time in subjective welfare. Taken together, these findings suggest that much subjective is going on when people evaluate their incomes; that "utility" is not a linear function of objective income. However, Diener et al. (1993) report evidence showing that relative standards such as social comparison and people's past income do not invariably influence the relation between income and SWB. Perhaps increases in income do not map neatly onto increases in perceived welfare because people's material desires also change at varying rates. The fact that educated, employed, married, healthy people in the Ravaillion and Lokshin study report higher monetary welfare supports our earlier conclusion that global feelings of well-being can affect people's financial satisfaction. In addition the finding that people in poorer areas were happier given a similar level of income is perhaps due to the fact that people there desire less expensive lifestyles. In both cases, however, the explanations are post-hoc, and we need direct measures of desires and comparison-others to directly determine what is occurring.

The conclusion that can be drawn from the existing data is that a more prosperous material world will not inevitably increase life satisfaction. If people's desires outstrip reality, it is likely that people would be more dissatisfied even in a very affluent world. People in wealthy nations may exhibit greater levels of SWB than people in poor nations because they have more of the desired goods. But the small increases in SWB in Japan, Belgium, the United States, and other nations experiencing high levels of economic growth are cautionary. An increase in income will not inevitably lead to greater SWB. The average person in the United States in 1946 would be considered poor today, but probably he or she did not feel poor. Thus it may be people's desires that determine whether they are psychologically rich or poor. Nevertheless, people's desires can be influenced by certain innate needs, and therefore income may have some effects on SWB that are not simply a reflection of transient desires.

One can achieve psychological wealth as much by constraining one's desires as by increasing one's income. The voluntary simplicity movement advocates that people purposefully limit their desires so as to use fewer resources. Whether this movement can gain widespread appeal is yet to be seen. It may be that people will move to other goals once they have achieved a certain level of material wealth, entering a post-materialistic (Inglehart 1990) phase in which intimacy and growth goals become paramount. However, it is also possible that competition and advertising will move people's desires ever higher, creating a cycle of economic growth that does not enhance SWB.

Effects of Poverty

Another conclusion drawn from the evidence is that it is not desirable to live in a poor nation. Not only is SWB low in these countries, but objective quality of life indicators such as longevity, literacy, gender equality, and crime (Diener and

C. Diener 1995a) also tend to indicate undesirable conditions in them. Furthermore it may in many ways be easier to be poor in a wealthy country than in a poor one. Even though poor people in rich countries do not receive a level of health care that they deserve, their health care in most cases is superior to that received by the poor in a poor society. Poor people in a wealthy society do not live as long as the wealthy, but they live longer than the average person in the poorest societies. Furthermore poor people in a wealthy society can benefit from the roads, parks, mass transit, schools, and other amenities that are more readily available in rich nations. We do not mean to justify poverty in rich societies. We only mean to suggest that being poor is not worse in wealthy societies than in poor ones.

In order to pursue the issue of poverty in more depth, we examined the SWB scores of the poorest people across nations. In the World Value Survey II, different income categories were used in different nations. Nonetheless, when we examined the lowest income group in the wealthiest nations, SWB on a 1 to 10 scale tended to be well above the neutral point of 5.5 (e.g., United States, 7.16; Netherlands, 7.44; Britain, 7.04; and Norway, 7.09), although usually not as high as for the richest group. In contrast, in the poorest nations, the poor group tended to score low on life satisfaction (e.g., India, 5.98; Poland, 4.81; South Africa, 4.88; and Hungary, 4.90), although this was not true of the poor in Latin nations. The poor in Latin countries such as Mexico, Brazil, and Chile showed relatively high SWB scores despite the large amount of inequality in these nations (means of 7.36, 7.45, and 7.38, respectively). This finding points to culture and expectations as important influences on SWB. Overall, however, our results suggest that it is worse to be poor in a poor country than in a rich one.

Future Research

The present chapter focused on the existing data on the relation between income and life satisfaction and financial satisfaction. However, there are additional interesting questions for future research. We should examine the relation between income and SWB using measures of pleasant and unpleasant affect because these are also major components of SWB. Although the World Value Survey II included Bradburn and Caplovitz's (1965) measure of these constructs, we found that this measure is somewhat weak (Larsen, Diener, and Emmons 1985) and therefore chose not to report on it in the present study. The measure does not broadly sample pleasant and unpleasant emotional feelings. In our international college student sample we did use a measure of emotional intensity and frequency regarding a number of specific emotion terms (e.g., joy, fear, sadness, and affection). We found correlations between income and affect even smaller than the values for satisfaction shown in table 8.1. However, we need better measures of pleasant and unpleasant affect in broadly representative samples of respondents before firm conclusions can be drawn. Ahuvia and Friedman (1998) suggest that certain aspects of income and consumption will predict life satisfaction, whereas other aspects will predict affective well-being. As of now, we restrict our conclusions to how income relates to life satisfaction and financial satisfaction. In the future we need to more carefully distinguish different components of subjective well-being such as life satisfaction, financial satisfaction, positive affect, and feeling poor.

We need greater use of experience sampling studies to explore momentary SWB, as well as to accurately assess desires and spending patterns. If we extrapolate Kahneman's (1999) extension of adaptation theory, we might surmise that richer people are happier in momentary experience than poorer individuals but require more happy moments to label themselves as having high global SWB. If so, experience sampling studies might, in unison with peer reports and memory measures, be able to uncover this pattern. The hypothesis is that momentary reports of mood will show larger differences between rich and poor people than global measures because expectations for happiness adapt, and this adaptation is reflected more strongly in the global measures.

In terms of methods, more sophistication is needed in future research in this area. For example, we need to more carefully differentiate types of income (e.g., earned individual income, household total income, or barter income), and also consider household size. There has been little research examining different types of income (e.g., earned income vs. inherited or investment income), or research on how people spend and invest the income they have. Although we have been blessed with large samples of individuals in this area of study, we now also need samples that include a large and diverse set of nations. In addition longitudinal panel designs will be very helpful.

We also need to gather measures of desires so that we do not have to infer them indirectly from other information. One problem in testing Maslow's model against the material desires model is that there are currently no large survey data in which material desires are specifically measured, and in which specific uses of money to meet various types of needs are also assessed. This forces us into the position of having to make inferences about need fulfillment and desires in our explanations of

SWB because the survey research does not include specific measures of these concepts that would help provide a more rigorous test of the models. One unanswered question in the material desires model is whether the desires must be conscious goals in order to influence SWB, or whether they can be implicit cognitive templates of the desirable life. Another issue in developing the materials desire model is to determine how one's past income and social comparisons might influence people's material desires. For the model based on Maslow's needs, researchers must be able to specify the needs and their fulfillment in enough detail so that they are directly measurable and the theory becomes falsifiable.

A fascinating question for future research is how the desire for new products relates to SWB. Many new products are created each year, and some, such as medical aids, undoubtedly enhance the quality of life. Some products are inherently desirable and other products require advertising to become desirable. Ryan et al. (1996) suggest that some goods are inherently more satisfying than others, and we suggest that this may extend to goods and services as well. A task for future research is to examine how both desires and consumption of various types of goods and services influence SWB. A plausible hypothesis is that economic growth cannot substantially enhance SWB in wealthy countries unless new products are created that are intrinsically very desirable.

A related question concerns how materialism interfaces with other values and goals. The belief that goods and services are more important than other values such as relationships appears to be detrimental to SWB (Kasser 2000). Reviews of the materialism literature can be found in Ahuvia and Wong (1997) and Sirgy (1998). As of yet, there is little research on how materialism interacts with income to predict SWB across cultures.

Conclusion

There may be something in our results to please everyone. For liberals, there is the finding that poor people are less happy on average. For conservatives, there is the finding that wealthy nations are happier, and that the degree of inequality in nations does not seem to adversely affect SWB. For those who believe that materialism is not the road to happiness, there is the finding that wealthy societies have not grown in SWB as they achieved even higher levels of wealth, and also the finding that believing money is very important is related to less life satisfaction. For the psychologist there is the finding that global feelings of well-being influence financial satisfaction in a top-down fashion beyond the bottom-up influence of objective income. And for the cross-cultural scientist there is the finding that culture and expectations seem to play a large role in people's SWB.

Subjective well-being is only one of our values, and it is only one of the outcomes we might examine in evaluating the effects of income on quality of life. Increased wealth can help reduce infant mortality, foster scientific pursuits, allow spending on parks and public facilities, and create more leisure time (Diener and Suh 1997). Thus we are not recommending that nations abandon the pursuit of wealth and economic growth but that they do need to question how increases in wealth will be used.

If wealthy societies are reaching the postmaterialistic point where added goods and services enhance SWB very little, we may be at a critical crossroads in terms of public policy and individual choices. People in wealthy nations feel an increasing time shortage, and yet many are working even longer hours than before. People seek a level of material wealth undreamed of by earlier generations, and they make sacrifices in time and personal relationships to attain it. However, despite the picture of a "good life" presented in the media and in advertising, people may want to reassess their priorities. To the extent that individuals or societies must sacrifice other values to obtain more wealth, the pursuit of income is not likely to be worth the costs. After World War II people had no computers or televisions, indoor plumbing was not taken for granted, and many people had ice boxes rather than refrigerators. Yet people report being about as happy as they are now. Thus we must question then whether we need a trip to Antarctica, a larger home with more bathrooms, and a high-status automobile to be truly happy. Certainly if these items require us to make sacrifices in self-growth, leisure time, and intimate relationships, they may interfere with happiness rather than enhance it. As long as people want more goods and services, they will tend to be somewhat dissatisfied if they do not get them. Thus the educational challenge is to convince people that other pursuits may sometimes lead to greater fulfillment than does the pursuit of more money.

Note

Our sincere thanks are extended to Ruut Veenhoven of Erasmus University and to Christopher Jencks of Harvard University for their insightful comments which most certainly improved this chapter.

References

Ahuvia, A., and Wong, N. 1997. Three types of materialism: Their relationships and origins. Unpublished paper. University of Michigan.

Ahuvia, A. C., and Friedman, D. C. 1988. Income, consumption, and subjective well-being: Toward a composite macromarketing model. *Journal of Macromarketing* 18: 153–68.

Bradburn, N. M., and Caplovitz, D. 1965. *Reports of Happiness*. Chicago: Aldine.

Brickman, P., and Campbell, D. T. 1971. Hedonic relativism and planning the good society. In M. H. Appley, ed., *Adaptation-Level Theory*. New York: Academic Press, pp. 287–305.

Brickman, P., Coates, D., and Janoff-Bulman, R. 1978. Lottery winners and accident victims: Is happiness relative? *Journal of Personality and Social Psychology* 36: 917–27.

Cohen, J. 1977. *Statistical Power Analysis for the Behavioral Sciences*. Hillsdale, NJ: Lawrence Erlbaum.

Cornoni-Huntley, J., Barbano, H. E., Brody, J. A., Cohen, B., Gledman, J. J., Kleinman, J. C., and Madans, J. 1983. National health and nutrition examination: Epidemiological followup survey. *Public Health Reports* 98: 245–51.

Diener, E. 1994. Subjective well-being in cross-cultural perspective. Paper delivered at the Twelfth International Congress of Cross-cultural Psychology, July 24–27, Pamplona, Spain.

Diener, E. 1995. A value based index for measuring national quality of life. *Social Indicators Research* 36: 107–21.

Diener, E. 1996. Subjective well-being in cross-cultural perspective. In H. Grad, A. Blanco, and J. Georgas, eds., *Key Issues in Cross-cultural Psychology*. Lisse: Swets and Zeitlinger, pp. 319–30.

Diener, E., Crawford, E., Oishi, S., and Wirtz, D. 1998. Goals and desires as the explanation for the relation of income to subjective well-being. Manuscript submitted for publication. University of Illinois.

Diener, E., and Diener, C. 1995. The wealth of nations revisited: Income and quality of life. *Social Indicators Research* 36: 275–86.

Diener, E., and Diener, M. 1995. Cross-cultural correlates of life satisfaction and self-esteem. *Journal of Personality and Social Psychology* 68: 653–63.

Diener, E., Diener, M., and Diener, C. 1995. Factors predicting the subjective well-being of nations. *Journal of Personality and Social Psychology* 69: 851–64.

Diener, E. and Fujita, F. 1997. Social comparisons and subjective well-beng. In B. Buunk, and F. X. Gibbons, eds., *Health Coping, and Well-being: Perspectives from Social Comparison Theory*. Mahwah, NJ: Lawrence Erlbaum, pp. 329–57.

Diener, E., Sandvik, E., Seidlitz, L., and Diener, M. 1993. The relationship between income and subjective well-being: Relative or absolute? *Social Indicators Research* 28: 195–223.

Diener, E., and Suh, E. 1997. Measuring quality of life: Economic, social and subjective indicators. *Social Indicators Research* 40: 189–216.

Diener, E., Suh, E., Smith, H. and Shao, L. 1995. National differences in reported subjective well-being: Why do they occur? *Social Indicators Research* 34: 7–32.

Droge, C., Calantone, R., Agrawal, M., and Mackoy, R. 1993. The consumption culture and its critiques: A framework for analysis. *Journal of Macromarketing* 13: 32–45.

Easterlin, R. A. 1974. Does economic growth improve the human lot? Some empirical evidence In P. A. David and M. W. Reder, eds., *Nations and Households in Economic Growth*. New York: Academic Press, pp. 89–125.

Hagerty, M. R., and Veenhoven, R. 1999. Wealth and happiness revisited: Growing wealth of nations *does* go with greater happiness. Unpublished study submitted for publication, University of California, Davis.

Inglehart, R. 1990. *Culture Shift in Advanced Industrial Society*. Princeton: Princeton University Press.

Kahneman, D. 1999. Objective happiness. In D. Kahneman, E. Diener, and N. Schwarz, eds., *Well-being: The Foundations of Hedonie Psychology*. New York: Russell Sage Foundation, pp. 3–25.

Kasser, T. 2000. Two versions of the American dream: Which goals and values make for a high quality of life. In E. Diener and D. R. Rahtz, eds., *Advances in Quality of Life Theory and Research*, pp. 3–12. Dordrecht: Kluwer Academic.

Krugman, P. 1998. Viagra and the wealth of nations. *New York Times Magazine*, August 23.

Kwok, O. 1998. Subjective well-being across nations: A hierarchical linear modeling approach. Masters thesis. Chinese University of Hong Kong.

Lapinski, J. S., Rieman, C. R., Shapiro, R. Y., Stevens, M. F., and Jacobs, L. R. 1998. Welfare state regimes and subjective well-being: A cross-national study. *International Journal of Public Opinion Research* 10: 2–24.

Larsen, R. J., Diener, E., and Emmons, R. A. 1985. An evaluation of subjective well-being measures. *Social Indicators Research* 17: 1–18.

Maslow, A. H. 1954. *Motivation and Personality*. New York: Harper and Row.

Michalos, A. C. 1991. *Global Report on Student Well-being*. New York: Springer.

Michalos, A. C., and Zumbo, B. D. 1998. Criminal victimization and the quality of life. Unpublished study. University of Northern British Columbia.

Oishi, S., Diener, E., and Lucas, R. E., and Suh, E. M. 1999. Cross-cultural variations in predictors of life satisfaction: Perspectives from needs and values. *Personality and Social Psychology Bulletin* 25: 980–90.

Oswald, A. J. 1997. Happiness and economic performance. *Economic Journal* 107: 1815–31.

Ouweneel, P., and Veenhoven, R. 1991. Cross-national differences in happiness: Cultural bias or societal quality. In N. Bleichrodt and P. J. D. Drenth, eds., *Contemporary Issues in Cross-cultural Psychology*. Amsterdam: Swets and Zeitlinger.

Parducci, A. 1995. *Happiness, Pleasure, and Judgment: The Contextual Theory and Its Applications*. Mahwah, NJ: Lawrence Erlbaum.

Ravaillion, M., Lokshin, M. 1998. Objective versus subjective welfare. Unpublished report. World Bank, Washington DC.

Ryan, R. M., Sheldon, K. M., Kasser, T., and Deci, E. L. 1996. All goods are not created equal. An organismic perspective on the nature of goals and their regulation. In P. M. Gollwitzer and J. A. Bargh, eds., *The Psychology of Action: Linking Cognition and Motivation to Behavior.* New York: Guilford Press, pp. 7–26.

Sandvik, E., Diener, E., and Seidlitz, L. 1993. Subjective well-being: The convergence and stability of self-report and non-self-report measures. *Journal of Personality* 61: 317–42.

Schyns, P. 1998. Crossnational differences in happiness: Economic and cultural factors explored. *Social Indicators Research* 43: 3–26.

Shao, L. 1993. Multilanguage comparability of life satisfaction and happiness measures in mainland Chinese and American students. Master's thesis. University of Illinois.

Sirgy, M. J. 1998. Materialism and quality of life. *Social Indicators Research* 43: 227–60.

Smith, S., and Razzell, P. 1975. *The Pools Winners.* London: Caliban Books.

Thoits, P., and Hannon, M. 1979. Income and psychological distress: The impact of an income maintenance experience. *Journal of Health and Social Behavior* 20: 120–38.

Torgerson, W. S. 1958. *Theory and Methods of Scaling.* New York: Wiley.

Veenhoven, R. 1991. Is happiness relative? *Social Indicators Research* 24: 1–34.

Veenhoven, R. 1993. *Happiness in Nations: Subjective Appreciation of Life in 56 Nations 1946–1992.* Rotterdam: Risbo.

Veenhoven, R. 1995. The cross-national pattern of happiness: Test of predictions implied in three theories of happiness. *Social Indicators Research* 34: 33–68.

Wachtel, P. L. 1983. *The Poverty of Affluence.* New York: Free Press.

World Bank. 1992. *World Development Report 1992.* New York: Oxford University Press.

World Value Survey Group. 1994. *World Values Survey, 1981–1984 and 1990–1993.* ICPSR. Ann Arbor, MI: Institute for Social Research.

9

National Differences in Micro and Macro Worry: Social, Economic, and Cultural Explanations

Shalom H. Schwartz and Gila Melech

This chapter examines national differences in worry, an aspect of subjective well-being that has begun to receive empirical attention across cultures only recently (Boehnke et al. 1998; Schwartz, Sagiv, and Boehnke 2000). We address a series of questions about worries with the aid of a set of data from 14 cultural groups: How can worries be conceptualized and measured? Is there sufficient cross-cultural similarity in the way people understand and report their worries to justify comparing worries across nations? How do different types of worry relate to other aspects of subjective well-being (SWB)—satisfaction with life, positive and negative feelings, frequency of being happy and sad?

The main focus of this chapter is on national differences in worry. We first note which worries are most salient across nations and how levels of the two major types of worry we identify vary. We then draw on various social, economic, and cultural variables in order to explain national differences in worry. Finally, we discuss some implications of what we have learned for the future cross-national study of worry and of SWB in general.

Worries: Their Nature and Measurement

We adopt the definition of worries proposed by Boehnke et al. (1998) and supported in their research: A worry is a disturbing cognition that a state of an object (micro or macro) in some domain of life (health, safety, etc.) will become (or become more, or remain) discrepant from its desired state. This broad definition applies both to the daily worries that may plague anyone and to the prolonged, intense, and uncontrollable worries associated with severe anxiety (Borkovec et al. 1983). This definition specifies two key facets of a worry: the object that is threatened and the life domain to which the worry refers.

Object of Worry: Micro and Macro

Most past theory and research has conceptualized worry as a subtype of anxiety whose presence indicates poor mental health (reviewed in Davey and Tallis 1994; Eysenck 1992). In a departure from this view, Boehnke, et al. (1998) argue that there are two distinct types of worry which they label "micro" worries and "macro" worries. Micro worries (e.g., "my being unattractive," "that my parents will die") have as their object the self or those with whom one identifies closely (in-group or extensions of self). Macro worries (e.g., "unemployment in our country," "people in the world dying of hunger") have as their object entities external to the self and one's in-group—the wider society, world, or universe.

With regard to micro worry, Boehnke, et al. (1998) theorized and presented data from three student samples showing that the more intense people's micro worries, the poorer their cognitive and affective SWB. In contrast, they found that the intensity of macro worries is often unrelated to well-being and sometimes even positively related (e.g., Boehnke 1995b; Doctor, Goldenring, and Powell 1987; Griffin and Prior 1990). A study of how the values important to people may influence their worries (Schwartz et al. 2000) further emphasized the distinctiveness of these two types of worry. People who attributed importance to power values reported more micro worry than others but less macro worry; the reverse was true for those who attributed importance to universal concern for others. These studies suggest that micro worries and macro worries differ both in their origins and in their consequences.

Life Domains

The second conceptual facet of worry refers to the domain of life in which an object is threatened. Boehnke et al. identified seven different domains of life in the lists of worries in the literature: health, safety, environment, social relations, meaning in life, achievement in work and studies, and economics. Every worry concerns a threat either to a micro or macro object in at least one of the domains of life. For example, the worry "hostility of people in the world to one another" concerns a macro object in the social domain, and the worry "my life being boring" concerns a micro object in the meaning domain. Thus the object and life domain facets of worry cross-cut one another and are conceptually independent.

Measuring Worry

Based on their conceptualization, Boehnke et al. developed an instrument to measure worries. It includes items intended to represent each combination of micro object or macro object with each life domain. Table 9.1 lists the items, each classified by object and life domain according to a priori classifications that were confirmed in research in Germany and Israel (Boehnke et al. 1998). For each item, respondents were asked to consider: "How worried, if at all, am I about . . . ?" A 5-point response scale was labeled "not at all worried" and "extremely worried" at its poles, and "somewhat worried" at its midpoint.

In this chapter we examine worry data from a much larger and more variegated set of countries and from adults as well as students. We studied university student samples from Belgium, Brazil, France, former East Germany, former West Germany, Hungary, Israel, Russia, Slovakia, Turkey, Uganda, and the United States, and primary and secondary school teachers from Brazil, Denmark, former East Germany, England, Hungary, Israel, and Slovakia.[1] This is but a small proportion of the world's nations. Still it is quite diverse, including samples from East and West Europe, North and South America, Africa, and the Middle East, but notably not the Far East. By studying two sets of samples, teachers and students, we can learn whether the observed associations hold across groups that differ in their stage in life and their social orientations. It would be best to study representative national samples, of course, but the current study may provide a reasonable first test of the universality of the proposed approach to worries. The first four columns of table 9.2 describe the samples.

The choice of samples raises two potential methodological limitations that may affect the interpretation of all the findings concerning national differences in worry that we report. First, because the current research is based on a limited set of nations, the range of variation in worries, SWB, and the main social and cultural variables may be restricted as compared with the range across a large set of nations. This would attenuate correlations and lead to under- or misestimation of associations among the variables. Only if the range of variation is relatively unrestricted will the sets of nations we studied provide assessments of association similar to what exists in the diverse global set of nations.

To evaluate whether restriction of range is a problem, we estimated how the sampling of nations in this study would have affected the two associations with SWB that Diener, Diener, and Diener (1995) found to be most powerful across a large and diverse set of nations. They reported that SWB correlated 0.58 with GDP per capita and 0.61 with cultural individualism, across 55 nations. We computed what these correlations would have been had the analyses been limited to the sets of nations available in the current study. The parallel correlations computed from the Diener et al. data, based only on the 12 nations in our student analyses, were 0.57

Table 9.1
Items in the worries questionnaire, classified by facets

Worry item	Object facet	Life domain facet
1. My getting cancer	Micro	Health
2. Conflict among groups in our society	Macro	Social
3. Worsening destruction of the environment	Macro	Environment
4. Someone in my family not having enough money to live on[a]	Micro	Economic
5. My country getting involved in a war	Macro	Safety
6. My life being boring	Micro	Meaning
7. Many people in XXX[b] living in poverty	Macro	Economic
8. My parents dying	Micro	Health/safety
9. XXX society not succeeding in maintaining high standards in education, science, and technology	Macro	Achievement
10. Someone in my family being in a traffic accident	Micro	Safety
11. Things not working out in my studies or job	Micro	Achievement
12. Someone close to me being infected with AIDS	Micro	Health
13. Damage to nature (forests, animals, etc.) in XXX	Macro	Environment
14. My not having any close friends	Micro	Social
15. The population explosion in the third world	Macro	Environment
16. My being unattractive	Micro	Social
17. A value crisis in society	Macro	Meaning
18. My own death	Micro	Health
19. Unemployment in our country	Macro	Economic
20. Politically motivated violence (incidence of terrorist attacks) in our country[c]	Macro	Safety
21. My life not really being meaningful	Micro	Meaning
22. Hostility of people in the world toward one another	Macro	Social
23. Pollution in my immediate neighborhood (air, water, noise, trash, etc.)	Macro[d]	Environment
24. Outbreak of a nuclear war	Macro	Safety
25. My getting into financial difficulties some day	Micro	Economic
26. Humankind not being wise enough to make responsible use of new scientific knowledge	Macro	Achievement
27. My closest relationship breaking up	Micro	Social
28. People in the world dying of hunger	Macro	Health
29. My not really being good enough to get a job	Micro	Achievement
30. People becoming addicted to hard drugs	Macro	Health
31. My being the victim of a violent crime	Micro	Safety
32. Nuclear power plant leaking or blowing up	Macro	Safety
33. Simply about the future[a]	Not specific	

a. Not included in the micro or macro index because of inconsistency across samples.
b. XXX indicates where the name of the respondent's country or people appeared.
c. Phrasing used for item depended on current realities in the country.
d. Designed as a micro but emerged as a macro in all SSA and factor analyses.

Table 9.2
Characteristics of samples

Country	N	Year	Mean age	Females (%)	GNP per capita	Income inequality, (Gini Index)	Inflation (%)	Rights violations	Hofstede individualism	Egalitarian versus hierarchy	Harmony versus mastery	Autonomy versus embedded
Students												
Belgium	355	1995	22.6	71	20,880	0.27	2.1	14.65	75	6.79	0.22	1.73
Brazil	148	1995	22.7	66	2,770	0.60	10.0	20.51	38	4.55	-0.89	0.57
East Germany	204	1994	23.8	56	9,800	0.33	1.5	16.58	52	6.08	0.15	2.25
France	671	1996	22.5	60	22,260	0.35	2.0	14.19	71	5.85	-0.01	3.42
Hungary	165	1995	23.0	70	5,000	0.27	23.5	14.84	50	5.08	0.60	0.50
Israel	428	1994	22.9	57	13,220	0.33	11.3	22.17	54	4.48	-2.60	0.57
Russia	242	1997	24.2	68	2,580	0.50	47.6	25.24	45	3.53	-0.50	-0.65
Slovakia	233	1996	19.6	64	5,200	0.20	5.8	16.25	49	5.55	-0.10	-0.88
Turkey	269	1995	21.7	51	1,980	0.49	80.3	28.43	37	3.56	-0.54	-0.66
Uganda	184	1995	22.6	23	159	0.41	7.2	26.96	27	2.34	-2.10	-1.97
United States	474	1996	24.7	37	23,240	0.34	2.9	13.39	91	4.25	-1.70	0.08
West Germany	193	1995	26.2	64	23,040	0.33	1.5	16.58	67	6.70	-0.44	2.51
Teachers												
Brazil	200	1995	36.8	49	2,770	0.60	10.0	20.51	38	4.55	-0.89	0.57
Denmark	706	1995	47.4	50	22,500	0.33	2.1	16.01	74	6.77	-0.26	2.02
East Germany	135	1994	28.8	74	9,800	0.33	1.5	16.58	52	6.08	0.15	2.25
England	208	1995	41.5	70	21,000	0.32	2.4	13.81	89	5.02	-1.23	1.69
Hungary	143	1995	42.3	79	5,000	0.27	23.5	14.80	50	5.08	0.60	0.50
Israel	88	1996	40.7	79	13,220	0.33	11.3	22.17	54	4.48	-2.60	0.57
Slovakia	191	1996	41.6	80	5,200	0.20	5.8	16.25	49	5.55	-0.10	-0.88

and 0.51, respectively. The correlations, based only on the 7 nations in our teacher analyses, were 0.57 and 0.46, respectively. Thus, the correlations of SWB were virtually identical with GDP and quite similar with individualism in the subsets and in the full 55 nations. This suggests that the subsets of nations in this chapter are not especially restricted, compared to the set of 55 nations in Diener et al. (1995). These data may therefore allow reasonable estimations of the associations among variables across nations around the world.

A second methodological issue is that we derive nation scores on worries from occupationally matched samples rather than from representative national samples. The matched sample approach (see Hofstede 1980, 1991; Schwartz 1994, 1997) does not assume that mean scores for student and teacher samples from a nation are the same as those for a representative sample from that nation. Rather, we assume that the *order* of a set of nations on the worries means, based on these matched samples, resembles the *order* one would obtain with representative samples from the same nations. Worries data from representative national samples are unavailable, so we cannot evaluate this assumption in the case of worries. However, it has been supported for values (Schwartz and Sagie, in press). In SWB research, moreover, Diener et al. (1995) reported correlations of 0.49 to 0.71 between the national SWB scores derived from college student samples and those derived from three national surveys. These correlations suggest a similar, but far from identical, ordering of nations.

If the assumption regarding the order of nations is plausible, then the national differences in worry, based on matched student and teacher samples, should relate systematically and predictably to other national characteristics. As we will see, several meaningful and predictable relationships are found. This suggests that the worry scores based on matched samples are viable, though not ideal, indicators of national levels of worry.

Are Worries Cross-culturally Comparable?

Does the conceptualization and method for measuring worries we have presented hold across cultures? Boehnke et al. (1998) confirmed the discrimination of both facets of worry as well as the assignment of items to these facets in three samples of university students in former East and West Germany and in Israel.[2] Here we pose a much stronger challenge to the cultural robustness of the theory of worries. Does it apply across 19 samples, including both student and adults, from 14 quite diverse nations? Specifically, we examine whether the structure of empirical relations among the worry items is similar in each sample. If so, does it confirm the theorized discriminations of micro and macro worries and of life domains?

Responses to the worries survey were analyzed separately in each sample using SSA (Borg and Shye 1993; Guttman 1968). This is a nonmetric scaling technique that represents items as points in a multidimensional space such that the distances between the points reflect the interrelations among the items. To test the claims of the worries theory, we examined whether the items intended to measure each type of worry form separate regions in the space. This is a "configurational verification" approach (Davison 1983; Dillon and Goldstein 1984).

To simplify the presentation, figure 9.1 displays the relations found among the worries in the grand sample of all respondents ($N = 6,030$) in a two-dimensional space. Worries close to each other in the space are highly positively intercorrelated; the farther apart any two worries, the less positive the correlations are between them. The spatial locations of the worries relative to one another also reveal the conceptual relations among them. Those close together share meanings, and they differ from those farther away.

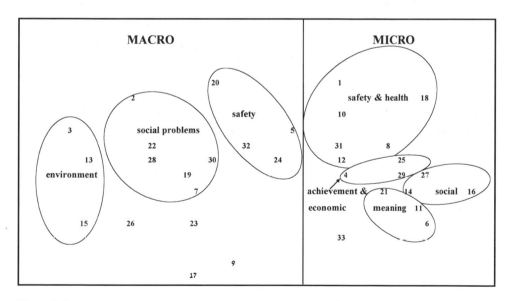

Figure 9.1
Two-dimensional similarity structure analysis of worries based on 19 samples from 14 nations.

Micro versus Macro Object of Worry

In figure 9.1 all of the micro worries are located on one side of the space and all of the macro worries on the other side. This spatial discrimination between micro and macro worries signifies that respondents reacted to them as conceptually different types of worry. The results imply that respondents experience the set of micro worries as sharing a common meaning and the set of macro worries as sharing a different common meaning. The empirical separation also implies that the intensity of worries is influenced substantially by whether their object is the self and its extensions (micro) or the wider society and world (macro). Single worries located near the micro/macro border in figure 9.1 express some degree of both micro and macro concerns. For example, worry 5 (my country getting involved in a war) is about a threat to society that also constitutes a threat to personal safety.

The empirical discrimination of micro and macro worries in the "grand sample" analysis in figure 9.1 also appeared in every one of the 19 separate analyses. That is, this discrimination replicated in the SSA analysis in every nation and type of sample. Hence we conclude that the micro/macro object facet of worries is meaningful and measurable across cultures.[3]

Having established that micro and macro worries are distinguished across cultures, we next consider relations between them. Our reasoning and past findings might seem to suggest that they are uncorrelated or even negatively related: they were clearly discriminated in the spatial and factor analyses and their observed relations with SWB in earlier research were different. Logically people who worry about their own health, income, or physical attractiveness may not be especially prone to worry that others in the wider society or world are living in poverty, dying of hunger, or suffering from a population explosion. Nonetheless, these two types of worry correlate positively with one another.

We averaged each individual's responses to the 14 micro worry items for a micro worry score and to the 17 macro worry items for a macro worry score. The correlation between micro and macro worry scores was substantial and positive in every one of the 19 samples (all $p < 0.05$), averaging 0.48 (SD = 0.12) across samples. This level of intercorrelation suggests that each person has a characteristic overall tendency to worry, or at least to report worrying, regardless of the specific content of worry. Some people tend to worry a great deal about almost everything; others to worry little about anything. What the SSA and factor analyses show is that whatever their overall level of worry, people do discriminate between micro and macro worry. They tend to be more consistent within the sets of micro worries and macro worries than they are between these sets.

The finding of an overall tendency to worry or to report worry adds a new twist to our investigation. We would like to uncover the correlates (causes and consequences) of micro and of macro worry, at the individual and the national level, unconfounded by this overall tendency. This can be achieved by partialing on one type of worry (macro or micro) when computing correlations of the other type of worry with other variables.

Life Domains of Worry

Now consider the life domains facet of worries. Is it too consistently discriminated across cultures? In the earlier research on three student samples (Boehnke et al. 1998), this facet contributed less to the intensity of people's worries than the object facet. The life domains distinction was subordinate to the object distinction. That is, the worries from the life domains formed six spatial regions within the broad region of micro worries and another six regions within the broad region of macro worries. For example, the micro health worries formed a region in the micro worry region of the space and the macro health worries formed a different region in the macro worry region. Worries about the environment formed one region in the broad macro worry region.

This complex set of discriminations among life domains of worry did not replicate fully across all 19 samples from 14 nations. However, seven life domains were consistently discriminated in the SSA analyses in each sample. The life domains that were discriminated consistently are portrayed as regions in the "grand sample" structure in figure 9.1. In all samples, environment and safety worries emerged as distinct regions in the larger macro worry region and meaning and social worries emerged as distinct regions in the larger micro worry region. Almost all of the macro social, economic, and achievement worries emerged together or in adjacent locations in the macro worry region in all samples. This signifies that they share a common core meaning and can be viewed as a broad, consistent set. This core meaning refers to the classical social problems of intergroup conflict, crime, poverty, unemployment, and drugs. Worries representing the remaining life domains of micro worry formed two broad sets that were also consistent across the 19 samples. Safety and health worries formed one set with a core meaning of concern about physical survival; achievement and economic worries formed another set with a core meaning of concern about financial, occupational, and educational failure.

The current findings indicate that the life domain facet of worry is meaningful. However, it includes a simpler set of distinctions than originally proposed by Boehnke et al. (1998). One might legitimately compare levels of worry across nations regarding the environment, social problems, and public safety, and regarding people's personal health and safety, social relations, educational and occupational success, and meaning in life. We limit ourselves in the remainder of the current chapter to the more basic micro/macro distinction. This poses sufficient complexity for an initial examination of national differences in worry.

Relations among Worries and Well-being: Are They Cross-culturally Robust?

How do worries relate to other forms of SWB? Causal analyses point to a close relationship with SWB for micro worry. It may cause poor SWB because worrying about possible threats to self is likely to increase anxiety or depression. Intense micro worry may undermine coping with threat, leading to poorer outcomes, to problems of adaptation, and to escalation of negative affect (Davey and Tallis 1994). On the other hand, poor SWB may increase micro worry. Potential problems are likely to appear more threatening to people who are anxious or depressed, and such people are likely to assess their own coping ability as less adequate, leading to more worry. Our reasoning about the nature of micro worry is not culture specific. We would therefore expect micro worry to correlate with poor SWB across cultures, as it did in the study of German and Israeli students (Boehnke et al. 1998). The current study assesses the universality of our understanding of micro worry by examining its correlations with SWB in a diverse set of nations.

Regarding macro worry, Boehnke et al. (1998) proposed the opposite link with SWB. They argued that individuals' general state of mental health causally influences their level of macro worry. Individuals who suffer from poor SWB may be so preoccupied with their own problems that they have neither the time nor the psychological energy to attend to problems external to the self or to extensions of self. Those enjoying positive mental health are less self-preoccupied. They are therefore able to attend to the problems in the society and world around them that concern the welfare of others. Thus poor SWB may preclude macro worry, and good SWB may permit it. This reasoning leads to the expectation of positive associations of macro worry with at least some types of SWB. Past research provided only minimal support for this expectation. Fourteen of 15 correlations of macro worry with different indicators of SWB in the German and Israeli student samples did not differ reliably from zero, though most were in the positive direction. The current study permits a test of the relations of macro worry to SWB across a diverse set of nations. It can help to clarify the meaning of this type of worry.

We used five of the most popular measures of SWB. The Satisfaction with Life Scale (SWLS: Diener et al. 1985), a cognitive measure of well-being, was included in 15 samples we studied. It contains five agree/disagree items (e.g., "In most ways my life is close to my ideal." "The conditions of my life are excellent."). The Bradburn (1969) positive/negative affect scale, included in 16 samples, yields independent positive and negative affect scores, each based on five items. Respondents indicate whether they have experienced each of ten feelings during the past few weeks (e.g., on top of the world, depressed, or very unhappy). A question on the percentage of the time that people feel happy, sad, or neutral (Fordyce 1978, cited in Larson, Diener, and Emmons 1985) was included in 14 samples. We used percent of time happy and percent of time sad as indexes of emotional well-being.

We computed the correlations of these measures of SWB with micro worry (partialed for macro worry) and with macro worry (partialed for micro worry) in each sample. The top panel of table 9.3 summarizes the findings for micro worry. In almost all samples, micro worry correlated negatively with satisfaction with life (15/15), positive affect (13/16), and percent of time happy (11/14), and positively with negative affect (16/16) and percent of time sad (14/14). Most of the correlations within samples were significant ($p < 0.05$) and the meta-analytic probability of the association with every one of the indexes across samples was significant ($p < 0.001$).[4] Thus the association of micro worry with poor SWB appears to hold across diverse cultures. The modest reliabilities of the SWB measures probably attenuate the magnitude of the correlations, so the correlations underestimate the true associations. The findings support the conceptualization of micro worry as a component of poor well-being related to anxiety.

As a component of SWB, how distinctive is micro worry as compared with the other five components we measured? The correlations of micro worry with the other components of SWB averaged 0.17 (the direction of some correlations was inverted before averaging, as appropriate). The average correlations of each of the components of SWB with the others were 0.36 for satisfaction with life, 0.26 for positive affect, 0.27 for negative affect, 0.37 for percent time happy, and 0.37 for percent time sad.[5] Comparing these correlations with those of micro worry, we conclude that micro worry has somewhat less in common with the other components of SWB than they have with one another and measures a unique aspect of

Table 9.3
Correlations of micro and macro worry with measures of subjective well-being within samples

	Satisfaction with life	Positive affect	Percentage of time happy	Negative affect	Percentage of time sad
Number of samples	15	16	14	16	14
Micro worries					
Number of correlations in hypothesized direction	15	13	11	16	14
Mean correlation	−0.17*	−0.10*	−0.12*	0.23*	0.22*
Standard deviation of correlations	(0.08)	(0.11)	(0.10)	(0.09)	(0.09)
Macro worries					
Number of correlations in hypothesized direction	14	14	12	13	11
Mean correlation	0.04	0.06*	0.09*	−0.09*	−0.05
Standard deviation of correlations	(0.09)	(0.07)	(0.07)	(0.08)	(0.07)

Notes: Macro was partialed from micro worry, and micro from macro worry. The asterisk (*) indicates meta-analytic probability across samples, $p < 0.001$.

SWB. Perhaps this is because worries are responses to specific threats to cherished objects whereas all the other components are descriptions of nonspecific states of feeling and satisfaction.

The bottom panel of table 9.3 summarizes the findings for macro worry. Most correlations within samples were very small and were not significant, but they were in the expected directions: positive with satisfaction with life (14/15), positive affect (14/16), and percent of time happy (12/14), and negative with negative affect (13/16) and percent of time sad (11/14). The meta-analytic probability of the association with three of the indexes across samples was significant ($p < 0.001$). The data hint that macro worry goes with good affective well-being. That is, people who worry about the problems of the wider society and world tend to be happier a larger proportion of the time and to have more positive feelings and fewer negative feelings than those who don't worry about macro problems. Although the associations of macro worry with positive well-being are very weak, they are consistent. The findings make clear that worrying about macro problems is not a sign of poor SWB.

In sum, the analyses of relations between worry and SWB within a diverse set of nations reveal that micro worry relates both to the affective and cognitive components of SWB, but that it constitutes a distinctive aspect of SWB. Across cultures, micro worry, with its focus on threats to one's personal welfare or the well-being of close others, is an indicator of poor mental health. On the other hand, macro worry, with its focus on the problems of others in the wider society and world, is not a form of SWB. People differ systematically in their tendency to worry about macro problems, and this is a meaningful individual difference variable across cultures. However, people who are especially concerned with social problems in society, with problems of the environment, and even with the general safety of people in their nation or the world do not suffer from particularly low levels of satisfaction with life or high levels of negative affect. Indeed, across different cultures there is a weak but consistent trend for these individuals to enjoy somewhat better mental health.

National Differences in Worry

Having established that the two types of worry have consistent meanings across cultures, we now turn to the examination of national differences in worry. We first describe some interesting differences among the nations we studied.

The simplest way to think about national differences is to ask about the most serious specific worries in each nation. Table 9.4 presents the 5 most serious worries in each of the 19 different samples from 14 nations. For each sample, we also list the most important single worry. For 5 nations (Brazil, former East Germany, Hungary, Israel, and Slovakia), there are data from both teacher and student samples. These data reveal that for both types of samples the same three or four worries were among the five most serious. We can therefore have some confidence that the most important worries reported here may characterize the nation rather than one particular subgroup in that nation.

The two worries most often rated especially disturbing by both students and teachers in various nations were "my parents dying" (worry 8) and "worsening destruction of the environment" (worry 3). These two worries were in the top five in more than half the nations. The other worries rated among the top five in at least five nations were: "someone in my family being in a traffic accident" (worry 10), "someone in my family not having enough money to live on" (worry 4), "damage to nature (forests, animals, etc.)" (worry 13), "people in the world dying of hunger" (worry 28). Thus the two categories of worry that were among the most intense

Table 9.4
Worries in different nations

	Top 5 worries	Most serious worry	Mean micro worry	Mean macro worry	Micro minus macro
Student samples					
Belgium	3, 4, 8, 10, 28	My parents dying	3.29	3.16	0.13
Brazil	7, 8, 9, 11, 28	People in poverty	3.32	3.29	0.03
East Germany	3, 13, 19, 20, 23	Destruction of environment	2.47	2.97	−0.50*
France	4, 7, 8, 11, 19	Trouble in studies/work	3.41	3.37	0.04
Hungary	3, 5, 6, 13, 23	Destruction of environment	2.84	3.04	−0.20*
Israel	5, 8, 10, 11, 20	Traffic accident	2.96	2.72	0.24*
Russia	4, 5, 8, 10, 27	My parents dying	3.58	3.21	0.37*
Slovakia	3, 8, 13, 22, 23	My parents dying	2.67	3.17	−0.50*
Turkey	4, 5, 8, 10, 24	My parents dying	4.05	4.09	−0.04
Uganda	3, 7, 8, 12, 19	My parents dying	3.55	3.73	−0.18*
United States	8, 10, 11, 25, 33	My parents dying	2.91	2.78	0.13*
West Germany	3, 13, 20, 22, 26	Destruction of environment	2.36	3.14	−0.78*
Teacher samples					
Brazil	7, 9, 10, 19, 28	People in poverty	3.24	3.51	−0.27*
Denmark	3, 13, 15, 22, 28	Destruction of environment	2.10	2.85	−0.75*
East Germany	3, 13, 20, 26, 28	Destruction of environment	2.56	3.17	−0.61*
England	3, 7, 9, 22, 28	Destruction of environment	2.40	2.83	−0.43*
Hungary	3, 4, 5, 6, 23	My parents dying	2.84	3.30	−0.46*
Israel	5, 8, 10, 17, 20	Traffic accident	3.09	3.12	−0.03
Slovakia	3, 8, 13, 20, 23	My parents dying	2.59	3.33	−0.74*

Notes: See table 9.1 for a list of the worries by number. The asterisk (*) indicates the micro/ macro difference is significant at $p < 0.01$ by the t test.

across nations were worries involving family members and worries about the environment. Only one of these worries referred to a personal problem of the self (worry 8), even indirectly. Three of the common, most intense worries were macro worries and three were micro worries.

Even with regard to the worries commonly rated most serious, there were major national differences. For example, of the four environmental worries included in the worries scale, not one appeared among the top five in Brazil, France, Israel, Russia, Turkey, and the United States. The environment is apparently not a very salient concern in these nations. In contrast, environmental worries were of particular concern in Slovakia, Hungary, East and West Germany, and Denmark, with at least two in the top five. Environmental worries may be more intense in the latter countries because they are densely populated, highly industrialized nations in which the struggle against pollution from obsolete factories in East–Central Europe has been high on the political agenda.

Table 9.4 also provides the mean scores for micro worry, for macro worry, and for the relative intensity of micro versus macro worry in each sample. Nations differ substantially in the average intensity of worries reported by their students and teachers. The ranges of the intensity of micro and of macro worry covered about 3 standard deviation units in both the student and teacher samples. Thus there is considerable cross-national variation to explain. The Turkish sample reported the highest levels of both types of worry. The Danish teachers reported the lowest level of micro worry, and the Israeli students reported the lowest level of macro worry.

Does the ordering of nations on intensity of micro and macro worry depend upon the type of sample from which the data come? The means in table 9.4 for the five nations for which there are data from both types of samples reveal that the ordering of nations does not depend upon the source of data. The order of nations on intensity of micro worry is exactly the same in both types of samples (Brazil, Israel, Hungary, Slovakia, East Germany). The order of nations on intensity of macro worry is also exactly the same for both teacher and student samples (Brazil, Slovakia, Hungary, East Germany, Israel).

The *relative* emphasis given to threats to personal or in-group welfare (micro worry) as compared with threats to the society and wider world (macro worry) also varies substantially across nations. The Russian, Israeli, and American students worried significantly more about micro than about macro problems. The West German, East German, Slovak, Hungarian, and Ugandan students emphasized societal and global concerns significantly more than personal and in-group concerns. In contrast, the teachers in all nations except Israel worried significantly more about macro than about micro problems. Overall, teachers worried more about macro issues than did students from the same nation, whereas both groups exhibited similar levels of micro worry.

We turn next to possible explanations for the wide cross-national variation in levels of micro and macro worry. We first discuss social and economic influences and then consider cultural dimensions on which nations differ as possible sources of influence on worry levels. Prediction of micro worry from social and economic characteristics of nations is fairly straightforward. Prediction of macro worry and prediction with cultural factors is quite complex, however.

Social and Economic Influences

In their study of national differences in life satisfaction and affective well-being, Diener et al. (1995) proposed that variables influence SWB to the extent that they affect people's ability to achieve their goals. Economic and social factors, like high income, human rights, and equality of opportunity, provide resources and opportunities for people to progress toward achieving a wide range of goals. Diener et al. confirmed their hypotheses that these factors predict national levels of SWB.

Is similar reasoning relevant for predicting national differences in worry? Recall the definition of worries we adopted: A worry is a disturbing cognition that a state of an object (micro or macro) in some domain of life (health, safety, etc.) will become (or become more, or remain) discrepant from its desired state. In other words, as Schwartz et al. (2000) have elaborated, people worry when they believe that a goal they value is threatened or blocked. Following Diener et al., we therefore propose that socioeconomic variables influence worry to the extent that they threaten, block, or enhance people's ability to achieve their goals. Low income, gross violations of human rights, and inequality of opportunity, should therefore predict high levels of worry. Such variables may increase worry through an additional process. They deprive people of the resources needed to cope with threat and thereby to reduce worry. If money, rights, and opportunities are available, people can mobilize these resources to restore the match between the observed and desired state of threatened objects.

We studied the three social and economic variables listed above (income, violation of human rights, inequality) as well as a fourth variable directly linked to economic insecurity—the recent experience of inflation in a country. These four variables certainly influence the ability of large numbers of people to achieve their personal goals and the goals of close others, so they should affect national levels of micro worry. We hypothesize that national levels of micro worry relate negatively to national levels of wealth and positively to national levels of income inequality, recent inflation, and violations of human rights.

It is less clear how these social and economic variables are likely to affect macro worry. On the one hand, we argued above that macro worry is less likely when people are preoccupied with their own problems. Low and insecure income, prevailing inequalities, and threats to one's human rights place heavy demands on people's physical and psychological resources as they struggle to keep body and soul together. People may therefore have little time or energy to attend to problems external to themselves and their families. These socioeconomic variables may predict low macro worry, that is, minimal concern with problems in the wider society and world.

On the other hand, these same variables exacerbate just those problems to which macro worry is directed. A weak and uncertain economy, inequality, and violations of human rights increase poverty, hunger, disease, unemployment, and social strife in the wider society, and they may contribute to environmental degradation. These same variables deprive society of the economic resources and the social will to relieve the problems they cause. If the objective incidence of such problems increases the tendency to worry about them, then these socioeconomic variables may predict greater macro worry.

There are thus two plausible but opposing processes that may link socioeconomic variables to macro worry. Difficult socioeconomic conditions may cause members of a society to be preoccupied with their own problems and hence to ignore the problems of others, thereby reducing macro worry. But, because difficult socioeconomic conditions increase the presence of problems in the wider society, such problems may more often capture peoples' attention and produce higher levels of macro worry. For micro worry, there is only one process that predicts a single direction of association—difficult conditions undermine individuals' ability to achieve their goals. Thus, even if the associations of socioeconomic variables with macro and micro worry are in the same direction, the associations for macro worry may be attenuated by countervailing processes. Consequently correlations of the *relative* seriousness of macro versus micro worry should be positive for GDP per capita and negative for the other socioeconomic variables.

Cultural Influences

Culturally different societies impart to their members different conceptions of what it means to be a person, of what constitutes competent and moral behavior, and of what goals are legitimate, desirable, or proscribed. People experience the impact of their culture through everyday exposure to customs, laws, norms, scripts, and practices that are shaped by and express prevailing cultural values. We explored the relations of worry to three dimensions of culture that have been validated in recent studies across more than 60 nations (Schwartz 1997, 1999; Schwartz and Bardi 1997, Schwartz and Ros 1995), and to individualism-collectivism (Hofstede 1980, 1991). These are bipolar value dimensions that describe the culturally valued ways societies respond to basic issues they must confront.[6] Next we outline each dimension briefly and derive hypotheses that relate it to national levels of micro and macro worry.

Egalitarianism/Hierarchy   The first basic issue societies face is how to assure responsible social behavior, to motivate people to consider others' welfare and to coordinate with them to manage their unavoidable interdependencies. High egalitarian cultures portray individuals as moral equals who share basic interests as human beings. Egalitarianism emphasizes the responsibility of autonomous individuals to transcend their selfish interests. People are socialized to internalize a commitment to voluntary cooperation with others and to feel concern for everyone's welfare. Low egalitarian cultures depend on a hierarchical system of ascribed roles to assure socially responsible behavior. They emphasize the legitimacy of an unequal distribution of power, roles and resources. People are socialized and sanctioned to comply with the obligations and rules attached to their roles.

The emphasis on hierarchy in low egalitarian cultures is likely to increase micro worry: it legitimizes imposing collective goals that may ignore or conflict with individuals' own goals, it justifies demanding that people meet role obligations that may oppose personal interests and sanctioning them for failure to do so, and it grants individuals little freedom to set and pursue their own goals. High egalitarianism, in contrast, discourages external pressures on individuals. It calls for voluntary cooperation among moral equals, allowing people to work out lines of action that protect or promote their personal interests. Hence cultural egalitarianism should relate negatively to micro worry.

Cultural egalitarianism is likely to increase macro worry. It encourages people to transcend selfish interests and concern themselves with the welfare of all others, to include members of the wider society and world in the moral universe of mutual human responsibility. Low egalitarianism, in contrast, is likely to decrease macro worry because it requires people to concern themselves only with the welfare of those to whom they are obliged through their ascribed roles. Role obligations are rarely directed to the wider society and world. Thus egalitarianism should relate positively to macro worry. We have hypothesized that egalitarianism/hierarchy influences micro and macro worry in opposite directions. Hence this cultural dimension should also affect the relative intensity of macro versus micro worry in a nation. Egalitarianism should correlate positively with the intensity of macro versus micro worry.

Harmony/Mastery   The issue underlying this cultural dimension is the place of humankind in the natural and social world: Is it more to submit, to fit in, or to exploit? High-harmony cultures accept the natural and social world as it is, trying to preserve rather than to change or exploit it. Harmony emphasizes fitting in, being in tune with others and with the physical environment, and valuing peace and harmony in the society and world. Low-harmony cultures encourage people to seek actively to master and change the natural and social world, to assert control, bend objects and people to their will, and exploit them to further personal or group interests. Such cultures emphasize getting ahead through active self-assertion.

Cultural harmony should decrease micro worry. A culture that emphasizes harmony discourages striving toward goals that are difficult to attain in the natural course of events. It calls for forgoing personal ambition and taking people and events as they come. In such a culture, people have less reason to worry about what could possibly go wrong, about personal success or failure. A low-harmony culture, in contrast, calls for an activist posture, for ambitiously pursuing goals and assertively overcoming barriers to them. People in such a culture must be vigilant about their fate in order to control it. They are therefore likely to worry a great deal about what could go wrong for them.

Cultural harmony should increase macro worry. By emphasizing peace and harmony among people and preservation of the natural environment, harmony directs attention to events that might threaten these states in the wider society and world. Harmony would thereby increase macro worry (even if it does not increase actions to address the causes of such worry). Low cultural harmony, with its focus on pursuing personal or group interests, legitimizes preoccupation with one's own strivings. It may therefore direct attention away from problems in the wider society and world and reduce the time and energy available for macro worry. A single directional hypothesis can encompass the postulated influences on both types of worry: Harmony correlates positively with the intensity of macro versus micro worry.

Autonomy/Embeddedness[7]   The basic issue this dimension addresses is the relationship between individual and group: To what extent are persons autonomous versus embedded in groups? High-autonomy cultures view the person as an autonomous, bounded entity who finds meaning in his or her own uniqueness. High autonomy cultures encourage people to pursue their own ideas and feelings and to express their own internal attributes (preferences, traits, feelings, motives). Low-autonomy cultures, in contrast, stress maintaining the status quo and restraining actions or inclinations that might disrupt the solidary group or the traditional order. In these cultures, people seek meaning in life largely through identifying with the group in which they are embedded and participating in its shared way of life.

The dimension of autonomy/embeddedness overlaps conceptually to some degree with *individualism/collectivism* (Hofstede 1980, 1991). Both concern the relationship between the individual and the collective and both contrast an autonomous with an interdependent view of people.[8] We therefore analyze the potential relations of both these cultural dimensions with worry together.

The location of nations on Hofstede's cultural individualism-collectivism dimension was the strongest predictor of national levels of SWB in the Diener et al. study. To explain the strong positive correlation observed, Diener et al. suggested that individualistic societies afford individuals more freedom to choose and to pursue their own goals and life course. Individuals in such societies presumably value personal well-being more highly, seek it more actively, and take more personal credit for their success. This analysis appears to imply that both the individualism and autonomy dimensions should relate positively to micro worry. Greater freedom to choose and pursue personal goals may reduce micro worry because it gives people a greater sense of control in life.

On the other hand, there are mechanisms that might link cultural autonomy and individualism to more rather than less micro worry. Cultural emphases on developing and expressing one's unique attributes increases attention to self and may thereby increase worry about one's personal outcomes. Encouraging people to pursue their personal aspirations and goals may increase their concern about personal success and failure. Moreover the absence of strong in-group solidarity may leave individuals with relatively little emotional and material support in the face of threat, thereby increasing micro worry. In sum, despite the fact that individualism and micro worry both relate substantially positively to SWB, cultural autonomy and individualism may not predict micro worry because of countervailing processes.

Prediction of macro worry with cultural autonomy/embeddedness and with individualism/collectivism is also hazardous. Autonomy and individualism might be expected to reduce macro worry because they legitimize preoccupation with self and one's own personal problems. This may reduce the psychological and physical energy people have left to concern themselves with others. Here too, however, other aspects of these cultural dimensions suggest an opposite prediction.

People in more autonomous, individualist cultures draw a less sharp line between members of their in-group and others in the wider society or world than do those in more collectivist cultures (Hofstede 1991; Triandis 1995). Concern for the welfare of strangers and other out-group members is not necessarily normative in more autonomous, individualist cultures, but it is weaker yet in more embedded, collectivist cultures. In the latter, in-group solidarity focuses attention on in-group concerns, so problems in the wider society or world may appear irrelevant. In sum, contradictory processes provide no unequivocal theoretical basis for generating hypotheses that relate these two cultural dimensions to macro worry.

Measurement of Variables

The data on worries were gathered from 1994 to 1997. We used measures of social and economic variables from shortly before or at the beginning of this period. This comports with the assumption that what people worry about most reflects current, recent, or persistent life conditions. Table 9.2, above, lists the nation scores on the predictor variables.

GNP per Capita   To measure the prevailing economic level in each nation, we used the gross national product of the nation divided by its population, for 1995 (Famighetti 1997).

Income Inequality   To measure inequality of income, we used income Gini coefficients for 1992 or 1993 (Tabai 1996; Veenhoven 1993). For Hungary, Russia, and Uganda, where no income Gini was available, we substituted the expenditure Gini which correlates substantially with it. Gini coefficients range from 0 (perfect equality) to 1.0 (complete inequality).

Inflation   To measure instability and uncertainty of financial resources as a source of threat, we used the inflation rate in each country, that is, the one-year change in consumer prices in the year preceding the gathering of worries data (Famighetti 1997).

Violation of Human Rights   To measure objective threats to human rights, we used discriminant scores provided by Gupta, Jongman, and Schmid (1994) which were based on three types of violations: gross human rights violations (e.g., disappearances, torture), civil rights violations (e.g., searches without trial, arbitrary seizure of property), and political rights violations (e.g., absence of freedom of press and assembly, no multiparty elections by secret ballot). Higher scores signify more violation of human rights. Data were for 1991.

Individualism   The individualism/collectivism cultural dimension was measured with scores that Hofstede (1991) derived from the evaluations of work goals made by IBM employees in each nation during 1967 to 1973. For Uganda, we used the score reported for East Africa. For East Germany, Hungary, Russia, and Slovakia, we estimated scores. We were guided by estimates by Triandis (reported in Diener et al. 1995) and by the status of these nations or regions on characteristics (social, economic, religious, and political) known to correlate substantially with individualism.

Schwartz Cultural Dimensions   These were measured with scores based on values data from our cross-national studies of 185 samples of teachers and students in 65 nations (Schwartz 1994, 1999, unpublished data). Respondents in each nation indicated how important each of 56–7 values is as a guiding principle in their life, on a −1 to +7 scale. Forty-five values demonstrated stable cross-cultural meanings. The sample means for these values were included in a culture-level, multidimensional space analysis. This analysis verified the existence of seven distinct types of values that formed the three bipolar cultural dimensions studied here (egalitarianism vs. hierarchy, harmony vs. mastery, affective and intellectual autonomy vs. embeddedness).

For the nations in the current study, there was at least one teacher and one student sample, gathered between 1988 and 1997, in all but Belgium and Denmark. To compute a single score for each nation on each cultural dimension, we averaged the scores for the multiple samples in that nation, giving equal weight to teacher and to student samples. For Belgium (two student samples only) and Denmark (two teacher samples only), the missing teacher and student scores, respectively, were predicted by regressing teacher and student scores on one another across nations. In every nation the samples in the current study comprised half or fewer of the samples on which the cultural dimension scores were based. The cultural dimension scores were computed by averaging the importance ratings of the values that measure one pole of each dimension and subtracting from them the average ratings of the values that measure the opposite pole of that dimension.

Results

Table 9.5 presents two correlations of each predictor with the three measures of worry. The first is for the 12 nations in which students provided worry data, the second for the seven nations in which teachers provided worry data. At this initial stage in the cross-national study of worry, it is important not to ignore potentially real associations. Therefore, and in light of the small number of cases, we treat hypothesized correlations that meet a criterion of $p < 0.10$ as worthy of note. Moreover the replication across two sets of samples permits us to assess consistency, not merely significance, of associations. As noted earlier, we wished to assess associations of micro worry and of macro worry net of the overall tendency to report worrying. To that end, we partialed on each type (macro or micro) when computing correlations of the other type with the predictor variables.

First, consider the socioeconomic factors. As expected, income inequality, inflation, and violations of human rights correlated positively with micro worry, and GNP per capita correlated negatively. The correlations were consistent in direction across the replications, though not all were significant. Thus difficult social and economic conditions apparently tend to increase micro worry just as they damage SWB in general.

There were no directional hypotheses for the relations of socioeconomic factors to macro worry, since we identified countervailing processes that may neutralize one another. The observed correlations (second column) for income inequality, inflation, and violations of human rights were quite weak and/or inconsistent across replications. GNP correlated negatively with macro worry, but the correlation across the 12 nations with student data was weak. This set of results might be interpreted as indicating that socioeconomic conditions are irrelevant to macro worry at the national level. It is just as likely, however, that they reflect the operation of the two opposing processes we identified. Difficult socioeconomic conditions may cause preoccupation with own personal problems and therefore lack of interest

Table 9.5
Correlations of social and cultural predictors with national levels of worry

Predictors	Sample type	Types of worry		Macro minus micro worry
		Micro worry	Macro worry	
Socioeconomic factors				
GNP per capita	ST	−0.30	−0.24	0.23
	TE	−0.40	−0.57	0.39
Income inequality (Gini)	ST	0.47	0.00	−0.40
	TE	0.42	−0.09	−0.46
Inflation	ST	0.42	0.23	−0.31
	TE	0.36	0.11	−0.40
Violations of human rights	ST	0.38	0.30	−0.27
	TE	0.70	−0.31	−0.71
Cultural factors				
Egalitarianism/hierarchy (Schwartz)	ST	−0.51	0.06	0.44
	TE	−0.87	0.58	0.86
Harmony/mastery (Schwartz)	ST	−0.34	0.32	0.34
	TE	−0.85	0.83	0.77
Autonomy/embeddedness (Schwartz)	ST	−0.25	−0.07	0.22
	TE	0.01	−0.48	0.12
Individualism/collectivism (Hofstede)	ST	0.06	−0.47	−0.07
	TE	−0.07	−0.88	0.21

Notes: We partialed macro worry from micro worry and micro worry from macro worry. Partial correlations are significant at $p < 0.10$, one-tailed test, if they equal or exceed 0.40 for students or 0.57 for teachers. ST = worry data from students, 12 nations; TE = worry data from teachers, 7 nations.

in societal problems. At the same time difficult socioeconomic conditions may produce such severe problems in the wider society that these problems force themselves into people's awareness. The pattern of correlations of socioeconomic variables with the relative seriousness of macro versus micro worry (column three) was consistent with our hypotheses, though many of the correlations were not strong. The more difficult the life conditions in a nation, the more people tend to worry about their personal problems and those of their family as compared to the problems in the wider society or world. Of the four socioeconomic factors, no particular one was clearly more important than the others.

We next consider relations of cultural factors to worry. In our view, cultural factors are as likely to influence levels of worry as are objective conditions. The positions of nations on various cultural dimensions reflect the ideal states to which individuals and groups aspire and the legitimacy attributed to the pursuit of particular goals rather than others. As noted in the introduction, the nature and intensity of people's worry depends on the goals they cherish and pursue. Their cultural environment is likely to affect worry by providing opportunities for or raising barriers to goal pursuit or by legitimizing or delegitimizing the goals people hold dear. We proposed clear directional hypotheses for the effects of cultural egalitarianism and harmony, but suggested that cultural autonomy and individualism may not relate in a straightforward manner to national levels of worry.

The bottom panel of table 9.5 presents the empirical findings for relations of cultural dimensions to national levels of micro and macro worry. As hypothesized, egalitarianism correlated negatively and substantially with micro worry in both sets of samples. The greater the cultural emphasis on hierarchy and the less on egalitarianism, the more people worry about personal and in-group problems. For macro worry, we proposed the opposite direction of association, a positive correlation of egalitarianism with the intensity of macro worry. This hypothesis was supported only in the set of teacher samples. However, correlations of egalitarianism with the relative seriousness of macro versus micro worry were positive and significant in both sets of samples, as hypothesized.

The total pattern of correlations suggests that an egalitarian emphasis in a culture reduces the tendency to worry about personal problems but increases concern with the problems of the wider society and world. In contrast, people in nations toward the hierarchy pole of this dimension worry more about micro than macro problems. The egalitarianism cultural dimension was the strongest and most consistent predictor of national level of worry among the eight variables we studied.

For the harmony versus mastery dimension, the directions of correlation with all three worry indexes were as hypothesized in both sets of samples, and the correlations in the set of teacher samples were significant. Micro worry is less intense across nations as the cultural emphasis becomes more on fitting harmoniously into the natural and social environment and the less on mastering and controlling the environment and assertively pursuing one's own goals. In contrast, an emphasis on harmony rather than mastery correlates positively with macro worry. A cultural emphasis on peace, smooth relations among people, and preservation of the natural environment rather than change and exploitation apparently focuses attention and concern on potential and actual threats in the wider society and world. Consistent (and redundant) with these findings, the relative emphasis on macro versus micro worry increases as national cultures are located closer to the harmony pole as opposed to the mastery pole of this cultural dimension.

Despite the fact that cultural individualism was the strongest predictor of national levels of SWB in the Diener et al. (1995) study, we proposed no hypotheses linking worry to individualism and to the related cultural dimension of autonomy. This is because we identified potential countervailing influences of these cultural dimensions on worry. Perhaps as a result of these countervailing forces little evidence of substantial association was found. With one exception, the observed correlations of autonomy and of individualism with micro and macro worry and with their relative intensity were near zero and/or inconsistent across the two sets of samples. The one significant and consistent finding was that individualism correlates negatively with macro worry. In cultures that emphasize the individual's responsibility for self and in-group rather than the integration of self into the larger collectivity, people exhibit less concern for the problems in the wider society and world. Although autonomy also correlated negatively with macro worry, the association was considerably weaker.[9]

Thus far we have examined associations of each predictor with worry independently of the others. With the small number of nations in this study, it is not possible simultaneously to control all other predictors statistically while examining each one. We can, however, examine the intercorrelations among the consistent predictors of worry. This enables us to identify where there is substantial overlap and assess redundancy in the findings we have reported. The appendix provides the intercorrelations among all of the predictors.

First, consider micro worry. Among its consistent predictors, cultural egalitarianism, rights violations, income inequality, and recent inflation were substantially intercorrelated. Harmony correlated substantially only with egalitarianism and rights violations. Thus there is considerable overlap, reflecting the intertwining of these predictors of micro worry in the real world of nations. If cultural egalitarianism is entered first into a regression to predict micro worry in either sample set, then none of the socioeconomic predictors account for significant additional variance. In contrast, egalitarianism, and harmony in the smaller set of nations, do account for significant additional variance in micro worry when entered into a regression following any *one* of the socioeconomic predictors. Were such findings to hold up across larger sets of nations, we might infer that much of the impact of objective socioeconomic conditions on micro worry is channeled through their influence on prevailing cultural orientations.

Two of the predictors of macro worry, cultural individualism and income (GNP per capita), were extremely strongly intercorrelated ($r > 0.87$), but their associations with the other predictor, cultural harmony, were negligible. Regression analyses suggest that the impact of income on national levels of macro worry may be mediated by individualism. Both cultural individualism and harmony may contribute independently to macro worry. Cultural egalitarianism predicted macro worry across the smaller set of nations, but this association was not independent of the association for harmony.

Cultural egalitarianism, harmony, and rights violations were the most consistent predictors of the relative intensity of macro versus micro worry. All three of these variables were substantially intercorrelated. The pattern of correlations and regression analyses suggest that cultural egalitarianism is the most important influence on the relative intensity of macro versus micro worry and that the impact of rights violations may be mediated by egalitarianism.

Overview and Discussion

This chapter first addressed the question of the cross-cultural applicability of a new conception and method for measuring worries (Boehnke et al. 1998). Results of structural analyses both within and across 19 samples from 14 countries, with two types of respondents, supported the approach proposed. In every one of the analyses, respondents made a clear distinction between what we have called micro worry and macro worry. That is, in every case there were two separate sets of worries. The micro set of worries concerned the welfare of the self or extensions of the self; the macro set concerned the welfare of others in the wider society or world.

Micro worry appears to be a component of subjective well-being. Within each nation studied, people who reported greater worry about their own health and safety and that of their dear ones, about success in their studies or career, and about the quality of their social relations also reported less satisfaction with life, more negative affect, less positive affect, more time feeling sad, and less time feeling happy. However, micro worry has less in common with these other components of SWB than they have with one another. The distinctiveness of micro worry makes it an aspect of SWB worthy of investigation in its own right.

Associations of macro worry with the various indexes of SWB make clear that macro worry is not a component of subjective well-being. Individuals who worry more than others about human suffering in society and in the world, about environmental dangers, and about international safety are just as likely to be satisfied with life, to experience positive rather than negative feelings, and to feel happy much of the time. Indeed, there is a weak tendency, consistent across nations, for people who worry about macro problems to enjoy better well-being. Boehnke et al. (1994, 1998) argued that poor SWB inhibits macro worry because it causes preoccupation with personal problems. But the weakness of the association suggests that SWB is not a major influence on macro worry. Macro worry is largely ideological. It may therefore be grounded in individuals' value priorities, as Schwartz et al. (2000) theorized and demonstrated in a recent cross-national study.

The current research also supported the second conceptual facet of worry, the specific life domain to which the worry is directed. However, fewer distinct life domains emerged consistently across all nations than in the original worries theory (Boehnke et al. 1998). For cross-national research, worries can be categorized reliably into the following life domains: among micro worries—social, meaning, economic/achievement, and health/safety domains; among macro worries—safety, social problems, and environment domains. Studying the impact of social and economic factors on the life domains of worry to which they are potentially most relevant might clarify how and why particular types of worry vary across nations. For example, crime rates are probably most relevant to worry in the micro health/safety domain, and ethnic and religious strife to worry in the macro social domain.

Cross-national comparison of the importance of worries revealed that the most intense worries in most nations concerned the environment and close family members. Other single worries varied greatly in importance. Moreover there was very substantial variation across nations in levels of micro worry and of macro worry and in the relative intensity of micro versus macro worry. Socioeconomic and cultural factors explained much of this variation.

Correlations of difficult life conditions (violations of human rights, income inequality, inflation, and—less reliably—low income) with national levels of micro worry suggest that objective conditions increase micro worry. In contrast, difficult life conditions, other than low income, failed to predict macro worry. This may reflect opposing processes that neutralize one another: difficult conditions exacerbate the problems in society that give rise to macro worry, but they also cause preoccupation with self that diverts attention from macro problems. If this analysis is correct, then low income is apparently an especially strong source of self-preoccupation. Overall, difficult socioeconomic conditions in a nation tended to increase concern for personal problems at the expense of societal problems.

Cultural egalitarianism (versus hierarchy) and harmony (versus mastery) correlated negatively with micro worry. That is, worry about self and close others is less to the extent that the national culture calls for transcending self-interests and accepting the world as it is. Micro worry is greater to the extent the culture calls for compliance with hierarchical role obligations and exhorts people to assert themselves to control and change the world. Interestingly, neither cultural autonomy nor individualism correlated with micro worry. This contrasts with Diener et al.'s (1995) finding that individualism strongly predicted good SWB across nations. Perhaps the cultural freedom to pursue personal goals that presumably contributes to SWB in individualist cultures is offset by weaker social support and greater emphasis on personal success and failure-avoidance that increase micro worry.

Cultural harmony and, less consistently, egalitarianism correlated positively with macro worry, whereas cultural individualism correlated negatively with macro worry. This fits the conception of harmony and egalitarianism as calling for concern with the preservation of nature, harmonious relations, and the well-being of others, and of individualism as legitimizing preoccupation with self. Cultural egalitarianism and harmony also predicted the extent to which people in a nation worried more about problems in the wider society and world as compared to personal and in-group problems.

Considering the total set of findings, it appears that the cultural factors were somewhat stronger predictors of national levels of worry than were the socioeconomic factors. Of course, it is necessary to study a substantially larger set of nations before accepting this inference as a firm conclusion. If this conclusion is valid, however, it implies that culture is a more important determinant of worry than objective conditions that pose threats to human well-being. In all events the findings indicate that culture is no less important than objective conditions. Let us consider how this can be so.

Cultural definitions of the states of affairs that are good or bad, of what people should aspire to, accept, or reject, transform the meaning of objective conditions. Where cultural egalitarianism prevails, for example, poverty is likely to be interpreted as an illegitimate state of affairs and a source of worry because it violates the cherished value of human dignity for all. Where cultural hierarchy prevails, the fact that some live in poverty and others enjoy wealth is more likely to be accepted as a normal state of affairs resulting from the "necessary" organization of society into hierarchically differentiated roles, each with its legitimate level of reward. Where hierarchy prevails, even the poor are socialized to view their state as normal and to aspire for little more. As a result the perceived discrepancies between their current and desired situations are likely to be smaller. Of course, extremely difficult objective conditions may cause worry regardless of the culture of the nation in which they occur. Ordinarily, however, culture is likely to moderate the impacts of objective conditions.

As regards macro worry, prevailing cultural values were considerably stronger predictors than were socioeconomic factors. This reinforces a conception of macro worry as largely ideological. The nation-level finding for macro and micro worry parallels the finding that individual differences in value priorities correlate more strongly with individual differences in macro worry than in micro worry (Schwartz et al., 2000). We infer from this that some of the impact of culture on macro worry is channeled through the personal values that the people in a society acquire due to prevailing cultural values.

Because of the substantial intercorrelations among many of the predictors of national levels of worry, it is impossible to tease apart their influences. For example, nations low as against high in cultural egalitarianism suffer more from violations of human rights and from income inequality. The intertwining of rights and inequality with cultural egalitarianism doubtless reflects mutual causal influences. Low cultural egalitarianism legitimizes disregard for human rights and inequality among citizens, and people and institutions modify their value priorities to be more compatible with the social conditions imposed upon them (see Schwartz and Bardi 1997, on adaptation to communist rule).

The statistical controls we were able to employ with the small samples of nations indicated that some variables were significant predictors (usually cultural factors) and others accounted for no additional variance in worry (usually socioeconomic). Research across a much larger sample of nations is required to ascertain which variables make unique contributions to national levels of worry. Such research might reveal effects for variables dropped by the regressions on small sample sets. However, an understanding true to the causal reality should recognize that it is the interplay of culture and social conditions that influences national differences in worry. Thus, for example, the level of cultural egalitarianism hinders or legitimizes the development of life conditions that cause micro worry, and these conditions in turn promote or inhibit the low egalitarianism that promotes micro worry.

We have assumed that the matched samples of students and teachers order nations on worries in a manner similar to the order one would obtain with representative national samples. This does not mean that the absolute levels of micro and macro worry observed here are equivalent to the absolute levels in representative samples. The processes postulated to link worry to life conditions imply that micro worry is probably lower for students and teachers than for the general population, and macro worry is probably higher.

Students and teachers are probably less personally vulnerable to difficult life conditions than the average citizen. Students tend to come from families with above average income, to be buffered temporarily from problems in the labor market, and, judging from their educational attainments, probably not to have suffered seriously from inequality or violations of their basic human rights. Although teachers in different nations typically have only modest incomes, their jobs are relatively secure, and their employment status indicates that they too probably endure fewer rights violations and less inequality than weaker groups.

Lower vulnerability to poor socioeconomic conditions implies less preoccupation with personal problems among students and teachers than in the general population. Hence the level of micro worry observed here may be lower than in representative samples. Lower vulnerability to difficult life conditions may affect macro worry in the opposite direction. Under less pressure from these conditions, students and teachers may be freer than other citizens, materially and psychologically, to attend to the presence or growth of threats to the welfare of others. Being more educated, they are also more likely to choose media (serious television programs, newspapers, and magazines) that draw attention to wider social problems (Luskin 1990). Hence the levels of macro worry observed here may be higher than in representative samples.

Future research on worry across nations might extend and improve on the current study by taking several steps. There is obviously a need to study a much larger sample of nations. Ideally data should be obtained from representative national samples. Representative samples from about ten nations that overlap with those studied here are especially critical. These samples are needed to assess the validity of our assumption that the matched student and teacher samples order nations on worry in a manner similar to what would be found with representative samples. If this assumption is verified, the path is open to expanding the number of nations without the exorbitant resources demanded by representative sampling in each nation. Once worry data are available from some 30 nations, hierarchical linear modeling can be employed to examine impacts of nation-level cultural and social conditions, together with individual differences, on micro and macro worry.

Suggestions for Improving Research on National Levels of Worry and SWB

Multiple Indicators

Researchers often combine multiple indicators to measure social and economic factors in order to increase reliability. For example, Diener et al. (1995) constructed principal component scores based on multiple indicators of wealth, inequality, rights, and individualism. However, these scores correlated with mean SWB scores only slightly more strongly than the best single indicators. We note two reasons to refrain from such an approach. Combining indicators requires dropping nations for which complete data are unavailable or, alternatively, using uncertain estimates for missing values. More important, combinations of indicators allow less unequivocal interpretation of presumed causal links than single indicators do.

For example, we used a single indicator of inequality limited to inequality of income. This permitted a straightforward interpretation of the positive association of inequality with micro worry. Large gaps in income create a sharp contrast for many members of society between the financial resources available to them and socially desired outcomes, giving rise to micro worry. Had we used a component score for inequality, combining financial inequality with inequality of longevity and gender inequality in secondary education as Diener et al. did, interpretation would have been equivocal. It would be hard to infer whether the correlation with micro worry suggested causal processes related to income, illness, gender identity, or other factors. Thus researchers must weigh possible gains of increased reliability using multiple indicators against possible losses of dropped nations, erroneous estimation, and confounded explanations.

Multiple Times of Measurement

We strongly recommend another way of improving the measurement of predictors. This recommendation derives from a theoretical concern with the timing of socio-economic and cultural influences. Over what intervals of time do different factors have their effects on worry and SWB? What are the implications of the different intervals and of the different rates of change in the predictors for their optimal measurement?

We measured each predictor at a single period in time, usually the period shortly or immediately prior to measuring worry. Such measurement is not problematic if the predictors do not change. However, most predictors do change over time, sometimes slowly but sometimes and in some places precipitously. Violations of human rights may suddenly increase or decrease with a change of regime (e.g., in Nigeria), for example, and inflation may spiral out of control or respond to dramatic economic measures (e.g., in Brazil). A burst of inflation may have stronger effects on SWB than equally high inflation that has persisted for several years. Increasing income inequality may damage SWB more than a stable high level of inequality to which people have adapted.

These observations suggest several improvements that may be feasible with existing archival data. First, one-time measures of predictors should be compared with measures over more extended periods. For example, average levels of the socioeconomic conditions over the preceding ten years could serve as predictors. It is also informative to compare prediction with the same measure taken at different intervals of time (e.g., one, five, and ten years) prior to measurement of worry. Rates and directions of change in the predictors over time (e.g., rising inequality, rapidity of deterioration in rights) are other useful types of measures. Examining the correlations of such different measures of social conditions with SWB would clarify the timing of effects. Which conditions, if any, have immediate and transitory effects? For which is the time lag of effects shorter or longer? Do the effects of some conditions emerge only if the condition persists over long periods?

The timing of cultural effects is more difficult to study because few measures of cultural dimensions are available for multiple time periods (but see Inglehart 1997). Culture tends to change quite slowly, even in response to major socioeconomic and political change (De Vos 1976; Moghaddam and Crystal 1997; Schwartz, Bardi, and Bianchi 2000). The time lag following measurement of cultural dimensions may therefore be less critical for understanding national differences in worry and SWB. There is evidence, nonetheless, that time lag matters for cultural variables too.

In their study of national differences in SWB, Diener et al. (1995) constructed a component score for cultural individualism that combined indicators from 1967 to 1973 (Hofstede's measure), 1993 to 1994 (Triandis's ratings), and 1992 (divorce rates). The Hofstede measure was the best of the three predictors in the component score, and it was the only one that was measured earlier than the surveys on which the SWB scores were based. In the current study the Hofstede individualism measure was a weaker predictor of micro worry and of the relative severity of macro versus micro worry than two other cultural dimensions. Here the time lag between measurements of individualism and worry was 20 to 28 years; it was 1 to 7 years for the other cultural dimensions. These findings suggest that it is important to consider change in cultural values and to study the timing of their influences.[10]

Future longitudinal studies that link cultural dimensions to worry and SWB would constitute a major contribution. Not only could they address questions of timing, but they could directly address the causal issue. We have postulated, on logical grounds, that both cultural dimensions and social and economic factors impact causally on worry. Testing whether changes in cultural, social, and economic factors lead to later changes in worry and SWB would validate or refute this view. Longitudinal studies could also reveal how stable or volatile national levels of micro and macro worry and SWB are over time. Cultural egalitarianism and harmony—variables that change quite slowly (Schwartz et al. 2000)—predicted substantial portions of the variance in the relative severity of the two types of worry. This suggests that national levels of worry may also change only slowly, perhaps with temporary large perturbations. Empirical evidence is needed.

Appendix

Intercorrelations among Variables

	GNP per capita	Income inequality	Recent inflation	Rights violations	Egalitarianism versus hierarchy	Harmony versus mastery	Autonomy versus embeddedness	Individualism (Hofstede)
GNP per capita		−0.32	−0.48	−0.64	0.56	−0.07	0.72	0.91
Income inequality	−0.12		0.48	0.64	−0.55	−0.27	−0.23	−0.47
Recent inflation	−0.50	−0.01		0.69	−0.50	0.06	−0.43	−0.45
Rights violations	−0.26	0.52	0.12		−0.78	−0.45	−0.64	−0.78
Egalitarianism versus hierarchy	0.47	−0.36	−0.52	−0.49		0.61	0.82	0.58
Harmony versus mastery	−0.27	−0.26	0.14	−0.67	0.56		0.43	0.11
Autonomy versus embeddedness	0.71	0.20	−0.46	−0.25	0.04	0.04		0.58
Individualism (Hofstede)	0.87	−0.31	−0.47	−0.56	0.32	−0.17	0.54	

Note: Correlations above the diagonal of blank cells are for 12 nations in which the worry data came from student samples. Correlations below the diagonal are for 7 nations in which the worry data came from teacher samples.

Notes

1. We are grateful to Hasan Bacanli (Turkey), Suzanne Beckmann (Denmark), Gabriel Bianchi (Slovakia), Klaus Boehnke (East and West Germany, Russia), Glynis Breakwell (England), Johnny Fontaine (Belgium), Dwight Frink (USA), John Munene (Uganda), Alvaro Tamayo (Brazil), Zsuzsa Vajda (Hungary), and Monique Wach (France) for gathering these data.

2. They employed two confirmatory approaches: confirmatory factor analysis (Joereskog and Soerbom 1989) and configural verification of a similarity structure analysis (Borg and Lingoes 1987; Davison 1983; Guttman 1968).

3. Exploratory factor analyses on the full sets of student and of teacher samples also yielded clear micro and macro factors. One factor included the micro worry items discriminated in the SSA analyses in each sample and in figure 9.1, the other included the macro worry items. Because the various analyses show that item 4 was not consistently micro or macro, we drop it from further consideration.

4. See Bortz, Leinert, and Boehnke (1990, p. 48) for the method of calculation.

5. We excluded percent time happy from the correlations for percent time sad, and vice versa, because their partial statistical interdependence might lead to an overestimation of their clustering with the various components of SWB.

6. For discussion of how these dimensions relate to those proposed by Hofstede (1980) and Markus and Kitayama (1991), see Sagiv and Schwartz (in press), Schwartz (1997), and Schwartz and Ros (1995).

7. Called "autonomy/conservatism" in some earlier publications.

8. The dimensions also differ. Autonomy/embeddedness strongly contrasts openness to change with maintaining the status quo; individualism/collectivism does not. Moreover many theorists associate individualism with the self-interested pursuit of personal goals (Kagitcibasi 1997; Triandis 1995). In contrast, Schwartz argues that selfishness cannot be an approved component of a cultural dimension, though some degree of selfishness might be tolerated. He therefore excludes selfishness from autonomy.

9. Correlations between individualism/collectivism and autonomy/embeddedness in the current sets of nations were only moderate (0.58 across the set of 12 nations and 0.54 across the set of seven), reinforcing the view that these are not the same cultural dimension.

10. Another explanation for the weaker prediction by individualism in the current study is that it is less relevant to worry. The fact that autonomy, the cultural dimension conceptually closest to individualism, was also a weaker predictor favors the lack of relevance explanation.

References

Boehnke, K., Regmi, M. P., Richmond, B. O., Chandra, S., and Stromberg, C. 1994. Worries, values and well-being: A comparison of East and West German, Nepalese and Fijian undergraduates. Paper presented at the XIIth Congress of the International Association for Crosscultural Psychology, Pamplona, Spain.

Boehnke, K., Schwartz, S. H., Stromberg, C. and Sagiv, L. 1998. The structure and dynamics of worry: Theory, measurement, and cross-cultural replications. *Journal of Personality* 66: 745–82.

Borg, I., and Shye, S. 1993. *Facet Theory: The Method and Its Application*. Newbury Park, CA: Sage.

Bradburn, N. M. 1969. *The Social Structure of Psychological Well-being*. Chicago: Aldine.

Davey, G. C. L., and Tallis, F., eds. 1994. *Worrying: Perspectives on Theory, Assessment and Treatment*. Chichester: Wiley.

Davison, M. 1983. *Multidimensional Scaling*. New York: Wiley.

De Vos, G. A. 1976. *Responses to Change: Society, Culture and Personality*. New York: Van Nostrand.

Diener, E., Diener, M., and Diener, C. 1995. Factors predicting the subjective well-being of nations. *Journal of Personality and Social Psychology* 69: 851–64.

Dillon, W. R., and Goldstein, M. 1984. *Multivariate Analysis*. New York: Wiley.

Famighetti, R., ed. 1997. *The World Almanac and Book of Facts: 1998*. Mahwah, NJ: K-III Reference Corporation.

Griffin, M., and Prior, M. 1990. Young people and the nuclear threat. *Journal of Youth Studies* 7: 40–43.

Gupta, D. K., Jongman, A. J., and Schmid, A. P. 1994. Assessing country performance in the field of human rights. *Human Rights Quarterly* 16: 131–62.

Hofstede, G. 1980. *Culture's Consequences: International Differences in Work-Related Values*. Beverly Hills, CA: Sage.

Hofstede, G. 1991. *Cultures and Organizations: Software of the Mind*. London: McGraw-Hill.

Inglehart, R. 1997. *Modernization and Postmodernization*. Princeton: Princeton University Press.

Larson, R. J., Diener, E., and Emmons, R. A. 1985. An evaluation of subjective well-being measures. *Social Indicators Research* 17: 1–7.

Luskin, R. C. 1990. Explaining political sophistication. *Political Behavior* 12: 331–61.

Markus, H., and Kitayama, S. 1991. Culture and self: Implications for cognition, emotion, and motivation. *Psychological Bulletin* 102: 72–90.

Moghaddam, F. M., and Crystal, D. S. 1997. Revolutions, Samurai, and reductions: The paradoxes of change and continuity in Iran and Japan. *Political Psychology* 18: 355–84.

Sagiv, L., and Schwartz, S. H. (in press). National cultures: Implications for organizational structure and behavior. In N. N. Ashkanasy, C. Wilderom, and M. F. Peterson, eds., *The Handbook of Organizational Culture and Climate*. Newbury Park, CA: Sage.

Schwartz, S. H. 1994. Beyond individualism/collectivism: New cultural dimensions of values. In U. Kim, H. C. Triandis, C. Kagitcibasi, S.-C. Choi, and G. Yoon, eds., *Individualism and Collectivism: Theory, Method and Applications*. Newbury Park, CA: Sage, pp. 85–119.

Schwartz, S. H. 1997. Values and culture. In D. Munro, S. Carr, and J. Schumaker, eds., *Motivation and Culture*. London: Routledge, pp. 69–84.

Schwartz, S. H. 1999. Cultural value differences: Some implications for work. *Applied Psychology: An International Journal* 48: 23–47.

Schwartz, S. H., and Bardi, A. 1997. Influences of adaptation to Communist rule on value priorities in Eastern Europe. *Political Psychology* 18: 385–410.

Schwartz, S. H., and Ros, M. 1995. Values in the West: A theoretical and empirical challenge to the individualism-collectivism cultural dimension. *World Psychology* 1: 99–122.

Schwartz, S. H., Bardi, A., and Bianchi, G. 2000. Value adaptation to the imposition and collapse of Communist regimes in Eastern Europe. In S. A. Renshon and J. Duckitt, eds., *Political Psychology: Cultural and Cross-cultural Perspectives*. London: Macmillan, pp. 217–37.

Schwartz, S. H., and Sagie, G. (in press). Value consensus and importance: A cross-national study. *Journal of Cross-cultural Psychology*.

Schwartz, S. H., Sagiv, L., and Boehnke, K. 2000. Worries and values. *Journal of Personality* 68: 309–46.

Smith, P. B., and Schwartz, S. H. 1997. Values. In J. W. Berry, M. H. Segall and C. Kagitcibasi, eds., *Handbook of Cross-cultural Psychology*, 2nd ed., vol. 3. Boston: Allyn and Bacon, pp. 77–118.

Tabai, H. 1996. *Statistics on Poverty and Income Distribution: An ILO Compendium of Data*. Geneva: International Labor Office.

Triandis, H. C. 1995. *Individualism and Collectivism*. Boulder, CO: Westview.

Veenhoven, R. 1993. *Happiness in Nations*. Rotterdam: Risbo.

10

Freedom and Happiness: A Comparative Study in Forty-four Nations in the Early 1990s

Ruut Veenhoven

"Freedom, equality, and brotherhood" was the credo of the French Revolution. This entreaty was linked to the concept of happiness, which was also under discussion by fashionable authors at the time. It was believed that people could live happier lives if more of society put these principles into practice. This classic view of the Enlightenment is still with us today. But is it realistic? Freedom, equality, and brotherhood are mixed blessings, and their realization is not always compatible.

For a long time this principle could not be tested empirically. The degree of freedom, equality, and brotherhood in society could barely be measured, and neither could the happiness of citizens. However, during the last decades most of the measurement problems have been solved. Fairly good data are now available on some 50, mainly developed, nations. The first explorations of these data yield intriguing results.

The presumed link between equality and happiness fails to appear, at least where income equality is concerned. Average happiness is as high in countries with great income inequality as in nations where income differences are small (Veenhoven 1997, p. 49). Happiness is also not higher in egalitaristic welfare states (Veenhoven and Ouweneel 1995). Brotherhood appears to be no sure ticket to happiness either, though we cannot be happy without good relations with our neighbors, we can live without relations of the brotherhood type. Average happiness appears to be higher in individualistic societies as against that in communitarian settings (Veenhoven 1998b). The next question is whether the freedom factor fulfills the promises of the French Revolution.

The Issue

Opinion about the impact of freedom on happiness is mixed. Different philosophies stress different effects and suggest different net outcomes.

Individualistic social philosophy stresses the possible positive effects. It is typically assumed that people themselves know best what will make them happy, and hence that they will enjoy life more if they can follow their own preferences. Conflicts of interest are seen to be solved by the invisible hand of the market, which is believed to yield more optimal solutions than prescription by king or custom. Though this intellectual tradition is not blind to the perils of free choice, it expects that the positive effects prevail.

Conservative thought tends to emphasize the negative consequences of freedom. Conservatives doubt that people really know what is best for them. The wisdom of tradition and the benefits of solidarity are seen to bring a better life than short-sighted egoism. Through the ages proponents of this view have complained that individual freedom has gone too far, that it is about to destroy vital institutions. Again, the other side of the coin is also acknowledged but deemed to be less relevant.

Some schools see different effects of different variants of freedom. Currently the New Right is quite positive about economic freedom, but at the same time it is critical about freedom in the private sphere of life. Free sex and the legalization of soft drugs are seen to lead to unhappiness. Likewise the leading view in South-East Asia is that economic freedom will improve the human lot but not political freedom.

Another theme in the discussion is that freedom will add to happiness only in specific conditions. The most commonly mentioned condition is that people are sufficiently "mature." If incapable to choose, people will fear freedom and seek refuge under authoritarian leaders and strict rules for life (e.g. Fromm 1941).

Three sets of questions are addressed in this chapter: The first is: Are the effects of freedom on happiness positive on balance? If so, how important is freedom relative to other societal predictors of happiness? The second is: What kind of freedom is most conducive to happiness? Do all freedom variants work out equally, or are some kinds more essential? One of the issues in this context is whether happiness depends more on freedom in private life than in public life, that is, the economy and politics. The third is: To what extent does the balance of effects depend on circumstances? Does freedom add to happiness only in so-called developed societies?

Answering these questions requires, first of all, that the concepts be defined and measured. To that end we will first consider freedom and then happiness. The next requirement is that the interrelationships be explored. The second half of the chapter reports on correlational analyses and discusses the findings.

Freedom

Concept of Freedom

Freedom can be defined as the *possibility to choose*. A person can be said to be free if his or her condition allows some choice and if that choice is not inhibited by others. In this sense absolute freedom is not possible. The human condition allows only a limited array of options. We cannot choose to fly or choose not to sleep any more. We cannot even choose to live on our own entirely. So mutual interdependence implies much interference. We deal here with the *degree* to which choice is limited.

The possibility to choose requires, first of all, that there be an *opportunity* to choose. This is an attribute of the environment. In the second place, it requires a *capability* to choose, which is, at last resort, an individual attribute.

Opportunity to Choose   The opportunity to choose involves two requirements: first that there be something to choose and second that choice not be blocked by others.

In the first sense, freedom depends on the societal supply of life style alternatives. That variety in life style options depends primarily on the mode of existence. For example, simple hunter-gatherer societies provide their members with a more limited assortment than highly differentiated industrial societies. Variety depends also on internal dynamics and on contacts with foreign cultures. In this meaning, the concept of freedom overlaps more or less with notions of material affluence, division of work, and cultural variety. This broad meaning will not be considered in this chapter. The reason is simply that it is too much to handle.

Provided that there is something to choose, opportunity to choose depends further on absence of restriction by others. Bay (1965) refers to this variant as social freedom. In this sense freedom is freedom from impediments, such as restrictive laws or oppression by the powerful. This is the kind of freedom pursued in the French Revolution. The focus of this study is on that latter freedom concept.

Capability to Choose   The possibility to choose requires more than mere opportunity. The opportunity must be seized. This requires an inner awareness of alternatives and the courage to choose.

A primary capability requisite is that the opportunity be acknowledged. The captives who fail to see that the door of their jail is open cannot flee, even though they would if they knew. In this sense freedom is determined by education and information. Bay (1965) calls it potential freedom.

The secondary demand is that recognition of opportunity is acted upon. This depends in the first place on an inclination to choose. The captives who see the open door may let that opportunity pass because they are not too eager to take their fate into their own hands. Inclination may depend on moral conviction and on reality beliefs. Even if one would like to seize the opportunity, there is still the problem that not everybody dares to. Choice involves mostly uncertainty and responsibility. Often people shy away from this. The reader may remember the last scene of *One Flew over the Cuckoos Nest*. In this context, Bay (1965) speaks of psychological freedom.

Measures of Freedom
As yet there is no comprehensive measure of freedom in nations, though there are partial measures. With respect to opportunity to choose, there are attempts to measure differences across nations in absence of restrictions in economic life and in political life. A new measure of nonrestraint in private life is proposed in this chapter.

Measures of capability to choose in nations are even more scarce. Though there are many good indicators at the individual level, there is little at the national level. New measures for this aspect are also proposed in this chapter.

Measures of Opportunity to Choose   Restrictions to choice can best be measured by considering spheres of life separately. We will review measures of freedom in economic, political, and private life below. Though these three domains do not constitute the whole of life, they cover at least much of it. The sum of restrictions in these fields is indicative of the room for choice in a society.

Economic Freedom   In the broad sense, economic freedom means opportunity for exchange of goods and services. That opportunity depends on many things, such as presence of a common language, mutual trust, and established custom. Without an economy there cannot be economic freedom. In the more limited sense used here, economic freedom means absence of restrictions on free trade, such as price control, excessive taxing, or closed-shop practices.

The latter meaning is operationalized in an index devised by the Fraser Institute, reputed to be a think tank of the New Right. This index is based on national ratings for security of money (4 items), free enterprise (6 items), freedom from excessive taxes (3 items), and freedom of money transfer (5 items). The items are presented in appendix A. This index has been computed for most nations of the world in the early 1990s. Scores on the index have been shown to predict economic growth quite well. Since the 1970s economic growth was higher in the economically most free nations (Gwartney 1996).

Political Freedom   Likewise political freedom in the broad sense requires that there be a political system. In the more limited sense the concept refers to restrictions on participation in the system.

That latter meaning is operationalized in two indexes kept by Freedom House, which is a liberalist pressure group, comparable to Amnesty International. The Freedom House indexes are a continuation of Gastril's (1987) registration of human rights violation in nations. One concerns civil rights such as free speech (11 items). The other deals with political rights and considers things like free elections (9 items). Scores on this index are available for most nations of the present-day world (Karantnycky 1996). This is presented in appendix A.

Private Freedom   Restriction in the private sphere of life can be measured in a similar way. One can consider various private domains and estimate the degree to which choice is limited in that domain. As yet no such attempts have been reported. A first shot is presented in this section.

Restriction of choice is most manifest in legal constraints. Legal restraints can be assessed by inspection of legislation and law enforcement reports. Comparative data on these matters are reported in several sources, for example, Humana (1992) and IPPF (1990). Many restrictions in private life are often informal, however, especially restrictions on sexuality. The degree of informal social control in nations can be estimated on the basis of attitudinal data. Most of these data can be found in the World Values Survey, which was conducted in 43 nations in the early 1990s.

On the basis of these sources of information I was able to approximate restrictions in the following fields: restrictions on the practice of one's religion, restrictions on travel in the country and abroad, restrictions on entering into marriage and getting divorced, restrictions on sexuality and reproduction, and finally restrictions on ending one's own life. No comparable data were found on restrictions on dress, use of drugs, and choice of vocation. The available data are presented in more detail in appendix A.

Measures of Capability to Choose   Two aspects of capability to choose were mentioned above: awareness of alternatives and inclination to choose. Neither matter has been the subject of earlier comparative research, so this chapter introduces new measures for these freedom variants.

Awareness of Alternatives   The best way to assess awareness of alternatives is to survey perceived options in the various life domains. Such data are not available. Second best is to use data on education and information, assuming that well-educated and informed people tend to see more alternatives. On these matters there are comparable data.

The level of education in nations is estimated on the basis of school enrollment and adult literacy. Data were found in the Human Development Report (UN-DP 1995). The level of information can, in principle, be assessed by estimating media variety, media attendance, and practice of criticism in the media. Unfortunately, data on these matters are not available for a sufficient number of countries.

Inclination to Choose   As noted above, the chance that people act on the opportunities they see will partly depend on their values and beliefs. Chances will be greater if people respect individual preference and an individualist identity. Currently the best indicators of adherence to individualist values come from studies in the tradition of Hofstede (1991), which assess adherence to individualist work-attitudes in nations. Some of these studies used nearly identical items. The combination of these studies has yielded 39 cases.

The possibility of choice will also be greater if people believe that they are in control of their fate. People who see themselves as a plaything of fate are less likely to seize the opportunities they see. Perceived fate-control was assessed in the World Values Survey by a single item. This score is available for 42 nations (Inglehart et al. 1998). For the purpose of this study, the national scores on work attitudes and perceived fate-control are combined in one index of inclination to choose.

Courage to Choose   Inclination to choose is often not sufficient, especially if the choice is contested; some courage is also needed. The measurement of this attribute requires information about stress tolerance and psychological assertiveness in nations. Unfortunately, comparable data on this matter are not available for a sufficient number of nations.

Table 10.1
Intercorrelations of freedom variants in 44 nations, early 1990s

Variants of freedom	Opportunity to choose			Capability to choose	
	Economic	Political	Personal	Information	Inclination
Opportunity to choose					
Economic freedom	—				
Political freedom	0.38*	—			
Personal freedom	0.23 n.s.	0.69**	—		
Summed opportunities	0.74**	0.86**	0.82**		
Capability to choose					
Information	0.24 n.s.	0.77**	0.70**		
Inclination	0.45**	0.45**	0.34*	0.38**	
Summed capabilities	0.49**	0.76**	0.59**	0.82**	0.83**
Comprehensive freedom					
Opportunities + capabilities	0.55**	0.84**	0.73**	0.81**	0.76**

Validity of the Measures of Freedom   The measures of freedom are summarized in table 10.1, left column. All these measures have considerable face validity, but do they really measure freedom?

One check is testing congruent validity, that is, assessing the correspondence of scores on these measures. Though the different aspects of freedom are not necessarily related, it is not unlikely that they root in common grounds and that they reinforce each other. So one could still expect sizable correlations. The intercorrelations are indeed sizable. Looking again at table 10.1, note that the bottom row is not corrected for autocorrelation.

Another check is testing for concurrent validity, that is, assessing correspondence with related matters. Some data are presented in table 10.2. The freedom measures do indeed appear to be highly correlated with individualism, human rights, and the emancipation of women. There is also a firm correlation with perceived freedom.

Freedom Rank of Nations
The three measures of opportunity to choose were combined in an average z-score per nation. The results are listed in appendix A and presented graphically in figure 10.1. In the bar chart China stands out as the nation that provides the fewest opportunities, closely followed by Cuba, Nigeria, Russia, and India. At the middle

Table 10.2
Freedom and related matters

	Human rights (Humana index)	Perceived freedom (WVS)	Women's emancipation (UNHDR 1995)	Individualism expert rating
Opportunity to choose				
Economic freedom	0.06 n.s.	0.47**	0.37*	0.55**
Political freedom	0.90**[1]	0.39*	0.65**	0.75**
Personal freedom	0.80**[2]	0.30 n.s.	0.75**	0.73**
Summed opportunities	0.82**[2]	0.54**	0.70**	0.79**
Capability to choose				
Information	0.75**	0.32 n.s.	0.74**	0.67**
Inclination	0.41**	0.56**	0.55**	0.65**
Summed capabilities	0.69**	0.57**	0.73**	0.78**
Comprehensive freedom				
Opportunities + capabilities	0.79**	0.56**	0.73**	0.82**

Notes: The Humana index of human rights overlaps to a large extent with the index of political freedom. Some items of the Humana index appear also in the personal freedom category.

of the chart we see countries like the Philippines, former Czechoslovakia, and Chile. Opportunity for choice appears greatest in Canada, Switzerland, and the Netherlands. The ranking fits fairly well with what a regular newspaper reader would expect. Only the low score of Israel comes as a surprise.

The measures of capability to choose were combined in the same way. The results are also listed in appendix A and presented graphically in figure 10.2. At the lowest end we see again Nigeria, India, and China. Yet Russia and Cuba perform better in this regard, mainly because the education in these countries is good. In the middle we have again the Philippines and Chile, while Czechoslovakia scores lower on capability than it did on opportunity. The top scorers are not too different either. Again, we see the United States, Switzerland, and Canada. Israel surprises us again, now with an unexpected high capability to choose. Apparently, Israel is a country that provides little opportunity for otherwise capable citizens.

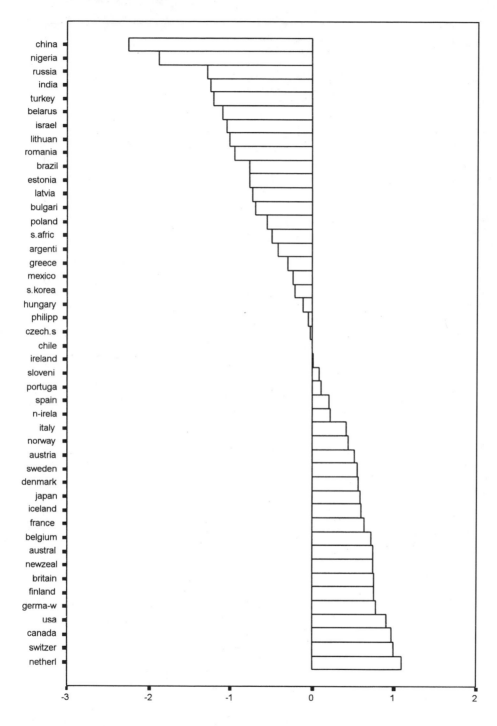

Value 1990 freedom: economic + political + personal

Figure 10.1
Freedom in nations: Opportunity to choose in 46 nations, early 1990s.

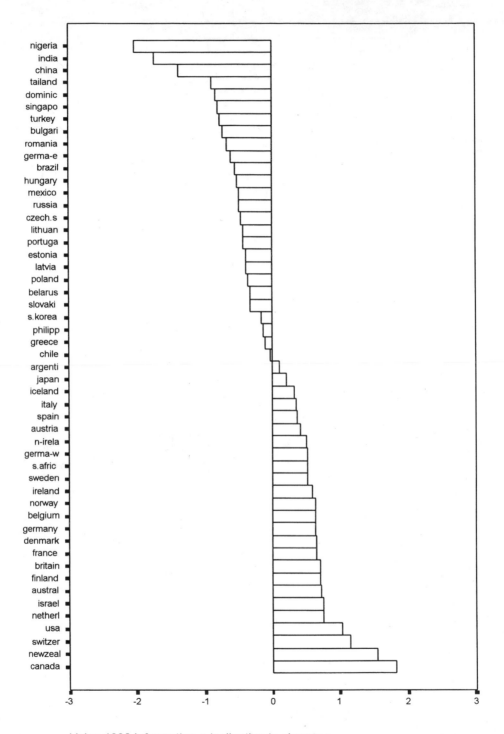

Value 1990 information + inclination to choose

Figure 10.2
Freedom in nations: Capability to choose in 46 nations, early 1990s.

The summed indexes of opportunity to choose and capability to choose were combined in a comprehensive measure of freedom. The rank order on that overall index is somewhat identical with the results presented earlier. Hence this chart is not provided. The scores are given in appendix A.

Happiness

Concept of Happiness

The term happiness can have different meanings, both objective and subjective meanings. In the objective sense, happiness is living in good conditions, such as material prosperity, peace, and freedom. In this interpretation, freedom and happiness are more or less synonymous words.

In the subjective sense happiness is a state of mind. This context refers to evanescent feelings as well as a stable appreciation of life. For our purposes the term is used only in the latter sense. *Happiness is defined as the degree to which someone evaluates positively the overall quality of his or her present life as a whole.* In other words, this is about how much one likes the life one lives. In this interpretation, freedom and happiness are different.

The term life satisfaction carries the same meaning and is often used interchangeably with happiness. An advantage of using the term life satisfaction over the word happiness is that it emphasizes the subjective character of the concept. Another current synonym is subjective well-being. Though this phrase makes clear that it is the subject who makes the appraisal, it is not so clear what the subject appraises. The term is not only used for satisfaction with one's entire life but also for specific discomforts and passing moods.

The concept of happiness denotes an *overall* evaluation of life. So the appraisal that life is free does not indicate that it is happy. There can be too much freedom in life and too little of other qualities. The overall evaluation of life involves all the criteria figuring in the mind of the individual: how good life feels, how well life meets expectations, how desirable life is deemed to be, and so on. The object of evaluation is *life in its entirety* and not a specific domain of life, such as the work life. The enjoyment of work adds to the appreciation of life, but it does not constitute it.

The appraisals of life can concern different periods in time: how life has been, how life is now, and how life will probably be in the future. These evaluations do not coincide necessarily; one may be positive about past life but negative about the future. The focus here is on satisfaction with the life one currently leads.

When we appraise how much we appreciate the life we live, we seem to use two sources of information: we estimate our typical affective experience to assess how well we feel generally, and at the cognitive level we compare life as it is with standards of how life should be. The former affective source of information seems generally to be more important than the latter cognitive one (Veenhoven 1996a, pp. 33–35). The word happiness is commonly used for these subtotals as well as for the comprehensive appraisal. I use the terms *overall happiness* or life satisfaction for the last judgment and refer to the affective and cognitive subappraisals as respectively *hedonic level of affect* and *contentment*. These concepts are delineated in more detail in Veenhoven (1984, ch. 2).

Measures of Happiness
All these variants of happiness can be measured by the self-report. Different questions have been developed for that purpose. For a review of the items and scales, see Veenhoven (2000). The most commonly used item is a single question: Taking all together, how happy would you say you are—very happy, fairly happy, not too happy or not at all happy? Another common question is: How satisfied are you with your life as a whole? The hedonic level is often measured by the ten-item Affect Balance Scale (ABS, Bradburn 1969), which concerns the occurrence of specific positive and negative affects in the past few weeks. The ABS method seems best suited for a cross-national comparison.

Since the 1970s happiness has served as a core variable in Quality of Life surveys in many developed nations. This has resulted in a growing body of data on average happiness in nations. These data have been collated in the World Database of Happiness (Veenhoven 2000).

Though currently used, these measures are much criticized. Three main objections have been raised. First, it is doubted that responses to such simple questions reflect true appreciation of life. Second, there are doubts about the comparability of such ratings across cultures. Third, it is claimed that subjective appraisals of life are meaningless. I will now present a short review of this criticism. For more elaborate discussions of the measurement problems involved, see Diener (1995), Headey and Wearing (1992), Saris et al. (1996), and Veenhoven (1993, 1996).

Validity of Self-reports on Happiness The first objection is that responses to questions about happiness do not adequately reflect how people really feel about their life. Several reasons have been suggested.

One of the misgivings is that most people have no opinion about their happiness. They would be more aware of how happy they are expected to be, and report on that instead. Though this may happen incidentally, it appears not to be the rule. Most people know quite well whether or not they enjoy life. Eight out of ten Americans think of it every week. Responses on questions about happiness tend to be prompt. The nonresponse rate on these items is low, both absolutely (± 1 percent) and relative to other attitudinal questions. The "don't know" responses are also infrequent.

A related claim is that respondents confuse their actual satisfaction with how satisfied other people view them, given their life situation. If this were so, people considered to be well off would typically report being happy, and people regarded as disadvantaged would avow themselves unhappy. This pattern does occur, but it is not widespread. For instance, in the Netherlands good education is seen to be a prerequisite for a good life, but among the best-educated respondents reports of happiness appear to be slightly lower.

Another objection concerns the presence of systematic bias in responses. It is assumed that questions on happiness are interpreted correctly, but that the responses are often inaccurate. People who are actually dissatisfied with their lives say that they are contented. Ego protection and social appearances are said to be the causes of these distortions. This bias is said to manifest an overreporting of happiness, with most people claiming to be happy and most perceiving themselves as happier than average. Other evidence of bias is suggested by the finding that psychosomatic complaints are not uncommon among the happy.

These observations could be correct, but the findings also allow other interpretations. First is the fact that the majority report themselves to be happy. This may not imply overreport but rather that most people are indeed satisfied with life. When living conditions are not extremely bad this could be a candid response. Second, there are at least three good reasons why many people could think that they are more satisfied than average. One is that we underestimate the happiness of our fellow citizen, since misery is more conspicuous than prosperity. Third, the presence of headaches and worries among the satisfied does not prove response distortion. Life can be a bitter trial at times but still be satisfying on balance. The proof is in demonstrating the response distortion. Some clinical studies have tried to do this by comparing responses to single direct questions with ratings based on in-depth interviews and projective tests. The results are generally not much different from responses to a single direct question posed by an anonymous interviewer.

The suspected flaws in self-reported happiness are discussed in more detail in Veenhoven (1984, ch. 3) and Headey and Wearing (1992, ch. 3). None of the doubts have been corroborated as yet.

Comparability of across Countries   The evidence above concerns the measurement of happiness within countries. It does not remove the questions about the comparability of responses across countries. These need to be addressed in separate tests.

A commonly voiced concern is that differences in language may hinder comparison. Words like "happiness" and "satisfaction" do not have quite the same meaning in different languages. Questions applying such terms will therefore measure slightly different matters. This hypothesis was checked by comparing the rank order of nations produced by three kinds of questions on the appreciation of life as whole: a question about happiness, a question about satisfaction with life, and a question that invites the respondent to give a rating between best and worst possible life. The rank orders turned out to be almost identical. As another check, responses to questions on happiness and satisfaction in two bilingual countries were compared, and they did not show a linguistic bias.

A second objection is that responses to questions on happiness are distorted by social desirability, and that these biases differ across cultures. One of the manifestations is more avowal of happiness in countries where happiness ranks high in the value hierarchy. This claim was inspected by checking whether reported happiness is indeed higher in countries where hedonic values are most endorsed. This appeared not to be the case. A second check was an inspection of whether reports of general happiness deviated from responses made few weeks earlier in these countries; the former measures being more vulnerable to desirability distortion than the latter. This notion was also disproved.

A third claim is that conventions in communication distort the answers dissimilarly in different countries. For instance, a collectivistic orientation might discourage "very satisfied" responses, since modest self-presentation is more appropriate in this cultural context. This hypothesis was tested by comparing happiness in countries differing in value collectivism, but no effect was found for the predicted direction. The hypothesis also failed several other tests.

A related claim holds that happiness is a typically Western concept. Unfamiliarity with it in non-Western nations is said to involve several effects: responses could be haphazard, and uncertainty could create a tendency to choose middle categories on the response scales, which results in relatively low average scores. If so, more "don't know" and "no answer" responses can be expected in non-Western nations; however, that appeared not to be the case. The frequency of responses was about 1 percent in all regions of the world.

All these claims imply that there is little relationship between average happiness reports and real quality of life in nations. Yet correlational studies show huge correlations with nation features such as economic prosperity, peacefulness, and schooling. Together such nation properties explain about 70 percent of the differences in reported happiness.

These empirical checks have been reported in more detail in Veenhoven (1993, 1996). There may be other distortions that only time will reveal us. For the present, it appears that self-reports of overall happiness can be meaningfully compared across nations.

Significance of Average Happiness   The last objection is that subjective happiness does not reflect real quality of life. This objection has two variants: one variant holds that happiness is relative, and the other that it is mere folklore.

Relative?   The first variant holds that happiness judgments draw on comparisons *within* the nation, so happiness cannot be meaningfully compared *across* nations. This view is based on the notion that happiness comes from comparative social standing. Some often cited investigations claim support for this theory. Easterlin (1974) saw the theory validated by his observation that happiness is as high in poor countries as it is in rich countries. Brickman et al. (1978) saw proof in the fact that lottery winners are no more satisfied with life than paralyzed accident victims. I have analyzed these sensational claims elsewhere (Veenhoven 1991, 1995), and the results can be summarized as follows:

In general, happiness is not the same in poor and rich nations, neither are accident victims equally as happy as lottery winners. The differences may be smaller than one might have thought, but they undeniably exist.

Some other implications of regarding happiness as relative also failed an empirical test. One is that changes in living conditions, for better or worse, do not have a lasting effect on happiness. To the contrary, there is good evidence that people do not adjust to everything. For instance, one does not adjust completely to the misfortune of having a handicapped child or the loss of a partner.

Another implication is that earlier hardship means later happiness. This hypothesis does not fit the data either. For example, survivors of the Holocaust living in

Israel were found to be less satisfied with life than Israelis of the same age who had not been persecuted.

A final empirical check to be considered is the correlation of happiness with income. The idea that happiness is relative predicts a strong correlation in all countries, irrespective of their wealth. Income is an important criterion in social comparisons, and it is typically compared within countries. Again, the hypothesis is not confirmed by the data. The correlation of happiness with income is high in poor countries but low in rich countries (Veenhoven and Timmermans 1998).

The idea that happiness is relative assumes that happiness is a purely cognitive matter and does not acknowledge affective experience. It focuses on wants and neglects needs. In contrast to wants, needs are not relative. An alternative affective theory is that we infer happiness from how we feel generally. If we feel fine, we gather that we must be happy. If we feel lousy most of the time, we conclude we must be unhappy. Unlike conscious comparisons between the ideal and real, affects are largely unreasoned experiences that likely signal the degree to which basic needs are met. The evidence for this theory is mounting. It denotes that happiness ratings reflect something universal that can be meaningfully compared cross-culturally.

Folklore?   A second variant of the insignificance objection is that reports of happiness have a superficial aspect and do not reflect the actual quality of life in a country. In this view, happiness ratings may be treated as local myths. Comparing happiness reports is like equating apples, pears, and bananas.

The theory of happiness behind this argument is also cognitive. Happiness is seen as a stereotypical attitude. Support for this view comes from some unexpected differences noted in the average happiness between nations, such as low happiness in France and the high happiness in the United States. The idea was also nourished by the finding that average happiness remained at the same level in postwar United States despite the doubling of the gross national product.

I have put this theory to several tests (Veenhoven 1992b, pp. 66–79, 1994, 1995). One implication is that differences in average happiness are unrelated to variation in the objective quality of life. Four such differences were considered: economic affluence, social equality, political freedom, and intellectual development. These national characteristics explained 70 percent of the differences in average happiness in a 28 nation set. Further there were instances of a change in average happiness following the improvement or a decline of quality of life in a country.

The residual variances should have been evident in regression charts. If the French national character is to understate happiness and the American to overstate it, we can expect to find the French less happy than predicted on the basis of objective welfare and Americans more happy than their situation justifies. No such patterns appeared.

Yet another test of happiness involved migrants. If happiness reflects the quality of the conditions one lives in, the happiness of migrants in a country must be close to that of autochthons. If happiness were a matter of socialized outlook, the happiness of migrants should be closer to the level in their motherland. The former prediction turned out to be true, the latter not.

Happiness Rank of Nations

Comparable data on average happiness for 48 nations in the early 1990s is now available. The scores are listed in appendix A and presented in the bar diagram of figure 10.3.

Sizable differences are evident. In Bulgaria the average score on this 1–4 scale is only 2.4, whereas in the Netherlands it is 3.4. This is 30 percent of the possible range. In this time period, happiness is lowest in the formerly communist countries and highest in the rich countries of Northwest Europe.

The scores in figure 10.3 are average responses to the single question: Taking all together how happy would you say you are? Responses to a ten-step life satisfaction scale and on the ten-item Affect Balance Scale show about the same rank order of nations. Earlier studies on a slightly different nation set yielded similar rankings (e.g., Cantril 1965; Inglehart 1990)

Freedom and Happiness

We compiled our data on both freedom and happiness for 44 countries in the early 1990s. The data are presented in appendix B. The responses led to the analysis of this chapter.

Does Freedom Raise Happiness?

The first question concerns whether freedom tends to work out positively. The responses are given in table 10.3.

The middle column of table 10.3 shows the basic correlations between the measures of freedom and happiness. All the correlations are positive and statistically significant. The last relationship is fully illustrated in figure 10.4.

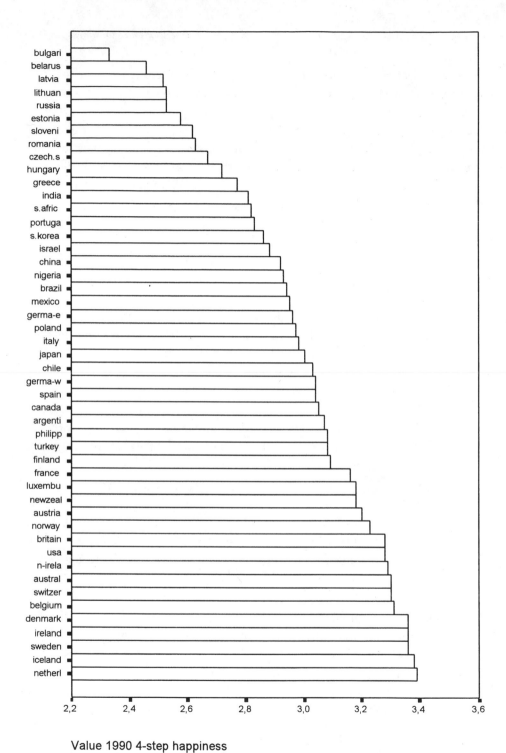

Value 1990 4-step happiness

Figure 10.3
Happiness in nations: 48 nations, early 1990s.

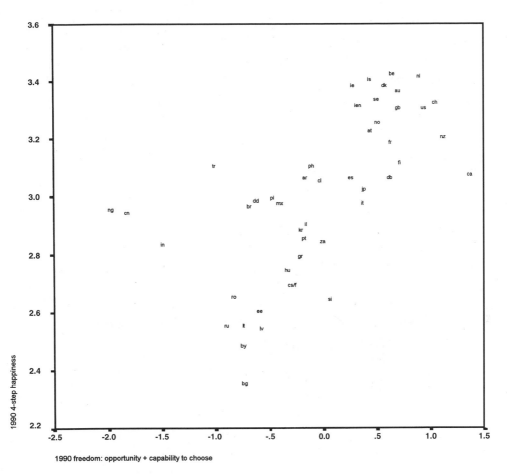

Figure 10.4
Freedom and happiness: 46 nations, early 1990s.

The scatter plot shows a cluster of free and happy nations in the upper right-hand corner. Represented in this cluster are the Netherlands (nl), Switzerland (ch), Iceland (is), Britain (gb), and the United States. Below this appears a cluster of formerly communist countries that were not yet entirely free after the fall of the Eastern bloc and were quite unhappy. Freedom scores are lower in Nigeria (ng), China (cn), and India (in). The great dispersion in the lower left-hand corner of the scatter plot may be due to a temporal happiness dip in the postcommunist countries caused by the turmoil of the transformation. In time this may change, but there is still evident a clear pattern to the data.

The distribution of data suggests a linear relationship. Except for Canada (ca) there is no evidence of diminishing returns. This is noteworthy because the relationship between happiness and the wealth of a nation does reveal a convex pattern (Veenhoven 1989; Veenhoven and Timmermans 1998). The implication is that freedom has not yet reached the level where its costs balance the benefits. If in figure 10.4 we leave out the Eastern European countries, we can see a tendency in the curve to rise, which suggests that the happiness yield of freedom increases at higher levels.

A look at figure 10.4 makes clear that the most free and happy nations are typically rich countries, while the unfree and unhappy nations tend to be poor. So the observed correlations may be spurious. To check this possibility, the wealth of nations was controlled for statistically. See the partial correlations in column 3 of table 10.3. Now all correlations are reduced to insignificance, except the correlation with economic freedom.

This control may be too strict. It removes all common variance with wealth, not only the variance caused by effects of wealth on freedom and happiness, but also possible effects of freedom on happiness through wealth, and vise versa. On the basis of this cross-sectional data we cannot disentangle these effects. So it is still likely that the true correlation is sizable.

Which Kind of Freedom?
The second question can be answered more easily. Table 10.3 shows that opportunity to choose is about as equally related to happiness as the capability to choose. The difference in correlation is not significant, neither is the difference in raw correlations nor the difference in partial correlation.

Looking at opportunities more closely, it is clear that economic freedom is strongly related to happiness; the zero-order correlation is +0.69 and the partial correlation is +0.43. Political freedom and private freedom are less related to happiness; the zero-order correlations are +0.39 and the partial correlations are also positive but insignificant. This is a pleasant surprise for the right-wing free market lobby but a disappointment for liberals like me. More surprising is that the correlation with economic freedom appears to be largely independent of wealth. The partial correlation is +0.43. This means that economic freedom must affect happiness in other ways than through economic growth.

Table 10.3
Happiness and freedom in 46 nations early 1990s

	Correlation with happiness	
Variants of freedom	Zero-order correlation	Partial correlation wealth of nation controlled
Opportunity to choose		
economic freedom	0.69**	0.43**
political freedom	0.39**	0.16 n.s.
personal freedom	0.39**	0.11 n.s.
summed opportunities	0.67**	0.29 n.s.
Capability to choose		
Information	0.32*	−0.19 n.s.
Inclination	0.59**	0.30 n.s.
Summed capabilities	0.59**	0.13 n.s.
Comprehensive freedom		
Opportunities + capabilities	0.64**	0.26 n.s.

Looking now more closely at the capability to choose, we see that information is less correlated to happiness than inclination to choose. The difference is particularly clear in the partial correlations.

In Which Conditions?
Although it is generally acknowledged that the relationship between freedom and happiness is conditional, there is no clear opinion on the kind of contingencies involved. Two possibilities are explored below.

Only When Opportunities Match Capabilities?   It seems logical that the opportunity to choose adds to happiness only when accompanied by a capability to choose. Chances one cannot pick are of no help. To test this hypothesis, we separated the countries that score low on capability from those that score high. The data are presented in table 10.4.

The hypothesis is confirmed for political freedom and private freedom. The opportunity to choose is negatively related to happiness among nations of low capability and positively in nations of high capability. The difference in correlations is considerable.

Yet the hypothesis is not confirmed for economic freedom. In fact economic freedom is more strongly related to happiness in low-capability nations than in high-capability nations ($r = +0.77$, respectively, $+0.34$).

This is an interesting outcome. Several explanations come to mind: one is that making economic choices requires different capabilities than making choices of a political or private nature. Possibly this is because the market choice is more structured. Another explanation may be that economic freedom affects happiness rather indirectly, such as by relieving dependency in oppressive family situations or by reducing social tensions. Such effects do not involve individual capabilities. Similarly one could argue that capability to choose will add to happiness only if there is an opportunity to choose. Capability may even give rise to frustration if it cannot be applied. The data are presented in table 10.5.

Table 10.4
Correlation of opportunity to choose with happiness by capability to choose

| | Correlation with happiness | | | |
| | Low capability ($N = 20$) | | High capability ($N = 25$) | |
Opportunity to choose	Zero-order correlation	Wealth controlled	Zero-order correlation	Wealth controlled
Economic freedom	0.77**	0.80**	0.34 n.s.	0.03 n.s.
Political freedom	−0.30 n.s.	−0.21 n.s.	0.76**	0.64**
Personal freedom	−0.21 n.s.	−0.10 n.s.	0.58**	0.37 n.s.
Summed opportunities	0.07 n.s.	0.25 n.s.	0.63**	0.44 n.s.

Table 10.5
Correlation of capability to choose with happiness by opportunity to choose

| | Correlation with happiness | | | |
| | Low opportunity ($N = 21$) | | High opportunity ($N = 26$) | |
Capability to choose	Zero-order correlation	Wealth controlled	Zero-order correlation	Wealth controlled
Information	−0.33 n.s.	−0.36 n.s.	0.47*	0.29 n.s.
Inclination	0.27 n.s.	0.30 n.s.	0.50*	0.34 n.s.
Summed capabilities	−0.04 n.s.	−0.05 n.s.	0.51*	0.33 n.s.

As table 10.5 indicates, the hypothesis is confirmed. Among nations where the opportunity to choose is low, happiness is unrelated to the summed capability to choose. Yet among nations that offer much opportunity to choose, the correlations are consistently positive and sizable. This pattern is largely due to the information factor. The correlations with inclination (individualist values + perceived control) differentiate less well.

Only in Affluence?   Another consideration is that freedom adds to happiness only among affluent nations. One reason may be that poor countries simply cannot afford the luxury of freedom, since all effort is dedicated to making ends meet. Another logic might be that freedom does not pay in poverty because there is little with which to choose. The data on this matter are presented in table 10.6.

In line with expectation we see that comprehensive freedom is unrelated to happiness in poor nations ($r = +0.-7$ ns) but is positive in rich nations ($r = +0.49^*$). Looking at the summed opportunities and the summed capabilities separately, we see the same pattern. Yet again, economic freedom behaves differently. In this case we see a strong positive correlation among poor nations and a smaller, nonsignificant correlation among rich nations.

Table 10.6
Correlation of freedom with happiness by wealth of nation

	Correlation with happiness	
Variants of freedom	Poor nations ($N = 22$)	Rich nations ($N = 25$)
Opportunity to choose		
Economic freedom	0.74**	0.24 n.s.
Political freedom	0.29 n.s.	0.54**
Personal freedom	−0.25 n.s.	0.38 n.s.
Summed opportunities	0.12 n.s.	0.45*
Capability to choose		
Information	−0.26 n.s.	0.39 n.s.
Inclination	0.38 n.s.	0.28 n.s.
Summed capabilities	0.01 n.s.	0.34 n.s.
Comprehensive freedom		
Opportunities + capabilities	0.07 n.s.	0.49*

Discussion

In view of these findings, we must acknowledge some limitations.

First, we must remember that this study deals with limited conceptions of both freedom and happiness. Freedom is considered in the emancipatory sense of limitation to interference by others, in particular, restrictions by governments. Happiness is considered as the subjective enjoyment of life. So the data presented here do not conclude philosophical debates in which these terms have been used with broader meanings.

Second, we must realize that measurements of these concepts are not perfect, especially with regard to the measurement of freedom. The opportunity to choose cannot be measured exhaustively to incorporate all possible restrictions. The three opportunity domains do not cover all relevant areas of life, and the measures of freedom in these domains do not regard all limitations. The measures of capability to choose are not ideal either. The level of education in a country is at best a dim reflection of its citizens' awareness of alternatives. Likewise adherence to individualist work values does not measure the inclination to choose very well. Though clearly incomplete, these measures do not seem systematically flawed in a particular direction. So the imperfections will probably attenuate the findings rather than produce deceptive relationships. If so, that means that the real relationships are even stronger than the observed correlations suggest.

Third, this study is greatly limited in that it covers only about half the world; it counts only 46 nations. As a result many of the differences observed do not reach statistical significance. So this study leaves doubt about these modest relationships. Still, several relationships were sufficiently strong to produce significant effects, among the differences that did not reach statistical significance, several are at least suggestive of the effect.

Last, we must remember that the postcommunist countries distort the picture somewhat. The data are from the early 1990s when economic and political freedom had just been proclaimed, but perils of transition depressed happiness. This effect is likely to have reduced the correlations as well.

Let us assume that the observed relationships are realistic. What then does that mean? The correlations mentioned above were interpreted as effects of freedom on happiness. I inferred that freedom makes life more enjoyable. Although freedom may have some negative effects, the positive effects dominate, in particular, when opportunities match capabilities and in conditions of material affluence. A pattern of diminishing utility was not observed in the data. In this respect, economic freedom was identified as a main condition for happiness in poor nations, and political freedom the differentiating factor in rich nations.

Although this interpretation is plausible, it is not the only one possible. The statistical relationships can also be due to effect of happiness on freedom. A high level of happiness in a country can foster a climate of tolerance and reasonableness in which freedom works. In other words, happy people can be better citizens. In this reasoning mass happiness is likely to breed opportunities to choose, that is, foster the development of nonrestrictive regimes. Similarly one could also imagine that happiness nurtures the capability to choose, for instance, by its effects on energy and self-esteem (Veenhoven 1988).

Yet we know from history that freedom often emerges from frustration. The French Revolution was not a hallmark of happiness. The present-day emergence of freedom in the postcommunist world was not the fruit of mass happiness either. So the effects of happiness on freedom seem at best secondary, in particular, the effects on economic freedom.

To settle this question of causality, we need to review trend data over long time periods in a sizable group of countries. Such data are not available yet, though the time series on all variables are growing. For the time being, I will assume that the data reflect effects of freedom in the first place.

If freedom does foster happiness, the next question is how. One could envision several mechanisms. Freedom may reduce the chance that people will harass each other; in particular, this regards political freedom. Further freedom in society may add to the chance that citizens live a way of life that fits well with their preferences and capacities. Conditions of freedom encourage the development of different lifestyles that allows individuals to experiment. In particular, private freedom can facilitate the selection of best fitting lifestyle. Next to these direct effects, freedom may contribute to happiness in indirect ways, for instance, to the growth of material wealth.

This is not to deny the negative effects of freedom. Freedom can also destroy happiness. Obviously economic freedom often gives rise to income inequality, which, according to Marx, contributes to the immiserization of the working poor. Likewise political freedom and private freedom can create anomie. Nevertheless, the positive correlations of freedom outweigh the negative correlations, though not equally in all circumstances.

Conclusions

The major conclusion is methodological. Empirical research can settle this matter which philosophers could not solve. Both freedom and happiness can be measured across nations. Though the measures are not yet ideal, and the data are limited, there is good feasible evidence.

The first substantive conclusion is that freedom does not always contribute to happiness, but it does not destroy it either. Significant negative effects of freedom have not been observed. The question is where do the positive effects occur? Second is that the data strongly suggest that economic freedom leads to happiness, especially for those in conditions of poverty and low capability. Third is the less certain data that political freedom and private freedom can add to happiness. This effect appears to be restricted to rich and capable countries.

Appendix A

Happiness and Freedom Ratings of 44 Nations, Early 1990s

Code	Nation	Happiness (scale 1–4)	Freedom (z-scores) Opportunity	Capability	Sum
AR	Argentina*	3.07	−0.71		−0.63
AU	Australia	3.30	−0.68	+0.80	+1.79
AT	Austria	3.20	−0.65	+0.86	+0.23
BE	Belgium	3.31	+0.93	+0.44	+0.98
BR	Brazil	2.94	−1.26	−0.75	−0.63
GB	Britain	3.28	+0.87	+0.85	+1.76
BG	Bulgaria	2.33	−0.90		−1.29
CA	Canada	3.05	+1.22	+1.58	+0.83
CL	Chile*	3.03	−0.42		−1.26
CN	China*	2.92		−1.89	−1.09
CZ	Czechoslovakia (former)	2.69	+0.34		−0.78
DK	Denmark	3.36	+0.82	+0.82	+1.78
EE	Estonia	2.58			−0.77
FI	Finland	3.09	+1.14	+0.78	+0.94
FR	France	3.16	+0.84	+0.47	+1.73
DB	Germany (former West)	3.04	+0.80	+0.78	+1.34
DD	Germany (former East)	2.96		+0.38	−0.69
GR	Greece	2.77	−0.40	−0.13	−0.93
HU	Hungary	2.72	−0.14	+0.26	−0.27

Appendix A (continued)

Code	Nation	Happiness (scale 1–4)	Freedom (z-scores)		
			Opportunity	Capability	Sum
IS	Iceland	3.38	+0.54	+0.32	
IN	India*	2.81	−1.86	−2.40	−0.53
IE	Ireland	3.36	−0.12	−0.08	+0.89
IL	Israel	2.88	−0.94	−0.34	−0.36
IT	Italy	2.98	+0.63	+0.40	+1.08
JP	Japan	3.00	+0.47	−0.28	−0.42
LU	Luxembourg	3.18		+0.44	
MX	Mexico	2.95	−0.55	−0.78	−0.85
NZ	New Zealand	3.18	−0.64	+0.72	+0.83
NL	Netherlands	3.39	+1.72	+0.83	+1.46
NG	Nigeria	2.93	−2.79	−2.50	−1.45
NO	Norway	3.23	+0.50	0.47	+1.10
PH	Philippines	3.08	−0.50	−1.04	−0.83
PL	Poland	2.97	−0.91	−0.18	−0.32
PT	Portugal	2.83	−0.02	−0.76	−2.89
RO	Romania	2.63	−1.35		−0.62
RU	Russia	2.53		+0.15	−1.10
ZA	South Africa	2.82	−0.74	−1.40	+0.28
KR	South Korea	2.86	−0.27	−0.76	−2.26
SI	Slovenia	2.62			+0.66
ES	Spain	3.04	+0.21	+0.89	+0.28
SE	Sweden	3.36	+0.69	+0.82	+1.04
CH	Switzerland	3.30	+1.19	+0.85	+1.33
TR	Turkey*	3.08	−1.74	−1.20	−0.99
US	United States of America	3.28	+0.99	+1.76	+1.97

Source: Happiness ratings are from the World Database of Happiness (Veenhoven 2000). Most of the data are from the World Value Study 2.
Note: The asterisk indicates that the happiness score is probably too high. The score is based on samples in which the poor rural population is underrepresented

Appendix B

Correlation of Happiness and Freedom Ratings of 44 Nations, Early 1990s

Indicators of freedom in nation	Zero order	Controlled for wealth	Data source correlation with average happiness (N)
Opportunity to choose			
Economic freedom (Gwartney 1996, table A1-1)			
Security of money			
* Little money expansion	+0.22 n.s.	−0.22 n.s.	38
* Little inflation variability	+0.37*	−0.10 n.s.	38
* Domestic foreign currency accounts allowed	+0.59**	+0.28 n.s.	38
* Deposits abroad allowed	+0.59**	+0.33*	38
Freedom to produce and consume (little government interference)			
* Little government consumption	−0.18 n.s.	+0.31 n.s.	38
* Little share government enterprises	+0.62**	+0.38*	38
* Little price controls	+0.61**	+0.33*	38
* Little interference on credit market	+0.36*	−0.10 n.s.	38
Freedom to keep what one earns			
* Low transfers and subsidies	−0.06 n.s.	+0.38*	38
* Low marginal tax rates	−0.06 n.s.	−0.09 n.s.	38
* No conscription	+0.28 n.s.	+0.26 n.s.	38
Freedom of exchange			
* Low trade taxes	+0.17 n.s.	−0.40*	38
* Little exchange rate controls	+0.71**	+0.47*	38
* Trade sector relatively big	+0.21 n.s.	+0.22 n.s.	38
* Little restraint on capital mobility	+0.63**	+0.24 n.s.	38
Index of the above based on expert weights	+0.73**	+0.43*	38
Political freedom (Karantnycky 1996)			
Respect of political rights	+0.35*	−0.11 n.s.	47
Respect of civil rights	+0.41*	−0.03 n.s.	47
Personal freedom			
Freedom of religion			
* Legal/practical opportunity (Humana 1992, item 38)	0.22 n.s.	0.14 n.s.	

Appendix B (continued)

Indicators of freedom in nation	Zero order	Controlled for wealth	Data source correlation with average happiness (N)
Freedom to travel			
* Legal/practical opportunity			
* Travel in country (Humana 1992, item 1)	+0.17 n.s.	+0.01 n.s.	46
* Travel abroad (Humana 1992, item 2)	+0.05 n.s.	−0.35*	46
Freedom of marriage			
* Legal/practical opportunity			
* Marriage (Humana 1992, items 36–37)	+0.19 n.s.	−0.17 n.s.	46
* Public acceptance			
* Divorce (World Value Survey 2, item 310)	+0.18 n.s.	+0.01 n.s.	42
Freedom of procreation			
* Legal/practical restrictions			
* Abortion PAI 1995	+0.13 n.s.	−0.21 n.s.	38
* Sterilization IPPF 1990	+0.18 n.s.	+0.02 n.s.	35
* Public acceptance			
* Abortion (World Value Survey 2, item 309)	−0.02 n.s.	−0.19 n.s.	21
* Planned single motherhood (World Value Survey 2, item 217)	+0.01 n.s.	+0.11 n.s.	41
Freedom of sexuality			
* Public acceptance			
* Homosexuality (World Value Study 2, item 307)	+0.72**	+0.38*	42
* Prostitution (World Value Study 2, item 308)	+0.35 n.s.	+0.07 n.s.	42
Freedom to die			
* Public acceptance			
* Suicide (World Value Study 2, item 313)	+0.29 n.s.	+0.09 n.s.	42
* Euthanasia (World Value Study 2, item 312)	+0.28 n.s.	+0.05 n.s.	42
Average private freedom (mean z-scores)			
Religion + travel + sex + marriage + death	+0.38	−0.13 n.s.	43
Average opportunity to choose (mean z-scores)			
economic + political + private	+0.60**	+0.04 n.s.	43
Capability to choose			
Awareness of alternatives			
Education			
* Literacy + school-enrolment (Human Development Report 1995)	+0.32*	−0.19 n.s.	47

Appendix B (continued)

Indicators of freedom in nation	Zero order	Controlled for wealth	Data source correlation with average happiness (N)
Inclination to choose			
Individualistic work-values (Hofstede 1991 + Smith 1997)	+0.52**	+0.30 n.s.	39
Perceived fate-control (World Value Survey 2, item 95)	+0.50**	+0.31 n.s.	42
Average capability to choose			
Information + inclination	+0.59**	+0.13 n.s.	46
Comprehensive freedom			
Opportunities + capabilities	+0.64**	+0.26 n.s.	46

Notes

1. Earlier versions of this chapter were presented at (1) International Conference of Psychology in Montreal, August 1, (2) International Conference Social Change in an Enlarged Europe, Collegium Budapest, May 1998, and (3) International Conference of Political Psychology, Amsterdam, 1999.

2. The Affect Balance Scale (ABS) has at least three advantages in a cross-national context. (1) The ABS is less vulnerable to language differences than the single happiness and satisfaction items. Since the ABS involves ten items, any distortions in translation and understanding are likely to neutralize each other. (2) The ABS is less vulnerable to desirability distortion, and therefore also less vulnerable to differential distortion of this kind. ABS concerns recent affective experience, which is more tangible than general happiness and satisfaction. Also admitting oneself to have felt bad within the last few weeks is less threatening than avowing to be unhappy. (3) The ABS does not require acquaintance with concepts such as happiness and satisfaction. Though single items on happiness do not appear to be vulnerable to these distortions either (Veenhoven 1993, ch. 5), the ABS is still a safer method.

3. Intercorrelations are as follows: happiness by life-satisfaction $r = +0.89$, happiness by affect balance $r = +0.57$, and life-satisfaction by affect balance $r = +0.55$.

References

Bay, C. 1965. *The Structure of Freedom*. Stanford: Stanford University Press.

Berlin, I. 1958. Two concepts of liberty. In *Four Essays on Liberty*. Oxford: Oxford University Press.

Blokland, H. T. 1997. *Freedom and Culture in Western Society.* London: Routledge.

Bradburn, N. M. 1965. *The Structure of Psychological Well-being.* Chicago: Aldine.

Cantril, H. 1965. *The Pattern of Human Concern.* New Brunswick, NJ: Rutgers University Press.

Diener, E., Diener, M., and Diener, C. 1995. Factors predicting subjective wellbeing in nations. *Journal of Personality and Social Psychology* 69: 851–64.

Fromm, E. 1941. *Escape from Freedom.* New York: Rhinehart.

Gastril, R. D. 1987. *Freedom in the World: Political Rights and Civil Liberties, 1986–1987.* New York: Greenwood Press.

Gwartney, J. D. 1996. *Economic Freedom in the World, 1975–1995.* Vancouver, BC: Fraser Institute.

Headey, B., and Wearing, A. 1992. *Understanding Happiness: A Theory of Subjective Well-being.* Melbourne: Longman Cheshire.

Hofstede, G. 1991. *Cultures and Organizations.* New York: McGraw-Hill.

Humana, C. 1992. *World Human Rights Guide.* New York: Oxford University Press.

Inglehart, R. 1990. *Culture Shift in Advanced Industrial Society.* Princeton: Princeton University Press.

Inglehart, R., Basenez, M., and Moreno, A. 1998. *Human Values and Beliefs: A Cross-cultural Sourcebook.* Ann Arbor: University of Michigan Press.

IPPF. 1990. Reproductive rights. International Planned Parenthood Federation. Wallchart distributed by *People* magazine, vol. 7, no. 4.

Karantnycky, A., Cavanaugh, C., and Finn, J., eds. 1996. *The Annual Survey of Political Rights and Civil Liberties.* New York: Freedom House.

Saris, W. E., Scherpenzeel, A. C., Veenhoven, R., and Bunting, B., eds. 1996. *A Comparative Study of Satisfaction with Life in Europe.* Budapest: Eotvos University Press.

UN DP. 1995. *Human Development Report, 1995.* United Nations Development Program. Oxford: Oxford University Press.

Veenhoven, R. 1984. *Conditions of Happiness.* Dordrecht: Kluwer Academic.

Veenhoven, R. 1988. The utility of happiness. *Social Indicators Research* 20: 333–54.

Veenhoven, R. 1989. National wealth and individual happiness. In K. G. Grunert and F. Olander, eds. *Understanding Economic Behavior.* Dordrecht: Kluwer Academic, pp. 9–32.

Veenhoven, R. 1991. Is happiness relative? *Social Indicators Research* 24: 1–34.

Veenhoven, R. 1993. Happiness in nations. Subjective appreciation of life in 56 nations, 1946–1992. RISBO, Erasmus University, Rotterdam. Updated version on Internet: http://www.eur.nl/fsw/research/happiness/.

Veenhoven, R. 1994a. Correlates of happiness: 7838 findings from 603 studies in 69 nations 1911–1994. RISBO, Erasmus University, Rotterdam. Updated version on Internet: http:/www.eur.nl/fsw/research/happiness/.

Veenhoven, R. 1994b. Is happiness a trait? Tests of the theory that a better society does not make people any happier. *Social Indicators Research* 32: 101–60.

Veenhoven, R. 1996. Developments in satisfaction research. *Social Indicators Research* 37: 1–46.

Veenhoven, R. 1997. Progress dans la comprehension du bonheur. *Revue Quebecoise de Psychologie* 18: 29–74.

Veenhoven, R. 1998. Quality of life in individualistic society: A comparison of 43 nations in the early 1990s. *Social Indicators Research* 48: 157–86.

Veenhoven, R. 2000. *World Database of Happiness.* http://www.eur.nl/fsw/research/happiness.

Veenhoven, R., and Ouweneel 1995. Livability of the welfare state: Appreciation-of-life and length-of-life in nations varying in state-welfare-effort. *Social Indicators Research* 36: 1–49.

Veenhoven, R., and Timmermans 1998. *Welvaart en geluk Economisch Statistische Berichten (ESB),* vol. 83, pp. 628–31.

World Value Survey. Cumulative file. ICPRS file 6160, Ann Arbor, MI. (See also Inglehart 1998.)

IV

Individual Differences

11

Age and Sex Differences in Subjective Well-being across Cultures

Richard E. Lucas and Carol L. Gohm

Subjective well-being researchers are interested in the factors that influence cognitive and affective well-being from the respondents' perspective. Both demographic and psychological factors are considered, and all consistent relations must be understood in the context of theories that explain the processes underlying SWB judgments. Thus far SWB researchers have made progress in cataloging the correlates of cognitive and emotional well-being (for a review, see Diener et al. 1999), yet the conclusions that can be drawn from these empirical findings are often limited by the reliance on Western samples. Cross-cultural replications of existing empirical findings benefit SWB theory in three ways: (1) cross-cultural studies establish the *generalizability* of empirical relations, (2) they can provide more accurate average effect size estimates derived from a broader sample of participants, and (3) they enable researchers to investigate the ways in which culture *moderates* the relations among SWB and psychological and demographic factors. All three questions have implications for our understanding of the processes underlying SWB. In this chapter we investigate the effects of age and sex on SWB across cultures using two large international samples.

It is important to note that SWB is not a single unitary construct. Instead, it comprises multiple, separable components (Andrews and Withey 1976; Lucas, Diener, and Suh 1996). People are said to have high SWB if they feel satisfied with the conditions of their lives (cognitive well-being) and experience frequent pleasant emotions and infrequent unpleasant emotions (affective well-being). The different components of SWB often have different demographic and psychological correlates. For example, personality researchers have found that extraversion tends to correlate moderately with pleasant affect but only slightly or not at all with unpleasant affect (Costa and McCrae 1980). For this reason it is important to investigate the separable components of SWB when examining the effects of age and sex. In this chapter we distinguish among the different components of life satisfaction, pleasant affect, and unpleasant affect when possible.

Sex Differences

In the first major review of SWB research, Wilson (1967, p. 294) concluded that sex had no effect on avowed happiness—the happy individual was "of either sex." Since that time, researchers have tried to reconcile this fact with the knowledge that women suffer from much higher rates of depression and other internalizing disorders (Nolen-Hoeksema 1990). But differential rates of clinical levels of emotional disorders do not necessarily reflect gender differences in normal ranges of emotional experience; and furthermore gender differences in unpleasant emotions are not directly tied to gender differences in positive aspects of SWB. Pleasant and unpleasant affect are only slightly correlated when assessed over long time periods (Diener and Emmons 1984; Diener, Smith, and Fujita 1995).

Recent reviews on gender differences in SWB consistently agree that women tend to experience higher levels of unpleasant affect than men (Brody and Hall 1993; Manstead 1992; Nolen-Hoeksema and Rusting 1999). Yet these differences are limited to what Nolen-Hoeksema and Rusting (in press) call "internalizing" moods. Women report more frequent and intense internally focused moods such as sadness, fear, nervousness, shame, and guilt. These differences mirror the elevated rates of internalizing disorders such as depression, anxiety disorders, and eating disorders experienced by women.

Not all emotions are internally focused, however, and gender differences are less clear when externally focused unpleasant emotions are examined. The most frequently studied example of an externalizing emotion is anger. In contrast to the findings for internalizing unpleasant emotions, women do not consistently experience anger more intensely or frequently than men. In some studies men experience more anger than women (Biaggio 1980; Doyle and Biaggio 1981), whereas in others, no significant differences are found (Allen and Haccoun 1976; Averill 1983; Brody 1993). Nolen-Hoeksema and Rusting (1999) suggest that sex differences in anger experience are situation-specific and that men and women may feel angry in response to different eliciting circumstances.

Equally complex are investigations into sex differences in positive emotional well-being. Of the three reviews cited above, Brody and Hall (1993) concluded that women experience more pleasant emotions than men, Nolen-Hoeksema and Rusting

(1999) concluded that results are inconsistent and sex differences change direction across studies, and Manstead (1992) concluded that consistent sex differences occur only in negative affect. Even the meta-analytic empirical reviews of the literature disagree. Haring, Stock, and Okun (1984) reported that men have a slight tendency to report higher levels of positive well-being, whereas Wood, Rhodes, and Whelan (1989) reported a slight benefit for women (particularly in measures of happiness and life satisfaction). They explained the discrepancy by noting that Haring et al. included measures that reflect unpleasant affect as well as pleasant affect and thus may capture gender differences on negative as well as positive dimensions of well-being. In both meta-analyses, however, effect sizes were small and males were very close to females on average levels of positive well-being.

Inconsistencies in sex differences may result from the confounding of two additional dimensions of emotional experience: intensity and frequency. Allen and Haccoun (1976), for example, found that females did not differ from males on the self-reported frequency with which they experienced four emotions, but females experienced greater intensity of experience on three of four emotions examined. Fujita, Diener, and Sandvik (1991) replicated this finding showing that females experienced greater intensity of both pleasant and unpleasant emotions than males, but there were no differences in frequency of emotional experience. Diener, Sandvik, and Larsen (1985) found that women experienced greater affect intensity over a wide range of age groups.

The pattern of sex-difference findings has led some to suggest that women are more emotional than men, and that this greater emotionality results from stereotypes and gender roles that women are required to fulfill (e.g., Wood, Rhodes, and Whelan 1989; Brody and Hall 1993). Wood, Rhodes, and Whelan, for example, state that:

The roles typically filled by men and women in our society differ importantly in terms of emotional experiences. Enactment of caretaker roles, which are typically filled by women in the home (e.g., mother, wife) and in paid employment settings (e.g., teacher, nurse), is likely to involve sensitivity to the needs of others and emotional expression. Men's roles are less likely to emphasize emotional experience. (p. 250)

Wood, Rhodes, and Whelan argue that enactment of gender-specific roles leads women to be more sensitive than men to their own and others' emotions. Brody and Hall (1993) argue that gender stereotypes include greater female emotionality and that these stereotypes may be self-fulfilling prophecies. Thus greater emotionality should translate into greater intensity of feelings when emotions do arise.

Few studies offer definitive answers regarding the causes of sex differences in SWB. Nolen-Hoeksema and Rusting (1999) reviewed a number of possible mechanisms and concluded that personality explanations and social context explanations are the most promising. Personality explanations focus on the traits, behavioral styles, cognitive styles, and coping styles that are associated with sex and gender. These differences include the above-mentioned affect-intensity differences, as well as greater investment in relations and dispositional empathy among women, and different patterns of attributional styles and coping styles across sexes. These personality differences may result in more intense emotional experience and possibly greater susceptibility to negative emotions on the part of women.

Social context explanations attribute sex differences in SWB to differences in status, roles, and social expectations of men and women. Women experience physical and sexual abuse more frequently than men do, and survivors of abuse have high rates of internalizing disorders such as depression and anxiety (Nolen-Hoeksema 1990). Women also experience less power in their relationships, and the resulting lack of control over daily decisions may influence internalizing moods and disorders (Nolen-Hoeksema and Rusting 1999). The differential expectations of men and women that result from stereotypes (Brody and Hall 1993) and gender roles (Wood, Rhodes, and Whelan 1989) also fall under the category of social context explanations. Nolen-Hoeksema and Rusting (1999) argued that in contrast to personality and social context explanations, biological explanations of sex differences in SWB have received little empirical support.

Other researchers have disavowed the "sex-differences" approach to studying emotions (e.g., Shields 1987) by examining the validity of emotion stereotypes. Feldman Barrett, Robin, Pietromonaco, and Eyssell (1998), for example, found that sex differences in global reports of emotions were not replicated when "on-line" moment reports of mood were assessed. Similarly Robinson, Johnson, and Shields (1998) found that participants used gender-stereotypes when predicting their emotional responses to hypothetical situations, but no stereotypical differences were found in actual emotional experiences. These results suggest that global reports of emotions and SWB may be influenced by gender-stereotypes, and sex differences may disappear when "on-line" momentary mood techniques are used.

The question of whether sex differences in SWB exist cannot be answered with a simple yes or no. The answer depends on the component of SWB that is being measured and the way these components are measured. Three reviews of the literature agree that women generally tend to report more intense and frequent negative, unpleasant, internalizing emotions than men. However, sex differences in the experience of externalizing emotions such as anger are less clear. Women may or may not experience more anger than men, and these differences probably depend on the circumstances and eliciting factors particular to the situation being investigated. Studies of pleasant emotions exhibit similar complexity, with some studies reporting greater pleasant affect among women, some reporting greater pleasant affect among men, and some reporting no sex differences at all. Explanations for sex effects are far from definitive, but the most support has emerged for personality and social context explanations. Gender roles and stereotypes about masculinity and femininity appear to influence emotional behaviors in which men and women engage, emotional attitudes that men and women hold, and emotion stereotypes.

Unfortunately, most studies of sex differences in SWB have been undertaken in Western countries, and the generalizability of sex differences is not known. In light of the hypothesized influence of social context and socially prescribed gender roles on emotional experience, the potential impact of cultural influences on sex differences must not be ignored. Cultural variation in gender roles may moderate sex differences in SWB. Social status differences and emotion stereotypes may vary across cultures, and these factors may influence sex differences in emotion. Furthermore cultural dimensions such as individualism/collectivism may influence the importance of gender roles in a particular culture. Triandis (1989) argued that in collectivist cultures, behavior is determined more by norms and social roles than it is in individualist cultures. Even if gender roles are similar across cultures, collectivist cultures may require more adherence to these socially appropriate roles. By examining the factors that moderate sex differences, theorists can develop stronger theories of the processes underlying these differences.

Age Effects

As with sex differences, age effects have been studied since the field of SWB emerged. In his review of the field, Wilson (1967) concluded that age does have an effect on avowed happiness, with younger individuals reporting higher happiness than older individuals. In the thirty years that have passed since this review, most studies contradict this simple interpretation of age effects on SWB (Diener et al. 1999). The relations depend on the component being measured and age-related declines in happiness may be due to the types of measures that are used (Diener and Suh 1998). Theories of age effects in SWB generally posit that (1) SWB is influenced by the objective conditions of our life (e.g., income, social support, health), and these conditions tend to worsen as we age (Diener and Suh 1998; Wilson 1967), or (2) SWB is influenced by our ability to regulate our emotions, and this ability tends to improve as we age (Carstensen 1995; Lawton 1996). Thus some theorists argue that SWB should decrease with age, while others argue that SWB should increase with age. Empirical support for these opposing viewpoints is mixed (see Mroczek and Kolarz 1998 for a review). Effect sizes are generally small and the direction of these effects often shifts across studies. Below we review evidence from cross-cultural studies of age and SWB.

In the first major cross-cultural study of the relation between age and SWB, Cantril (1965) examined the life satisfaction ratings of individuals from 14 nations. Although limitations in the data make correlations or mean differences across age groups difficult, Cantril's data show that approximately the same percentage of older adults as middle-aged or young adults report high life satisfaction. Using a series of studies conducted in the 1980s, Inglehart (1990) replicated this finding, noting only small differences in life satisfaction across age groups. For example, 80 percent of young adults and 81% of those aged 65 and older reported being satisfied or very satisfied with their lives.

More recent cross-cultural examinations of age effects have used better measurements of SWB that allow for more precise hypothesis tests. Okma and Veenhoven (in press), for example, studied the relation between age and SWB in 8 European nations between 1980 and 1990. Unlike previous studies, Okma and Veenhoven examined the cognitive and affective components of SWB separately, and they examined more precise age groups instead of simply comparing young and old. From age 18 to 90, mean levels of life satisfaction exhibited almost no change whatsoever. Affective well-being, on the other hand, showed consistent declines across the life span. Specifically, affect balance (defined as the difference between pleasant and unpleasant affect) declined slowly from ages 18 to 48, and more dramatically after age 65.

Diener and Suh (1998) examined the decline in affect balance and other age effects in more detail using the World Values Survey II (World Values Study Group 1994), a survey of approximately 60,000 respondents from 43 nations. Replicating previous findings, Diener and Suh reported that when plotted against age, life satisfaction scores formed an almost perfect flat line—from age 18 to age 90 mean levels of life satisfaction were stable. The separable affective components of positive and negative emotions exhibited slightly different patterns. Positive affect showed a slow but steady decline across all age groups from respondents in their 20s to respondents in their 80s. Negative affect also showed a slight decline from the 20s to the 60s, but then rebounded slightly among respondents in their 70s and 80s. Diener and Suh conclude that because positive affect declines steadily throughout the life span, the decline in affect balance reported by Inglehart (1990) is due to declines in pleasant affect rather than emotions as a whole.

Recently Gross, Carstensen, Pasupathi, Tsai, Skorpen, and Hsu (1997) examined specific aspects of emotional experience in four ethnically and culturally diverse samples. Gross and colleagues separated emotional experience from emotional expression and emotional control. The most consistent finding from these four studies was that emotional control increased across the life-span. Gross et al. also found some evidence that negative emotional experiences decrease with age, but this effect was only replicated across studies for the emotion "anger." In one study, age was slightly associated with greater happiness experiences ($r = 0.07$, $p < 0.05$, $n = 1,080$), but this finding was not replicated in the second study, which assessed changes in happiness experiences.

Several consistent findings emerge from cross-cultural studies of age effects on SWB. In all major international studies of SWB, life satisfaction shows little, if any change across the life-span. Affective well-being appears to decline with age, but Diener and Suh (1998) suggested that this decline is due to more to decreases in pleasant affect than increases in unpleasant affect. Diener and Suh reported that at least until the 60s negative affect also declines. This finding of general declines in emotional experience is supported by findings of decreased affective intensity (Diener, Sandvik, and Larsen 1985) and greater emotional control (Gross et al. 1997) with age. These trends seem to be consistent across nations and across diverse cultural and ethnic groups.

Yet examining the generalizability of age effects on SWB is only one goal of cross-cultural investigations. Cross-cultural research can also benefit theory by providing more accurate estimates of effect sizes from broad samples of individuals. Most of the cross-cultural studies described above do not report any clear effect sizes from which we can judge the importance of age effects. Perhaps even more important, by focusing on the generalizability of age effects, the cross-cultural studies reviewed above often ignore the differences that exist between nations and across cultures. It would be useful to know how age effects differ across nations, even if the direction of the effects are consistent. For example, the impact of the elderly's poorer health on SWB may be greater in nations where access to medical care is limited, or the impact of reduced income among the elderly may be magnified in nations with poor economies. Examining the effects of cultural variables will help to elucidate the processes underlying age-related changes in SWB.

Goals

The goal of this chapter is to understand the effects of sex and age on SWB across cultures. One technique for accomplishing this goal is to treat samples from different nations as a single broad sample from which we can test the generalizability of relations found among exclusively Western samples. Such an approach ignores differences among nations, however, and is thus not desirable. An alternate approach is to treat each nation as a separate study and examine the distribution of effect sizes in this population of studies. Using meta-analytic techniques, average effect sizes can be determined by weighting individual effect sizes and averaging. Furthermore meta-analysis allows researchers to test hypotheses about how different effect sizes are from each other. More specifically, we can test whether the variability in effect sizes that is observed is due to sampling, and whether the observed effect sizes come from a single population. If no significant heterogeneity is detected, we cannot interpret differences between effect sizes as anything more than sampling error. If, on the other hand, the variability is greater than what would be expected by chance, we can go on to make substantive claims regarding trends in effect sizes across studies.

Based on previous research, we can ask several questions about age and sex effects across nations. Most studies find that women experience more unpleasant affect than men do, but it is unclear whether this difference results from greater frequency or greater intensity of unpleasant emotional experiences and whether it applies to all unpleasant emotions equally. Wood, Rhodes, and Whelan's (1989) meta-analysis suggests that women also experience more pleasant affect, but the effect is small and inconsistent. We will examine gender differences in frequency and intensity of pleasant and unpleasant affect, as well as more specific emotions such as fear and anger. Our goal is to provide an estimate of average effect size using a broad international sample, but also to examine the amount of variability in effect sizes found in different nations. Similarly we will estimate the average effect of age on life satisfaction, pleasant affect, and unpleasant affect, again focusing on differences between nations.

Method

The current chapter analyzes data from two large international studies: the World Values Survey II (WVS II; World Values Study Group 1994) and the International College Student Data study (collected by Ed Diener and colleagues). Age cohort analyses from the WVS II were originally reported in Suh and Diener (1998) and are re-analyzed here using the meta-analytic approach. Sex difference analyses have not been published previously.

World Value Survey II

The WVS II data set includes approximately 57,000 respondents from 41 nations (see Suh et al. 1998, for a list of nations). All populated continents were sampled, and the nations that are included are quite diverse. In most nations, stratified multi-stage random sampling was employed, and the resulting sample is quite representative of the populations being studied.

Three SWB measures were included in the WVS II. Life satisfaction was measured on a scale ranging from 1 ("dissatisfied") to 10 ("satisfied"). Pleasant and unpleasant affect were measured using Bradburn's (1969) Affect Balance Scale (ABS), a 10-item measure with five questions reflecting pleasant affect and five questions reflecting unpleasant affect. Respondents answer no (1) or yes (2) to each of the ten questions, and responses are summed to create pleasant and unpleasant affect scores that range from 5 to 10.

International College Student Data

The second data set includes responses from over 6,000 college students from 39 nations around the world. Again, nations from all populated continents were included, and the sample of nations is quite diverse (see Suh et al. 1998 for a list of nations). Questionnaires were administered to college students by colleagues in each of the universities studied. Since only college students were included, this data set is not analyzed with respect to age effects.

Because the International College Student Data (ICSD) project was designed to assess personality and SWB constructs, more psychometrically sound measures of SWB were included. Life satisfaction was measured by the Satisfaction with Life Scale (SWLS; Diener et al. 1985), a five-item measure with high reliability, temporal stability, and construct validity. Pleasant and unpleasant affect were measured by assessing the frequency and intensity with which respondents experienced each of 8 emotions: fear, anger, sadness, guilt, affection, joy, contentment, and pride. Thus we had four affect measures: frequency and intensity of pleasant and unpleasant affect. Each emotion can also be examined separately. To provide more reliable measures for each emotion, we summed frequency and intensity scores for each emotion when analyzing emotions individually. Thus the ICSD complements the WVS II by providing better measures of SWB and a sample of emotions that can be examined separate from global dimensions.

Analytic Procedure

We first calculated effect sizes for each nation and then examined the distribution of effect sizes across all nations. In the case of sex differences, we calculated Hedge's d statistic, which is the mean difference between males and females divided by the pooled standard deviation (positive effect sizes reflect greater intensity or frequency for males, and negative effect sizes reflect greater intensity or frequency for females). The resulting standardized mean difference is then corrected for bias (Rosenthal 1994). For age effects we used regression analyses to examine the linear and quadratic effects of age on each of the three components of SWB in each of the 41 nations. The quadratic effect was significant 6 times for life satisfaction (5 positive, 1 negative), 6 times for pleasant affect (3 positive, 3 negative) and 14 times for unpleasant affect (all positive). Because of the infrequent and inconsistent quadratic effects in life satisfaction and pleasant affect, the quadratic term was dropped from the model and correlation coefficients were computed as effect sizes.

Because there were consistent quadratic effects in predicting unpleasant affect, both linear and quadratic effects were included in the meta-analysis. Unfortunately, the linear and quadratic terms are correlated with each other as well as with the dependent variable, which makes computing effect sizes for the linear effect separate from the quadratic effect difficult. In this case, however, we are interested in the amount of variance that each variable contributes to predicting unpleasant affect. Cohen and Cohen (1975) argue that when testing the importance of quadratic effects, the linear effect should be tested first, and the quadratic effect should be tested by examining the additional variance that is accounted for when the quadratic term is entered into the equation. Following this rationale, we use the correlation between age and unpleasant affect as the effect size for the linear effect and the semi-partial correlation between the quadratic term and unpleasant affect controlling for age (which is equivalent to the square root of the change in R^2 when the quadratic term is entered) as the effect size for the quadratic term.

The mean of the effect sizes are computed by weighting each effect size by the inverse of its variance (which is dependent on the sample size of the study). A homogeneity statistic (Q_w) determines whether the inconsistency in effect sizes across studies is large enough to reject the hypothesis that the studies are drawn from a common population. This estimate has an approximate chi-square distribution with $k-1$ degrees of freedom, where k is the number of effect sizes included in the meta-analysis (Shadish and Haddock 1994). If the Q_w value exceeds this chi-square value, the variability in effect sizes is greater than what would be expected by chance, which suggests that some feature of the individual studies has influenced the size of the effect.

For each variable we examine, we will attempt to answer a number of questions. First, does significant heterogeneity in effect sizes exist? In most meta-analyses, individual studies have been conducted by researchers with varying theoretical orientation who use different measures and procedures. Thus it is often unreasonable to expect homogeneity before specific aspects of the individual methodologies are taken into account. In the WVS II and the ICSD, however, the same measures were administered in the same format across all nations. Thus methodological factors are relatively constant, and variation in effect sizes should be due to cultural characteristics of the nations. If effect sizes are homogeneous, we can assume that all studies come from the same population. In other words, if we had an infinite number of samples from each of the nations, we would expect the mean of all samples from all nations to equal the mean found in our meta-analysis. When we reject the null hypothesis of homogeneity, we cannot make this assumption and must assume that the effect sizes vary across nations. The existence of significant heterogeneity suggests that cultural factors moderate the size of the relation between SWB and sex and SWB and age.

Once we determine whether heterogeneity exists, we calculate the weighted average effect size across studies. The weighted average indicates how strong the relations between sex and SWB and age and SWB are on average. If the effect sizes are homogeneous, then the individual effect sizes do not significantly differ from this mean, and we do not need to look for cultural differences that affect the size of the relation (Shadish and Haddock 1994). If heterogeneity exists, however, we will examine the distribution of effect sizes further. Specifically, we will examine whether the effect sizes differ in magnitude only, or if they actually change direction across studies. For example, women tend to experience greater amounts of unpleasant affect in the West. If there is significant heterogeneity in the effect sizes across nations, it will be interesting to see whether variability exists only in the magnitude of this effect, or if the direction of the effect actually changes in some nations.

Furthermore, if there is significant heterogeneity, we can begin to formulate hypotheses about the cultural factors that influence effect sizes. Specific procedures exist for testing hypotheses about the factors that influence effect sizes (e.g., see Hedges 1994), and we will proceed mainly in an exploratory manner. For sex differences, we will examine whether the individualism/collectivism of the country (Triandis 1989), the level of freedom in the country (Lewis 1999), and the status of women in the country (Estes 1983) moderate the size of the relation. These variables enable us to test the tentative hypotheses that the extent to which social roles are enforced (individualism/collectivism, freedom) and the content of social roles (which may be reflected in the status of women indicator) may influence sex differences in SWB. For age effects we will examine the individualism/collectivism (Triandis 1989), strength of economy (Lewis 1999), and quality of health (Lewis 1999) of the nation. We hypothesize that in collectivist cultures, extended families are more important, and thus the elderly may not lose social support and may be buffered from the effects of limited income. Furthermore, in nations with poor economies and poor health-care, older adults may suffer more severe SWB decrements as resources to meet basic needs diminish. We will also examine nations in the tails of the distribution of effect sizes. This will enable us to identify potential cultural factors that may be tested more rigorously in future research.

Results

Sex Differences

Table 11.1 presents the weighted average effect size, the 95 percent confidence interval around this mean, and the range of scores observed in each sample of nations. The heterogeneity statistic (Q_w) and its probability are also reported for each variable. If the probability is less than 0.05, we can reject the hypothesis that the effect sizes come from the same population. For three out of five variables in the ICSD (frequency of unpleasant affect, intensity of pleasant affect, and life satisfaction), we cannot reject the hypothesis that these studies come from the same population, since the Q_w statistic does not exceed the critical chi-square value with $p < 0.05$. For frequency of pleasant affect and intensity of unpleasant affect, however, the Q_w statistic is significant. In other words, for three out of five SWB vari-

Table 11.1
Sex difference effect sizes

	ICSD				WVS II			
	FreqPA	FreqUA	IntPA	IntUA	SWLS	PA	UA	LS
Lowest	−0.62	−0.87	−0.89	−0.79	−0.66	−0.21	−0.38	−0.24
Lower 95% CI	−0.24	−0.26	−0.18	−0.25	−0.21	0.01	−0.18	−0.01
Average	−0.19	−0.21	−0.13	−0.20	−0.16	0.03	−0.17	0.01
Upper 95% CI	−0.14	−0.16	−0.08	−0.15	−0.10	0.04	−0.15	0.03
Highest	0.38	0.30	0.32	0.54	0.28	0.20	0.08	0.17
Q_w	58.12	52.85	52.15	72.20	52.93	133.06	201.31	111.20
p	0.03	0.07	0.08	0.00	0.07	0.00	0.00	0.00

Note: FreqPA = frequency of pleasant affect; FreqNA = frequency of unpleasant affect; InPA = intensity of pleasant affect; IntUA = intensity of unpleasant affect; SWLS = Satisfaction with Life Scale; PA = pleasant affect; UA = unpleasant affect; LS = life satisfaction.

ables in the ICSD study, we cannot say that the variability in effect sizes is greater than what we would expect by chance, and thus the effect sizes can adequately be summarized by the weighted mean effect size.

In the WVS, on the other hand, the Q_w statistic is significant for all three variables (pleasant affect, unpleasant affect, and life satisfaction), suggesting that substantial heterogeneity in effect sizes exists. However, this difference between studies must be interpreted cautiously. As with many statistical tests, power to reject the null hypothesis increases with increased numbers of respondents. The average number of respondents per nation in the WVS II (1,373) is almost 8 times greater than the average number of respondents in the ICSD (175). In fact, even though homogeneity is rejected in the WVS II but not in the ICSD, the range of scores is greater in the ICSD than in the WVS II, illustrating the effects of sample size on the Q_w statistic. Based on the rejection of homogeneity in the study with greater power, and the inconsistent significance of Q_w in the ICSD study, we conclude that sex differences in SWB are not equal across nations and thus can be influenced by features of the particular nations being studied.

Accepting that there is variability in sex effects across nations, we can still go on to examine the average effect size and the range of effect sizes across nations to get a sense of how large sex differences are on average. Furthermore we can examine how the effect sizes change across nations. Do the sex differences found in the West reverse in other nations, or are the direction of effects the same, with variation only occurring in the magnitude of sex differences?

In the ICSD we find that the average effect sizes mirror those found in many Western studies: women appear to experience greater frequency and intensity of both pleasant and unpleasant emotions, and they experience greater life satisfaction. While the size of this effect is not large (ranging from approximately one-tenth to one-fifth of a standard deviation), it is consistent across variables (see table 11.1). On average, the difference between men's and women's experience of unpleasant affect is the same as the difference between men's and women's experience of pleasant affect and life satisfaction. This supports the notion that women tend, on average, to be more emotional than men.

However, only the sex differences in unpleasant emotions are replicated across both studies. As table 11.1 illustrates, of the three variables measured in the WVS II, only unpleasant affect shows sex differences. The weighted average effect size for unpleasant affect is -0.17, which is very close to the average found in the ICSD sample. The 95 percent confidence interval for life satisfaction includes zero, and the 95 percent confidence interval for pleasant affect comes very close to zero (0.01). In this sample, men and women appear to experience approximately equal amounts of pleasant affect and life satisfaction.

Why are there differences across studies? The first answer that comes to mind is that the ICSD consists entirely of college students, whereas the WVS II samples a broader population of citizens from each nation. Perhaps sex differences in pleasant affect and life satisfaction only occur among young adults. However, when we examine respondents in their 20s from the WVS II, the same pattern emerges: there are sex differences in unpleasant affect but not pleasant affect or life satisfaction. When we examine trends in sex differences across cohorts, we find that sex differences in all three components tend to increase across the life span (see figure 11.1). Women experience even more unpleasant affect than men in older age cohorts, while older men begin to experience more pleasant affect and life satisfaction than older women. Thus sex differences change across age cohorts, but differences in age are not responsible for the differences found across studies. We cannot rule out other demographic differences across samples that may be responsible for the different results.

We also cannot rule out the effects of the specific SWB scales used. The WVS II is a large survey that was not specifically focused on SWB. The measures are short and may not be as psychometrically sound as those used in the ICSD. For example, the

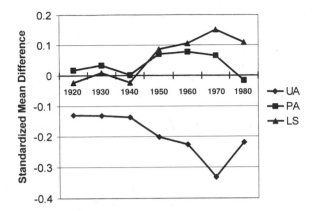

Figure 11.1
Sex differences across age cohorts.

life satisfaction measure is a single item, and the Bradburn Affect Balance Scale has been shown to have less validity than other commonly used affect scales (Larsen, Diener, and Emmons 1985). Perhaps with better measurements the pattern from the ICSD may have been replicated in the WVS II. Even with these limitations, we can draw some conclusions from the two studies. It is clear that women have a tendency to experience slightly more unpleasant affect than men. This is the most consistent finding in the literature, and it is consistently found across samples here. Also we found that women experience *at least as much*, if not more, pleasant affect than men. The greater unpleasant affect that women feel is not reflected in decreased pleasant affect and life satisfaction.

Furthermore, although the magnitude of the sex difference varies from nation to nation, the majority of nations in both studies exhibited greater unpleasant affect for women than for men. For example, in the ICSD sample, 85 percent of nations had a negative effect size for frequency of pleasant affect and 83 percent of nations had a negative effect size for intensity of unpleasant affect. In the WVS II sample, 83 percent of nations had negative effect size for unpleasant affect. Thus, whether we examine the mean effect size or the number of nations showing greater emotionality among women when compared to men, we find consistent sex differences in unpleasant affect. The variability in effect sizes appears to be in the magnitude rather than the direction of the effect.

To examine potential moderators of sex differences in SWB, we used weighted least squares regression to predict effect sizes from the individualism of the nation, the status of women in the nation, and the freedom in the nation. In general, there are few significant effects, and only one that is replicated across both samples: as predicted, individualism of the nation is inversely related to the magnitude of sex differences in frequency of pleasant affect (ICSD: $\beta = -0.30$; $p < 0.05$) and pleasant affect (WVS II: $\beta = -0.44$; $p < 0.05$). In individualist countries, women are likely to experience more pleasant affect than men. Similarly, in nations with greater freedom, women are likely to experience more pleasant affect than men (though this effect is only significant in the ICSD sample: $\beta = -0.37$; $p < 0.05$).

The status of women influences unpleasant affect in the predicted direction in the WVS II sample ($\beta = 0.45$; $p < 0.01$): in nations where women have higher status, the difference between men's and women's SWB is not as strong (mean differences are closer to zero). This effect is not replicated in the ICSD sample, perhaps because the college students sample is not affected by the factors measured by the status indicator (the indicator reflects the percent of eligible girls in secondary school, the female adult illiteracy rate, and the age of constitutional documents affecting the legal rights of women). In addition this indicator is based on data from 1983, so it may not reflect current conditions in these nations.

Table 11.2 lists the five nations with the lowest effect sizes (i.e., where the difference between women and men is most in favor of women) and the five nations with highest effect sizes (where the difference between women and men is most in favor of men) for each of the SWB variables. It is difficult to discern any pattern of high and low effect sizes across nations. Diverse nations fall into the tails of the distributions of each of the SWB variables. Thus there are no simple cultural factors that seem to explain the variability in effect sizes across nations.

In addition to examining the broad components of SWB, it is also useful to investigate gender differences in specific emotions. Nolen-Hoeksema and Rusting (1999) suggest that sex differences are more likely to be found in internalizing unpleasant emotions such as fear, sadness, and guilt than in externalizing emotions such as anger. Weighted average effect sizes, 95 percent confidence intervals, and the range of effect sizes for each of the eight emotions measured in the ICSD are presented in table 11.3. In support of the internalizing hypothesis, the emotions fear and sadness are experienced more frequently and intensely by women compared to men, and this difference is larger than the sex difference for anger. However, there is a slight tendency for women to report more anger than men, as well. Furthermore the smallest effect size is for guilt, which could be considered to be an internalizing emotion. Thus there is some support for the pattern of results found in Western samples.

Table 11.2
Nations in the tails of the distribution of sex difference effect sizes

	Nations with lowest effect sizes	Nations with highest effect sizes
Frequency of PA	Colombia, Slovenia, Peru, India, Lithuania	Guam, Bahrain, Greece, Nepal, Germany
Frequency of UA	Turkey, Guam, Finland, Italy, Lithuania	Hong Kong, Egypt, Hungary, Nepal, Taiwan
Intensity of PA	Denmark, Finland, Austria, Ghana, Indonesia	Greece, Singapore, Bahrain, Guam, Portugal
Intensity of UA	Denmark, Finland, Germany, Austria, Italy	Peru, Singapore, Hong Kong, India, Egypt
LS	Estonia, Slovenia, India, Singapore, Peru	Japan, Guam, South Africa, Pakistan, United States
PA (WVS II)	Britain, Bulgaria, Canada, Iceland, United States	Portugal, Slovenia, Byelorus, India, Switzerland
UA (WVS II)	Byelorus, West Germany, Poland, Russia, Brazil	India, Nigeria, Finland, Japan, Iceland
LS (WVS II)	Nigeria, Turkey, Iceland, Mexico, Norway	Portugal, Brazil, Italy, Estonia, Romania

Table 11.3
Sex difference effect sizes for specific emotions

	Affection	Joy	Content-ment	Pride	Fear	Anger	Sadness	Guilt
Lowest	−0.78	−0.78	−0.64	−0.43	−0.89	−0.57	−0.87	−0.88
Lower 95% CI	−0.34	−0.29	−0.16	0.03	−0.36	−0.13	−0.31	−0.09
Average	−0.29	−0.23	−0.11	0.08	−0.31	−0.08	−0.26	−0.04
Upper 95% CI	−0.23	−0.18	−0.05	0.13	−0.26	−0.03	−0.20	0.01
Highest	0.23	0.43	0.44	0.51	0.14	0.37	0.32	0.45
Q_w	76.29	51.27	54.42	42.44	63.00	51.67	58.43	65.73
p	0.00	0.09	0.05	0.33	0.01	0.08	0.02	0.01

Among negative emotions, the largest effect sizes occur among internalizing emotions of fear and sadness, whereas smaller sex differences are found for anger. Guilt is somewhat anomalous and should be explored more carefully in future research. Perhaps two categories of unpleasant emotion (internalizing and externalizing) are not enough to fully explain sex differences in emotion.

Among pleasant emotions the strongest effect size is for affection, with women scoring over one-third of a standard deviation higher than men, on average. The differences are smaller for joy and contentment, and men actually score higher on pride than women. This pattern is also in line with theories that suggest women are socialized to perform care-giving roles and that these experiences make them more empathic and more affectionate toward others.

In sum, the pattern of results confirms the generalizability of many findings from studies of sex differences among Western samples. In two international studies women report more intense and more frequent unpleasant emotions. Differences are particularly strong in the internalizing emotions of sadness and fear, and less strong for the externalizing emotion of anger. The greater unpleasant affect that women experience does not result in decreased pleasant affect or life satisfaction. Instead, it appears that women experience at least as much, if not more, pleasant affect and satisfaction than men. Women are particularly likely to experience more affection than men, but men report more pride than women. Although significant heterogeneity in effect sizes exists, suggesting that cultural factors affect the magnitude of sex differences across cultures, the direction of sex effects in unpleasant affect is quite consistent: in the vast majority of nations, women report greater unpleasant affect than men.

Age Effects

Using the same data set analyzed in this study (WVS II), Diener and Suh (1998) report that life satisfaction is stable across age cohorts, pleasant affect tends to decline, and unpleasant affect stays about the same (though there was some evidence that unpleasant affect rebounded in older adult cohorts). However, their analyses treated all respondents as a single sample and reported no effect sizes for the three SWB components. In the current analyses we calculate average effect sizes and examine the variability in the distribution of effect sizes to examine how age effects vary across nations.

Table 11.4 presents average correlations between age and life satisfaction, pleasant affect, and unpleasant affect. In addition the semi-partial correlation between

Table 11.4
Age effect sizes

	LS	PA	UA	UA quad
Lowest	−0.11	−0.27	−0.24	−0.05
Lower 95% CI	−0.01	−0.13	−0.06	0.04
Average	0.00	−0.12	−0.05	0.04
Upper 95% CI	0.01	−0.11	−0.05	0.05
Highest	0.18	0.09	0.11	0.13
Q_w	239.90	358.61	327.89	81.19
p	0.00	0.00	0.00	0.00

Note: LS = life satisfaction; PA = pleasant affect; UA = unpleasant affect; UA quad = quadratic term (age squared).

the quadratic term and unpleasant affect, controlling for the linear effect of age is reported (as discussed above). The range of correlations, the 95 percent confidence interval, the Q_w statistic and its probability level, are also reported. Although r's are reported in the table, all r's were transformed to Z's before weighting and averaging and were transformed back to r's for the table.

All homogeneity statistics are significantly different from zero, and thus significant heterogeneity exists among effect sizes. However, it is still informative to examine the average effect size and range of effect sizes in the sample. For life satisfaction the results are clear: on average there are no changes in life satisfaction across the life span. The weighted average correlation between age and life satisfaction is 0 and the correlations only range from −0.11 to +0.18, suggesting that even in the nations where the effect is strongest, age accounts for very little variance in life satisfaction scores (1 to 3 percent).

For affective well-being, the results are slightly more complicated, but we can still draw several conclusions. First, on average the correlation between pleasant affect and age is −0.13. Pleasant affect decreases slightly as individuals age. This decline in pleasant affect is consistent across nations. Ninety percent of nations exhibit a negative correlation between age and pleasant affect (ranging as high as −0.27). Positive correlations between age and pleasant affect are found in only four nations, and these effects are not large (maximum = 0.09). Thus, although variation in effect sizes is probably not due to chance alone, it appears that cultural factors only influence the magnitude of the relation between age and pleasant affect. But they are unlikely to change the direction of this effect.

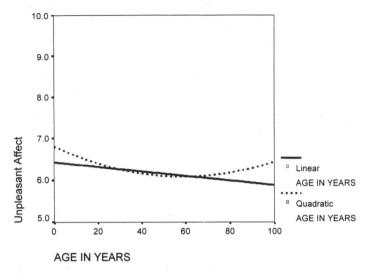

Figure 11.2
Regression line for unpleasant affect.

We find similar results for unpleasant affect, though the effect sizes are not as large. On average, the correlation between age and unpleasant affect is -0.05. Unpleasant affect declines slightly across the life-span. Furthermore this decline occurs in 73 percent of nations. However, in 78 percent of nations there is also a positive semi-partial correlation between the square of age and unpleasant affect (though the size of this effect is usually small), reflecting a U-shaped curvilinear relationship between age and unpleasant affect. For part of the life-span, unpleasant affect declines faster than the -0.05 correlation would suggest, but there is a curvilinear effect such that unpleasant affect begins to increase slightly in later years (though the overall trend across the life-span is a slight decline). Figure 11.2 illustrates the regression line predicting unpleasant affect from the linear and quadratic effect of age (for the entire combined sample). Although this equation is estimated from the combined sample, the distribution of linear and quadratic effect sizes suggest that the pattern is quite consistent across most of the nations in the sample.

Using weighted least-squares regression, we examined the effects of individualism, economy, and health on the four age effect sizes. Again, there are few significant effects, and the effects were not always in the predicted direction. As predicted, age has a more negative relationship with life satisfaction in individualist nations than

Table 11.5
Nations in the tails of the distribution of age effect sizes

	Nations with lowest effect sizes	Nations with highest effect sizes
Pleasant affect	West Germany, Austria, Iceland, Netherlands, Ireland	Poland, Chile, Lithuania, Czechoslovakia, Romania
Unpleasant affect	Sweden, Latvia, Finland, Canada, Denmark	Poland, Hungary, Portugal, Slovenia, Bulgaria
Unpleasant affect (quadratic effect)	Northern Ireland, South Africa, Brazil, Poland, Estonia	Norway, Sweden, Byelorus, Japan, Canada
Life satisfaction	Hungary, Estonia, Slovenia, Nigeria, Austria	China, Northern Ireland, Chile, Brazil, Switzerland

in collectivist nations ($\beta = -0.36$; $p < 0.05$). However, the effect of health of the nation on the age effect size is counter to predictions. The relation between age and life satisfaction becomes more negative in healthy countries ($\beta = -0.49$; $p < 0.01$). An examination of the data shows that this is due to a number of very healthy European countries (e.g., France, Austria, Iceland, Germany, Netherlands) that have strong negative associations between age and life satisfaction.

Furthermore health is positively associated with the size of the quadratic effect ($\beta = 0.41$; $p < 0.01$): in healthy nations the quadratic effect is significantly stronger. In other words, unpleasant affect rebounds more strongly among older cohorts in more healthy nations. Perhaps this is due to the fact that healthy nations tend to be individualist nations, and although the elderly may be healthier in these nations, they may receive less social support as they age. Unfortunately, the strength of the economy, the health of the country, and individualism/collectivism are all strongly correlated and it is impossible to tease apart the effects of these variables. Table 11.5 lists the five nations that fall in each tail of the distributions of age effect sizes for each of the four variables examined. Again, there are no clear patterns revealing cultural factors that can distinguish nations at opposite extremes in the distributions.

These results extend those presented by Diener and Suh (1998) by calculating the average effect size and examining the distribution of effect sizes among nations. The homogeneity statistic suggests that cultural factors can influence the size of the relation between age and SWB, but cultural variation usually occurs in the magnitude of the effect, rather than in the direction of the effect. If only the direction of the effect is examined, the results are quite consistent across nations: life satisfaction does not change, pleasant affect decreases slowly, and unpleasant affect decreases slightly and then gradually increases in later life.

Discussion

Cross-cultural investigations of the correlates of SWB help to determine the generalizability of relations obtained among Western samples, the average size of these relations, and the ways in which the relations vary across cultures. All three pieces of information aid in the development of theories that can explain the processes underlying SWB phenomena. The current study used two large international samples to examine age and sex effects in predicting SWB.

A number of consistent findings emerged. First, in accordance with previous research, women showed a slight tendency to experience greater unpleasant affect than men. Women reported approximately one-fifth of a standard deviation higher unpleasant affect scores than men. This sex difference was found both in measures of frequency and intensity of unpleasant affect, and it tended to increase among older age cohorts. When individual emotions were examined, sex differences were largest in the internally focused emotions of fear and sadness (though guilt did not show the same pattern). Women did report experiencing more anger than men, but the difference was not as large as it was for fear and sadness. Although previous research suggests that men suffer from externalizing disorders more often than women, this difference is not reflected in the experience of the externalizing emotion anger.

Results for pleasant affect were not as consistent across the two studies, but one important conclusion can be drawn: the increased unpleasant emotion that women experience does not lead to a concomitant decrease in pleasant affect and life satisfaction (except, possibly in older women). Women reported similar levels of pleasant affect and life satisfaction as men in the WVS II sample, and women scored higher than men on these measures in the ICSD sample.

As with sex, age exhibited unique relations with each of the components of SWB. Replicating previous findings, age had no effect on life satisfaction (average $r = 0$). Even in the nations where the strongest relations were found, age accounted for only 3 percent of the variance in life satisfaction scores. Pleasant affect, on the other hand, decreased steadily (average $r = -0.12$) throughout the life-span, and unpleasant affect showed a curvilinear relation with age, decreasing at first and then increasing among the elderly.

Importantly, the meta-analytic techniques demonstrated two facts about the distribution of scores. First, there was usually enough variability in effect sizes to reject the hypothesis that the effect sizes were homogeneous. Because the same measures were used in each nation (within each larger sample), we concluded that differences in effect sizes were likely due to cultural factors that varied across the nations. However, we must make two points about this variability. First, although effect sizes varied in magnitude, the direction of the effects were extremely consistent across nations. For example, 90 percent of nations exhibited decreasing pleasant affect with increased age, and in 83 to 85 percent of the nations, women experienced more unpleasant affect than men. Culture may have an effect on these relations, but there are striking similarities across very diverse nations.

Second, although the same measures and same response format were used across all nations, there may be slight methodological differences that have significant effects on sex and age effect sizes. Heterogeneity could be found because of differences in translation quality or sampling techniques across nations. Thus age and sex effects may be even more homogeneous than our study indicates.

What implications do the differences that are found in age and sex effects have for SWB theory? First, if sex differences in SWB are due to social context and socially prescribed gender roles, there must be considerable consistency in ideas and stereotypes of gender across cultures. Women experienced more unpleasant affect than men in the majority of diverse nations studied. Social context explanations must not rely on features of gender roles that are unique to Western cultures in explaining the differences that exist in Western samples. Although some of these features may make sex differences larger or smaller, our results suggest that sex differences in SWB result from factors that are relatively constant across cultures. It is unclear, however, whether these consistencies are due to biology or to consistent socialization across cultures.

Second, trends in SWB across the life-span do not support Carstensen's (1995) idea that greater emotional control will lead to increased pleasant affect and decreased pleasant affect in later life. Both pleasant affect and unpleasant affect decline with age, and unpleasant affect actually rebounds among 60, 70, and 80 year old cohorts. This suggests that emotionality in general may decline with age, perhaps because of decreased affect intensity (Diener, Sandvik, and Larsen 1985; Suh and Diener 1998). It is unclear why unpleasant affect starts to increase again later in life, but this may be due to increased negative circumstances and problems that occur later in life. Diener and Suh (1998) reported that the curvilinear effect of age on unpleasant affect is stronger among unmarried individuals than married individuals and stronger among men than women. Given that men tend to react more negatively than women to the end of a relationship (Stroebe and Stroebe 1983), and that curvilinear effect is greater for unmarried individuals, the increase in unpleasant affect may result from the loss of resources including social support from a spouse and the loss of income that occurs with retirement. Fortunately, the loss of these resources does not have similar effects on pleasant affect and life satisfaction.

Unfortunately, the SWB measures used in the WVS II sample were not the most psychometrically sound measures that are available. Therefore it is difficult to interpret inconsistencies that arise between the samples. Furthermore individual emotions were not examined in the WVS II, and thus we cannot see how different emotions change across the life-span. Large-scale cross-cultural survey research necessarily requires brief measures of the constructs under investigation. However, a number of short, psychometrically sound measures of cognitive and affective well-being exist. Future researchers must choose strong measures if we are to make further advances in the understanding of cross-cultural differences in SWB.

This chapter demonstrates the utility of examining distributions of effect sizes across nations in large-scale cross-cultural studies of SWB. Treating each nation or culture as a single study and using meta-analytic techniques to summarize the distribution of scores enables researchers to understand typical effect sizes as well as variability in these effect sizes across cultures. Since both pieces of information aid in our understanding of SWB phenomena, we recommend that meta-analytic techniques be used in cross-cultural research in the future.

Cross-cultural research on the correlates of SWB has enormous potential for furthering our understanding of the processes underlying SWB constructs. In the current studies we were able to test the cross-cultural generalizability of relations that had been found mainly among Western samples. Furthermore we were able to examine the variability in effect sizes to determine how strong an influence culture has on these relations. While the relation between sex and SWB and between age and SWB varies across nations, there is remarkable consistency in these effects. The more details we know about the size of these effect and the ways they are modified by culture, the more we know about the processes that underly SWB phenomena.

References

Allen, J. G., and Haccoun, D. M. 1976. Sex differences in emotionality: A multi-dimensional approach. *Human Relations* 29: 711–22.

Andrews, F. M., and Withey, S. B. 1976. *Social Indicators of Well-being.* New York: Plenum Press.

Averill, J. R. 1983. Studies on anger and aggression: Implications for theories of emotion. *American Psychologist* 38: 1145–60.

Biaggio, M. K. 1980. Assessment of anger arousal. *Journal of Personality Assessment* 44: 289–98.

Bradburn, N. M. 1969. *The Structure of Psychological Well-being.* Chicago: Aldine.

Brody, L. R. 1993. On understanding gender differences in the expression of emotion: Gender roles, socialization, and language. In S. Ablon, D. Brown, E. Khantzian, and J. Mack, eds., *Human Feelings: Explorations in Affect Development and Meaning.* New York: Analytic Press.

Brody, L. R., and Hall, J. A. 1993. Gender and emotion. In M. Lewis and J. M. Haviland, eds., *Handbook of Emotions.* New York: Guilford Press, pp. 447–60.

Browne, A. 1993. Violence against women by male partners: Prevalence, outcomes, and policy implications. *American Psychologist* 48: 1077–87.

Cantrill, H. 1965. *The Pattern of Human Concerns.* New Brunswick, NJ: Rutgers University Press.

Carstensen, L. L. 1995. Evidence for a life-span theory of socioemotional selectivity. *Current Directions in Psychological Science* 4: 151–55.

Cohen, J., and Cohen, P. 1975. *Applied Multiple Regression/Correlation Analysis for the Behavioral Sciences.* Hillsdale, NJ: Lawrence Erlbaum.

Costa, P. T., and McCrae, R. R. 1980. Influence of extraversion and neuroticism on subjective well-being: Happy and unhappy people. *Journal of Personality and Social Psychology* 38: 668–78.

Diener, E., and Emmons, R. A. 1984. The independence of positive and negative affect. *Journal of Personality and Social Psychology* 47: 1105–17.

Diener, E., Emmons, R. A., Larsen, R. J., and Griffen, 1985. The Satisfaction with Life Scale. *Journal of Personality Assessment* 49: 71–75.

Diener, E., Sandvik, E., and Larsen, R. J. 1985. Age and sex effects for emotional intensity. *Developmental Psychology* 21: 542–46.

Diener, E., Smith, H., and Fujita, F. 1995. The personality structure of affect. *Journal of Personality and Social Psychology* 69: 130–41.

Diener, E., and Suh, E. 1998. Subjective well-being and age: An international analysis. In K. W. Schaie and M. P. Lawton, eds., *Annual Review of Gerontology and Geriatrics*, vol. 17. New York: Springer, pp. 304–24.

Diener, E., Suh, E. M., Lucas, R. E., and Smith, H. E. 1999. Subjective well-being: Thirty years of progress. *Psychological Bulletin* 125: 276–302.

Doyle, M. A., and Biaggio, M. K. 1981. Expression of anger as a function of assertiveness and sex. *Journal of Clinical Psychology* 37: 154–57.

Feldman Barrett, L., Robin, L., Pietromonaco, P. R., and Eyssell, K. M. 1998. Are women the "more emotional" sex? Evidence from emotional experiences in social context. *Cognition and Emotion* 12: 555–78.

Fujita, F., Diener, E., and Sandvik, E. 1991. Gender differences in negative affect and well-being: The case for emotional intensity. *Journal of Personality and Social Psychology* 61: 427–34.

Gross, J. J., Carstensen, L. L., Pasupathi, M., Tsai, J., Skorpen, C. G., and Hsu, A. Y. C. 1997. Emotion and aging: Experience, expression, and control. *Psychology and Aging* 12: 590–99.

Haring, M. J., Stock, W. A., and Okun, M. A. 1984. A research synthesis of gender and social class as correlates of subjective well-being. *Human Relations* 37: 645–57.

Hedges, L. V. 1994. Fixed effects models. In H. Cooper and L. V. Hedges, eds., *The Handbook of Research Synthesis*. New York: Russell Sage Foundation, pp. 285–99.

Inglehart, R. 1990. *Culture Shift in Advanced Industrial Society*. Princeton, NJ: Princeton University Press.

Koss, M. P. 1993. Rape: Scope, impact, interventions, and public policy responses. *American Psychologist* 48: 1062–69.

Larsen, R. J., Diener, E., and Emmons, R. A. 1985. An evaluation of subjective well-being measures. *Social Indicators Research* 17: 1–18.

Lawton, M. P. 1996. Quality of life and affect in later life. In C. Magai and S. H. McFadden, eds., *Handbook of Emotion, Adult Development and Aging*. San Diego, CA: Academic Press, pp. 327–48.

Lucas, R. E., Diener, E., and Suh, E. 1996. The discriminant validity of well-being measures. *Journal of Personality and Social Psychology* 71: 616–28.

Manstead, A. S. R. 1992. Gender differences in emotion. In A. Gale and M. W. Eysenck, eds., *Handbook of Individual Differences: Biological Perspectives*. New York: Wiley, pp. 355–87.

Mroczek, D. K., and Kolarz, C. M. 1998. The effect of age on positive and negative affect: A developmental perspective on happiness. *Journal of Personality and Social Psychology* 75: 1333–49.

Nolen-Hoeksema, S. 1990. *Sex Differences in Depression*. Stanford, CA: Stanford University Press.

Nolen-Hoeksema, S., and Rusting, C. L. 1999. Gender differences in well-being. In D. Kahneman, E. Diener, and N. Schwarz, eds., *Well-being: The Foundations of Hedonic Psychology*. New York: Russell Sage Foundation, pp. 330–52.

Okma, P., and Veenhoven, R. (in press). Is Langer Leven Nog Wel Leuk? Levensvoldoening van hoog-bejaarden in 8 EU-landen [Is a longer life a better life? Happiness of the very old in 8 EU-countries]. *Sociale Wetenschappen* 43.

Robinson, M. D., Johnson, J. T., and Shields, S. A. 1998. The gender heuristic and the database: Factors affecting the perception of gender-related differences in the experience and display of emotions. *Basic and Applied Social Psychology* 20: 206–19.

Rosenthal, R. 1994. Parametric measures of effect size. In H. Cooper and L. V. Hedges, eds., *The Handbook of Research Synthesis*. New York: Russell Sage Foundation, pp. 231–44.

Shaddish, W. R., and Haddock, C. K. 1994. Combining estimates of effect size. In H. Cooper and L. V. Hedges, eds., *The Handbook of Research Synthesis*. New York: Russell Sage Foundation, pp. 261–81.

Shields, S. A. 1987. Women, men, and the dilemma of emotions. In P. Shaver and C. Hendrick, eds., *Sex and Gender: Review of Personality and Social Psychology*, vol. 1. Newbury Park, CA: Sage, pp. 227–45.

Stroebe, M. S., and Sroebe, W. 1983. Who suffers more? Sex differences in health risks of the widowed. *Psychological Bulletin* 93: 279–301.

Wilson, W. 1967. Correlates of avowed happiness. *Psychological Bulletin* 67: 294–306.

Wood, W., Rhodes, N., and Whelan, M. 1989. Sex differences in positive well-being: A consideration of emotional style and marital status. *Psychological Bulletin* 106: 249–64.

12

Perceived Control and Subjective Well-being across Nations and across the Life Span

Alexander Grob

The interest in the notion of agency has a long history in philosophy and religion. Its success as an empirical construct can be traced to Julian Rotter's publication in 1966 entitled "Generalized expectancies for internal versus external control of reinforcement." Rotter was interested in the extent to which people believe that they are able, through their actions, to obtain desired outcomes, particularly the extent to which they see control as located internally or externally. Rotter's paper seized the imagination of psychologists, with a consequent outpouring of theoretical studies, empirical findings, and an ever-widening variety of scales. After more than three decades of research in that field, a number of psychologists are taking stock, asking what has been learned and what the next steps are (summary in Bandura 1995, 1997). A central proposition in this research tradition is that people strive to exercise control over the events that affect their lives (Flammer 1990; Seligman 1975; White 1959). By exerting influence over the flow of positively and negatively reinforcing events, people maximize their utility (Headey and Wearing 1992).

An overview of previous work on perceived control has been provided by a number of writers (Bandura 1997; Flammer 1995; Furnham and Steele 1993; Rotter 1990; Skinner 1996; Strickland 1989). I think these reviews identify three questions as fundamental: First, to what extent is perceived control general or specific to particular domains? Second, is perceived control a one- or a multifactor construct? And, third, how is perceived control related to people's level of well-being?

Before looking at these issues in more detail, we clarify the aspects of control that are discussed in this chapter. We investigate control belief or perceived control, that is, the subjective agentic representation of or belief about one's capability of exercising control (Flammer 1990; Grob and Flammer 1999). Perceived control ideally refers to actual control or controlling. Actual control means regulating certain processes, specifically the attainment, the maintenance, or the avoidance of certain states of affairs. There is no doubt that certain people have more control in some domains than other people. As people are more or less aware of these individual differences, they should be reflected in personal control beliefs. Being in control of certain states of affairs presupposes at least two things, that is, real causal relations between specific means and specific goals, and the availability of such means to the given actor (Bandura 1977; Skinner 1996; Skinner, Chapman, and Baltes 1988).

In order to believe in one's own control or lack thereof, people must typically be aware of their own former successes or failures. Although most control beliefs are rooted in personal control experiences, some may originate from other people's feedback, and another—relatively rare—possibility stems from the observation of comparable others (Bandura 1977). However, there is no doubt that perceived control does not always exactly represent actual control, that is, the level to which a person or a system regulates the process itself. Many studies have shown that people typically overestimate their control competencies (Alloy and Abramson 1982; Langer 1975; Taylor and Brown 1988).

Specificity versus Generality of Perceived Control

Perceived control concerns people's perception of their control in particular situations. However, perceived control is a concept usually defined as dispositional, both in terms of stability over time and in terms of relative generalizability over domains (Nowicki and Strickland 1973; Phares 1976). In practice, though, locus of control has been treated more or less as domain-specific, with only the number of domains and their extent being a matter for argument (Krampen 1989).

The view that locus of control develops only as a result of experience, and depends on what particular experiences people have, would hold that locus of control is primarily situation-specific, and this reflects the acquisition of competence in these specific situations. This view, deriving from learning theory, allows the possibility of generalization, but it implies that an analysis of control in a wide range of situations would yield a multi-factor rather than a one-factor solution (Paulhus and Christie 1981; Skinner 1996).

The literature that addresses this question concludes that at the very least the number of persons involved in the control behavior context is important. The kind and possibility of effective control behavior varies as a function of this dimension (Flammer, Grob, and Lüthi 1989; Grob 1998; Schneewind 1995). Therefore it is crucial to investigate perceived control in different life situations which—among other characteristics—differ in the number of persons possibly sharing control over the outcome of a specific event. It is apparent that the occurrence of specific events differs tremendously with respect to the number of individual, social, and physical conditions that are involved. For example, the number of people who collaborate for a clean environment, or the number of people who have to share control during a peace mission is enormous. However, each person's relative control in his or her domain is crucial for the success of the whole undertaking. Therefore each person contributes to a certain degree to the occurrence of a particular event, and indeed has personal control. There are other events, such as writing scientific articles or playing sports, in which the amount of personal control is actually much greater. Hence the level of personal control varies at least as a function of the number of persons contributing toward a specific outcome, the degree of required collaboration among these persons, and as a function of the physical conditions in which an action takes place. We expect a priori three domains in which the levels of perceived control differ importantly. These domains are the personal, the interpersonal, and the societal domain.

Dimensionality of Perceived Control

In extending Rotter's (1966, 1990) single-factor concept of locus of control, perceived control has been understood as a composite of contingency beliefs and competence beliefs (Flammer 1990; Weisz and Stipek 1982), or outcome expectancy and efficacy expectancy (Bandura 1977, 1986), or means-ends beliefs and agency beliefs (Chapman, Skinner, and Baltes 1990; Skinner et al. 1988). Both components together make up what we call *control expectancy*. The above-mentioned frameworks share in common an emphasis on the cognitive component of perceived control. However, the relevance of an action for the person has been largely neglected.

We think that it is worthwhile to consider the importance to the person of the domains in which perceived control can operate, in addition to the expectancy component. Following Lazarus's (1966; Lazarus and Folkman 1984) general framework, we use *control appraisal*, the second component of perceived control, as a general term to reflect the process of the assessment of importance. This dimension of perceived control has rarely been studied, although it seems evident that it is important. Not being in control of subjectively important events certainly affects one's life more than not being in control of subjectively unimportant events (Abramson, Seligman, and Teasdale 1978). The literature on hopelessness and on depression has shown that helplessness alone might not be psychologically detrimental as long as one's stake is not vital (Barber and Winefeld 1987; Miller and Norman 1979). Nevertheless, the importance dimension was ignored in research about the consequences of perceived control and noncontrol. There might be two reasons why this happened, one methodological and one substantive. The methodological reason has to do with the interest of most researchers to investigate control mechanisms only in areas that are self-evidently important, such as proving to be intelligent, maintaining one's health, or making money. Thus, if the importance variable is basically held constant, there is nothing to be learned about this variable. The second reason has to do with the fact that perceived control is correlated with the importance one attributes to the respective domain and the control expectancy in this domain. If this would be the case, it is redundant to assess a second component of perceived control. However, we seriously doubt that importance and expectancy are substantively correlated.

Perceived Control and Subjective Well-being

Understanding humans as active and constructive beings, and believing that people are instrumental in their own development (Lerner 1982), we think that actions themselves and their cognitive antecedents affect people's subjective well-being. In addition to the biological, economic, cultural, social, and biographical conditions, we assume in line with many other researchers that especially cognitive-evaluative processes affect subjective well-being. This process is characterized by an overall calculation between demands and resources on individual, social, and societal levels. The purpose of this evaluative process is to better understand the actual situation, and its role in the codetermination of subjective well-being.

A far-reaching approach was proposed by Lazarus and his colleagues (1966; Lazarus and Launier 1978; Lazarus and Folkman 1984, 1987). Under this perspective, stress is defined in the person-environment transaction. Psychological stress occurs if a person perceives him- or herself in danger because the demands with which he or she is confronted exceed his or her coping capacities. Lazarus and his colleagues differentiate between two processes, cognitive appraisal and coping behavior. Of major interest for our purpose are the concepts of appraisal. Primary appraisal refers to the evaluation of an event as being challenging or threatening, whereas secondary appraisal refers to, among other things, the evaluation of whether the stressor is perceived as controllable or not. Both processes affect directly and conjointly people's well-being. The fact that a person concludes that something important is at stake, and that this situation or event is personally controllable, leads a person to perceive the same situation as being more of a challenge than a threat. Consequently the person experiences less stress and a higher level of subjective well-being. In short, the fact that one feels in control leads to a positive reappraisal of the situation.

These considerations concerning the person–environment–transaction are in accordance with many theories of well-being. Theories of subjective well-being span, by and large, two basic approaches: cognitive oriented and affect oriented. Cognitive-oriented theories generally maintain that deficits in meeting one's needs lead to ill-being and that positive discrepancies between perceived reality and personal aspirations lead to well-being (Brickman, Coates, and Janoff-Bulman 1978; Duncan 1975; Headey and Wearing 1992; Michalos 1985; Wills 1981). From this viewpoint, people compare an actual situation with an intended, expected, or ideal situation. Accurate appraisals and positive discrepancies between actual and intended states are evaluated favorably, and lead to satisfaction (Cantril 1965). Affect-oriented theories of well-being suggest that satisfaction is enhanced by short-term positive experiences or reducing aversive states (for overviews, see Diener 1984, 1994). From this perspective, well-being reflects the feelings people experience during their everyday lives (Bradburn 1969; Diener and Larson 1993).

In our studies we operationalized well-being as a positive attitude toward life, a generally positive sense of self-esteem, an enjoyment of life, and low levels of depressed mood (Grob 1995; Grob et al. 1991). Given that these aspects of well-being are influenced by cognitive- and affect-related processes (Diener 1984), they are enhanced when numerous antecedents are successfully managed (see Evans 1994, for an overview). Some of these antecedents include a stable historical, cultural, and social context (Bronfenbrenner 1986), accomplishing well-defined normative and age-specific developmental tasks (Havighurst 1948), accomplishing desired nonnormative developmental tasks (Brim 1992; Grob 1991), having meaningful life goals and future perspectives (Brunstein 1993; Emmons 1992; Nurmi 1992), and especially having the personal conviction that one is in control in important life domains (Bandura 1997; Flammer 1995; Seligman 1975).

Evidence across Cultures and across the Life Span

In this section we show evidence across cultures and across the life span for the three general assumptions: that perceived control is best described by control expectancy and control appraisal, that perceived control operates in three domains, and that perceived control is an important predictor of subjective well-being.

Control Expectancy and Control Appraisal

In our longitudinal study across adolescence (Flammer et al. 1989; Grob and Flammer 1997), 4,201 participants aged 14 to 20 years old completed a questionnaire about perceived control in nine everyday situations either once, twice, or three times with a two-year time lag. The nine situations represented three life domains, that is, the personal (personal appearance, future working place, personality development, and pocket money), the interpersonal (conflict with parents and intimate friendship), and the societal (demise of forests, school subject, and local politics). Each situation contained a short description. For example, "physical appearance" was described in the following terms: "You are standing in front of a mirror and are looking at yourself, your eyes, your face, your hair, your entire body. Perhaps you think you are good-looking, perhaps you think you are not."

After the presentation of each of the situations the participants had to answer a series of questions concerning different aspects of control (for details, see Grob, in press). Confirmatory factor analyses were conducted with the same seven items in each of the nine situations. All analyses were carried out in the same manner. First, a one-factor model—assuming the seven variables measure a single construct—was fitted to the data. Second, a two-factor model was fitted to the data with two components: *control expectancy* (four items about how much control the participants expect for themselves) and *control appraisal* (three items about how important control is for them). The indexes for each of the confirmatory factor analyses showed unequivocally that the two-factor solution provided a superior fit to the data than did the one-factor solution. These analyses gave evidence that perceived control is composed of two factors, control expectancy and control appraisal, that hold across very different life situations. The data from the longitudinal sample confirmed the two-factorial pattern of perceived control across the nine life situations, across individuals, and across time.

Life Span We presented 1,631 participants (aged between 14 and 89 years) the same three life situations, that is, personal appearance, handling a conflict with the partner, spouse, or parents, and a natural environmental problem (Grob, Little, and Wanner 1999). The life-span data showed that the latent correlations among the control constructs were statistically the same, both across the three life situations and across the age cohorts. This outcome indicates that the correlational structure among the control constructs is generalizable across the three life situations *and* the age cohorts. Control expectancy and control appraisal overlapped approximately

18 percent within each domain. Notably, the identical nature of the structure among the control constructs within each domain and across each age cohort highlights the robust nature of the psychological meaning of these constructs across the life span.

Sociocultural Context   The next question was whether we would find this same pattern of perceived control across different sociocultural contexts. We tested this assumption with 3,844 adolescents from 14 different sociocultural contexts in Eastern Europe (Bulgaria, Czech Republic, Hungary, Poland, Romania, Russia, Transylvania), Western Europe (Finland, France, Germany, Norway, French-speaking part of Switzerland, German-speaking part of Switzerland), and the United States (Grob et al. 1996). The socioeconomic profiles of each sample were comparable (for more details about the sample, see Alsaker, Flanagan, and Csapó 1999). Three life situations were assessed in the protocol (personality development, workplace, and school subject). Again, we used the same four items to measure control expectancy, and the same three items to measure control appraisal as in the studies mentioned earlier.

In short, the two-factorial model was confirmed using MACS analyses (Little 1997). The expected indicator-to-latent-factor model fit the data in each of the 14 sociocultural contexts, and the equality-constrained model did not decrease the goodness-of-fit indexes. Furthermore, in each of the 14 sociocultural contexts, the correlation between control expectancy and control appraisal could be constrained to $r = 0.44$. The dominant outcome was that the individual-difference relations among the two constructs in each of the 14 sociocultural settings was the same.

Overall, we have evidence that there is a cross-nationally generalizable two-factorial pattern of perceived control, that is, control expectancy and control appraisal. The disattenuated overlap between control expectancy and control appraisal varies between 18 and 25 percent, and it was demonstrated with a large sample from various sociocultural contexts across adolescence and across the life span. Hence it is worthwhile to consider separately the expectancy and the appraisal component in which perceived control operates. Although the two components overlap, they do not serve at all as a proxy for each other.

Domain Specificity of Perceived Control

In our studies on perceived control we were interested in reducing the number of situations to a reasonable higher-order cluster. We assumed that the level of perceived control varies as a function of the number of persons involved in a specific outcome, and that this difference would manifest itself across personal, interpersonal, and societal domains.

In the adolescence study the participants were given nine everyday situations representing these three life domains. The analyses, however, indicated that only two domains could be empirically discerned (Grob, Flammer, and Wearing 1995). The everyday situations covering the personal and interpersonal domain loaded into one domain (personal appearance, future working place, personality development, pocket money, conflict with parents, and intimate friendship), but the societal domain emerged separately (natural environment, school subject, local politics). However, it is noteworthy that the methodology for testing the independence of the domains was not as strong as in the subsequent analyses in which we employed MACS analyses.

The life-span study included three everyday situations, that is, personal appearance (for the personal domain), handling a conflict with the partner or parents (interpersonal domain), and problems with the natural environment (societal domain). A high degree of discrimination emerged among the three domains. In particular, the perceived control constructs in the societal domain and the same constructs in the personal domain showed no overlap. The constructs showed low but positive correlations between the societal and social domains and between the social and personal domains. These low correlations of the control constructs across the three life domains provide evidence for the domain specificity of psychological control. Also the systematic differences in the between-domain correlations suggest that the social domain shares some commonality with both personal and societal issues, but that personal and societal issues are quite independent domains.

Trajectories of Perceived Control

So far we showed that control expectancy and control appraisal are different facets of perceived control and that they operate in three domains, that is, the personal, the interpersonal, and the societal domain. However, we have not discussed age- and culture-related mean-level trajectories.

In the adolescence study the participants were questioned three times over a four-year period. The results indicated that over this time period (1986 to 1990) the adolescents' control expectancy increased, whereas control appraisal stayed the same. The time effect did not interact with the adolescents' gender or age. Under a perspective that investigates how social change affects people's representation of their life, this result is important. Control expectancy increased steadily from age 14 through age 17 and remained at a high level until age 20 in both of two domains, the personal and the interpersonal, respectively. The level of expected control in these two domains was importantly higher than the level of expected control in the societal domain. In addition age did not vary with control expectancy in the societal domain. Interestingly female adolescents expected higher levels of personal control in societal matters than male adolescents did. The pattern for *control appraisal* was different from that of control expectancy. Each of the three domains was rated as more important by female adolescents than by male adolescents. Again, the societal domain was appraised as being less important than the other two domains. In addition the importance of control appraisal decreased with the adolescents' age in the societal domain but not in the personal and interpersonal domains.

Life Span   Consistent with our expectations, control expectancy and control appraisal assessed across the three life domains showed substantially different life-span trajectories. Across the life span, control expectancies in the personal and social domains were rated higher than in the societal domain. Although the slopes for the personal and social domains did not differ, the intercept did. The paths showed an increase from adolescence to about the third life decade, followed by a decrease into old age with some slowing after around age 60. The trend for societal concerns, in contrast, showed a steadily linear decrease, and, in terms of absolute levels, was rated quite low across each age cohort.

The trends for control appraisal differed substantially from those of control expectancy. The social and societal domains were rated as more important than the personal domain. Social relations were viewed as equally important across the life span, while the importance of societal concerns increased, surpassing the importance of the social domain around age 55. In contrast to the social and societal domains, the trajectory for the personal domain showed a pronounced decrease from adolescence to about age 65, followed by a general stability into old age.

Sociocultural Context   The mean level trajectories were also examined across sociocultural contexts. It is noteworthy that none of the mean-level differences were related to measurement artifacts nor to differential mental representations of perceived control. Instead, there were valid differences because of the measurement equivalence and the similar correlational structure among the constructs. The overall control expectancy and control appraisal levels in *all* contexts were high. Furthermore we found that the Eastern European countries had higher values of control expectancy and control appraisal than the Western countries. In terms of the national context patterns, the French adolescents and French-speaking Swiss adolescents were consistently lower than their Western peers in perceived control, and the Hungarian adolescents were consistently lower than their Eastern peers on the perceived control dimensions. On the other hand, the American adolescents were consistently higher than both their Western European and Eastern European compatriots on control expectancy, and the Russian adolescents were among the highest in control expectancy and control appraisal. Despite these interesting national patterns, the most striking result concerns the fact that adolescents from Eastern contexts reported higher levels of perceived control than their Western peers.

To understand this pattern, we think that two processes may be involved. The high control expectancy of the American adolescents is consistent with the educational and sociocultural emphasis that basic capabilities, coupled with personal effort and opportunity, will lead to one's desired outcomes (see also Little et al. 1995). But this attitude regarding achievement probably does not apply to the adolescents from Eastern contexts. To understand the high control expectancy levels of the Eastern adolescents in general, we focus more on the changing social context of these adolescents. Specifically, historically oriented social comparisons to adolescents of former generations may accentuate for the adolescents living in the changing societies—in our study those living in formerly socialist countries—the impact of the shift from relatively rigid institutions to more democtractic systems. Replacing institutional-based restrictions and privileges with the opportunity for personal achievement in democratic settings may give these adolescents the conviction to personally contribute to the ongoing change and therefore to believe in personal control in private and social life. Such an accentuation of one's control expectancy may be a by-product of the comparative contrast between perceived restrictions and perceived opportunities. In this sense, establishing democratic rules in a society (Eastern contexts) is a process with subjectively more degrees of freedom than after it has been well established (Western contexts). This interpretation assumes that adolescents readily adjust to the demands of a given sociopolitical and sociohistorical context. However, this interpretation needs more empirical evidence, and it would be especially strengthened by cross-cultural longitudinal data.

National Characteristics and Perceived Control

Furthermore we examined economic descriptors and indicators of the nations involved in our study, that is, the nations' GNP in 1992, country size, population, population density, and degree of urbanization, and we related these indicators to perceived control. The subsequent analyses therefore were conducted with the respective means per country. In order to enlarge the scope, we calculated a Global Perceived Control index out of the different control components (control expectancy and control appraisal) across the three domains (details in Grob and Flammer 1999). The GNP correlated negatively with Global Perceived Control. Furthermore the results for country size and its population across the three domains indicated that adolescents from bigger countries and from countries with more inhabitants believed they had more control than adolescents from countries that were less populated and smaller in size. The nations' population density and the degree of urbanization showed less consistent effects on the components of control than did the above-mentioned indicators. However, all existing relations between population density and control components were negative, indicating that adolescents from countries with high population densities reported less personal control than did adolescents from countries with lower population density.

The next set of analyses was conducted to shed light on the unique effects of the country indicators on the control components. The other indicators were partialed out in each analysis in order to identify the *unique* effect of the respective indicator on perceived control. Hence, for example, when we partialed out country size, population, population density, and degree of urbanization, the remaining correlation between Global Perceived Control and GNP was no longer significant. The same occurred for country size and population density. However, population size still correlated positively, and the degree of urbanization correlated negatively with perceived control. These results of the partial correlations were controlled for the fact that the sample included heterogeneous countries in terms of economic and geographic descriptors.

Because we assume that the objective degrees of freedom were at least not larger in either country, it is not likely that these differences reflect differences in actual controlling. Hence it seems worthwhile to relate individual scores on perceived control to the population of the country of origin and its degree of urbanization. These results go in parallel with a possible historical consequence of nationalistic thinking in so far that people from larger populated countries feel stronger and more in control than those from smaller countries. This would be a kind of spillover from identification with the own country.

Perceived Control and Subjective Well-being

We hypothesized that a positive sense of control fosters people's self-esteem and satisfaction (individual differences analyses). Therefore we split the participants in the *adolescent study* into a low and high control expectancy group. The adolescents with high levels of control expectancy indeed reported higher levels of positive attitude toward life, higher levels of self-esteem and joy in life, and lower levels of depressed mood than did adolescents with low levels of control expectancy (Grob 1997).

However, the pattern became more complex by referring to the longitudinal sample. We investigated the dynamics among satisfaction, control expectancy, and control appraisal in a three-wave study across adolescence. The model indicated that each of the three constructs was stable across time. It is noteworthy that the predictive constellation of the concepts across time was consistently negative. That is, once controlled for stability, there were negative paths from perceived control at a former time to satisfaction two years later, and so on. This result was even more convincing, given that the paths between the second and third wave were constrained to the same levels as the same paths between waves one and two without a loss of fit of the structural equation models (Grob 1997, 1999). Nevertheless, these robust findings were not expected, and they therefore need some post hoc interpretation.

Under a cross-sectional perspective the results indicate that a positive sense of control leads to well-being. However, the longitudinal data did not confirm this result. Referring to the literature that has shown that people in general overestimate their control competencies (Alloy and Abramson 1982; Taylor and Brown 1988), one might assume that the adolescents in our study overestimated their control competencies. It is noteworthy that this fact is not detrimental per se. If, however, the adolescents were not able to justify their level of control expectancy across the two-year period, this fact might have a negative impact on their well-being. This particular interpretation highlights the functionality of control illusions. Taylor and Brown (1988, 1994; for a recent critique, see Colvin and Block 1994) argued that positive illusions foster well-being in each case, whereas Baumeister (1989) argued for optimal levels of illusion. Interpreting our results in this light, it might be that control optimism becomes dysfunctional if the adolescents were not able to actualize their high level of perceived personal control in everyday experiences. This hypothesis assumes that unjustified levels of control might be detrimental for future well-being. However, it is evident that further research is needed on this particular question.

In the cross-national study we conducted regression analyses in which the background variables were entered first, followed by the agentic variables (for details, see Grob et al. 1999). Overall, the data support the generality of the proposed two-level model of subjective well-being by providing evidence of its cross-cultural invariance. Given sociocultural, political, and economic differences between the countries sampled, the cross-cultural consistency in the structure of well-being with respect to the underlying measurement model was remarkable. Specifically, the analyses revealed similar reliability coefficients of the scales employed in the study across the sociocultural settings, which suggests that the meaning of the scales was the same for the adolescents throughout the settings. Moreover there were consistent patterns in predictive effects from the variables of both levels (i.e., background and agentic) on subjective well-being in adolescents across all of the samples.

The amount of daily strain had—compared with all other measures in the study and regardless of the macrosocial contexts—the strongest impact on adolescents' well-being. That is, the more hassled adolescents felt they were, the lower was the level of their subjective well-being. At the same time the adolescents' well-being was hardly affected by gender and age. Furthermore the adolescents' well-being was predicted by a low preference for emotion-oriented coping reactions, a high preference for problem-oriented coping reactions, and a positive belief in personal control.

A high overall mean level of subjective well-being was found, confirming findings from other research (e.g., see Diener and Diener 1995; Headey and Wearing 1992). In general, adolescents feel well, and in each context the mean level of subjective well-being was above the midpoint of the scale. The adolescents report on their future as looking good and that they are able to do things as well as other people can. However, differences between the countries exist, even though they were not large. Considering the possible range of the well-being scale the highest level of subjective well-being (German-speaking Switzerland) was only 13 percent higher than the lowest level for adolescents from the Czech Republic).

Again, the mean-level differences in subjective well-being were almost consistent with the distinction between the two macrocontexts, the countries of Eastern and Central Europe, that is, formerly socialist countries, on the one hand, and countries of Western Europe and the United States, that is, Western type democracies on the other. Except for the French samples, every Western country was higher on subjective well-being than every formerly socialist country.

Because the economic situation in these two macrocontexts was very different at the time of the study in 1991, with the economies of Eastern European countries being much weaker than those of Western countries, we regard this finding as further support for the assumption that subjective well-being of adolescents is also linked to the income levels or wealth of the country where they live (Diener, Diener and Diener 1995). The few exceptions to this rule (e.g., French sample) suggest that other macro-level factors than economic affluence have an impact on the levels of subjective well-being in adolescents. These factors are difficult to trace in the present study, but further research could shed light on this question.

Although the data suggest that security and economic stability favor subjective well-being, they demonstrate an additional process, namely that everyday strain impairs subjective well-being and individual properties, such as having a positive sense of personal control enhance subjective well-being. Taken together, strain and the three agentic type variables (control expectancy, emotion- and problem-oriented coping reactions) accounted for 26 percent of the 31 percent explainable variance in subjective well-being. These data support the hypothesis that both sociohistorical conditions and personal competencies affect subjective well-being importantly.

In conclusion, the broad comparative framework allowed us to escape the confines of a one-society perspective. This approach is of special importance because self-related cognitions in adolescents, which serve as a prerequisite for their future decisions and therefore guide their future paths, are of great significance. The impact of sociocultural factors might be quite strong, since this life period is characterized by growing demands and needs of integration into given societal, political, and economic structures. All the countries represented in the sample belong to modern societies in that they have comparable levels of industrialization, urbanization, family structure, and education. Simultaneously they differ significantly from one another for example with respect to economics, political traditions or intracultural diversity. Given these culturally determined differences and similarities, the adolescents showed a highly similar predictive pattern of subjective well-being across all the cultural units.

Conclusions

Broadly speaking, a number of important points can be derived from our studies. The points differ with regard to their significance for theory and practice. The first two conclusions should be implemented as standards in control research; the next two deal with open questions. The final conclusion is a meta-level comment on perceived control and subjective well-being which is related to increasing individualization in modern societies.

First, perceived control is a multidimensional construct. We identified two components of perceived control: control expectancy and control appraisal. The correlational structure of these components was stable across three life domains, across the life span, and across different sociocultural contexts. This finding highlights on one side the robustness of the interrelations between control expectancy and control appraisal, and on the other side the importance of the motivational component of perceived control. Specifically, the expectancy component refers to generalized cognitive estimates of the amount of control one possesses, whereas the appraisal component refers to the valuation or perceived importance of the situation at stake. These two features of the perceived control system are in accordance with well-known expectancy-value theories (e.g., see Weiner 1992). For that reason we think that it is worthwhile to include both components of perceived control in control theory.

Second, the constructs' low correlations across the three life domains highlights the distinctive, domain-specific nature of perceived control. The differentiation between life domains certainly depends on the domains that are under study. This is why such studies never can definitely answer the question of how many and what kind of domains have to be distinguished. However, the three dimensions that came out of our studies represent fundamental divisions. The distinctive feature of our division is the number and kind of people having a share in perceived control.

Third, although the relation of control expectancy and control appraisal are consistent across life domains, age-cohorts, and different sociocultural contexts, their mean-level trajectories are quite variable. Pronounced differences emerged for control expectancy. Adolescents and adults at all ages reported low amounts of control expectancy for societal concerns. Furthermore this relative lack of control expectancy decreased steadily with age. On the other hand, the expectation of attaining one's goals in the social and personal domains was quite high. Although the three life domains were quite distinctive and heterogeneous, they were appraised as being important across the life span. We think that these various life-span patterns are interpretable with regard to three superordinate approaches, that is, biophysical aging processes, meeting culturally shared developmental tasks (Havighurst 1948) or life cycles (Erikson 1959), and the selection, optimization, and compensation of different life task across the life span (Baltes 1987). A challenge for future research will be to focus on specific predictions regarding how, when, and in which cultural settings certain control expectancies in specific life domains increase while others decrease, and still others remain stable.

Fourth, regarding the correlational pattern between subjective well-being and perceived control, control appraisal had a low relationship with well-being, whereas control expectancy had a considerably higher relationship. These correlational patterns were almost identical across the sociocultural settings. The positive direction of the correlations between well-being and perceived control supports the idea that people who believe they are able to exert influence over the flow of events also show higher levels of self-esteem and perceive their world in a more positive light. This system of relations is consistent with a causal model in which control expectancy is an important self-regulatory component of one's well-being. However, the modest levels of this relationship indicate that these components of the self-system are not locked together in a fixed system. Instead, the antecedents of well-being and perceived control may encompass different features of people's social psychological world, and the nature of this system of relations remains an open question for future research.

The fifth conclusion concerns the meaning of control in people's lives at the end of the twentieth century at large. Our data showed that adolescents from Eastern European countries believed themselves to have more control than their Western peers. We assume that the objective degrees of freedom were the same in both cultural contexts. However, compared to the West, the perception of control in the East might indeed have increased since the Iron Curtain disappeared. It might also be that the situation did not change for the best at once, and therefore it is also plausible that adolescents living in Eastern contexts anticipated an even better future. Although these interpretations are preliminary, they represent important directions for future research. Adolescents from two very distinct macrosocial contexts report high levels of personal control, and the adaptive psychological interface among these aspects of personal control and well-being appear to be robust in the face of sociopolitical fluctuations in both sociocultural environments. Furthermore similarily high levels of perceived control and subjective well-being were found across the life-span.

Hence one might relate these findings to the *Zeitgeist*. At the end of the twentieth century, people live in a world where very many events are expected to be caused by personal agency and competence: a person is what she or he personally does. This contemporary understanding of how the world functions is largely shared cross-contextually and across the life-span. It appears to us that high levels of perceived control are not only descriptive of individuals but also descriptive of modern societies. There might be even a societal pressure for having high levels of personal control. If this account has some accuracy, the study of individual perceived control also tells us about societies at large.

An Outlook and Preliminary Answer

On a very broad level the notion that the individual can and must responsibly determine his or her life course and sense of well-being is taken for granted in modern societies. Modern societies no longer uniformly define what well-being is, nor how it is related to aspects of the life course or significant life events. However, in modern societies a normative pressure exists to permanently realize oneself in a original manner. Such a pressure on permanent self-actualization can be taken as an indicator for a new understanding of development: traditional developmental tasks seem to be increasingly less given by society and less bounded to specific ages. In place of that the individual has to state personal goals. This developmental understanding makes human beings more than ever to architect their own fortune. To meet the architecture, individuals have to satisfy two conditions: to decide from a large number of possible goals for a few distinct goals along their life course, and to decide for appropriate ways to their successful realization. Such an understanding of development demands high degrees of self-responsibility and a strong belief in available psychosocial resources.

We recently started to test this assumption with people from three age cohorts (Grob 1998), that is, people who were born between the wars (born 1920–1925), people who were early baby boomers (born 1945–1950), and people from the "generation X" (born 1970–1975). The results provide evidence that this modern understanding of life and development holds true, especially for people from younger cohorts. People from younger cohorts have a concept of their own development that values self-defined goals positively, and that for them a successful life consists in realizing the intended life course. In contrast, people from older cohorts have a developmental concept that is more related to satisfy traditional developmental tasks and to meet societal and familial demands. It goes without saying that these findings have to be replicated with different methods and in different cultural settings. Nevertheless, they indicate that human development in general and the regulation of subjective well-being in particular is not only dependent on individual competences within cultural settings, but is strongly dependent on time-specific knowledge and norms.

Note

The writing of this manuscript was supported by a grant of the Swiss National Science Foundation (11–45780.95). I thank Adrian Bangerter for his valuable editorial help.

References

Abramson, L. Y., Seligman, M. E. P., and Teasdale, J. D. 1978. Learned helplessness in humans: Critique and reformulation. *Journal of Abnormal Psychology* 87: 49–74.

Alloy, L. B., and Abramson, L. Y. 1982. Learned helplessness, depression, and the illusion of control. *Journal of Personality and Social Psychology* 42: 1114–26.

Alsaker, F. D., Flanagan, C., and Csapó, B. 1999. The issues of sampling in cross-national/ cross-cultural research. In F. D. Alsaker, and A. Flammer, eds., *The Adolescent Experience: European and American Adolescents in the 1990s.* Hillsdale, NJ: Lawrence Erlbaum, pp. 15–32.

Baltes, P. B. 1987. Theoretical propositions of life span developmental psychology: On the dynamics between growth and decline. *Developmental Psychology* 23: 611–26.

Bandura, A. 1977. Self-efficacy: Toward a unifying theory of behavioral change. *Psychological Review* 84: 191–215.

Bandura, A. 1986. *Social Foundations of Thought and Action: A Social Cognitive Theory.* Englewood Cliffs, NJ: Prentice Hall.

Bandura, A. 1997. *Self-efficacy. The Exercise of Control.* New York: Freeman.

Bandura, A., ed. 1995. *Self-efficacy in Changing Societies.* New York: Cambridge University.

Barber, J. G., and Winefeld, A. H. 1987. Three accounts of learned helplessness effects. *Genetic, Social and General Monographs* 112: 143–63.

Baumeister, R. F. 1989. The optimal margin of illusion. *Journal of Social and Clinical Psychology* 8: 176–89.

Bradburn, N. M. 1969. *The Structure of Psychological Well-being.* Chicago: Aldine.

Brickman, P., Coates, D., and Janoff-Bulman, R. 1978. Lottery winners and accident victims: Is happiness relative? *Journal of Personality and Social Psychology* 36: 917–27.

Brim, O. G., Jr. 1992. *Ambition: How We Manage Success and Failure throughout Our Lives.* New York: Basic Books.

Bronfenbrenner, U. 1986. Ecology of the family as a context for human development: research perspectives. *Developmental Psychology* 22: 723–42.

Brunstein, J. C. 1993. Personal goals and subjective well-being: A longitudinal study. *Journal of Personality and Social Psychology* 65: 1061–70.

Cantril, H. 1965. *The Pattern of Human Concerns.* New Brunswick, NJ: Rutgers University Press.

Chapman, M., Skinner, E. A., and Baltes, P. B. 1990. Interpreting correlations between children's perceived control and cognitive performance: Control, agency, and means-ends beliefs? *Developmental Psychology* 26: 246–53.

Colvin, C. R., and Block, J. 1994. Do positive illusions foster mental health? An examination of the Taylor and Brown formulation. *Psychological Bulletin* 116: 3–20.

Diener, E. 1984. Subjective well-being. *Psychological Bulletin* 95: 542–75.

Diener, E. 1994. Assessing subjective well-being: Progress and opportunities. *Social Indicators Research* 31: 103–57.

Diener, E., and Diener, M. 1995. Cross-cultural correlates of life-satisfaction and self-esteem. *Journal of Personality and Social Psychology* 68: 653–63.

Diener, E., and Larson, R. J. 1993. The experience of emotional well-being. In M. Lewis and J. M. Haviland, eds., *Handbook of Emotions.* New York: Guilford, pp. 405–15.

Diener, E., Diener, M., and Diener, C. 1995. Factors predicting the subjective well-being of nations. *Journal of Personality and Social Psychology* 69: 851–64.

Duncan, O. D. 1975. Does money buy satisfaction? *Social Indicators Research* 2: 267–74.

Emmons, R. A. 1992. Abstract versus concrete goals: Personal striving level, physical illness, and psychological well-being. *Journal of Personality and Social Psychology* 62: 292–300.

Erikson, E. H. 1959. Identity and the life cycle. *Psychological Issues* 1: 50–100.

Evans, D. R. 1994. Enhancing quality of life in the population at large. *Social Indicators Research* 33: 47–88.

Flammer, A. 1990. *Erfahrung der eigenen Wirksamkeit* [Experiencing one's own efficacy]. Bern: Huber.

Flammer, A. 1995. Developmental analysis of control beliefs. In A. Bandura, ed., *Self-efficacy in Changing Societies.* New York: Cambridge University, pp. 69–113.

Flammer, A., and Grob, A. 1994. Kontrollmeinungen, ihre Begründungen und Autobiographie [Control beliefs, their justification, and autobiographical memory]. *Zeitschrift für Experimentelle und Angewandte Psychologie* 41: 17–38.

Flammer, A., Grob, A., and Lüthi, R. 1989. Swiss adolescents' attribution of control. In J. P. Forgas, and J. M. Innes, eds., *Recent Advances in Social Psychology: An International Perspective.* Amsterdam: Elsevier Science, pp. 81–94.

Furnham, A., and Steele, H. 1993. Measuring locus of control: A critique of general, children's, health, and work-related locus of control questionnaires. *British Journal of Psychology* 84: 443–79.

Grob, A. 1991. Der Einfluss bedeutsamer Lebensereignisse auf das Wohlbefinden und auf bereichsspezifische Kontrollmeinungen von Jugendlichen [The impact of significant life events on subjective well-being and domain specific control attributions]. *Schweizerische Zeitschrift für Psychologie* 50: 48–63.

Grob, A. 1995. Subjective well-being and significant life events across the life span. *Swiss Journal of Psychology* 54: 3–18.

Grob, A. 1997. Entwicklung und Regulation des Wohlbefindens [Development and regulation of subjective well-being]. Habilitationsschrift. Faculty of Philosophy and Humanities. University of Berne, Switzerland.

Grob, A. 1998. Identifying societal change by studying biographics of people from different cohorts. Invited lecture at the Preconference entitled "Societal Change and Adolescents' Development." 6th Biennial Conference of the European Association for Research on Adolescence. Budapest, Hungary.

Grob, A. 2000. Dynamics of perceived control across adolescence and adulthood. In W. J. Perrig and A. Grob, eds., *Control of Human Behavior, Mental Processes, and Consciousness.* New York: Lawrence Erlbaum.

Grob, A., and Flammer, A. 1997. Der Berner Jugendlängsschnitt: Design und ausgewählte Resultate [The Berne adolescent study: Design and selected results]. *Zeitschrift für Sozialisationsforschung und Erziehungssoziologie* 17: 244–55.

Grob, A., and Flammer, A. 1999. Macrosocial context and adolescents' perceived control. In F. D. Alsaker, and A. Flammer, eds., *The Adolescent Experience: European and American Adolescents in the 1990s*. Hillsdale, NJ: Lawrence Erlbaum, pp. 99–113.

Grob, A., Flammer, A., and Wearing A. J. 1995. Adolescents' perceived control: Domain specificity, expectancy, and appraisal. *Journal of Adolescence* 18: 403–25.

Grob, A., Little, T. D., and Wanner, B. 1999. Control judgements across the life span. *International Journal of Behavioral Development* 23: 833–54.

Grob, A., Little, T. D., Wanner, B., Wearing, A. J., and Euronet. 1996. Adolescents, well-being and perceived control across fourteen sociocultural contexts. *Journal of Personality and Social Psychology* 71: 785–95.

Grob, A., Lüthi, R., Kaiser, F. G., Flammer, A., Mackinnon, A., and Wearing, A. J. 1991. Berner Fragebogen zum Wohlbefinden Jugendlicher (BFW) [Berne questionnaire on subjective well-being (BSW-Y)]. *Diagnostica* 37: 66–75.

Grob, A., Stesenko, A., Sabatier, C., Botcheva, L., and Macek, P. 1999. A model of adolescents' well-being in different social contexts. In F. D. Alsaker, and A. Flammer, eds., *The Adolescent Experience: European and American Adolescents in the 1990s*. Hillsdale, NJ: Lawrence Erlbaum, pp. 115–30.

Havighurst, R. J. 1948. *Developmental Tasks and Education*. New York: McKay.

Headey, B., and Wearing, A. J. 1992. *Understanding Happiness: A Theory of Subjective Well-being*. Melbourne: Longman Cheshire.

Krampen, G. 1989. Mehrdimensionale Erfassung generalisierter und bereichsspezifischer Kontrollüberzeugungen [Multidimensional assessment of generalized and domain specific locus of control]. In G. Krampen, ed., *Diagnostik von Attributionen und Kontrollüberzeugungen*. Göttingen: Hogrefe, pp. 100–106.

Langer, E. J. 1975. The illusion of control. *Journal of Personality and Social Psychology* 32: 311–28.

Lazarus, R. S. 1966. *Psychological Stress and the Coping Process*. New York: McGraw-Hill.

Lazarus, R. S., and Folkman, S. 1984. *Stress, Appraisal, and Coping*. New York: Springer.

Lazarus, R. S., and Folkman, S. 1987. Transactional theory and research on emotion and coping. *European Journal of Personality* 1: 141–70.

Lazarus, R. S., and Launier, R. 1978. Stress-related transactions between person and environment. In L. Pervin, and M. Lewis, eds., *Perspectives in International Psychology*. New York: Plenum, pp. 287–327.

Lerner, R. M. 1982. Children and adolescents as producers of their own development. *Developmental Review* 2: 342–70.

Little, T. D. 1997. Mean and covariance structures (MACS) analyses of cross-cultural data: Practical and theoretical issues. *Multivariate Behavioral Research* 32: 53–76.

Little, T. D., Oettingen, G., Stetsenko, A., and Baltes, P. B. 1995. Children's action-control beliefs about school performance: How do American children compare with German and Russian children? *Journal of Personality and Social Psychology* 69: 686–700.

Michalos, A. C. 1985. Multiple discrepancy theory. *Social Indicators Research* 16: 347–413.

Miller, I. W., and Norman, W. H. 1979. Learned helplessness in humans: A review and attribution-theory model. *Psychological Bulletin* 86: 93–118.

Nowicki, S., and Strickland, P. R. 1973. A locus of control scale for children. *Journal of Consulting Psychology* 141: 277–86.

Nurmi, J.-E. 1992. Age differences in adult life goals, concerns, and their temporal extension: A life course approach to future-oriented motivation. *International Journal of Behavioral Development* 15: 487–508.

Paulhus, D., and Christie, R. 1981. Spheres of control: An interactionistic approach to assessment of perceived control. In H. M. Lefcourt, ed., *Research with the Locus of Control Construct*, vol. 1. New York: Academic Press, pp. 161–88.

Phares, E. J. 1976. *Locus of Control in Personality*. Morristown, NJ: General Learning Press.

Rotter, J. B. 1966. Generalized expectancies for internal versus external control of reinforcement. *Psychological Monographs*, vol. 80, no. 609.

Rotter, J. B. 1990. Internal versus external locus of control of reinforcement. *American Psychologist* 45: 489–93.

Schneewind, K. A. 1995. Impact of family processes on control beliefs. In A. Bandura, ed., *Self-efficacy in Changing Societies*. New York: Cambridge University Press, pp. 114–48.

Seligman, M. E. P. 1975. *Helplessness*. San Francisco: Freeman.

Skinner, E. A. 1996. A guide to constructs of control. *Journal of Personality and Social Psychology* 71: 549–70.

Skinner, E. A., Chapman, M., and Baltes, P. B. 1988. Control, means-ends, and agency-beliefs: A new conceptualization and its measurement during childhood. *Journal of Personality and Social Psychology* 54: 117–33.

Strickland, B. R. 1989. Internal-external control expectancies: From contingency to creativity. *American Psychologist* 44: 1–12.

Taylor, S. E., and Brown, J. D. 1988. Illusion and well-being: A social-psychological perspective on mental health. *Psychological Bulletin* 103: 193–210.

Taylor, S. E., and Brown, J. D. 1994. Positive illusions and well-being revisited: Separating fact from fiction. *Psychological Bulletin* 116: 21–27.

Weiner, B. 1992. *Human Motivation*. Newbury Park, CA: Sage.

Weisz, J. R., and Stipek, D. J. 1982. Competence, contingency and the development of perceived control. *Human Development* 25: 250–81.

White, R. W. 1959. Motivation reconsidered: The concept of competence. *Psychological Review* 66: 297–333.

Wills, T. A. 1981. Downward comparison principles in social psychology. *Psychological Bulletin* 90: 245–71.

Index

Page numbers in italics refer to illustrations.